THE GRAMMAR OF SOCIAL RELATIONS

THE GRAMMAR OF
SOCIAL RELATIONS

The Major Essays of Louis Schneider

Edited by
Jay Weinstein

With an Epistolary Foreword by
Robert K. Merton

Transaction Books
New Brunswick (U.S.A.) and London (U.K.)

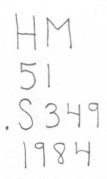

Copyright © 1984 by Transaction, Inc., New Brunswick, New Jersey 08903. Foreword copyright © 1984 by Robert K. Merton.

Library of Congress Catalog Number: 83-17949

ISBN: 0-87855-474-2 (cloth)

Printed in the United States of America

Library of Congress Cataloging in Publication Data

Schneider, Louis, 1915-
    The grammar of social relations.

    Bibliography: p.
    Includes index.
    1. Sociology—Addresses, essays, lectures.
2. Social sciences—Addresses, essays, lectures.
3. Religion and sociology—Addresses, essays, lectures.
I. Weinstein, Jay A., 1942-   . II. Title.
HM51.S349   1984   301   83-17949
ISBN 0-87855-474-2

Acknowledgments

The editor gratefully acknowledges the following publishers and publications for permission to reprint copyrighted material:

"Dialectical Orientation and the Sociology of Religion," *Sociological Inquiry* 49 (1979):49-73.

"The Role of the Category of Ignorance in Sociological Theory," *American Sociological Review* 25 (August 1962):492–508; and "Dialectic in Sociology," *American Sociological Review* 36 (August 1971): 667-78.

"The Sociology of Religion: Some Areas of Theoretical Potential," *Sociological Analysis* 31 (Fall 1970):131-44.

"Mandeville as Forerunner of Modern Sociology," *Journal of the History of the Behavioral Sciences* 6 (July 1970):219-30. Clinical Psychology Publishing Company, Inc.

"Ironic Perspective and Sociological Thought," in Lewis A. Coser, ed., *The Idea of Social Structure: Papers in Honor of Robert K. Merton.* New York: Harcourt Brace Jovanovich, 1975, pp. 323-37.

"Adam Smith on Human Nature and Social Circumstance," in Gerald P. Driscoll, Jr., ed., *Adam Smith and Modern Political Economy: Bicentennial Essays on the Wealth of Nations.* Ames: Iowa State University Press, 1979, pp. 44-67.

"The Scope of the 'Religious Factor' in the Sociology of Religion," *Social Research* 41 (Summer 1974):340-61.

"Memorial to Louis Schneider," by Walter I. Firey, *Journal for the Scientific Study of Religion* 18 (September 1979):336.

"Tension in the Thought of John Millar," *Studies in Burke and His Time* 13 (Winter 1971-72):2083-98. Texas Technological University Press.

"Introduction," in *Essay on the History of Civil Society,* by Adam Ferguson. New Brunswick: Transaction, 1979, pp. x-xxviii.

"Inspirational Religious Literature: From Latent to Manifest Functions," *American Journal of Sociology* 62 (1957):476-81.

"Pitirim A. Sorokin: Social Science in the 'Grand Manner,' " *Social Science Quarterly* 49 (June 1968):142-51; and "On Frontiers of Sociology and History," *Social Science Quarterly* 50 (June 1969):6-24.

"Some Psychiatric Views on 'Freedom' and the Theory of Social Systems," *Psychiatry* 12 (1949):251-64. William Alanson White Psychiatric Foundation.

Contents

Texts, Contexts and Subtexts:
An Epistolary Foreword

Robert K. Merton

Mrs. Louis Schneider
Havenwood Drive
Austin, Texas 78759   October-November, 1983

Dear Jo,

It was good to talk with you the other day, if only by exceedingly long
distance telephone, and to have you agree that, in light of Jay
Weinstein's superb general introduction and his introductions to the
several parts of Lou's volume, a foreword written in the ordinary way
would simply be redundant. Redundancy has its uses, of course, in making for reliability in a swiftly conveyed coded message, but not, I believe,
in a foreword. And so, as you agree would be in order, I shall try, as
briefly as can be, to introduce the reader to texts and documents that
provide otherwise inaccessible contexts and subtexts[1] for this carefully

---

1.   Since Lou was almost as addicted to expository footnotes as I, holding firm
     to the conviction that these supplied contexts that readers should not be
     asked to search out for themselves, yet contexts that could not be elevated
     into the text itself without so disrupting its sought-for flow as to have it
     turn into a meandering Shandean stream of freely-associated ideas, and
     since you, I know, take cognitive pleasure in such contextual footnotes, I
     shall introduce them as occasion seems to require.
        Thus to begin: The Louis Schneider I knew would have taken interest in
     the historical and cognitive roots of the concept "subtext" which denotes
     the variously implicit allusions, structural cues, and direct references to
     earlier texts that make for a deep understanding of the text under examina-
     tion. The notation has been variously used in literary analysis but I have

selected and ordered collection of his papers. In doing so, I shall draw upon letters which Lou and I exchanged intermittently during the past forty years, ever since he left his graduate studies at Columbia University for war-related work in the early and mid-1940s. And I shall obey your stern injunction to try to maintain the kind of distance from the contents of my letters to him that Lou achieved in distancing himself from his own scholarly writings as he reexamined them with a critical eye. That is, I shall feel free, as you ask, to quote "shamelessly"—we both recognize this as one of Lou's self-deprecating, distancing terms—from his letters to me and from mine to him, whenever these passages bear on themes exemplified in this collection of papers. The foreword thus becomes a gloss on a few episodes and themes in Lou's life as a scholar since the time I first encountered him on Morningside Heights back in 1941 when, like his slightly later fellow graduate student Alvin Gouldner, he turned up as a mature young scholar, mature in critically sifted sociological knowledge and understanding rather than in years.

From the start, one recognized the quiet, responsible dignity of Lou's scholarly demeanor and judgment that found expression in both style of thought and style of exposition. In Lou's case, Buffon is surely right: the

---

found no *locus classicus* that anatomizes it. Drawing upon Taranovsky (who, writing in Russian, is inaccessible to me), David Borker has identified the criteria and components of a subtext: manifestly, it must precede the text chronologically; it must be known to the author or at least be accessible in the local subculture; its surface indicators include lexical overlapping with a prior text of key words or phrases, thematic parallelism or paraphrases, and, of course, direct citations. Such decodings complicate the task of understanding a text while deepening its meaning by providing private associations of the author. Should you find yourself interested in this idea of subtext, you might start with David Borker, "Annenskij and Mallarmé: A Case of Subtext" in the *Slavic and East European Journal* 21 (1977):46-55, whose references will take you to Taranovsky, Lotman, Ivanov, and others. Quite independently of this tradition, the term "subtext" is a staple in the vocabulary of the theatre where it refers to a more speculative sort of reading between and beneath the lines of the text. It is rooted in "the theatre of the unexpressed" of J.-J. Bernard (1883-1970, who had his predecessors) with its accent on pauses, silences, and other tactics of allusion and intonation designed to orient the director, actors, and audience to underlying personal relationships, the personality and temperament of the characters in the play, and nuances of its evolving plot. For this context, see Kester A. Branford, *A Study of Jean-Jacques Bernard's Théâtre de l'inexprimé* (University, Mississippi: Romance Monographs, 1977).

style truly is the man himself.[2] The consistency of intellectual style, as we know, continued through his life. Committed as he was to integrity of intellectual effort as well as result, Lou meticulously rejected posthumously idealized discussions of scholars that easily lapse into hagiography. And yet, it must be said that the portrait emerging from these pages is indeed that of a scholar wholly dedicated to self-defined tasks of enlarging our sociological understanding. Over long stretches of time, not invariably, as when he simply did not like what he found himself thinking or writing, but in the main, he was clearly taking joy in exploring sociological ideas of enduring interest. Readers of this volume of far-seeing sociological essays will thus come to know the man as well as his ideas through his work.

It is almost inevitable that I should have been put in mind of Buffon's dictum from Lou's favorite century of the Scottish moralists. For, as you noticed, Lou and I shared an abiding interest in the question of styles of intellectual work. I rummage through our correspondence and soon find him comparing the "intellectual styles" of two contemporary social scientists

> in terms of temperament, in terms of variations in senses of humor, in terms of disposition of "builders"—one of whom (with vast ability but a bit overgrimly) builds by piling one stone on top of another and adjusting asymmetries and imbalances by bringing up still more stones, while the other (also with huge ability but with a grin rather than grimness) builds and connects rather more exquisitely, with more scepticism of the flat dictum that a stone is a stone *et voilà*, with more of a geological and artistic eye for the character of individual stones themselves, their layering, weight, veins, color [25 October 1975].

-----

2.   Buffon's dictum "le style est l'homme même" appears in his short but, after the accepted manner, high-flown address to the French Academy at the time of his election in 1753. (The originally untitled address has since become known as the *Discours sur le style*.) The seemingly self-contained maxim of everyday wisdom is imbedded in a context that gives it special point here since it distinguishes the easily transmissible substance of scientific knowledge that is "external to the man" from "style" which, as the dictum has it, "is the man himself," that is, the composite of telling ways in which we each formulate our ideas and thoughts. In that sense, the papers collected in this volume consistently reflect Lou's preferred intellectual style as Jay Weinstein, in his capacity as compiler, informs us when he explains that Lou's probably best-known paper was omitted in part because "its style contrasts sharply with the rest of the book."

To this passage that moves toward a Stevensonian analysis of technical elements in sociological rather than literary style,[3] I replied in short and dull albeit forthcoming fashion:

> The hastiest of notes in response to your tantalizing letter of late October. This business of intellectual styles of work is one that has intrigued a good many of us but I know of no one [*pace* Wilhelm Ostwald] who has found an effective way of characterizing styles in science (including, if you will allow it, social science). If you do move ahead with this, I hope that you will keep me in touch [2 December 1975].

To me, an especially impressive component of Lou's intellectual style is his having lived up to the institutionalized norm known for some time as "organized skepticism," which calls for scientists and scholars to scrutinize and assess with care the cognitive standing of claims to knowledge in their fields of inquiry. Lou did so to the full. He was ever the disinterested sociological critic. He adopted at least as demandingly critical a stance toward his own scholarly work as toward the work of others placed in distant times or in the present day. And unlike some of the rest of us, angered by seeming violations of scholarly standards, he took no malicious joy in questioning or refuting ideas advanced by other thinkers. He was intellectually vigilant but not an intellectual vigilante confidently meting out a brand of summary "justice." Rather, he was concerned to clarify, as best he could, what seemed to be their tenable or intellectually interesting ideas. As the critical pages in this book attest, nothing in his criticism ever declined into *Schadenfreude* or into doctrinal squabbles: witness only his complex appraisals of some of Max Weber's classic formulations.

His capacity for sustained and disinterested self-criticism also finds ample expression in this volume. But perhaps this capacity for strong criticism of his own work is most fully registered by the case of a paper that is deliberately *not* included here, for reasons indicated in Jay's introduction. Some time back Lou decided, without public fuss or feathers, that the consequential article for which he is perhaps best known—the article being "The Deferred Gratification Pattern" written with Sverre Lysgaard thirty years ago—simply was not up to the standards of substance and form that he had come to set for his published writings. I happen to believe that Lou was excessively hard on

---

3.   The allusion is to "Some Technical Elements of Style in Literature," reprinted in *The Letters and Miscellanies of Robert Louis Stevenson* (New York: Charles Scribner's Sons, 1898), pp. 243-64.

himself (and derivatively in this case, his collaborator). After all, the paper did crystallize the idea of a basic behavioral pattern and did propose an interesting hypothesis about its theoretically expected distribution among the social classes. It was, moreover, a consequential paper since it led to a considerable body of detailed research on the central hypothesis. Exceedingly self-critical authors are not always the best judges of their own work.

Incidentally, as I once intended to write Lou but never did, his tough-minded appraisal of the paper on deferred gratification is reminiscent of the comparative judgments Nobel laureates in the sciences often make of the work that won them the prize. As Harriet Zuckerman learned from her interviews with numbers of them, nearly half, "while conceding the scientific significance of their research, were convinced that it was not their best work."[4] In much the same way, authors of papers and monographs that are defined as "citation classics"—works that have been most cited by fellow scientists and scholars—not infrequently express surprise that it was that particular piece of work rather than other work more to their liking which proved to be most cited.[5] That fellow sociologists and psychologists thought much of the idea of deferred gratification is indicated by the attention they lavished upon it. Long after its publication, in the period of 1966 to 1982, the paper was cited at least fifty-four times.[6] We can only estimate the considerably larger

---

4. Should you want more on these judgments by laureates, consult Harriet Zuckerman, *Scientific Elite: Nobel Laureates in the United States* (New York: Free Press, 1977), pp. 210-14. She notes that similar judgments are also made at times by scientific peers of the laureates, as when one of them remarked that he "would have liked to see him get [the prize] for something else."

5 . Authors of "citation classics" speculate about the reasons for such frequent use of their work in the bibliographical resource *Current Contents,* which is published weekly by the Institute for Scientific Information for the social and behavioral sciences as well as severally for the life sciences, the physical, chemical, and earth sciences, the arts and humanities, and so on.

6. To see this in perspective, you must know that the vast majority of published scientific and scholarly articles receive very little recorded notice from the community of scientists and scholars. Less than half of 1 percent of some 11 million papers published in the physical, chemical, and life sciences received as many as 51 citations in the five-year period 1975-79, and those figures include recent papers published during this period or just before. If you are interested in this, often ironic, fate of much scholarship, examine the succinct, authoritative book by the inventor of the Science Citation Index: Eugene Garfield, *Citation Indexing: Its Theory and Application in Science, Technology, and Humanities* (New

number of citations to it in the thirteen-year period immediately following publication (a period in which the great bulk of citations usually occur), since the Social Science Citation Index has not yet developed a data base for citations before 1966. There is no doubt that the paper on deferred gratification qualifies as a citation classic. I suspect that Lou was bemused by the irony that the paper he thought so little of received so much notice from his peers.

As Jay also reports in his introduction, and as you are abundantly aware, Lou developed an increasingly critical, not to say jaundiced, opinion of his first book, *The Freudian Psychology and Veblen's Social Theory* (1948, reprinted 1974). Now that the statute of limitations on breaking confidence in such matters has surely run its course, I can tell you about the early personal contexts of the book which have now become historical contexts. As you know, it began as Lou's dissertation. But, as you may not know, the dissertation was substantially drafted as early as 1943, before Lou left for Washington to work for the War Production Board. In accord with the practice back in those days, the sponsor of the dissertation selected a group of readers who would eventually serve as the examining committee. From the long retrospect of some forty years, it is apparent that I did not make things easy for Lou. Here is the exceptionally suitable but formidable and perhaps minatory group who agreed to serve as academic referees for Lou's evolving dissertation: the distinguished practicing psychoanalyst Abram Kardiner, who had been analyzed by Freud himself,[7] and who, as adjunct professor at Columbia, had recently begun the collaboration with the anthropologist Ralph Linton that eventuated in his well-known volumes tracing the reciprocities of culture and personality;[8] the

---

York: Wiley, 1979); you might also glance at its Foreword. For an algorithm providing estimates from partial data on aggregated citations, see Nancy L. Geller, John S. de Cani, and R. E. Davies, "Lifetime-Citation Rates to Compare Scientists' Work," *Social Science Research* 7 (1978): 345-65. I am indebted to Dr. Eugene Garfield and the Institute for Scientific Information which he directs for searching out the citations to the paper on deferred gratification.

7.   This, of course, meant much to Kardiner. For the account, see Abram Kardiner, *My Analysis with Freud* (New York: W.W. Norton, 1977).

8.   By way of reminder: Abram Kardiner, with two ethnological reports by Ralph Linton, *The Individual and His Society* (New York: Columbia University Press, 1939); Abram Kardiner, with Ralph Linton, Cora du Bois, and James West, *The Psychological Frontiers of Society* (New York: Columbia University Press, 1945); Abram Kardiner and Lionel Ovesey, *The Mark of Oppression: A Psychosocial Study of the American Negro* (New York: W.W. Norton, 1951).

economist Joseph Dorfman, who, almost a decade before, had published his magisterial full-scale biography, *Thorstein Veblen and His America;* with these Freudian and Veblenian orientations being supplemented by the sharply contrasting sociological styles of thought distinctive of Robert S. Lynd, of *Middletown* and *Knowledge for What?* fame, and Robert M. MacIver, the pungent Scottish-American theorist and author of many books, including *Community, Social Causation,* and *Society.* As the relatively young sponsor of Lou's dissertation, I brought up the rear.

This collection of diverse intellects was not one to be easily satisfied by any given piece of scholarly work. Consider, by way of tacit background, that just a few years before, Robert MacIver—no one ever called him "Bob"—had published what was then regarded as a blistering review of Bob Lynd's *Knowledge for What?*, which contrary to his usual practice soon elicited a sturdy reply in print from Bob. By the standards, say, of seventeenth-century scientific controversy or, for that matter, of today's endemic disputes of an *ad hominem* variety in parts of the philosophy of science and other polemicized disciplines, the tone of this public exchange would be judged as rhetorically even-tempered and cognitively sharp, the sort of thing that leads the scholarly reader as the ever-present third party to respect both the principals in the debate and their announced, though contrasting, sociological principles.[9] Nevertheless, this proved to be an episode which enlarged the personal rift between MacIver and Lynd, scarcely allowing them to see eye to eye on most intellectual matters in the department.[10]

---

9. The debate may still hold interest for its concise archetypes of contrasting philosophies of social science; see Robert M. MacIver, "Enduring Systems of Thought," and Robert S. Lynd, "Intelligence Must Fight," *Survey Graphic* 28 (August 1939):496-99.

10. By way of still further context of the sort you want to know more about, here is Robert MacIver's penitent testimony on the matter some thirty years later. He writes of a period during which Lou began his resident graduate work that there "was a sharp cleavage within the department. I had been its chairman for more than a decade, and now there was an active revolt. The leader of the opposition was my major colleague, Robert Lynd. From the beginning we had differences of viewpoint on the focus of sociology and on the function of university instruction. He wanted to professionalize the teaching, to make it primarily utilitarian, preparing the students for profes-sional service. I laid stress on the significance of sociology for the under-standing of society and the development of a coherent science of society, claiming that our students were provided . . . with a broad training that would enable them to play their parts in responsible positions. I had always welcomed differences of viewpoint within the department and was aware of Professor Lynd's position before inviting him to join us. . . . What brought the issue to a head was a rather injudicious action of my own. Professor

All this happened in the late 1930s; Paul Lazarsfeld and I came along somewhat later. In his autobiography, MacIver tells how that occurred:

> One thing both sides agreed on was that the department of sociology was seriously undermanned [and reading that text today, one must add, even more seriously underwomanned], but each side had different ideas about the choice of new members. My first choice was Robert Merton, a Harvard graduate [and now, Jo, I shamelessly continue with the quotation, just as you said I must do in such cases] whom I regarded as the most promising of our younger sociologists. Professor Lynd and some others particularly favored Paul Lazarsfeld, a Vienna graduate who had transferred from mathematics to research in social psychology and sociology and was a forceful proponent of quantitative methods in the social sciences. The upshot was that both of these scholars were elected [MacIver 1968, p. 141].

That, then, is how it was that in due course I became sponsor of Lou's dissertation after those stormy years. Lou enjoyed the irony that Paul

---

Lynd had published a book entitled *Knowledge for What,* in which he emphasized the utilitarian conception of education. I was invited to write a review of it—and did so, trenchantly enough. That was the breaking point. [And then, after due reflection, Robert concludes:] It was unwise to write a highly critical review of a book by a colleague." MacIver's account appears in his autobiography, *As a Tale that is Told* (Chicago: University of Chicago Press, 1968), pp. 137-38. Charles Page, who was there first as graduate student and then briefly as lecturer, provides a more detailed account of the troubled 1930s and early 1940s in the Columbia department. See his recent autobiography, cited properly by reversing the published title and subtitle, thus: *A Lucky Journey: 50 Years in the Sociological Enterprise* (Amherst: University of Massachusetts Press, 1982), chapter 2. A perceptive, critical, and beautifully composed analysis of MacIver's sociological thought appears in chapter 6 of Robert Bierstedt, *American Sociological Theory: A Critical History* (New York: Academic Press, 1981). As you may know, Bob Bierstedt and Robert MacIver's daughter, Betty, have been married for some forty-five years; that makes his even-handed analysis all the more impressive. The most detailed discussion of Bob Lynd's sociological work known to me appears in a special issue of *The Journal of the History of Sociology* (2 [Fall 1979-80]: 1-152), edited by Gillian Lindt, who provides an apt introduction, "Robert S. Lynd: American Scholar-Activist." Irving Louis Horowitz provides a succinct biographical account in "Robert S. and Helen Merrell Lynd" in the *International Encyclopedia of the Social Sciences: Biographical Supplement,* edited by David L. Sills (New York: Free Press, 1979), vol. 18, pp. 471-77.

and I, who had never met before, were brought together as proponents of supposedly opposed sociological orientations.

A more immediate and more disconcerting context than the MacIver-Lynd rivalry which threatened the official acceptance of Lou's dissertation was Kardiner's memorandum, here quoted in full, on an early draft. Kardiner managed to sandwich a meaty paragraph of rare praise between two scorching paragraphs of overdone blame:

Dr. A. Kardiner
1095 Park Avenue
New York City

January 17, 1943

I have received the thesis of Mr. Louis Schneider, and have read it over once. As a preliminary report on this work I can say this: I am in no position to evaluate the sociological side of his thesis. My impression is that he has undertaken a foolish task and one impossible to consummate. The reason is very simple. Psychology and sociology do not operate with concepts on the same level of abstraction and hence their results can in no way be compared.

Apart from this however those portions of the thesis which deal with psychoanalysis and the trends in psychoanalysis and recent developments are really excellent. They show an exhaustive knowledge, a sympathetic study and a fairness of presentation which was to me delightful to read. It is in fact the only time I have had an opportunity in the last six years to see a report of recent developments in psychoanalytic theory insofar as they pertain to sociology presented in a dispassionate manner and with fairness to the various workers. Here and there he falls down for reasons that are quite obvious. I do not happen to know whether Mr. Schneider has been analyzed, but even if he were it would make little difference. He understands the development of psychoanalysis as well as it is possible for an outsider—that is, the clinical difficulties that made many of these recent innovations necessary. This is not to his discredit. However the uses that he makes of his psychoanalytic knowledge to solve the sociological problems are not convincing, and the thesis as a whole, particularly with regard to Veblenism seems to me to be extremely weak.

If you wish I shall give you a more complete report on the psychoanalytic aspects of this paper with some suggestions about how it might be followed more fruitfully. I think Mr. Schneider has gone about as far as one can with the sources that he has at his disposal, but he evidently cannot go beyond the point that the so-called psychoanalytic sociologists have gone. This is not his fault.

If this is not a thesis for the degree I would certainly discourage Mr. Schneider from proceeding with his endeavor; and if it is too late to change his course, I can affirm that the psychological side is very diligently and carefully done. But it stands apart from the main thesis of his work.

Sincerely yours,
A. Kardiner, M.D.

As I soon indicated to Abe Kardiner, he was of course profoundly mistaken in asserting that Lou had embarked on a fool's errand by attempting to *compare* the results provided by psychological and social theory. That was not at all the objective. Rather, Lou had agreed to take on the focused task of examining Freud's psychology and Veblen's social theory in order to analyze socio-psychological mechanisms linking social structure and individual behavior, not in order to compare their efficacy in accounting for the "same" phenomena. It would be ironic were Abe to continue in this misconception since the aim of the dissertation was formally, not substantively, much like Abe's own aim in his book *The Individual and His Society* (and, as only a seer could then have known, in several of his later books as well). Substantively, the dissertation drew upon quite another sociological orientation. That ongoing theoretical perspective was partly directed toward working out the socio-psychological dynamics of structural locations with regard both to patterns of individual choice among socially structured alternatives of behavior and the socially patterned development of character structure.[11] Lou's dissertation had the distinct potential of contributing to that sociological perspective, and since Abe's middle paragraph was in unwonted praise of Lou's "exhaustive knowledge . . . sympathetic study and . . . fairness of presentation" of psychoanalysis, should not this early draft of the dissertation be approved in principle? In the event it was, but not before further vicissitudes.

---

11. For a deeply informed and uncannily precise analysis of this evolving line of theoretical inquiry, see Arthur Stinchcombe's detailed analysis in Lewis Coser, ed., *The Idea of Social Structure* (New York: Harcourt Brace Jovanovich, 1975), pp. 11-33, esp. pp. 25-26 that deal with the "transformation of levels" of theorizing. In accord with the terminological and conceptual usage initiated by Imre Lakatos, such a line of inquiry would nowadays be described as an SRP (scientific research program). Should you be interested in that metatheory, see Imre's detailed discussion, "Falsification and the Methodology of Scientific Research Programmes," in Imre Lakatos and A. Musgrave, eds., *Criticism and the Growth of Knowledge* (Cambridge University Press, 1970), pp. 91-196.

Unknown to me as sponsor at the time this discussion with Kardiner was taking place, Joseph Dorfman, the authority on Veblen, has sent his opinion of the manuscript to Bob Lynd, then chairman of the department. Dorfman's letter supplies other contingent difficulties in the evolving saga of the dissertation:

January 14, 1943

It seems to me that the Schneider dissertation is concerned basically with Freud. The discussion of Veblen appears to be for the purpose of filling out the dissertation, and its omission would not be noticed. There is really only one chapter on Veblen (Chapter 3) of twenty-eight pages. I think the reader will get the impression that it is rather vague, aside from the idea that Veblen emphasizes the irrationality of human nature.

The author's short analysis of *The Theory of the Leisure Class* at the end (pp. 137-138) is not very enlightening. The author's assertion that this book is concerned with "the pervasiveness of the 'pecuniary motive' in modern social life" may be true, but history is full of thinkers, literary figures, and pulpit orators who have presented the same theme.

I think the question of the acceptability of the dissertation turns on the question whether his discussion of Freud is original and enlightening.

Sincerely,
Joseph Dorfman

Meanwhile, Robert MacIver advises me that the dissertation is acceptable as "a first draft" and, in a rare meeting of minds, Bob Lynd takes the same position. I give Lou my suggestions for revision and he is encouraged by the word that the dissertation has been approved in principle, though subject to much revision and development. But immediate further work on the dissertation must be set aside as Lou moves on to Washington, first to fill a post as economist for the War Production Board and then for the Office of Price Administration. He plows into these new assignments with concentrated vigor. After a spell, he manages to get back to the dissertation, by this time more accurately described as "the book" since we had reason to assume that it would be published. That assumption was based in part on the merits of the dissertation as a distinct contribution to theoretical sociology and in part on the long-standing requirement at Columbia, terminated only in 1950, that doctoral dissertations must be published. (If memory does not deceive, Columbia was one of the two last American universities to retain that requirement, designed to maintain high standards for dissertations by having them subject to organized skepticism, i.e., widespread scrutiny in the scholarly community.)

Lou digs into the manuscript in increasing earnest and by mid-summer of 1946, submits the penultimate draft. The dissertation saga moves toward conclusion. MacIver writes Lou that he has read through the revised dissertation, that it is greatly improved, and that he finds in it

> some excellent pieces of analysis. I am entirely in favor of acceptance. There are some positions taken in the study that may be controversial, but I have not touched on these. On the other hand there are quite a few special points and a few larger questions that I would like you to consider for a final revision. These I have indicated in a fairly long series of pencilled annotations. But I am sending the MS to the Department since I wanted Professor Merton to see the nature of my comments. [This is late summer, and MacIver is happily ensconced in his Chilmark haven on Martha's Vineyard.] I hope in this way that we can facilitate the last stages of your progress to the degree [8 August, 1946].

The pace quickens. Bob Lynd reports his satisfaction with the revision. I visit Abe Kardiner for a long evening session, replete with his favorite Scotch, which is entirely given over to a detailed discussion of Lou's greatly revised manuscript. Abe requires no persuasion; he is impressed by Lou's clear treatment of the modes of connecting institutional and individual levels of analysis, the sort of thing that you remember I had been urging upon Abe several years before as the theoretically derived objective of the inquiry. Joseph Dorfman is away from Columbia at this time and there is no immediate word from him. Further delay is unthinkable. After all, a consensus among the theoretically assorted four of us— MacIver, Lynd, Kardiner and myself—was sure to carry the day in the event that Dorfman were to dissent. At long last, I am able to write Lou an official letter of acceptance, along with a somewhat more personal note, inevitably tinctured with allusions to editorial suggestions for the published version:

November 18, 1946

Dear Schneider:

> Let me congratulate you on having written a good contribution to social theory. The dissertation remains consistently on the very highest level of systematic thinking and I, for one, regard it as a

major event. So far as I am concerned, it is entirely satisfactory for you to proceed with arrangements for publication. Do feel free to ignore any or all [of the] suggestions I have scribbled on the margins. I happen to think that the work would be somewhat improved if you were to eliminate some of the "extraneous" material, but [and here comes an apt Freudian slip] that is ultimately a matter of text [! taste, of course]. It would also help, I think, if you were to cut down the very numerous phrases which are of a purely introductory character: e.g. "At this point we must have reference to a matter which we have considered above. . . ." But that again is entirely trivial. I am sending you my copy of the dissertation and shall be glad to discuss it with you if you want to take up further details.

Again, I want to tell you how highly I regard the entire work and to express my regret in the delayed reading.

Almost two months later, Dorfman returns and conscientiously sends on his judgment of the final draft. At the time, it seemed anticlimactic; today, it provides further context for the complexity of Lou's initial and developing attitudes toward his first and, to my mind, seminal book.

January 9, 1947

Dear Merton:

I think that my opinion of Schneider's dissertation is summed up in the reference to me in the preface [see below]. Our differences rest on matters of interpretation of Veblen, but that is a matter, perhaps, of opinion. I think that Mr. Schneider has lost sight of the "fact"—that is, a fact to me—that Veblen's contrast between "business" and "industry" runs through all of Veblen's work. Schneider might ask himself, for instance, when discussing Veblen's psychology at such length, how it has come to pass that Veblen, although having presumably the same psychology as James, McDougall, and Wallas, reaches different conclusions in regard to the social order. Another example is in connection with a footnote by Schneider on page 323. He says "There is a definite tendency in his [Veblen's] thought to regard all human activities not undertaken in the interest of industrial efficiency or procreation as pathological aberrations." [The footnote, essentially unchanged, appears on p. 219 of the published book.] The author, I think, misses the point that Veblen is in reality discussing the industrial efficiency of activities that are presumed to make for industrial efficiency. The "sports" Veblen is discussing are the combats of the captains of finance.

I do not know that these matters make much difference. Perhaps the most important questions in the thesis are in connection with Freud, on which I am less than a novice.

                              With high regards,
                              Dorfman

Dorfman's wry allusion to Lou's preface is more perceptive than he could have known. But now that this relatively detailed life history of the dissertation is before you to supply both context and subtext, you can readily read between the lines of Lou's not wholly *pro forma* preface to the first printing of *The Freudian Psychology and Veblen's Social Theory*. Here it is:

Preface

This writer wishes to express his gratitude and appreciation to the following persons:

Professor Robert K. Merton, who afforded encouragement and numerous valuable suggestions when this study was initially worked out, and stimulated its writer to better efforts;

Professor Robert M. MacIver, Professor Robert S. Lynd and Doctor Abram Kardiner, all of whom gave the writer a conviction of the feasibility of the study at times when he was inclined to waver on this point;

Professor Joseph Dorfman, who was tolerant of an effort to put Veblen to what may well have appeared to him to be strange uses.

Lou was not entirely satisfied with the dissertation even after it saw print. Neither was I. However, I thought much more of it than he. You might think my opinion suspect since the occasional piety of a student for an erstwhile teacher is as nothing compared with the occasional piety of a teacher for an erstwhile student come to full maturity. The book took on a life of its own which I do not undertake to trace through the initial reviews, its use by successive cohorts of scholars as loosely signalled by citations to it, and the continuing interest in it as indicated by its having been reprinted a decade ago. Lou's growing ambivalence toward the book which he expressed to you, Jo, and your beloved Valerie as well, finds ample expression in the prefatory note whose inclusion in the new printing he made a condition of republication. In that note, you will hear echoes from this composite life-history and saga of the dissertation:

Prefatory Word: 1973

This book was written a quarter of a century ago. In that span of time my views of many things have inevitably changed considerably. There are statements here with which I would certainly disagree and others with which I would be acutely uncomfortable. Even in 1948 it was most unwise to support Elton Mayo's views of economic theory. Veblen himself has limitations I would have done well to recognize more clearly and fully. I am less enamored of various neo-Freudian ideas than I once was.

Nevertheless, I still believe that some of the effort here made was not entirely misguided. I think it was worth while to attempt to work out an apparatus for analysis of connections between psychological and social phenomena. What I did in this regard might have been done better, but at the time I made my venture there was even less available than there is now to give one help. I take advantage of this opportunity to refer the interested reader to a slightly later venture of the same general sort but with a different accent, namely, my paper entitled "Some Psychiatric Views on Freedom and the Theory of Social Systems," *Psychiatry* 12 (1949), 251-264 [reprinted as Chapter 5 of this volume].

My book was also quite peculiarly a product of its post–World War II time, in ways, indeed, that I could not realize twenty-five years ago. Thereby, whatever its defects, I think a certain historical interest attaches to it. There appears to be some demand for it, in any case, and I trust that the present Greenwood Press reprint will be useful to a number of readers.

Another word to indicate anew that, in Lou's case, the style is indeed the man himself and I am done with this story of the dissertation years. Not unlike his Scottish moral philosophers, Lou paid punctilious, almost courtly attention to politesse in his personal relations just as he paid scrupulous attention to intellectual details in his style of thought. From the time we met in 1941 until the time of the final acceptance of the dissertation in 1947, he meticulously addressed me, in conversation and in letters, as Professor Merton or Dr. Merton, thus successfully resisting my every suggestion that we drop such formality, and thus, also, requiring me to address him as Mr. Schneider or, in letters, as Schneider. Although we did not differ much in age, in Lou's scheme of things, I was, after all, his mentor and the sponsor of his dissertation. And so by example he quietly insisted on an appropriate symbolism of structural distance. No sooner was the final draft of the dissertation accepted than I was alerted to the change by his easy shift to "Robert" and "Bob" with the clear intimation that I might now feel free to address him as "Louis" or even "Lou." And so I did, in 1947, the sixth year of our association.

If the dissertation can be taken as the peak event in Lou's intellectual life of the 1940s, then his consequential year at the Center for Advanced Study in the Behavioral Sciences can surely be taken as the peak event in both his intellectual and personal life in the 1950s, as you, Jo, above all others, have ample reason to know. I resist the temptation to rehearse the prehistory and beginnings of the Center, pausing only to express the hope that a systematic historical account of that venturesome innovation in the social sciences will be forthcoming one of these days. But I must not resist reviewing a little of Lou's experience at the Center as an enduring basis and context for much of his work on religion in society, a portion of which comprises Part III of this volume.

That phase of the story begins with Lou writing me in early 1954 from Purdue University, where he had been teaching for five years after a two-year stint at Colgate:

January 22, 1954

Dear Bob:

My departmental chairman has been kind enough to nominate me for a fellowship with the Center for Advanced Study in the Behavioral Sciences. I have just filled out a form for the Center and have taken the liberty of using your name as reference. I trust this will not evoke excessive ire on your part.

This year, thus far, has been a particularly hectic one. I stand in need of thorough spiritual repair, but I hope you are doing much better.

The expressed need for "spiritual repair" recurs periodically in Lou's letters to me—as we shall see, about every ten years—but more of that later. Here I note only that Lou had no way of knowing that his chairman's nomination had come at a most opportune moment; seldom again in the now thirty-year history of the Center could a nomination be acted upon so promptly. As the Center became institutionalized, it accumulated a large, growing backlog of nominations sifted and sorted by national panels of referees in each of the major disciplines with the result that the relatively large numbers of young scholars approved for fellowships are typically required to wait for some time before room can be found for them in a particular cohort. But 1954-55, you remember, was to be the very first year of the Center. This meant that though the first several cohorts of prospective senior Fellows could readily be agreed upon by the advisory committee of the Center, able younger scholars of far less visibility had to be drawn to their attention.

Time was running down with decisions on prospective Fellows to be made at least by the end of the academic year. For reasons now unknown to me, I did not respond to Lou's quietly urgent letter for two weeks:

February 4, 1954

Dear Louis,

You evidently have no idea that you have been so much with me these past weeks. I was delighted to learn that your chairman had nominated you for the fellowship, particularly since I had been doing so for some time before. It all promises to be an intellectually exciting place and I do hope that you will find your way there. If ever you have doubts on the matter, please check with me before you say "no." I am taking precisely the same position with the Director of the Center with respect to your nomination. In short, I believe the Center and you were made for each other.

. . . There's simply no sense in anyone like you having a hectic time of it. If spiritual repair is needed then, by Heaven, let's get it started.

Within four days—this was the less inhibited postal system of the 1950s—I have Lou's expression of deepening interest in the Center and his assurance that "the process of spiritual repair has already been initiated by your good letter. I feel the 'conquering mood' coming back and am looking forward to new enterprises." He goes on to tell of "the rather vasty text on *Power, Order, and the Economy* which I wrote with two others here [that] should be off the presses before very long."

Time passes and pressure evidently builds. On March 31st, there is the brief, urgent yet restrained inquiry: "If you have the information, and it is ethical to divulge it, I'd like to know what prospects I may actually have of getting one of the Center's fellowship awards." The evolving process of selection at the Center runs its course and it is mid-May before Lou and I simultaneously learn that he will be in the first cohort of Fellows. I write him about the shared sense that new things are astir:

I am delighted to know that you'll be at the Center this next year. Although the first year is bound to be less crystallized than the years scheduled to follow, it may be all the more interesting and instructive on that very account. Since I think of it now, might I suggest that you consider writing me about your experiences from time to time if only because of my obvious interest in knowing about the emergence of an "institution" almost from scratch.

The Book [*Power, Order, and the Economy*] has just come to hand and I find myself intrigued by the organization of what you have set out to do. I get the impression that you proceeded simply to inter-disciplinize (!) without bothering to announce that the event is taking place. And that, it must be said, is all to the good [12 May 1954].

The appearance of this interdisciplinary text (written with M. B. Ogle and W. J. Wiley) could scarcely have been more symbolically and intrinsically apt. By design and aspiration, the Center was to be an interdisciplinary home for all the behavioral sciences (focused on the core of the social sciences) and Lou had done much thinking on these matters. Lou's perspective, incidentally, was foreshadowed during his graduate studies when he took as many courses in economics and anthropology together as in sociology, an uncommon configuration in those days.

At the Center, you will recall, Lou finds himself in the company of many a stalwart in the various behavioral sciences: one group comprises the Viennese biologist and polymath Ludwig von Bertalanffy; the physiologist and polymath Ralph W. Gerard; the economist Kenneth E. Boulding; and the Russian-born mathematical biologist Anatol Rapoport, who, during their year as fellow Fellows, launched the international research program known as General Systems Theory and Research. The psychologists that year include the experimental social psychologist Alex Bavelas; the psychoanalytically oriented formulator of the concept "intolerance of ambiguity," Else Frenkel-Brunswik; and as frequent visitors, Bob Sears and Jack Hilgard from neighboring Stanford. The consequential anthropologists are Clyde Kluckhohn, John P. Gillin, and Allan Holmberg, while political science takes manifold form in the singular person of Harold D. Lasswell, who, among his many pioneering works, had long before taken the lead in consolidating political analysis with ideas drawn from Freud. Finally, in sociology, the pervasive senior scholar is Paul F. Lazarsfeld and the decidedly youthful one, Sanford M. Dornbusch. All told, an intellectual microenvironment that can hardly fail to be of interest to Lou with his own multi-disciplinary curiosity, and one in which he can continue with his program of spiritual repair. Or to vary the figure, one in which Lou can store up intellectual capital on which he will draw immediately and for years to come.

As the year at the Center comes to a close, Lou sends me some reflections on it. Lou's letter provides context for the beginnings of his enduring interest in the sociology of religion, hints at the subtext of his distinctively functional orientation toward problems in that field, and conveys a little of the atmosphere in the first year of the Center. It warrants quotation in full:

July 29, 1955

Dear Bob:

It has been an extremely pleasant year, and, I cannot help feeling, a quite profitable one. Paul Lazarsfeld cornered me some nights ago and subjected me to close inquiry about what I had done here, how the Center had contributed to it, etc.[12] I freely admit I could not satisfy him in his desire to elicit something very specific in justification of my enthusiasm for this place, but I retain the unconquerable sentiment that my time has been very well spent. Morale sustains itself even at the present critical point, when a number of the new Fellows have arrived and the pioneers are constrained to fold their tents. I've made some friends whom I expect to retain. As matters

---

12. This probing was not at all idle curiosity on Paul Lazarsfeld's part. It was, rather, an expression of his long-standing vision of an institute given over to advanced study in social research. The Center for Advanced Study as instituted in 1954—and as it has continued ever since—departed from that vision of advanced training for theory-oriented and policy-oriented social research as laid out in a position paper a few years before. The elucidative note to that paper—"A Professional School for Training in Social Research," eventually published in 1972—conveys Paul Lazarsfeld's sense of defeat even as it hints at the otherwise invisible prehistory of the center, which had meant so much to Lou and to many other scholars since. The note reads: "Written with Robert K. Merton. This memorandum, written in 1950, was widely circulated in mimeographed form. A faculty committee at Columbia University discussed the matter but found that no funds were available to carry out the plan. The memorandum was then submitted to the Ford Foundation, which in turn appointed a committee. In the course of discussions, alternative ideas were considered which finally led to the creation of the Center for Advanced Study in the Behavioral Sciences. [And then Paul's elegiac observation:] Its structure is quite different from the one proposed in the present memorandum." Pp. 361-91 in P.F. Lazarsfeld, *Qualitative Analysis: Historical and Critical Essays* (Boston: Allyn & Bacon, 1972).

finally turned out, my closest relations have perhaps been to Ken Boulding and Sandy Dornbusch. I think very well indeed of these two.

I did not get much writing done. But Sandy and I have been collaborating for months on a content analysis of inspirational religious literature, the *Peace of Mind—Power of Positive Thinking* sort of thing, from about 1880 on. We've had two coders busy on this affair for quite a long time and I'm hopeful that we'll get some worthwhile things—possibly, material for a small book. I think we may find a shift somewhere around 1935 from a view that "following the principles of Christianity" will make one a worldly success to a view that it will make one (emotionally) healthy. We may also find some interesting things relating to "suffering": Whereas other and older religious orientations involved the notion that "suffering" was in some sense transparent, in that one could look behind or through it and detect a transcendent, dramatic significance in it, I make the guess that the literature we're investigating will de-value suffering radically and look on it as a kind of brute, non-transparent thing, best gotten rid of as quickly as possible. I'm fooling with a category of "presentization," i.e., bringing into the present things that used to be regarded as "last things"—Father Divine's followers, claiming that Divine is God, so that it is not necessary to wait until a next life in order to see God, illustrate what I mean, as does the whole powerful emphasis that salvation is in the here and now. Instrumentalization seems to me a pertinent category too: in this literature the stress on utilization of the deity seems to be very strong, and at times all his ancient presumptive appurtenances fade into the background, I suspect, in favor of his one function as a kind of especially effective phenobarbital pill. Perhaps I convey something of what we're after. If it looks as if we're likely to get anywhere, I think I see ways of fleshing out the results of the content analysis with some pertinent historical and sociological considerations. For the rest, I have an odd piece coming out in *Phylon* and two or three half-finished, problematic kinds of things hanging around.

On the personal side, it's been a year of tremendous re-invigoration. My ordinarily rather slatty frame has taken on some twenty pounds. I shall return to Purdue in a storm of energy. I hope you're very well yourself and I trust you've accomplished a good deal. When the spirit moves me, I shall certainly write again. You will remark on the increasingly theological cast of my style. To judge from Ken Boulding's reaction to the work that Sandy and I have been doing, the new style is merely appropriate. When we reported on and asked for criticism of this work, Ken threw a rather delicious tantrum, condemned what he conceived as a misplaced quantitative emphasis, and accused us of pursuing "inspirational science." Voilà!

I shall be leaving the Center in about two weeks, but it's been a memorable year.

Evidently the year for spiritual repair has done its work. Witness the private testimony that he leaves "in a storm of energy" and the immediate, publicly visible result in the collaborative paper with Sandy Dornbusch "Inspirational Religious Literature: From Latent to Manifest Functions" (reprinted in this volume as Chapter 12) and the later collaborative monograph *Popular Religion.* I do not pause here to remark on the intimation of Lou's growing and enduring interest in the unanticipated consequences of purposive social action which is registered in the subtitle of the paper "From Latent to Manifest Functions." That is best considered later.

What cannot be postponed, however, is the unanticipated, unintended, and, in principle, unforeseeable consequence of Lou's year at the Center that surpasses all others, one which Lou characteristically tells about in a severely understated postscript to a note dated January 7, 1956. You have probably never seen this postscript written in unmistakably Schneiderian prose and so I quote it in its entirety:

P.S. Do you remember Jo Sundine, Ralph Tyler's secretary at the Center during the first year? I am unashamed to aver that I took the "best thing" the Center had to offer: Jo and I were married January 3.

I rather suspect that, as director of the Center, Ralph Tyler did not greatly appreciate this surpassing moment of Lou's spiritual repair.

All apart from that unique prize, it was the variously consequential year at the Center in Palo Alto, I believe, which led Lou, a decade later, to want another time of renewal. At any rate, it was then that he wrote me to say that he would like to have a semester for thinking and writing at that other Center for Advanced Study, the one at the University of Illinois, where, I gather, Lou had been enjoying his stint of teaching for the preceding four years. In our highly credentialed society, even scholars of distinction must be vouched for by colleagues-at-a-distance asked to serve as referees. And so this resulted in the following letter to the Illinois authorities which at least now has the belated value of indicating how some of us then perceived Lou's place in the domain of sociological scholarship and his evolving research program in theoretical sociology.

December 29, 1964

Dear Dean ———,

. . . Louis Schneider has a very special niche in contemporary American sociology. He is one of the comparatively few who alerts the rest of the fraternity to significant theoretical problems that have been unjustifiably neglected. His work on a sociological theory of ignorance or on patterns of deferred gratification or on unanticipated consequences of social action represents particularly well known cases of this kind. He has a knack for examining works in classical social theory and finding new contemporary relevance in them. Several of us here at Columbia are especially glad to hear that he intends to make a close study of the 18th-century Scottish theorists Ferguson, Millar, Adam Smith, Hume and the others, since Professor Lazarsfeld and I have become persuaded of the importance of these theorists in the course of the seminar we are giving jointly.

It would be presumptuous of me to tell you that Professor Schneider enjoys a merited reputation as one of the more incisive sociological theorists in this generation. I very much hope that you and your colleagues can give him the opportunity he so amply merits to write the book which many of us would like to read.

In the event, many of us did enjoy reading *The Scottish Moralists on Human Nature and Society* (1967) and the subsequent papers on these "roots of modern social science," which, intermittently published during the next fifteen years, comprise Part I of this volume.

By the way, my note on behalf of that anticipated fruitful semester at the Illinois Center at once elicited a three-sentence note from Lou. The last sentence exhibits his engaging capacity for self-mockery and for joy in private life:

January 4, 1965

The content of [your] note made me strut for two days, until I had to desist for the ridiculous effect I saw being produced in our small, highly imitative daughter. [As I recall, Valerie would have just celebrated her second birthday.]

Having found spiritual repair at the Palo Alto Center in 1955 and at the Illinois Center in 1965—both to the enduring benefit of his fellow sociologists—Lou again seems ready, in 1975, for another such time of renewal. Here is his self-diagnosis in the concluding paragraph of a long letter otherwise and typically given over to some of my work, recent and ancient:

October 27, 1975

Somehow, lately, I've been involved in too many things I haven't deeply wanted to do, although there have happily been two or three I *have* wanted to do. I sense a certain staleness in me. My teaching has been rather more uninspired this year than in a long while and I'm going to try to get some time free for refreshment. (I estimate I have taught some five thousand students since I came here in 1967.) [Evidently, the University of Texas at Austin does have classes on the appropriately mammoth scale.] There's one bright spot on the horizon. I was invited some months ago to be one of nine speakers at the University of California at Santa Barbara this coming winter in a lecture series to celebrate the bicentennial of the publication of *The Wealth of Nations.* This brings me back to an abiding interest. I've begun work on my own lecture and it's the one thing this year that has given me a measure of zest. So, anyway, I do not sink quite into stagnancy.

My reply to this declaration is emphatic and confidently optimistic:

You "stagnant"! I accept the reported imagery only because I know the feeling so well. But I am confident that you will soon be yourself again and preparing that lecture in which you can mobilize so many of the ideas that have been haunting you through the decades.

The optimism was of course well founded. The zestful lecture, with its focus on "so salient a matter as 'unanticipated consequences of purposive social action,' " was delivered and now appears as the second essay in this volume.

I attach no significance, symbolic or intrinsic, to the decadal periodicity with which Lou announced a state of spiritual deficit and cognitive fatigue. After all, he may not have told me of other, equivalent bad times. I do have the impression, however, that for Lou, as for many of us, the times of melancholy and despair had a way of coming soon after the completion of a piece of work long in the doing. He evidently suffered an acute postpartum depression upon being separated from a favorite brainchild which he had ushered into the often harsh world of critical scholarship. This observation may, of course, be pure illusion since Lou was publishing books or major articles with some regularity throughout his scholarly life. Still, Lou himself linked by subtextual proximity a newly finished book with his concurrent state of mind. That was soon after the appearance of his (collaborative) book—the first since the dissertation six years before—when he was applying to the newly founded Center for Advanced Study in Palo Alto. We can scarcely overlook the juxtaposition of "spiritual disrepair" and appearance of the new book that appears in his letter dated February 7, 1954:

> The process of spiritual repair has already been initiated by your good letter. I feel the "conquering mood" coming back and am looking forward to new enterprises. By the way [was it truly by the way?], the rather vasty text on *Power, Order, and the Economy* which I wrote with two others here should be off the presses before very long.

Not being a materialist, Lou preferred the metaphor of obtaining spiritual repair to the alternative metaphor of acquiring new intellectual capital. However that might be, his need for an unencumbered stay at the Illinois Center for Advanced Study was expressed a decade later, soon after he had completed editing and writing parts of the two volumes, *Problems of Economics and Sociology: Essays by Carl Menger* and *Religion, Culture and Society.*

One more instance. As Jay Weinstein reminds us in his general introduction, Lou's "early years at Texas were the most productive of his life." So it was that in the spring of 1975, not long before his letter reporting a state of stagnation, he had published his comprehensive, consolidating book, *The Sociological Way of Looking at the World.* Searching through our correspondence during this period, I come upon my blurb for the book directed to what I took to be its central theme:

> A book focussed on sociological irony in the forms of "unanticipated consequences of purposive social action" and the "self-fulfilling prophecy" is bound to be of immense interest to sociologists. When that book is written in the commanding style that Louis Schneider brings to everything he writes, it should be of interest to everyone concerned to learn something about the workings of human society.

I write Lou of my pleasure in the book and, striving to temper his own critically based pleasure in it, he characteristically devotes himself to what he rightly regards as a barely perceptible defect. Organized skepticism is being rigorously self-applied.

May 6, 1975

Thank you for the comments about my book. I have been looking it over and have thus far found only one passage of a page or two in which I think I was rather too careless and forgetful of something important that should have been put in by way of clarification and expansion. But I suppose we all have our private owls of Minerva that fly by night. (My own owl is a hard-working bastard not content with getting his stint around midnight but insistent on an extra shift usually between 3:00 and 5:00 A.M.) Also, to be guilty of only one large burr in a book is so good for me that I am inclined to share some of your optimism with regard to this new item.

It is this passage, I believe, that led to my (undated) note for the files which reads in its entirety thus:

Louis Schneider exhibits a double "trained incapacity" (to adopt a term-and-concept drawn from his well-understood Veblen): an incapacity for poor thinking and a collateral incapacity for obscure writing. Not, of course, that he wholly avoids error or never writes an obscure sentence. Who on earth does? But so critical of his own work is he that, almost invariably, he detects and expunges the error or the obscurity. He provides a superb example of that most difficult aspect of organized skepticism which calls for being at least as critical of one's own work as of the work being put forward by one's peers.

And now, after reading our exchange of letters over the years, I see that this aspect of Lou's character as sociological scholar is more interesting than that. Always imposing heavy demands on himself, sometimes expressing regret that he was not doing even more by way of scholarship, he did not, in privately masochistic fashion, systematically belittle himself. In that regard, he was like another scholar of magnitude, Goldsworthy Lowes Dickinson, of whom E. M. Forster was able to say in his inspired biography: "He never exalted himself, and even resisted the more congenial temptation of self-deprecation." Here is an apt case in point from one of Lou's long letters mostly devoted to the anatomizing of my own work but directed here to looking inward:

October 19, 1976

You remember the Westminster Creed as cited by Max Weber, with its reference to that "state of sin and death in which they are by nature.'' Well, theologies change (even to the point of being no longer called theologies) and I would hardly think of myself as having started out in a "state of sin and death." But it does seem to me that I've had a kind of long, long struggle away from ignorance and intellectual ineptitude. (Be not concerned that I undervalue myself! That isn't the point at all and I don't think I do, anyway.) How anyone can come through with first-rate papers, in sociology especially, before he's thirty or thereabouts is a mystery to me: I don't fathom it at all.

Lou may not have been able to fathom such moments but I believe that in his own twenties and thereabouts he was laying a basis for his lifelong scholarship. This he began doing in the dissertation-book which he came to undervalue. We have only to examine the subtext of *The Freudian Psychology and Veblen's Social Theory*—its thematic intimations and lexical cues—to find the promise of analytical things to come, a promise largely fulfilled, and not least in the carefully selected sociological papers and essays that make up this volume. If you will bear with me in the concluding pages of this lengthening effort to provide context and subtext for a good many of those papers, I in turn shall try to be brief though not, I trust, cryptic.

All along and increasingly in the most recent years, Lou and I were variously aware of parallels and intersections in our sociological work. This congeniality of tastes ranged from broad similarities in patterns of work, problems and modes of exposition, to theoretical orientations, foci of scholarly attention and, in some measure, styles of thought. These parallels now become all the more striking to me as I reread the array of papers in this volume and the letters we exchanged over the years. The following letter expresses my pleasure in this affinity of outlook registered in the paper that appears as Chapter 10 in this volume:

Sunday, 14 September, 1975

Dear Lou,

Your letter reached me yesterday. . . . It could not have come at a better time. I had just settled down to read rather than only to scan your paper in the Festschrift before telling you again how very much I treasure your having contributed to it. Your decision to write on ironic perspective was itself a symbolic statement, one that unites our joint pasts and, if you'll allow me to say so, our joint styles of thought.

It is an altogether brilliant piece—evocative of whole sets of ideas and possibilities, informed in what it leaves unsaid, and altogether *controlled*. The last of these is evident throughout the paper. But, in this time of subjectivism run riot, I particularly appreciated your crisp reminder that "there can be such a thing as irony-mongering or paradox-mongering." And as always in your writing, I take pleasure in your powers of vigorous understatement.

That you should have also managed to weave deep-seeing allusions to some of my own specific interests in irony and paradox into the close-woven texture of your paper testifies once again to your sure control over the ideas you are elucidating.

The past thirty years have rushed by for some of us. It is good for me to know that we have shared them.

Now that I have read the paper again, I continue to find it luminous and evocative in every aspect, altogether suitable for inclusion in this fine anthology of Lou's sociological essays.

In speaking of the parallels between us, I do not, of course, for a moment suggest that any of these were confined to Lou and me; but the varied array of similarities does narrow things down. In one respect and, so far as I know, in only that respect, did we begin as similars and end as dissimilars. That has to do with details in styles of daily work. He was the lifelong owl, sometimes terminating his nocturnal work in the early morning hours at a time when I, also once an owl but then transmuted into a lark, would be beginning my matutinal work. But being alike simply in such workaday details would scarcely have made us sociological congeners.

We evidently remained akin in quite another aspect of style of work. We were both addicted to oral publication, continually and sometimes for years revising our thoughts in lectures before putting them into print. Indeed, this pattern of delayed print lay behind the circumstance that Lou was the second scholar and the first sociologist to refer in print, this in his published dissertation, to the paired concepts of "manifest and latent functions." Noting this as my terminology, he went on to refer the reader for my usage of the concepts to a monograph by the distinguished anthropologist Clyde Kluckhohn.[13] This may appear as an odd and possibly mistaken citation but it was not that at all. True, I had been developing the concepts and their associated problematics for a dozen years in lectures at Harvard and Columbia. But "Manifest and Latent

---

13.   Clyde Kluckhohn's monograph, should you want to look at it, is *Navaho Witchcraft,* Papers of the Peabody Museum of American Archaeology and Ethnology, Harvard University (Cambridge: Peabody Museum, 1944), XII, no. 2.

Functions'' did not find its way into print until 1949, a year after Lou's dissertation was published, when it appeared as the first chapter of *Social Theory and Social Structure*. Thus, Lou could cite only the monograph by Kluckhohn, who, having audited my lectures at Harvard, was taken with the analytical value of the concepts and, with my full assent, put them in use in his monograph. When my account of the concepts did finally appear I could draw upon Lou's dissertation as collateral background for my claim that Veblen had tacitly adopted the logic of latent-function analysis in setting out the pattern of conspicuous consumption. And, in this continuing chain of interactive developments of the central idea, Lou could in turn draw upon that reanalysis of conspicuous consumption to convey and to utilize the distinction between the two kinds of functions, in his Chapter 3 of the collaborative book, *Power, Order and the Economy*. I now round out this cluster of connected but unplanned episodes by again noting as further context that the eleventh essay in this volume—"Inspirational Religious Literature: From Latent to Manifest Functions of Religion" (written with Sandy Dornbusch)—originated during Lou's year at the Center in Palo Alto where, as it happens, not only Sandy but Clyde Kluckhohn were fellow Fellows.

Just as with our temporal work patterns and our sustained use of oral publication before going to print, Lou and I also shared with one another various agonies of exposition. I refer to only one of these, a problem that continued to plague us both for years. We are in December of 1948; the dissertation is now once and for all behind Lou; and he is writing me, in kindly, typically restrained style that he "rather especially enjoyed for its lucidity the article on 'The Self-Fulfilling Prophecy' in the *Antioch Review.*" Then, without pause, he goes on to say:

> There's a manuscript on my desk right now which, with some exasperation, I can only describe as "gnarled." I suspect that at least part of the trick is to be set to write just *one* paper when one is writing a paper, and to run it concurrently with two or three others which keep overflowing into the footnotes and which simply *must* be included.

The subtextual force of this juxtaposition was surely clear to both of us. The juxtaposition was saying that, in the case of the piece on the self-ful-filling prophecy, I had finally managed to write a single-minded paper while he was still struggling with the temptation to twist several distinct papers into one. Lou's gnarled manuscript in due course became thoroughly ungnarled, appearing the next year in the journal *Psychiatry,* under the title "Some Psychiatric Views on 'Freedom' and the Theory of Social Systems," and now reappearing as Chapter 5 in this volume. I suspect that Lou continued to wrestle with this ever-present temptation of trying to say too many things at once and, judging from the evidence found in this anthology of his major essays, all written much later than this one, he succeeded to a degree that I seldom did.

Another parallelism between us solidified our friendship as it reinforced our sociological commonalities. I believe that Lou would have told of this aspect of our friendship were he, far more appropriately, writing a foreword to a posthumous collection of my writings. I will try to do as much. As I say, we enjoyed the reciprocities of friendship as well as a mutuality of sociological interests. Especially in the latter years, Lou was watching over his former mentor just as, I am sure, he had long watched over his former students.

Here he is in 1968 writing me to say: "I do hope you'll find the time this summer for a new introduction to the older science-technology monograph. The relevant literature is of course still replete with references to it even where it disagrees." Just a summer later,[14] I am following Lou's quiet suggestion; the new edition with its new long introduction appears soon afterward. In that introduction, I explored the import of Lou's careful scholarly reminder, repeated in several of the essays in this book, that the monograph was not beyond criticism. Only another instance of Lou's commitment to the norm and practice of organized skepticism.

A few years later, he is again persuasively urging me to publish:

October 27, 1975

I want to ask whether you have any plans for bringing out another collection of your papers. There are so many of your things I have

---

14.   Lou was writing me in June of *1968* and so the year's delay in following his suggestion needs no gloss (even for one like myself with a notorious propensity for delaying publication). Still, as context, here is Lou's paragraph on the student revolt: "As regards Columbia, I can only wish for a peace reasonably satisfactory to all concerned. The turmoil, as you certainly know, is very widespread and the students, it seems to me as to numerous others, have their measure of justification despite their deplorable devices. There is an intensely concerned group of them here also. Were it larger, there might be some highly newspaperable consequences. I must say that I sometimes find a little alarming the level of political sophistication with which they approach a number of local problems. A gas-station owner who was apparently rotten toward a young Negro recently found himself faced with a strategy of opposition that would have done credit to a highly trained corps of Bolsheviks."

missed. And then there is the business of fallible memory for the
contents of scattered papers. Paul's [Lazarsfeld's] comment on
"Sociological Ambivalence" made me re-read it. I think I read it
originally about the time it appeared, a dozen or so years ago. On
re-reading, I discovered I had forgotten a salient point which, had I
been in possession of it, would have resulted in a better statement
of a matter I took up in a recent publication. If "Sociological
Ambivalence" were solidly walled into another collection of your
papers and accordingly handy of access, this sort of thing would
not happen. So, I am sure I enhance your motivation. But I really
am most curious about whether you do contemplate another
collection.

The volume of essays, *Sociological Ambivalence,* appeared the next
year. And now you have context for the sentence in its preface: "I must
thank Paul F. Lazarsfeld and Louis Schneider for having independently
suggested that the essays 'Sociological Ambivalence' [written with Elinor
Barber] and 'The Unanticipated Consequences of Purposive Social
Action' be made more widely accessible." I was being looked after by a
colleague close at hand and by another, at a distance.

In all this, it seems that Lou was exhibiting a pattern of behavior
complementary to what Harriet Zuckerman describes in *Scientific Elite*
as role-reenactment: the behavior and attitudes of mentors toward
students that reproduce what the mentors had themselves experienced
when they were students. In repeatedly manifesting concern for his one-
time *mentor* become colleague-at-a-distance, Lou was reproducing
behavior and attitudes which that mentor had long before manifested
toward *his* mentor, Talcott Parsons. There are differences, of course,
between these complementary kinds of role-reenactment, principally in
the mechanisms of transmitting the patterns, but no matter. I must,
however, testify that Lou's suggestions made much better sense to me
than my suggestions to Talcott apparently made to him.

In drawing these diverse parallels, I am not remote from Lou's own
perceptions, I believe. At times, Lou himself would draw a parallel
between us, in the shape of formally similar though substantively
different lines of interest. Witness this self-assessment in a note dated
November 9, 1973:

What I'll be doing in the near future is not altogether certain. I'm
probably diffused over too much. I remember your telling me
about ten years ago, in Urbana, that you were resolved to stick
pretty exclusively to the sociology of science. I should summon a
like resoluteness . . . on the lines of sociology of religion or (some)
other line. . . .

As the bibliographic record shows, Lou did continue with his theoretical work on the history and systematics of social science with a focus on religion as well as culture and social change.

Lou and I traveled parallel lines backwards through time. I had lived a half-dozen years or so in seventeenth-century England, spending my days there first with Bacon and then with Newton, Harvey, Boyle, Hooke, Halley, and a good many of the lesser members of that band of natural philosophers who were bringing about a new era in the development of Western science. Lou spent at least as many years, by my reckoning, living in eighteenth-century Scotland, consorting there chiefly with the band of moral philosophers—Adam Smith, John Millar, Adam Ferguson, and more occasionally, David Hume, Thomas Reid, Francis Hutcheson, and Dugald Stewart—whose work, as Lou takes pains to show in Part I of this volume and elsewhere, can be regarded as the root of basic themes in contemporary social science. Now that I reread these essays about his old friends, the Scottish moralists, I am again persuaded that Lou felt more at home with them than with many a social scientist of his own time. In the company of those Scots, he was seldom glum. They were for him a source of sociological excitements. As he studied their often magisterial works, he discovered much sociology in them, both in and between the lines—sociological discoveries, I would argue, often resulting from the interaction between those eighteenth-century texts and their critically sympathetic and creative twentieth-century reader.

It was a little later that, in the same concentrated way, Lou turned a discerning eye to another denizen of his favorite century, the Dutch-born English thinker Bernard Mandeville, in the paper which originally appeared in 1970 and reappears as the first essay in this volume. I still treasure my offprint of that paper inscribed: "Courtesy of R.K. Merton!" That amiable inscription was a private subtext for the two of us, bearing on our shared interest in Mandeville. Lou had sent me the manuscript in my capacity as an associate editor of the *Journal of the History of the Behavioral Sciences.* I studied it with more than ordinary critical care to counterpoise my partiality for both the author and subject; the result, nevertheless, required me to inform the editor of the *Journal,* the psychologist Robert I. Watson, that I found it a "distinguished piece of work." What is more in point, since it bears directly upon the character and style of Lou's earlier papers on the Scottish moral philosophers and particularly on his developing interest in Mandeville, is the further report to Watson that

> Schneider is in thorough command of his materials and, unlike many who write on early forerunners, never overstates the case.

Evidently, he is sensitive to the dangers of "Whig" interpretations of history. I know that sociologists will find the paper of great interest and I should hope that other behavioral scientists would too. In fact, the only fault I can find in the paper is an occasional reference to me but I suppose that that can't be helped.[15]

Here is Lou's note to me upon hearing from Watson that the paper had been accepted for publication; it is a prelude to what would become, during the decade of the 1970s, Lou's ever-growing interest in Mandeville as a proto-functional analyst, an interest, as we know, that culminated in the book-length manuscript which has still to see print:

If Mandeville's ka—and I admit that this is most unlikely—but if his ka has been waiting around for this item for over two centuries, it should now be very pleased. On second thought, to heck with the ka; *I'm* most pleased.

Mandeville's scholarly ka should have been especially pleased by Lou's perceptive and evenhanded sensitivity to his divers ideas, not only to his "various sociological insights," but also to "the provocative ways in which he could be wrong." I like to think too, in accord with the hypothesis that the fundamentals of Lou's continually developing ideas were tucked away in that brilliant dissertation, that in part he turned his systematic attention to Mandeville because Mandeville's style of thought was in certain formal respects akin to Veblen's, even when they differed substantively. (Kin are not always agreed.) Lou was not, of course, the first or the last to compare Mandeville and Veblen; as he says, Joseph Spengler in particular had been there before him. But Lou was alone in those analytical observations—greatly expanded in his book-length manuscript—which variously link Mandeville, Veblen, and Freud. I am mindful, for one example, of a passage in the paper that echoes the unmistakable Veblenesque tone in the course of adopting a Freudian imagery:

---

15.   Just as Lou took pride in some of his students, so he took pride in one of his mentors. Thus it was that he wrote in the longish second footnote of the paper: "A rare instance of mention of Mandeville by a sociologist in recent years is afforded by Robert K. Merton, in his *On Theoretical Sociology* (New York, 1967), p. 21, where he refers to Spengler's paper. This reference can now also be found in Merton's *Social Theory and Social Structure* (New York, 1968), *q.v.,* at pp. 20-21 (and also at p. 475 for a much earlier reference to Mandeville)." We were both quite aware of our parallelisms of interest.

There may well be a deeper connection between Mandeville's short-comings in understanding social control and his limitations in understanding religion. [Now comes the Veblenesque stylistic echo.] We may be allowed to state the matter in laconic Freudian language. Mandeville is strong and apt and convincing where he has to deal with man's id (and ego) and various manifestations thereof, but less strong, apt and convincing where he confronts the task of understanding the superego and its manifestations: where he cannot break up (or break "down") moral furniture to his liking he becomes exceedingly suspicious of it and perhaps wishes to believe it does not exist.

In this same paper, Lou speaks of "the crude intimations of structural-functional analysis" to be found in Mandeville's work. As readers of the first paper in this volume will see for themselves, he then proceeds to sketch those "adumbrations" in methodical form, while resolutely avoiding the cardinal sin of "adumbrationism."[16] All of which brings me, briefly and mercifully, to the last of the parallel and intersecting sociological paths that Lou and I explored over the years: the theoretical orientation of structural and functional analysis, and most especially, its linkage with the idea of unanticipated and unintended consequences of social action.

Jay Weinstein has it altogether right, I believe, in his several intro-ductions to this book. Throughout his work, Lou retained a functional and structural perspective, one which he subjected to ongoing critical examination and use. In his critical appriasals and extensions, he took care to avoid patterned misunderstandings of what he was reading. He remained unperturbed by those excesses of functional and structural analysis which derived from prime if not exclusive attention to shared values and consensus just as he was unperturbed by those excesses of criticism that stereotypically ascribed to that mode of analysis what was not there. He would have none of those critics who, neglecting all evidence to the contrary, would reiteratively attribute to all forms of functional and structural analysis an Arcadian sociology in which everything mysteriously works together for good in society. Instead, he recognized as one of the fundamental problems of theoretical sociology the development of a conceptual scheme that would help us discover the

---

16.   The scholarly tracing of the history of ideas is one thing; the sin of adumbration*ism* is quite another. As I have noted elsewhere, "At the extreme, the adumbrationist describes the faintest shadow of resemblance between earlier and later ideas as virtual identity."

sources and consequences of the nonrationalities as well as rationalities that are perpetuated in social structures and their associated cultures. An enduring interest in this problem provided part of the basis for Lou's and my lifelong obsession with the phenomena of unanticipated and unintended consequences of social action.

All the other parallelisms and intersections between Lou and myself were shared by many others, with regard to some of them by myriad others. Owl and lark temporal patterns of work, the intensive use of oral publication, agonies of composition, an interest in one's mentors as well as one's students, even a prolonged visit to another century are peripheral contexts that are of course common beyond easy measure in academic life. And so, too, of course, with the central and publicly visible context provided by the successively modified theoretical orientation of functional and structural analysis which we shared with large numbers of sociologists.

I know of no other pair of present-day sociologists, however, who have been obsessed throughout their long working lifetimes by a belief in the fundamental importance in human society of unanticipated and unintended consequences of action, along with such kindred themes and special cases as manifest and latent functions and dysfunctions, the self-fulfilling and self-defeating prophecy, and the continuing play of irony in social structure and social change. To my knowledge, outside the domain of sociology, the only other contemporaries exhibiting that enduring obsession are Karl Popper and F.A. Hayek. Happily, what has long been an obsession for some of us now shows promise of becoming a sustained focus of sociological inquiry by others. One is happy to note in more recent years the important contributions to our understanding of such patterned types of unintended consequences by the French sociologist Raymond Boudon and by the Norwegian sociologist Jon Elster.

In referring to Lou's lifetime interest in this theme, I am being quite literal. From the time of his dissertation, when he took note of my mid-1930s piece on unanticipated consequences, to publication of his lecture on Adam Smith in 1979, he returned to the theme with growing frequency. The open text rather than subtext of the latter paper (which appears as Chapter 2 in this volume) contains both a retrospective and a programmatic statement of the theme with its reiterated lexical cue of UCPSA:

> A contemporary sociologist has made familiar to social scientists the rather long but useful phrase, "the unanticipated consequences of purposive social action." Adam Smith never employs just this

phrase, but what it points to interests him again and again. . . .
Indeed, so salient a matter as "unanticipated consequences of
purposive social action," which has played so large a role in the
philosophy of history and social science, has unexpectedly attracted
much attention before and must again [p. 53].

Temporally intermediate between Lou's earliest published allusion to
the theme in his 1948 *Freudian Psychology and Veblen's Social Theory*
and the paper on Adam Smith in 1979, was his iterated emphasis on the
intellectual history of the theme in his 1969 paper, "On Frontiers of
Sociology and History: Observations on Evolutionary Development and
Unanticipated Consequences" (which appears as Chapter 7 in this
volume). He refers to this as an "intellectual tradition" and then,
indulging his one-time mentor as we shall see, continues:

> The contemporary sociologist stands in this tradition when, after
> Merton, he speaks of the unanticipated consequences of purposive
> social action. In Merton's article under this title, a listing of the
> modern theorists who have (although not in equally significant
> ways) treated of unanticipated consequences gives the names of
> Machiavelli, Vico, Adam Smith, Marx, Engels, Wundt, Pareto,
> Max Weber, Graham Wallas, Cooley, Sorokin, Gini, Chapin and
> von Schelting. [In kindly tones, Lou then proceeds to further soften
> his mild notice of some of my youthful omissions.] Merton also
> indicates that "some later classical economists" after Smith might
> be included and indeed he might have added numerous other
> names, such as those of Mandeville, David Hume, Adam
> Ferguson, and the economists Carl Menger and Friedrich Hayek
> [pp. 170-71].

Lou goes on to observe that "the development of the entire idea of
unanticipated consequences of purposive social action is itself a matter
of tremendous interest in intellectual history." In making this apt
observation, Lou spares his old friend further mild embarrassment. He
does not ask when I intend to redeem the promissory footnote included,
with innocent arrogance, in the 1936 paper that announces:

> Some of the terms by which the whole or certain aspects of this
> process [of unanticipated consequences] have been known are:
> Providence (immanent or transcendental), *Moira, Paradoxie der
> Folgen, Schicksal,* social forces, heterogony of ends, immanent
> causation, dialectical movement, principle of emergence and
> creative synthesis. [And then comes the promissory note embar-
> rassedly eradicated from more mature reprintings:] The present

writer hopes to devote a monograph now in preparation to the history and analysis of this problem.

It is, of course, Louis Schneider who provided much of that intellectual history in his detailed interpretations of the array of Scottish moral philosophers just as he also contributed to the contemporary elucidation and substantive application of the idea of the unanticipated and unintended consequences of purposive social action. In his beautiful paper "Ironic Perspective and Sociological Thought" (Chapter 10 in this volume), Lou begins by reminding us that "ironic outcomes of action involve an element of the unintended or unexpected" and then goes on to develop in grand analytical style "the notion of strong affinity of structural-functional analysis with ironic perspective."[17]

These strands of interest in the theme of which Lou and I were addicted our lives long seemed about to be gathered up in a thematic session arranged by David Caplovitz for the 1978 annual meeting of The Society for the Study of Social Problems. The stated theme was "the idea of social problems as unanticipated consequences revisited." Asked to contribute to it were one Louis Schneider and one Robert Merton. Lou wrote me to express his pleasure in the plan for the session, which included Sam Sieber and Richard Henshel, and his further pleasure in my proposal after the session that Raymond Boudon and Gary Marx also be asked to contribute to the volume I was putting together under the title *Unanticipated Consequences of Social Action: Variations on a Sociological Theme.* Lou's oral presentation, "Unanticipated Consequences of Social Action: Beneficent and Maleficent," overlapped a later version which, owing to changed emphasis, adopted the subtitle "From Theology to Social Theory." So far as I know, this partly revised manuscript was Lou's last. His death meant that it fell to me, as editor of the planned volume, to consolidate his two drafts. And now I confess: *mea culpa.* Although the other completed chapters have been in hand for some three years, the consolidation of Lou's draft-manuscripts is still only partly done. *Mea maxima culpa.* It is little solace to have you know that the volume, containing Lou's paper, is being readied anew for

---

17. Since the essay is here at hand, I resist the acute temptation to discuss the theme of irony in the considerable length it eminently deserves. You will have seen the apt discussion by Lou's onetime student Richard Machalek, "Thorstein Veblen, Louis Schneider and the Ironic Imagination," *Social Science Quarterly* (60 (1979): 460-64.

publication. But it is a great comfort to have this superb and comprehensive collection of Lou's writings see the light of day.

Yours, as ever,

Bob

P.S. This is the place to thank the National Science Foundation for a grant in
support of work on unintended consequences of social action and the MacArthur
Foundation for their generous support. I also thank Rosa Haritos for finding
several hard-to-find sources in the Columbia Libraries.

Introduction

Jay Weinstein

Sociology is a difficult science. In the proper hands and the appropriate circumstances there is no more powerful discipline for gaining insight into human nature. Under less than ideal conditions, it seems to be singularly prone to abuses such as scientism, trivialization, and ideology mongering. No one was more aware of this "strain" in the calling of sociology than Louis Schneider. He became interested in the social sciences when an undergraduate, and early in his long career he came to appreciate how elusive is the line between their proper uses and abuses. If one were constrained to summarize in a word the program or agenda upon which the work of Schneider was based—and of which he was conscious (at least some of the time)—it would be that he was a *guardian,* a voice of conscience who spoke with clarity, rigor, true expertise, and, not least, deep respect when he spoke of things sociological. He was virtually obsessed with underscoring the wisdom in sociological and related social thought of the last two hundred years—and more—and of more than a dozen nationalities, and equally with exposing the charlatanry and false consciousness (intended or otherwise) characteristic of doctrines and approaches ranging from classic Marxism to Norman Vincent Peale's popular religion. In the process of performing this "guardian" role, he made several authentic contributions to the history of social science, sociological theory, and the sociology of religion; indeed, his own carefully wrought, painstaking research was clearly pursued in the light of these ideals.

There is in Schneider's writings a quality that made him an effective scholar and teacher but also something of a sociologist's sociologist, that is, tremendous drive and energy that allowed (or compelled) him to elaborate, qualify, illustrate profusely, call upon literary and documentary sources in several languages and spanning centuries. No discipline, scientific, humanistic, or mixed, can boast of a man who worked harder and with more substantial intellectual gifts in a conscious effort to advance his field of learning. His colleagues in academe and outside it—including his critics—knew him well for this, and all knew that they had something to learn from him because of it. If it also tended to cause preoccupied undergraduates in his "Intro." lectures to squirm, or if it caused his book sales—especially of a book like the masterful but unusual introductory text *The Sociological Way of Looking at the World*—to be modest when they might have been, if not phenomenal, at least substantial, then this is perhaps a cost of Schneider's type of greatness. It is our fondest hope that this volume will help make his work more accessible to those who might otherwise have overlooked his profound but exacting vision.

All this was expressed better and with characteristic grace by Walter I. Firey, Jr., who continues to be one of the liveliest and most original thinkers in American academic circles and was a close friend and colleague of Schneider at the University of Texas. In an obituary published in the *Journal of the Scientific Study of Religion,* Firey observed that when Schneider died

> he was at the peak of his career. A few weeks earlier he had completed the manuscript of a book on the social thought of Mandeville, and he was in the midst of several papers dealing with the work of the Scottish Moralists. Still other papers were in mind for the future. The loss of this distinguished and humane scholar is an irreparable one. . . . [His] publications reflect the vision of social science for which Lou Schneider is known—a consistently structural point of view, a respect for methodological diversity, and an appreciation for the intellectual continuities to which social science is heir.
>
> Lou Schneider's scholarship was an integral part of the man. It was his vocation. He imposed high standards of excellence upon himself and he instilled those standards in his students. To colleagues he was the genial and supportive critic and a never failing resource for ideas and perspective. In faculty councils he could be counted on for unerring good judgment and statesmanship.
>
> Lou's loyalty to his friends, and his affection for his family, were prominent in his day-to-day conversations on and off the job. He was a man with strong and deep feelings, and a man with compassion and magnanimity.

A Biographical Note

Schneider was born in Vienna, Austria, on March 22, 1915, and emigrated with his family to the United States at age six. He was reared in the Bronx during the Great Depression and became a U.S. citizen at age twelve.

Schneider attended primary school in New York and graduated from DeWitt Clinton High School, the Bronx, in January 1932. There is every indication that he was an excellent student: He accumulated honors in languages, French and Latin especially, and was an unusually able four-wall handball player. (He was a tall, 6'1", lean man with very strong hands.) He took his B.A., Phi Beta Kappa, at the College of the City of New York in 1935, and served as a reader (fellow) in sociology there in 1935-36. The following year, 1937, he began work as tutor (instructor) in sociology at Brooklyn College, where he remained on the faculty until 1943.

In 1937 he also began graduate study in sociology and economics at Columbia University. There he received his M.A. (1938), with the thesis "Some Sociological Aspects of Marx's *Capital*," and—with an interruption of studies during the war—his Ph.D. At Columbia he came into contact with several distinguished men who, during Schneider's early student days, helped make the Sociology Department there the leading one in the country, shifting the very center of social science research in the United States from Chicago to the East. Among these is Robert K. Merton, who was Schneider's mentor and for whom he had tremendous respect, Paul Lazarsfeld, and Hans Zetterberg.

His early work at Columbia shows a pronounced interdisciplinary orientation, an appreciation of the classic social thinkers, and a concern for reconciling psychiatric and economic perspectives on rationality. Of particular interest to him, as it was to Merton at that time, is the play and byplay of rational and irrational features of motivated action. His first published work, "Toward an Institutional Psychology," appeared in the *Journal of Social Philosophy and Jurisprudence* in 1942; it draws on Thorstein Veblen's "school" of institutional economics as a corrective or supplement to Freudian and neo-Freudian psychoanalytic theory. This paper ultimately became his Ph.D. dissertation.

Schneider moved to Washington during the war. There he served as labor economist for the War Production Board between 1943 and 1945 and, for the following two years, as an economist at the Office of Price Administration. On May 27, 1946, Schneider married Betty Sancier— with whom he had two children, David and Dana, before their divorce in 1954. He completed his Ph.D. studies at about the same time as his marriage and submitted his dissertation on Freud and Veblen to Columbia in 1947 (it was later published as *The Freudian Psychology and Veblen's Social Theory*). He received his degree in 1947—at age thirty-two—and from that time spent his entire career as a university teacher.

The dissertation is a carefully researched and well-argued discussion of several key themes in the works of Freud, Veblen, and many other social theorists—especially themes that bear on freedom, rationality, and motivation. On his vita prepared in 1977, in the entry for this work, Schneider writes: "Will probably omit reference to this book more and more since I now disagree with it so basically." Lou would have been pleased that the present volume contains nothing from the dissertation as such (though it was hardly possible to "omit reference" to it altogether). The reader need not take Schneider at his word, however—for there are substantial continuities between this and work done during and after 1977; the Greenwood Press edition remains in print.

Schneider's first job after getting his Ph.D. was at Colgate University, where he was assistant professor of sociology from 1947 to 1949. In 1948 Kings Crown Press in New York published his dissertation, and the following year an article based on it was published in *Psychiatry*. This article is reprinted in the present volume as Chapter 5.

In 1949 Schneider moved to West Lafayette, Indiana, where he was hired as associate professor at Purdue University. From that time—except for a brief stint as visiting professor at Dartmouth, in 1959-60, and an occasional summer—this New York-bred scholar did not return to live on the East Coast. Indeed, in a half-joking manner, he would tell his students how he enjoyed contemplating social history in the long view, like Sorokin, over centuries and eons; for then he could imagine Manhattan reduced to dust, with no trace of the civilization that so smugly acts as if it exists in perpetuity.

Between 1950 and 1954 Schneider continued his research on psychiatric and economic perspectives and the sociology of religion, and he began to develop his interests in applied sociology—in 1950 he published a fine critique of industrial sociology in *Antioch Review*. During this period he published seven articles and his second book, this a collaborative effort with M. B. Ogle and J. B. Wiley, of which about one-third of the chapters are by Schneider. Included among these articles is the first paper for which Schneider was widely cited, "The Deferred Gratification Pattern," written with Sverre Lysgaard. "Deferred gratification" is one of those social science concepts that many researchers of the present generation use—sometimes implicitly—without knowing whence it came, though the article was later distributed as Number 250 in the Bobbs-Merrill Reprint Series in the Social Sciences.

The decision not to include it in this volume was made again partly on the basis of Schneider's own wishes—he considered this article among his worst—and partly because its style contrasts sharply with the rest of the book. It is a tersely written, heavily empirical report on an attempt to operationalize the concept. Deferred gratification, for those who may not know the pattern by this name, is the practice of postponing relatively small immediate rewards for the sake of greater rewards in the future. Schneider and Lysgaard proposed and, to an extent, demonstrated that this pattern varies in presence, absence, and intensity among social categories, specifically social classes. Thus, it might —they suggested—explain why middle- and upper-middle-class youth continue their education through college and professional studies while working-class youth quit school and go to work at the first opportunity. The connections between this work and Schneider's earlier and later writings are somewhat obscure, though there is a clear interest here, too, on the workings of rationality and, as is implied in the article, in the role of the Protestant ethic in modern society. The article was cited by other social scientists, at least for a time; but as Schneider knew, the concept also has been widely abused in support of a kind of middle-class ethnocentricism. Nevertheless, it remains an intriguing idea and the article is accessible to those who are interested in knowing more about the concept's background and—of particular interest—how it might be measured.

Schneider's first published work on religion, also written during his earlier days at Purdue, was the brief statement "Three Views on Religion" that appeared in the University Hillel Foundation magazine.

In 1954 Schneider was promoted to professor of sociology at Purdue, in which position he served until 1959. That year he also won a fellowship to the Center for Advanced Study in the Behavioral Sciences at Stanford, California, and took leave until the fall of 1955. On January 3, 1956, he married Josephine Sundine in Moline, Illinois.

Between 1955 and 1959 he published two articles and his third book, largely based on work done at the center and with the fruitful collaboration of Sanford M. Dornbusch. This was his first major work on religion, and it continued to serve as a foundation for his research in this area thoughout his career. The focus, as revealed in the title of the book, *Popular Religion,* is on the best-selling books of Norman Vincent Peale and other "inspirational religionists." The study has some unique theoretical and methodological twists, which are evident in the chapter reporting the results and in our commentary, included in Part 3 of this volume.

From the fall of 1959 until the spring of 1960, Schneider was a visiting professor at Dartmouth College. In March of 1960 Schneider became head of the Department of Sociology at the University of Illinois. At Illinois he came into a department that had known the likes of Florian Znaniecki and through which had passed an occasional rising star like Alvin Gouldner. In his four years as head, Schneider was an activist. The faculty included Joseph Gusfield, Bennett Berger, Bernard Karsh, and Bernard Farber, and while Schneider was head, Mark G. Field, Norval D. Glenn, Harry M. Johnson, and Alexander Vucinich were hired, giving Illinois one of the strongest departments in the country. He worked on raising Ph.D. admission standards and on making its program more rigorous (at the beginning of a period of general lowering of standards).

Among his students of this era was Ronald Maris, now head of the Department of Sociology at the University of South Carolina and president of the American Association of Suicidology—the first nonpsychiatrist ever to hold that post.

During his tenure as head and then professor at Illinois, Schneider published four articles, including his major paper on the category of ignorance in the *American Sociological Review* (reprinted here as Chapter 8); two edited volumes, including his collection *Religion, Culture, and Society,* for which he wrote about 25,000 words and translated several of the papers from French and German; and three entries in Gould and Kolb's *Dictionary of the Social Sciences.*

This was also a time during which he developed his already strong professional contacts. He was an active member and fellow of the American Sociological Association, a visiting scientist in the association's National Science Foundation Program in 1963, and just before coming to Illinois he had served for one year as president of the Ohio Valley Sociological Association. Later he was to play prominent roles in the Society for the Scientific Study of Religion and the Society for the Study of Social Problems, and he served on both the MacIver and Sorokin Award Committees of the ASA.

He took his teaching with characteristic seriousness, and always sought and applied connections between his classroom lecturing and his field and literary research. At Illinois he took on the dreaded Sociology 400 General Sociology Seminar, a known "flunk out" course required of all first-year graduate students. Schneider piled on the work. The class was expected to read—in fifteen weeks and for one of four units in a regular course load—Durkheim's *Elementary Forms of the Religious Life* (in English if absolutely necessary), the better part of Merton's *Social Theory and Social Structure,* his own *Popular Religion,* and Sorokin's *Social and Cultural Dynamics*—Schneider very reluctantly conceding that the one-volume abridgement (about nine hundred pages) would have to do because of a shortage of the "real," four-volume work. Moreover, his multilingual lectures were packed with enough material, references, and suggested "related themes" to keep a student well occupied when exam time came. And the exams. In-class, closed-book, comprehensive essay type (with limited choices), closely proctored by the professor himself. For his students—and to an extent his colleagues—who were willing to work, to read, and to engage with the "big ideas," Schneider had the time and the patience that mark a dedicated teacher. For those who did not share his enthusiasm and work ethic regarding sociology, he could be less than Socratic.

This might suggest that Schneider was not interested in communicating with the "uninitiated," but this is simply not true. He was constantly attempting to render some of the more abstruse concepts of the social sciences—*dialectic, ignorance,* and *eufunction*—more comprehensible to a wider public. He looked upon his freshman introductory courses with the same sense of professional responsibility as he did his postdoctoral proseminars. And, perhaps above all, he wanted to write an unusual introductory text, a foreword or preface to sociology. Schneider began work on this enterprise at Illinois, or perhaps earlier.

In December 1962 the Schneiders' daughter Valerie was born. They remained at Illinois, with Lou as professor and, for a semester, associate member of Illinois's Center for Advanced Study, through the 1966-67 academic year. During this period he did his most intensive research on Mandeville and the Scottish Moralists. Between the time of his retirement from the headship and his departure from Illinois he published a brief paper and his collection *The Scottish Moralists on Human Nature and Society.* It was also during this period that he came in close contact with—and developed a strong personal regard for—Harry M. Johnson, whom he had hired to the Illinois faculty in 1964. Johnson, who is a fair match for Schneider in physical presence, depth of commitment to sociology, and erudition—including in the field of religious studies—is a dedicated Parsonian functionalist. In their first few meetings it became clear that there was much to be discussed—and argued—between them. Subsequently, for the few years that they spent together at Illinois and whenever the occasion presented itself after Schneider left Urbana, they carried on an often heated dialogue on the merits of the Parsonian framework vis-à-vis the Mertonian one and smiliar subjects, and there emerged from it a genuine mutual respect.

In the fall of 1967 Schneider moved to Austin, Texas, a city he loved, where he spent an extremely productive twelve years as professor of sociology until his death.

Schneider came to Texas during the administration of Lyndon Johnson, at a time of expansion of the entire state university system, and when the Austin campus was asserting itself as a national leader in many fields. In coming to Austin, Schneider clearly benefited from the university's considerable resources. In the department were a number of first-rate sociologists and students, including his former Illinois colleague Norval D. Glenn and several new colleagues with whom Schneider would collaborate during his tenure: Charles M. Bonjean, Sheldon R. Ekland-Olson, Cookie White Stephan, and Louis A. Zurcher, Jr. He also had strong collegial relationships with Walter I. Firey, Jr., Joseph Lopreato, and Gideon A. Sjoberg. Among his Ph.D. students at Texas were Judith Fruchter, who taught for a time at Purdue University after completing an excellent dissertation on technological determinism (and with whom Schneider explored—and "exploded"—the work of Jacques Ellul), and Richard Machalek, who worked with Schneider on the sociology of religion and is now on the faculty of Trinity University in San Antonio. Schneider's intellectual influence on his students and the warmth of his relationship with them is nicely captured in Machalek's essay "Thorstein Veblen, Louis Schneider and the Ironic Imagination" (*Social Science Quarterly,* 1979) and in his contributions to an introduction for a symposium dedicated to Schneider's memory (*SSQ,* 1979).

It was with Zurcher that Schneider participated in his most extensive fieldwork on the sociology of religion. His last years at Illinois and his first few years at Texas coincided with the turbulent period of the New Left, antiwar, civil rights, and campus protests. As expressed most clearly in his chapter on the counterculture in *The Sociological Way,* he was in sympathy with but also critical of these movements. Though not always easy to discern from his writings, Schneider's personal politics had a distinct liberal orientation. He was much intrigued by the rebellious, the antinomian, and the antiestablishment tendencies that always appear to accompany organized social life, and this interest deepened with the years. His orientation toward the counterculture was to admonish and instruct—some of these young people, "technocracy's children" Theodore Roszak called them, were after all Schneider's students; to show how really very old and how ironically conservative are their "new" ideas about sex, drugs, religion, technology, and the "straight world"; and to impress upon them what a strange and trying business it is to attempt to create a better society even through a movement that stresses peace, love, freedom, and other obviously good things.

For the most part Schneider's views were based upon secondary sources, news reports, and informal experience. With Zurcher, however, he came across what appeared to be countercultural "meaning" in the unlikely context of a dispute between a group of priests and their archbishop in San Antonio. Following the first public reports of the controversy, Zurcher and Schneider undertook to study the archdiocese and the events surrounding the dispute in depth. Intensive interviewing and testing of attitudes revealed several interesting—and some ironic—features of the "case of the dissident priests," including basic verification of the hypothesis that though the context was a religious one, the conflict was in many ways a variant of confrontations between "youth" and "authority" occurring throughout the United States (and the world) at that time. We have noted points in the text of this volume where this study is discussed, but the full-length report that appeared in the *Journal for the Scientific Study of Religion* in 1970 is not included here.

A brief note on the San Antonio study first appeared in *Social Science Quarterly* in March 1969. This was Schneider's second paper in the journal—which has its editorial offices at Austin and is an official publication of the Southwestern Social Science Association. The first was a memorial essay on P. A. Sorokin that we have included here as Chapter 6. With these two papers Schneider began a most fruitful and personally close relationship with *SSQ* and its editor Charles M. Bonjean.

SSQ's orientation coincided nicely with Schneider's own interdisciplinary, methodologically diverse inclinations. Its very presence and the close relationship with Bonjean were mutually rewarding. As a result, between 1967 and his death he published six articles in the journal; was coeditor or special editor of two issues and seven symposia, including a symposium on Veblen that appeared after his death; prepared two volumes with Bonjean of work that appeared in the journal; and acted as referee, editorial board member, and consultant in countless instances. Certainly, as Bonjean has acknowledged, Schneider played a central role in *SSQ*'s development and emergence as a major interdisciplinary journal.

Schneider's early years at Texas were the most productive of his life. Between 1968 and 1973 he continued and deepened his interests in the history of social theory and "the religious factor," and during that period he published thirteen articles—many reprinted here—including one in Italian and a seminal article on the dialectic in the *American Sociological Review* (Chapter 9 of this volume), his text *The Sociological Approach to Religion,* and a coedited issue of *SSQ* and subsequent bound volume, *The Idea of Culture in the Social Sciences,* with Bonjean. In addition, he remained quite active in the profession, including service as associate editor and consulting editor, respectively, of *Sociological Analysis* and *Journal for the Scientific Study of Religion.*

During the last five years of his life Schneider began to work toward a synthesis of his approaches to religion, intellectual history, and social theory. *The Sociological Way of Looking at the World* was published in 1975. It forced Schneider—or so he approached the task—to organize material in such a comprehensive and general way that connections previously unnoticed or unexplored now became apparent. The Scottish Moralists, the dissident priests, the counterculture, Sorokin's views, functionalism, the abuses to which social science is prone, and other interests had to be brought within one, albeit loose, framework. The result was the shaping of a distinctively "Schneiderian" approach, appropriately named in the title and explained at length in his preface to the text.

This distinctive approach, while certainly adumbrated in Schneider's earlier work, is explicit and self-conscious in his last few writings. In addition to *The Sociological Way,* with a 1979 Argentinian edition in Spanish, his last publications include an important paper on irony for Lewis Coser's collection in honor of Robert K. Merton (Chapter 10 of this volume), the short text *Classical Theories of Social Change,* an essay originally delivered as the Girvitz Memorial Lecture on Adam Smith at the University of California in 1976 (Chapter 2 of this volume), an essay on the history of social science in the United States for *Social Science in America* (coedited with Charles M. Bonjean), and an introduction to the Transaction Books edition of Adam Ferguson's *Essay on the History of Civil Society* (Chapter 14).

Through the years 1977 and 1978 Schneider continued working on the social problems text, a book on Mandeville, and a variety of other projects. At the time of his sudden and unexpected death from a pulmonary embolism on March 17, 1979, he had completed the Mandeville volume and was in the process of negotiation about it with publishers. He also left unpublished a completely new edition of his collection on religion, a long study of the history of social thought, *The Heritage of Sociology,* and several papers, proposals, outlines, and plans at various stages of completion. As is clear from Firey's remarks, his loss is deeply felt by his colleagues and his family.

An Overview of Schneider's Work

As suggested, one can divide Schneider's career into two periods: the longer, formative period, which lasted through his years at Illinois; and the latter period of synthesis, chiefly during the second half of his tenure at Texas. It is tempting to see his earlier works as pieces of an already-whole cloth, as products of a well-formulated theoretical perspective, for there are strong continuities between the "earlier" and "later" Schneider, strong enough to cast doubt on this or any other attempt to periodicize his work. (And we have, largely, avoided doing so in the ordering of this collection.) Nevertheless, it should be emphasized that until moving to Austin Schneider tended to work in distinct "problem areas," always able to borrow insights from one to apply to another but feeling no special need to evolve a covering model, perspective, or orientation. Indeed, much of his elusiveness as a writer, his tendency to qualify and understate, can be traced to a conscious disavowal of, a tendency to dissociate himself from, anything that mildly resembles a "doctrine": This would be far too authoritarian, too "Hegelian" for an American pragmatist intellectual like Schneider.

But by the force of the logic of the ideas themselves, Schneider's constant association and dissociation of them, and—not least—through the project of "putting it all together" in a general text, an identifiable "sociological way" did evolve, perhaps despite Schneider's goals (or we might ask, in a half-serious way, was he always pursuing the goal of developing "his own" perspective through indirection?).

Preceding each section of Schneider's papers in this volume is a summary and discussion of the work. It is through these essays that I have attempted to identify, describe, and comment upon Schneider's sociological way. I believe that I have made it clear there that Schneider was largely successful in avoiding the kind of closure and stultification of the "research instinct" that intellectual doctrines can entail. As we note, if he is a functionalist or a Marxist or a Mertonian or a Parsonian or an ironist or, for that matter, something of a preacher, it is always as a *plain* one—cautiously avoiding the excesses of such perspectives identified by C. Wright Mills as "vulgarization" and "sophistication." His is an open system, one that is self-conscious of the real and significant limitations of such useful, but often too "cute," concepts as irony, dialectic, latent function, and contradiction. It is a system that is methodologically tolerant—though demanding that methods be exercised in the pursuit of other ends and not as a self-contained activity, inherently interdisciplinary, and ideologically open and self-critical.

With this said, certain key features of Schneider's sociological way can be listed:

1. The perspective is decidely structural-functionalist, with strong emphasis on the interaction between cultural and social elements. This, in brief, focuses the attention of the sociologist on the systemic properties of social relations: Parts and wholes affect one another in intricately complex and consequential ways, and social scientists—and psychiatrists and other professionals as well—cannot afford to ignore this.

2. There is a critical interest in problems of reason and freedom, at the individual level, especially in connection with structures and functions at the social and cultural levels. Schneider sees in the "protosociology" of Mandeville and earlier authors, and in the authentic social science of any age, a constant struggle to understand and to reconcile the tension between individual intentions and motivated action, on one hand, and collective outcomes, on the other. This interest is expressed in Schneider's historical writings, his commentary on psychiatry, and in all of his work.

3. There is a special role given to the institutional sphere—and to deviations from institutionalized ways—in understanding the relationship between individual and collectivity. Institutions, such as religion and especially religion, cut across cultural dimensions as

organized belief systems and social dimensions as organized—even ritualized—behavior. If we wish to understand "human nature," we must certainly know how "social circumstance"—institutions —operates. And, always of special interest, what do behavior and belief at or beyond the limits of the institutionalized reveal about society and the individual?

4. There is a decidedly humanist bent to the perspective. This is reflected in two principal ways in Schneider's work: One is his striving for interdisciplinary ties with history, the literary arts, philosophy, and theology; the other is his own, classical, humanist values and a forthright commitment to use these values in the role of sociologist. While, as noted, it is sometimes difficult to locate on an ideological continuum Schneider's political orientation, there is no doubt that he is "for" freedom, equality, the little man, self-realization, and a more rational social order, and he is "against" alienation, trivialization of work, and racism. But he can rarely, if ever, allow such noble causes to be mentioned without subjecting them—concept and construct—to detailed analytical scrutiny. For Schneider, and—as he suggests—for any social scientist sensitive to the human condition but also sensitive to the complexity of values and value-inspired causes, it is always and eminently possible that the freedom fighter and the equality seeker will end up contributing to the forces of oppression and oligarchy, or that the oligarchs will broaden the base of democracy. These things can happen and do happen, and though they do not excuse moral paralysis, awareness of the tendency for such unanticipated, ironic outcomes should certainly make social scientists circumspect in applying their values to their data.

In addtition to, or emerging from, these general features, Schneider's work is "laced" with commentary on two other subjects: psychiatry and the notion of contradiction. In the earlier writings these are treated with interest but relatively separately; later they become important components of the sociological way.

Beginning with his first published article and his Ph.D. dissertation, Schneider was engaged in an intense dialogue with psychological and psychiatric thought. He read extensively the works of Freud, Jung, and numerous contemporary and neo-Freudian writers. He saw in this work both tremendous insight and tremendous limitations. He certainly could identify, in some remote way at least, with Dr. Freud of Vienna, and yet he considered Freud's sociological views queer and incomplete; and, in his later years, Schneider became increasingly interested in iatrogenesis— physician-induced illness—and its implications for what Thomas Szasz had called "the manufacture of madness."

The other subject that served as an important background theme in Schneider's work is contradiction. This is certainly one of what Schneider considered to be the "big ideas" in social thought, but—or perhaps consequently—it is one that is widely misunderstood and widely abused. Extended discussion of contradiction, in society and in language, is contained in Chapters 9, 10, and 14 of this volume—often in the footnotes, and at various other points in his work.

By considering these features of his work we can perhaps begin to get the "feel" of Schneider's sociological way, of the cues that, he believed, the analyst ought to follow. It is a demanding, careful, often cynical, but fundamentally humanistic way. With it (or with the whole of his output, if I have erred in oversimplifying by trying to precipitate out a single, distinctive perspective) Schneider enriched social science in the United States and elsewhere, and left to his students and colleagues a substantial sense of direction for research long into the future.

A Note on the Collection

This collection is divided into three sections that correspond to the principal areas in which Schneider conducted research: history of social thought, principles of social theory, and sociology of religion. There are grounds to argue that another classification might have been more appropriate, that, for example, Schneider's intererst in culture or race relations is not well represented. To be sure, these are not the only areas of interest to Schneider—to the contrary, it is clear that he read just about anything, and was able always to find "beauty in the bellow of the blast." We are also not hereby saying that Schneider consciously divided his attention or his writings neatly among these three topics. There are several instances in which it is not self-evident that a chapter placed in one section might not better fit in another (e.g., Chapter 14), and others for which the "fit" is strained (e.g., Chapter 6). Nevertheless, with the benefit of hindsight, it does help make this collection cohere to view these as three major substantive strains that Schneider came to draw together, with greater explicitness, toward the end of his life.

It is also true that Schneider's earlier writings and his more empirical and overtly methodological work are underrepresented here. This was not intentional, and in fact it is unfortunate. Schneider did think of his own mathematical training as deficient, and he regarded the uses of mathematics in social science often with cautious skepticism, but also sometimes with—undeserved—awe. But his work (with Dornbusch) on popular religion, on deferred gratification (with Lysgaard), on the dissident priests (with Zurcher), and his own essays on methodology in the last two chapters of *The Sociological Way* prove that he was not a "mere library sociologist." He had great respect for empirical research and for, properly used, mathematical approaches; and his own work demonstrates, at a minimum, a competent grasp of these matters and, at points, real ingenuity. We regret that because of space limitations and similar reasons the volume can give only the barest indication of this side of Schneider.

One constraint under which we operated was to include nothing here that appeared first as a chapter or section of a book, though a few of the papers have appeared in edited collections. This perforce eliminated much interesting material on religion, Norman Vincent Peale especially, some on social change, and of course the whole of *The Sociological Way*. In addition, it was decided to issue at this time only works previously published, this after considerable deliberation. There is, as mentioned, a long volume on the history of sociology that includes essays on Mandeville and the Scots but also chapters on French sociology—from Saint-Simon to Durkheim, including an addendum on the work of the Belgian Adolphe Quetelet; on Herbert Spencer; on German contributions, including a long section on Marx, Simmel, and Weber; on Pareto; and on the founders of American sociology, William Graham Sumner, Thorstein Veblen, W. I. Thomas, Robert E. Park, Charles Horton Cooley, and George Herbert Mead. There was a temptation to include in this volume several of these essays, especially from the latter part of the book, in order to give some sense of the extent and depth of Schneider's knowledge about the sociological heritage. In the end, however, we resisted; the book deserves to be published as a volume in its own right, and this is our plan for it. Schneider also left what appears to be a portion of a book on culture, including a long (over sixty pages of typescript), complete chapter, "Religion as Culture." But because there are still some gaps in it, because it is so long, and because most of the main points are covered in other parts of this volume, it, too, will be published in another separate form.

Within these limitations and allowing for some arbitrariness in our organization and criteria of inclusion, this volume does, I believe, give us the "Best of Lou Schneider"—a title we jokingly used in referring to a collection that was to appear while Schneider was alive. We are pleased and honored to have a part in disseminating the writing of this truly outstanding modern thinker.

Finally, I want to register my deepest appreciation to Jo Schneider for allowing me to enter her life at a trying time and to help in the bittersweet task of keeping her husband's spirit alive. In addition to providing archival assistance, Jo typed the final typescript of this volume. I also am grateful to the others whose contributions to the man, to his work, and to this volume, were so essential: to Robert K. Merton for his kind Foreword, to Irving Louis Horowitz for his help and encouragement at every stage of his project, to Sanford M. Dornbusch, Richard Machalek, Walter I. Firey, Jr., Joseph Lopreato, Charles M. Bonjean, Harry M. Johnson, and Schneider's other colleagues who were willing—most willing—to share their memories with me. Typing, retyping, correcting, and related work on early drafts of this manuscript were ably undertaken by Té Burt, Jane Wilson, and Judy Rogers at Georgia Tech and Len E. Thompson in Hyderabad, India. Thanks are also due to the American Studies Research Centre in Hyderabad for its aid and auspices during the final stages of the project, to Russell Dynes for his personal interest in our work, and to Marilyn for her editorial assistance and constant support.

I, of course, assume final responsibility for all editorial decisions, errors, and oversights.

Part I
THE ROOTS OF MODERN SOCIAL SCIENCE

Introduction

This first section consists of four chapters on the works of the eighteenth-century social philosophers Bernard Mandeville, Adam Smith, Adam Ferguson, and John Millar. The essays, which are written in the style of the intellectual historian—copiously footnoted, carefully and, at times, elaborately qualified, and employing a close comparative examination of textual sources—introduce a central thesis in Schneider's writings on social thought, one that is posed and discussed at length in *The Scottish Moralists,* in earlier sections of *The Sociological Way, Classocial Theories of Social Change,* the unpublished book "The Heritage of Sociology," and elsewhere. In brief, it is that these four men deserve special consideration as founders of modern social science.

Aware that the search for roots is inevitably fraught with practical and verbal difficulties, Schneider cautions at the outset of Chapter 1 that "one could reach back almost endlessly for antecedents of sociological thought." Indeed, in order to account for possible exceptions, but also to illustrate what is distinctive about modern social scientific approaches (regardless of their chronological age), he nominates, at various points, Vico (a contemporary of the four), and Ibn Khaldun and Machiavelli (who predate the four by centuries) as others whose perspectives might be counted as "protosociological." Nevertheless, he marshals a convincing case to show that certain philosophical projects begun in England and especially Scotland around the year 1750—and of which the works of Mandeville, Smith, Ferguson, and Millar are exemplary—marked a true turning point in intellectual history: For the first time, a serious attempt was undertaken to apply systematically scientific principles to the task of understanding (and of controlling) human relationships. The major problems encountered by Mandeville and Smith and the other Scottish Moralists in their attempt and the solutions offered by them are, Schneider argues, identical to, cognate with, or, at least, "suggestive" of major problems and solutions still current in academic social science disciplines such as sociology.

Unintended Consequences

The most important point of contact, for Schneider, between

19

Mandeville, the Scots, and social scientists today lies in their shared fascination which the unintended and / or unanticipated outcomes of collective action. The concept of unintended consequences appears in several variations, guises, and permutations throughout Schneider's work: as the ironic focus, in relation to the utility of ignorance; as "indirection"; as a dialectical principle; and—often—as latent functions and dysfunctions. Several of these variations are taken up as the object of closer scrutiny in Part 2 of this volume. Here, however, the focus is on the great use made of the concept of unintended consequences in the writings of the four, with constant reference to the fact that the concept continues to be pervasive in contemporary social science, especially—but not exclusively—in functionalist sociology.

Other instances of continuity than these are identified at various points in the first four chapters. For example, one or more of the philosophers is cited for innovations in theories of socialization, early reference to the problem of objectivity—the "impartial spectator," foundation theories about the social impact of technology and the alienation of labor, and the beginnings of modern social evolutionism—and of the sociological critique of social evolutionism. But certainly the main argument of this section is that Mandeville, Smith, Ferguson, and Millar are properly considered founders of social science largely because, through their interest in unintended consequences, they are also the founders of what is now known as the structural-functionalist perspective—but, it must be added, of the conflict and dialectical perspectives as well (see, for example, the latter sections of Chapter 3, where the works of Marx and Gumplowicz are connected with Ferguson's).[1]

The notion of unintended consequences appears first in the context of Mandeville's views on evolution. After a brief introduction in which some "scattered insights" are identified, the chapter takes up Mandeville's reaction to the appearance (revolutionary for its time) that history can be meaningfully altered and shaped by great men, bold plans, and dramatic events. In Mandeville's response Schneider sees a clear adumbration of Smith's treatment, and that of Ferguson, Millar, and several of their contemporaries, of what was obviously a major philosophical issue of the early industrial era, that is, the idea that people *can* rationally control their own destinies. Mandeville's response to the apparent, new-won control of nature and history—which is the characteristic reaction of the Scots, of the age, and, Schneider insists, is or ought to be recognized as the proper sociological response even today—is that society does change in a very gradual manner as the outcome of the multitude of factors or forces in which, significantly, human intentions and rational planning play a surprisingly minor role. Despite the appearance of control and rationality, and despite the good intentions of social reformers who wish to exercise such control for what they perceive to be human betterment, the actual outcomes of collective action often differ significantly from that which is intended or anticipated by key actors. Society evolves not because people consciously strive to achieve certain general ends; rather it is transformed "behind the backs of men," most of whom are spurred on by short-run personal motives and inclinations. Thus, as in *The Fable of the Bees*, in which a great incongruity appears to exist between the behavior of the individual bees and the general state of the hive, "private virtues" may become "public vices" and private vices can turn out to be public virtues.

Before we consider how this idea recurs in the work of Mandeville, the Scots, and in contemporary sociology, it might be useful to analyze it into what are in fact its two separate parts or innovations. First is the recognition by Mandeville that a disjunction exists between individual acts or intentions and social outcomes, that social outcomes cannot be "reduced" by straightforward transformations (e.g., arithmetic) to individual motives. It is this point that more than a century later preoccupied Durkheim in his *Rules of Sociological Method,* as he attempted to establish an authentic "emergent" social level of causation and, thus, authentic sociological laws and explanations. But in addition to this recognition we find in *The Fable* and in Cleomenes' commentary, especially, the modern understanding that virtue and vice are everywhere bound by social circumstance. Here we have a foreshadowing of the distinctively sociological way of dealing with ethics and morality, as objects to be studied scientifically and with the same type of analytical detachment that the physicist brings to the study of the properties of the pulley or the motion of spheres on an inclined plane (though, as we shall see in a moment, such detachment does *not* imply support of "ethical relativism"). These two insights—that individual acts and collective outcomes are disjoint, and that morality can be treated objectively—are at times confounded by Schneider, in large part because they are confounded by Mandeville and the others, but by understanding them as distinct (though obviously closely related) we can perhaps appreciate better the magnitude of the contributions of these philosophers.

Unintended consequences (or their operation and effects) are discussed throughout the writings of Mandeville and the Scots. Moreover, the idea plays a major role in these writings. It is not a casual observation or a chance discovery; rather it is at the very core of this "school" (which, at times, can include Hume, John Stuart Mill, and others) of eighteenth-century social philosophy. In Chapter 1, Mandeville's position as precursor of the Scots is established in several ways that are related to the focus on unintended consequences (with the implication of both "emergence" and moral objectivity kept in mind). He is, for example, credited with introducing into social inquiry the concepts (though not the terms) "the cunning of reason" and "the invisible hand." In Chapters 1 and 3 Schneider identifies these concepts as "conversion mechanisms," structures or processes through which individual acts are transformed into, often ironically discrepant, collective results. Because this focus on conversion mechanisms helps to explain the disjunction between individual intentions and collective outcomes—which, in turn, has implications for the treatment of morality and the emergent level of social causation—it is "one of the most fundamental insights or perspectives in the social sciences."

A related insight, prominent in the writings of Mandeville, Smith, and especially in the historical works of Ferguson and Millar, is that man's ordinary acts can have "higher" ends—and the corollary that, as indicated in Part 3, forms the basis for Schneider's major research in the sociology of religion, that men's sacred acts can have ordinary ends. This understanding was applied by Mandeville and the Scots in connection with their "incrementalist" views on evolution, in their characteristic stress on the *latent* consequences—or dialectical outcomes—of joint action (for example, in the case of the outcome of the signing of the Magna Carta or the consequences of Rome's successes at road building), in the concerns of Smith, especially, about the limitations of rationality, and in other ways. As Schneider stresses at several points, this insight continues to inform sociological research today—his own research on religion and that in many other areas.

A final example of a theme cognate with unintended consequences that Schneider traces through Mandeville, the Scots, and the present is first encountered in Mandeville's now classic critique of "the vulgar ideology of positive thinking." Mandeville and the others made great effort to separate good *will* from good *results*. Clearly this was part of their larger project, again traceable to value issues that had newly arisen in industrializing England and Scotland, of understanding the scope and limits of freedom—and which is still of concern, at least as background, to most social science researchers today. The critique, as Schneider points out, introduced into social thought a healthy skepticism about the operation of psychological factors in human history. It cannot possibly satisfy careful students of Mandeville and the Scots—which is to say the sociologists of any era who are conscious of their roots—to be told, for example, that economic depression is caused by negative thinking and that economic recovery comes when people begin to "accentuate the positive." Those familiar with Schneider's early work on the philosophy of Norman Vincent Peale (discussed in this volume in Chapter 11) will understand why he attaches special importance to the similarities between Mandeville's, Smith's, and current views on the power of positive thinking.

The Priority of Mandeville and the Scots over the French Sociologists

Ultimately, Schneider's case in favor of Mandeville and the Scots as inventors of social science relies upon such demonstrations of continuity between their concerns and contemporary ones; and it is this project that occupies most of his attention. But also implicit in these essays is a more indirect, sociology of knowledge analysis (which is presented in somewhat greater detail in other works cited) to the effect that England and Scotland during the industrial revolution, and in the wake of political union between the two nations, provided an especially fertile environment for the birth of social science.

The momentous changes that occurred there in the middle of the eighteenth century, including the rise of institutionalized science, massive population migrations, a clear and growing gap between rural-agricultural and urban-industrial sectors, and the spread of new techniques of production, brought to the fore what we now recognize as modern questions and responses about human freedom, morality, and technology's impact on social relations. Prior to that time, and outside Britain, men of learning (and, one could speculate, ordinary people as well) were concerned with problems of more traditional (Comte would have said "religious" and "metaphysical") scope. As the new ideas, forms of social organization, and machinery of the industrial revolution were diffused and assimilated, the older, more rigid, and—in general—morali*stic* ways of understanding human freedom and ethical behavior proved increasingly inadequate. The social changes that occurred in Scotland and England in the early industrial era seemed to mean, for many, that man had at last taken hold of his own fate; that with the aid of science and technology people now had the capacity to shape nature—including human nature—to whatever purpose they desired. It was this appearance that challenged the Dutch-born physician Mandeville and, later, the Scots to rethink the relationship between man, nature, and human nature and, as a result, to invent a discipline or a branch of moral or natural philosophy[2] that is recognizable today as social science.

In some respects, one might say at a very deep level, Mandeville and the Scots shared in this enthusiasm for science, technology, and progress. As self-identified men of science, they were as insistent as any of their contemporaries or successors that we understand clearly what *authentic* progress entails and what its achievement actually requires. But in other respects, their response had a perverse twist, one that characterizes Smith's and Ferguson's gradualist treatment of evolution and the shared, all-important, focus on unintended consequences.

Within this argument Schneider summarizes an alternative—formulated more or less intentionally by several economists, intellectual historians, and sociologists—to the view, still commonly held, that modern social science was born in France at the end of the eighteenth century. This is a qualified alternative because, for Schneider, Saint-Simon and Comte continue to deserve credit for early contributions to, or even for an independent discovery of, social science (but, it should be realized, they were familiar with and often referred to the work of the Scots); they, especially Comte, were evidently the first systematizers of the new science of man and they introduced a new vocabulary—including the word *sociologie* itself—into scholarly discourse about human relationships. Moreover, the influence of the French social philosophers, Saint-Simon but also Condorcet, Say, Proudhon, and Saint-Just, upon Marx is sufficiently well documented to win for revolutionary and postrevolutionary France a very special place in the development of modern social thought. And if events were propitious for the first attempts at a systematic application of scientific principles to human relationships in England in 1750, they were, it could be argued, equally or even more propitious in France in 1800 (as Durkheim and Mannheim argue in their histories of early French sociology). While granting this, it remains true for Schneider that a certain bias exists in a reading of the history of a social science discipline such as sociology that begins not with Mandeville or Smith but with Saint-Simon or Comte. (He is also curious at times about the possibility that this may be a "convenient" or an interest-serving bias.)

His reasons for calling attention to this bias are instructive, and they bring us once more to the main thesis of these chapters concerning the continuity between earlier and current themes in social science. It is here, also, that Schneider comes closest to *prescribing* what good modern sociology should be as opposed to merely describing the similarities between, e.g., Smith's views on economic rationality and contemporary functional analysis.

While it may be true that the French "Fathers" were the first to engage in self-conscious discussions of social science, Mandeville and the Scots were *practicing* that science earlier, as what Joseph Ben-David has called "amateur men of learning"[3] and/or under the label of older academic disciplines such as moral philosophy and political economy. One link, significant for Schneider, with contemporary themes that emerges in this comparison is that, properly, sociology is rooted in a more general and ethically committed perspective than that encompassed today by the strict confines of the discipline. This is to say that an historical account that omits or underestimates the contributions of Mandeville and the Scots supports a style of sociology that is insufficiently interdisciplinary and overly prone to favor disciplinary purity, insufficiently engaged with or concerned about social problems, and overly prone toward "detached" treatment of sociological "problematics."

It is possible that, in what is essentially Schneider's statement of his considered opinion that interdisciplinary, ethically committed styles of sociology are better (more useful, more authentic, etc.) than other styles, the contrast between the English/Scottish founders and the French founders is exaggerated (compare these remarks with those in *Classical Theories of Social Change and* "The Heritage of Sociology," which include separate chapters and sections on the French sociologists). The bias away from interdisciplinary and committed styles—to the extent that it exists in sociological research today—may be the effect of other, later events and not necessarily the result of an overemphasis on the roles of Saint-Simon and Comte. For the French "Fathers" clearly meant by *"sociologie"* a field that is, precisely, far more encompassing of other disciplines and far more ethically committed (e.g., to progress) than what is practiced by the majority in the name of sociology today. But, with these points granted, the utility of beginning our history with Mandeville remains undiminished. Without neglecting the innovations of Saint-Simon and Comte, sociologists would do well to recall that their intellectual roots coincide with those of the economist, the social historian, and the moral philosopher, and to realize thus that their powers as sociologists would be enhanced to the extent that they are able to put into interdisciplinary practice this historical fact.

Interdisciplinarity

As indicated, the main interdisciplinary connections Schneider seeks to trace in the first four chapters are between sociology and economics, history, and, secondarily, philosophy. By establishing the importance of the contributions of the English industrial revolution, the economic dimension of social thought is stressed as an alternative to what might be labeled the "political determinism" that arises from exclusive emphasis on the French origins. Chapter 2, for example, is essentially a comparative essay on Smith's two major works, *The Theory of Moral Sentiments* and *The Wealth of Nations*. It argues that the differences between these two books—one a tract on ethics and the other a discourse on the workings of the economy—have been exaggerated. It is not, as some historians have asserted, that *The Wealth of Nations* either refutes or is tangential to the earlier work. Rather, the later work is in several important respects noted a recapitulation, a refinement, and an *application* of the earlier. This reconciliation between the two books serves as a vehicle whereby Schneider can demonstrate how "human nature" and "social circumstance" are intimately bound together for Smith (and the other Scots), how his sociological insights and economic ones complement each other, and how as a consequence this complementarity persists in the modern academic disciplines of sociology and economics.

Schneider also sees in the views of Smith and the others a foreshadowing of what later came to be known as institutional economics, the approach pioneered by another frequently underestimated—and interdisciplinary—contributor to contemporary social science, Thorstein Veblen. The establishment of this linkage between the Scots and academic economics/sociology via Veblen is most perceptive and it is of sufficient importance to Schneider to be echoed at several places in his work (beginning with his Ph.D. dissertation). Here, in defense of Smith's economic theories against those who view them as overly mechanistic or morally insensitive, Schneider provides a faithfully Veblenesque critique of "economic science." This critique, in seeking to correct narrow (and possibly opportunistic) interpretations of classical economics, explicates a sociological, even anthropological, model of economic man, complete with irrational motivations, driven by vanity, and prone to such "uneconomic" behavior as conspicuous consumption, self-aggrandizement, and emulation. It opposes the model, still apparently favored by some academic economists, in which behavior is essentially the result of the "simple" calculation of self-interest. Significantly, this critique places the work of Smith and, to a lesser degree, that of Ferguson and Millar, firmly in the anthropological "irrationalist" tradition.

Schneider's appreciation of the historical strain in the foundation works of social science arises in discussions of Smith, of Millar—where we are reminded "not to worry overmuch" whether Millar's school is properly labeled "sociological" or "historical"—and especially of Ferguson, the principal historian among the Scots. Here, in a concise proposition that Schneider attempted to illuminate and apply throughout his intellectual life (see, for example, Chapter 7 of this volume) he notes how, for Ferguson, "sociology enriches history" and "history enriches sociology." And, perhaps, the most evident connection between the two fields for Mandeville and the Scots is their general and frequent reference to social evolution or, simply, their "evolutionary view." Indeed, that

these philosophers were interested in exploring evolution in a recognizably modern way, some decades before and in what is arguably a more
sophisticated analytical manner than Saint-Simon or Comte, is a key bit
of evidence in favor of them as founders.

Ethical Commitment

In addition to the stress of interdisciplinarity, Schneider finds in the
works of Mandeville and the Scots a clear preference for ethically committed social research. He is well aware that this discovery may challenge
those sociologists and historians who, somewhat vaguely, trace to Smith
and classical economics generally a "value-free" orientation; and he intends his remarks to serve as a corrective for such practices—again
speaking prescriptively about modern social science. It is, thus, of some
importance that, for example, in his response to critics of functionalism
(at the end of the first section of Chapter 2) he can establish that in
Smith's views moral purpose—on the part of the investigator—is not incompatible with scientific sociology. In fact, the classical model of the
investigator—one that was to an extent self-consciously developed by
Smith and the others in grappling with the problem of the "impartial
spectator"—is as much a *medical* model as any other type. Neither
Mandeville, the physician and social pathologist, nor his successors saw
any special difficulty in seeking "objective" solutions to problems that
arise in the pursuit of highly partisan ends: Like the physician who dis-
passionately seeks the truth about the patient and his disease for the
highly committed purpose of saving one and destroying the other, the
social investigator can exercise his skills as an impartial observer even
(and perhaps especially) when he does so in order to promote social progress, encourage virtue, discourage vice, etc.

The collective view of Mandeville and the Scots on the place of the investigator's own values and interests is perhaps best summarized by Ferguson. In Chapter 3, Schneider makes reference to Ferguson's major
works in support of the idea that no strict separation exists between
sociological inquiry and moral purpose. Here he is saying quite explicitly
that "ethical concern" has an important place in social research and that
the classical economists—including Mandeville—did not refuse to make
value commitments. Ferguson, in particular, formulated a bold argument against cultural relativism in which considerable scope is given for
the intrustion of judgments about success, failure, progress, and regres-
sion. But, characteristically, such judgments intrude in an often cynical,
often ironic way: as when success brings failure to Rome's design to rule
the world. Thus, it is not that good social research must avoid value
judgments and ethical concerns, but that it must—if it is to take advan-

tage of the innovations of Ferguson and the others—raise one's awareness of the role of values and ethics (including those of the investigator himself) to a truly modern, *dialectical* level.

The final chapter of this section deals in a very direct way with the Scots'—in this case Millar's—interest in the place of ethical concern in social science. As the title indicates, Schneider's focus here is on "tensions" in Millar's views. Several such tensions, or discrepancies, are identified, including the instructive "asymmetry" between Millar's "low" regard for the rational efficacy of most social institutions and the great credit he gives to the clergy of the Roman Catholic Church for shaping history to its private ends. But as Schneider suggests, perhaps this and most of the other tensions resolve in a single one, the one to which, properly, modern social scientists are the heirs: the tension beween "truth for propaganda and truth for science." That this "double truth" is integral to Millar's method—and, thus, to that of his fellow Scots—helps us better understand the ethical complexities of laissez faire and the ambiguous sort of "progress" that attends increasing division of labor (which leads both to efficiency and to the trivialization of work). And, not least, the fact that the double truth of eighteenth-century philosophy resounded with force in the work of Marx—whose singular influence on modern social science is firmly established—helps to underscore another significant point of continuity between that century and ours.

In a most general sense, the type of social science that Louis Schneider is describing (and prescribing) in these—and subsequent—chapters is distinguished from other types by its ethical concern, but its preference for some questions or lines of inquiry over others, and for its specific commitment to certain humanistic values. Like the philosophies of Mandeville, Smith, Ferguson, and Millar, it is a social science that is *not* indifferent to problems of justice, virtue, alienation, and human betterment. But, as a science, it carries to the solution of these problems a (modern) commitment to skepticism—organized skepticism, to be sure—about such matters as the meaning of justice, the vices of virtue, the benefits of alienation, and the degradation that the pursuit of human betterment can cause. In this sense, the value judgments of the ironist, the skeptic, the seeker of contradiction, and the student of unintended consequences are useful ones; they serve the important purpose of inspiring true scientific insight into the human condition. As is amply emphasized and reemphasized in this section (but with characteristic understatement), for Mandeville, the Scots, and for their successors today, "a touch of the sardonic helps in its way to launch sociology into the world."

Notes

1. An effective defense of structural-functionalism (note how Schneider warns against the mistakes that can occur when one forgets that "functionalism" is an ellipsis) accompanies the main argument that Mandeville and the Scots were early users of the approach—in these chapters and elsewhere. It is instructive to follow this defense not only because it illuminates the "big debate" in sociology of the 1950s and early 1960s but also because it interprets structural-functionalism in such a way that the approach appears vital and relevant to sociologists today (though Schneider stops short of asserting, as Kingsley Davis and others have argued, that functionalism is equivalent to sociological analysis itself). Here, Schneider uses Smith's thoughts to respond decisively to critics of functionalism and to "vulgar functionalists," alike, on the supposed disjunction between moral purpose and scientific sociology.

2. The drawing together of moral and natural philosophies is, itself, a major achievement of the era and, perhaps, the basic turning point in the innovation of social science. Schneider comments on this connection at length in the essay on Smith, and at other points, with reference to biographical factors, e.g., Ferguson, "preeminently a moral philosopher and historian," who also "a teacher of physical science subjects." This point is also taken up at some length, following Schneider's lead, in the first section of our *Sociology/Technology* (New Brunswick, N.J.: Transaction, 1982).

3. Joseph Ben-David, *The Scientist's Role in Society* (Englewood Cliffs, N.J.: Prentice-Hall, 1971). Following Ben-David's formulation, one might also properly consider Saint-Simon and Comte to be amateurs or, at most, amateur-academics. Thus, the contrast between them and the Scots—the most important of whom were academic scholars—is not as great as implied here.

1
Mandeville as Forerunner of Modern Sociology
(1970)

The idea that Bernard Mandeville may be regarded as in some sense a forerunner of modern sociology is not novel.[1] Yet, on the whole, Mandeville has received little attention from sociologists, and appears to be receiving very little indeed from them today.[2] It is true, of course, that one could reach back almost endlessly in a search for antecedents of sociological thought. But Mandeville's sociological thought is outstandingly meritorious for its time,[3] and in terms of time, moreover, Mandeville is rather strategically placed. Whether we take his relevant endeavors as "presociological" or "protosociological,"[4] their merit would seem to call for a more thorough critical consideration of his work than has yet been offered. The object of this chapter is to afford such a consideration, within limits of inevitable brevity.[5] The reader familiar with Mandeville's work will note how large a proportion of that work lends itself readily to inclusion under sociological rubrics.

It is convenient and helpful in obtaining a general view of Mandeville as a sociologist or forerunner of sociology to attend to four main matters: (1) scattered sociological insights, (2) elements of what has been called evolutionary thought on Mandeville's part, (3) suggestions or adumbrations of structural-functional analysis, and (4) a disposition in Mandeville to stress what we shall label "asymmetry." Reservations about Mandeville's thought can hardly be avoided. In the following section, for example, as the section heading indicates, we concern ourselves with "limitations" as well as with "insights."

Some Insights and Limitations

In referring to scattered sociological insights, we mean to suggest various perceptive notions of Mandeville's that are not developed in great depth and that are at the same time easily comprehended without necessarily being related to the central concerns subsequently considered.

31

"Scattered" should not be taken as equivalent to "trivial." The category "scattered insights" is useful for expository purposes. It aids in effecting an "introduction" to Mandeville the sociologist, while under later headings we seek to penetrate more deeply into his work.

The whole range of the broadly sociologically "interesting" or "insightful" Mandeville is too considerable to capture here. We must make choices. It is well to turn first to Mandeville on the subject of socialization, a matter of no small importance and one on which his ideas are excellent. Socialization is understood as the proceess whereby the human being is made distinctively human in virtue of his internalizing or making part of himself the values and standards upheld by others about him. "Men become sociable," says Cleomenes-Mandeville, "by living together in Society";[6] and he sees the importance of man's relatively prolonged youth for the whole socialization process:

> Another thing to be consider'd is, that tho' some Animals perhaps live longer than we do, there is no Species that remains young so long as ours; and besides what we owe to the superior Aptitude to learn, which we have from the great Accuracy of our Frame and inward Structure, we are not a little indebted for our Docility, to the slowness and long Gradation of our Encrease, before we are full grown: the Organs in other Creatures grow stiff, before ours are come half to their Perfection.[7]

Cleomenes develops the argument that men become sociable in virtue of society itself by observations thoroughly worthy of a discerning psychiatrist and sociologist. He contends that "Natural Affection" impels mothers to take care of their children to the point of feeding them and keeping them from harm while they remain helpless; but, he adds, "where People are poor, and the Women have no Leisure to indulge themselves in the various Expressions of their Fondness for their Infants, which fondling of them ever encreases, they are often very remiss in tending and playing with them." The consequences of this? "This want of pratling to, and stirring up the Spirits in Babes, is often the principal cause of an Invincible Stupidity, as well as Ignorance, when they are grown up; and we often ascribe to natural Incapacity, what is altogether owing to the Neglect of this early Instruction." Cleomenes is even sagacious to suggest that "the more healthy and quiet" the less than adequately cared-for children are, "the more they are neglected."[8]

Two additional statements on the subject of socialization may be noted. In one, Mandeville asserts that it is "hard to guess what Man would be, entirely untaught," but adds that we have "good Reason to believe, that the Faculty of Thinking would be very imperfect" in any human who had "nothing to imitate" and had not "any body to teach him." And in a second statement, Cleomenes contends that while speech is "a Characteristick of our Species," still "no Man is born with it," to which he adds that "a dozen Generations proceeding from two Savages would not produce any tolerable Language; nor have we reason to believe, that a Man could be taught to speak after Five and Twenty, if he had never heard others before that time."[9] This is all that need be noted in regard to language and socialization, but Mandeville on language must soon concern us again.

This very brief, selective recall of "scattered insights" may be brought to an end with reference to one other. Whatever one may decide about Mandeville's possible influence on the Thorstein Veblen of *The Theory of the Leisure Class*,[10] it would be hard to gainsay the penetration of the following passage (as it would be hard to miss its importance for Mandeville's views of pride and self-liking, which do not concern us in this particular context):

> People, where they are not known, are generally honour'd according to their Clothes and other Accoutrements they have about them; from the richness of them we judge of their Wealth, and by their ordering of them we guess at their Understanding. It is this which encourages every Body, who is conscious of his little Merit, if he is any ways able, to wear Clothes above his Rank, especially in the large and populous Cities, where obscure Men may hourly meet with fifty strangers to the Acquaintance, and consequently have the Pleasure of being esteem'd by a vast Majority, not as what they are, but what they appear to be: which is a greater temptation than most People want to be vain.[11]

It would appear that there is sufficient "scatter" in going from socialization to conspicuous consumption.

One must inevitably note here also that Mandeville exhibits errors or ineptitudes over a wide range of phenomena. He will suggest, with regard to fear, that the more you "work upon it," the "more orderly and governable" man will be.[12] Presumably London in the eighteenth century was not altogether unlike the same city in the twentieth. It can at least be strongly argued that it is not fear alone (nor pride nor the desire for a good name alone) that keeps men within certain bounds in the two centuries. Mandeville's understanding of "social control," of the phenomena that keep men orderly in society, leaves out or "reduces" too much. He is too ready to overlook (or to misunderstand by way of specious reduction to self-interested motives) elements of "control" that have been developed in men to collaborate with external authority. This particular kind of reduction on his part certainly antedates him, but its relative antiquity is evidently no warrant of its truth. (It is still the case, to be sure, that his reductionism is, as it were, one face of a coin whose other face shows forth his impressive power in tracing to such motives as fear and pride various actions that only speciously lay claim to nobler motivation.)

Let us again switch abruptly to something that appears very different, at least initially. Mandeville could be acute about numerous religious phenomena. Much of this acuteness is shown in his tract in favor of toleration.[13] Yet his comprehension of religion in sociological and psychological terms, for all its shrewdness, remains seriously defective. Cromwell was "a vile wicked hypocrite," in his outlook. He gives ground for the view that he considers Puritanism and "hypocrisy" to have close affinities and that this is an extremely significant thing about Puritanism.[14] Throughout the volume in which these notions are expressed he shows a certain skill in the consideration of the perversion of Christianity to the uses of politics and war—a skill one might indeed expect of him. But he tends in his discussions of religion (which run to some length) either to exhibit this particular skill or to insist that man, in virtue of his "darling Lusts," cannot live up to the requirements of Christianity[15]—and with these things he stops.

There may well be a deeper connection between Mandeville's shortcomings in understanding social control and his limitations in understanding religion. We may be allowed to state the matter in laconic Freudian language. Mandeville is strong and apt and convincing where he has to deal with man's id (and ego) and various manifestations thereof, but less strong, apt, and convincing where he confronts the task of understanding the superego and its manifestations: where he cannot break up (or break "down") moral furniture to his liking, he becomes exceedingly suspicious of it and perhaps wishes to believe it does not exist.[16]

The above selection perhaps suggests sufficiently the cogency and variety of various sociological insights of Mandeville's as well as something of the provocative ways in which he could be wrong. But it is well to turn now to the evolutionary component in his thought as an instance of at least the beginning of systematic structure in the work he accomplished.

The Evolutionary View

For Mandeville, human wisdom was the child of time.[17] Human institutions, human establishments in the broadest sense, did not originate in perfection overnight, by way of the planning of clever men. We revert briefly to the matter of language, in this context. Horatio asks how any language could ever "come into the World from two Savages."

Cleomenes answers, "By slow degrees, as all other Arts and Sciences have done, and length of time; Agriculture, Physick, Astronomy, Architecture, Painting, etc."[18] In the light of the previous statement we have already quoted from Mandeville on the subject of "savages" and language, it is a fair presumption that he would have contended that the development of human language was a very slow affair indeed. He afforded a brief sketch by way of a plausible "conjectural history" of language, and the sketch further enforces the view that developed language was the product of a long historical course in which one generation improved upon the work of another.[19] He has Cleomenes say that "it is the Work of Ages to find out the true Use of the Passions, and to raise a Politician, that can make every Frailty of the Members add strength to the Whole Body, and by dextrous Management turn *private Vices into Public Benefits.*"[20] Here we must attend particularly to the words "the Work of Ages." Once again, human wisdom is the child of time, and although skilled "politicians" perform very useful services their role is limited. When Cleomenes avers in the *Enquiry into Honour* that honor is an idol reared on a foundation of human pride and by human "Contrivance,"[21] even here the word *contrivance* must be understood with qualifications. Mandeville is not really inclined to attribute very much in human affairs to deliberate, reasoned invention or manipulation. What he called "Human Sagacity labouring with Design *a priori*"[22] always had decided limitations in his view.

The evolutionary point of view is brilliantly suggested by Mandeville when he deals with human inventions and shows how their final forms are unintended affairs, remote indeed from the fumbling efforts and limited human purposes which initially launched them. Cleomenes speaks: "To Men who never turn their Thoughts that way, it certainly is almost inconceivable to what prodigious Height, from next to nothing, some Arts may be and have been raised by human Industry and Application, by the uninterrupted Labour, and joint Experience of many Ages, tho' none but Men of ordinary Capacity should ever be employ'd in them."[23]

The wisdom built into a ship (like that which may be built into a system of kinship, although Mandeville does not specifically refer to this) is once more seen as cumulative, and Cleomenes further asserts that "we often ascribe to the Excellency of Man's Genius, and the Depth of his Penetration, what is in reality owing to length of Time, and the Experience of many Generations, all of them very little differing from one another in natural Parts and Sagacity."[24] The repetition involved here is after all Mandeville's and may presumably be construed as a sign of the importance he attaches to these evolutionary views. The point of the discrepancy between what is envisaged in limited initial purposes, on the one hand, and what is witnessed in imposing outcomes over time in a process of development, on the other, is made particularly clear in the following statement, also by Cleomenes:

> The Chevalier *Reneau* has wrote a Book, in which he shows the Mechanism of Sailing, and accounts mathematically for everything that belongs to the working and steering of a Ship. I am persuaded, that neither the first Inventors of Ships and Sailing, or those who have made Improvements since in any Part, ever dream'd of those Reasons, any more than now the rudest and most illiterate of the vulgar do, when they are made Sailors, which Time and Practice will do in Spight of their Teeth.[25]

In the outlook that Mandeville develops in connection with such observations as these, then, men were constantly acting with ends in view which terminated in outcomes often very useful to their societies even if the originating ends or actions had little to do with those outcomes—those "useful results for others which they [individuals] did not anticipate or perhaps even know," as Hayek puts the matter. Hayek further observes that in his elaboration of this kind of thesis "Mandeville for the first time developed all the classical paradigmata of the spontaneous growth of orderly social structures: of law and morals, of language, the market and of money, and also of the growth of technological knowledge."[26] Despite his relative brevity in these matters, Mandeville deals with them very strikingly. Conservative thought understandably inclines to stress the wisdom putatively built into traditional institutions and it is not always so careful as it might be in distinguishing institutional spheres from technological ones (where criteria of utility and efficacy are inevitably clearer). Ideological constraint can then evidently operate upon sociological, economic, and political thinking. But whatever components of ideology and whatever impulses toward sustaining a status quo there may have been in Mandeville's views with regard to the evolution of institutions and inventive arts, there can be no doubt that he was offering in the area we have reviewed a core of sound and very apt notions important for sociology as well as for other social science disciplines. For here Mandeville was showing how men inadvertently created that order to which, as we have noted, Hayek refers—an order "formed without design," to use Hayek's precise words—an order in human society whose sheer existence lays a foundation for theoretical inquiry. But the understanding that Mandeville exhibits in the area we have just reviewed is also significant for the crude intimations[27] of structural-functional analysis which his work exhibits and to which attention may now be given.

Adumbrations of Structural-Functional Analysis

There is no occasion to afford here a detailed outline of structural-functional analysis[28] and its variant forms and the controversy that is going on about it within sociology. But several points essential for the purposes of this article may be reviewed.

An initial point, thoroughly familiar to sociologists, is that, in any enterprise in functional analysis, it is desirable for the sake of clarity and precision to specify the structure whose function it is intended to explain. The absence of a fairly firm notion of what structure consists in and what structure it is that one is concentrating upon is bound to lead to trouble. (A physiologist studying the functions of that structure called the liver would obviously be ill advised to lose sight of the circumstance that it was specifically the liver whose functions he was studying.) And this holds at the social as well as the physiological level. (Likely candidates for inclusion under the rubric of structure at the social level are phenomena of the type of social roles, group organization, values, and standards and attitudes legitimated in interaction.)[29] It is not to be expected that Mandeville should have had any penetrating conception of structures; that he should have self-consciously discriminated and labeled shrewdly various structural elements in a social system and sought to analyze their functions with care; that he should have postulated that certain structures may be interchangeable for certain purposes; or that he should have elaborated notions of the line of "dysfunction" and "strain" that have become very much a part of contemporary sociological thought. Mandeville's thrusts in the direction of functionalism were in significant ways indeed primitive.

But on a second point, Mandeville is considerably closer to modern analysis. The point has been well put by Merton, who writes that "the concept of function involves the standpoint of the observer, not necessarily that of the participant. Social function refers to *observable objective consequences,* and not to subjective dispositions (aims, motives, purposes)."[30] It is one of the most salient features of Mandeville's orientation to society and economy that he is aware that men act with certain intentions but that the social consequences of their action often transcend (and in some cases may well baffle) the intentions with which they began. (Here the rudimentary functional analysis that can be found in Mandeville plainly connects with his evolutionary outlook.) The matter is important enough to call for consideration in some detail. It has repeatedly been observed that a biological—or sub-social or sub-cultural—necessity for any society is that it must replace its personnel over time and must do so largely by reproduction (since other ways of doing so, as by capture of offspring from other societies, would be subject to grave difficulties). Let us treat this as if we were dealing with an unequivocably "social" necessity—what in the sociological literature might be called a functional requisite or functional imperative. It is then evident that the general requisite of group reproduction is one to which, in particular societies, few men may give any thought at all and one which the many can meet by actions designed simply to express love or attain pleasure (or, at most, designed to obtain offspring for particular men and women). In a notable passage in the *Fable,* Horatio proposes that "the End of Love, between the different sexes, in all animals, is the Preservation of their Species." Cleomenes responds: "But . . . the Savage is not prompted to Love from that Consideration. He propagates, before he knows the consequence of it; and I much question whether the most civilized Pair, in the most chaste of their Embraces, ever acted from the Care of the Species, as a real Principle."[31] One may contend, of course, that "a most civilized Pair" could well want their own offspring, but even if they did they could clearly not reproduce the species or the membership of a society and presumably would not ordinarily have such ends in view. And in societies where considerable ignorance of reproduction prevails, such large-scale results would hardly be connected with the sexual behavior of various individual pairs.

The impression that Mandeville shrewdly distinguishes purpose from objective outcome is variousely reinforced. We have already noted that Cleomenes is concerned with the effect of fast-days upon the morale of soldiers who fast, not with the object of fast-days in the line of gaining divine favor, which concerns Horatio. Here Horatio dwells on purpose; Cleomenes on function. In the case just reviewed, related to "the End of Love," there is a reversal of emphases. Horatio proposes a "function" (or at any rate a socially significant biological consequence) of love while Cleomenes appeals to the motive or purpose in love-making. It is worth remarking on Mandeville's already impressive skill in these premises. He can shift from purpose to function or from function to purpose with considerable effect, and he can shift adroitly from one purpose to another.[32]

A third point in functional analysis has again been put succinctly by Merton, who marks, as "the central orientation of functionalism," the practice of "interpreting data by establishing their consequences for larger structures in which they are implicated."[33] The practice of so doing is inveterate with Mandeville (always within limitations imposed by the undeveloped character of his functionalism). He discusses, in what one may call a functional "spirit," the ignorance of the poor and lowly, prostitution, and duelling. In the case of ignorance, it is not only the poor and lowly who will benefit from their lack of knowledge of a variety of things, but also society as a whole, which will profit from not experiencing that unrest that too much knowledge on the part of subordinate orders is likely to generate. Accordingly, we find "Ignorance recommended as a necessary Ingredient in the Mixture of Civil Society."[34] As regards prostitution, Mandeville's position is that the prostitution of some, sustaining the chastity of others, rebounds to the general benefit.[35] Finally, as regards duelling, the essential view urged is that the honor expressed in and through the practice of the duel spreads good breeding in a society, although not all duel—and although individual deaths do occur. Obviously, any of these positions could be seriously challenged. It may be quite significant that just after Cleomenes remarks on the contribution that duelling makes to "Politeness of Manner and Pleasure of Conversation," he adds: "But that Politeness itself, and that Pleasure, are the things he [Mandeville] laughs at and exposes throughout his book."[36] This clearly suggests that Mandeville depreciated the very function of diffuse sustaining of good breeding that he imputed to the duel. Possibly this was due to a perception that *other* (or additional) functions which men would be likely to cherish *less* than the sustaining of good breeding could reasonably be imputed to the practice of duelling.[37]

If it is possible that Mandeville had such a perception, it is certain that he did not explicitly consider "other functions." But with all due reservations, his performance as a functionalist is still noteworthy.

Asymmetry

We recall that it was a central thesis of Mandeville's that out of "vice" would come "paradise." True—and important—the conversion of private vices into public benefits required what he called dextrous management by skillful politicians. This reservation should certainly not be overlooked. It is much too easy to misunderstand Mandeville if one does overlook it. But our stresses here must fall on different things. Mandeville sees that numerous necessities for the operation of a society ("fuctional requisites") are in fact met by indirection and even inadvertently. He would have been in thorough sympathy with Adam Smith's observation, "I have never known much good done by those who affected to trade for the public good."[38] Rather, public good (under appropriate conditions) will tend to emerge from efforts oriented to private good. We can grant that there are for Mandeville different kinds of "vice," some more socially serviceable than others. We may note his argument that, when he says that societies cannot attain wealth and power without vice, he is not thereby recommending vice. We may note his saying after Bayle that the utility which vice may have does not mitigrate the character of vice.[39] After all possible cautions have been observed and all needed qualifications made, however, it is still true that for Mandeville, in an important sense, "vice" leads to "paradise." This marks a theme of asymmetry which is very insistent in his thought. He does not give it this name, but it is a helpful name to give simply in order to draw special attention to a distinctive turn of his mind.

If vice is opposed to or asymmetrical with paradise, it is certainly possible to conceive the vices that Mandeville thought of as culturally molded or patterned. His doggerel on vice and paradise, with its important supporting text, would not be at all difficult to construe or restate in modern functionalist terms. When he avers that it is "Pride, Sloth, Sensuality, and Fickleness" that are "the great Patrons that promote all Arts and Sciences, Trades, Handicrafts, and Callings,"[40] evidently we may take this as simply a specifying of the meaning of vice leading to paradise, still featuring asymmetry in that pride, sloth, and so on are ordinarily conceived as bad; arts, sciences, and so on as good. We could still make a fit with a functionalist framework. Moreover, Mandeville's functional—and asymmetrical—bias far transcends the economic sphere. The asymmetry inevitably strikes us as a frequent correlate of the crude functionalism where Mandeville's preoccupations are not at all economic. But we have just said "frequent," not "invariable," and we leave open the question of whether all of Mandeville's asymmetrical play could profitably be regarded as coming within a functionalist framework in some significant sense. The powerful asymmetrical thrust of his thought, however, is in itself worth further notice.

Cleomenes, in referring to human nature, asserts that "a most beautiful Superstructure may be rais'd upon a rotten and despicable Foundation."[41] The suggestion of asymmetry between beauty and rottenness is plain, and it is also plain that Mandeville means to stress it. He will say very generally: "The short-sighted Vulgar in the Chair of Causes seldom can see further than one Link; but those who can enlarge their View, and will give themselves the Leisure of gazing on the Prospect of concatenated Events, may, in a hundred Places, see *Good* spring up and pullulate from *Evil,* as naturally as Chickens do from Eggs."[42] And the asymmetrical play goes on, sometimes clearly suggesting a functionalist outlook, sometimes perhaps not. Envy and love of glory make schoolboys do well in their studies. Envy prompts painters to improvement as they try to outdo their superiors. Married women are generally guilty of the "vice" of envy and seek to arouse the same "passion" in their husbands. And where they have succeeded in this, "Envy and Emulation have kept more Men in Bounds, and reform'd more Ill Husbands from Sloth, from Drinking and other evil Courses, than all the Sermons that have been preach'd since the time of the Apostles.''[43] Truly, evil generates good. Mandeville is most perceptive on the point that "low" passions can have great value.[44] *This* is emphatically *not* cynicism.[45] It is clearly an important line of thought, important for psychology (and sociology) and ethical theory.

The significance of all this at the "large" and "macro" social level must be emphasized at the risk of emphasizing the by-now obvious. The vulgar ideology of "positive thinking" tells us that bad thoughts bring bad outcomes in society and economy as a whole as in more restricted psychological or interpersonal contexts. Adherents of this ideology can trace a phenomenon such as a great economic depression to pessimistic, unpositive thinking on the part of too many; while a prosperity supervening after depression is traceable to an appreciable upswing in optimistic mentation. This is a very particular example, certainly, of "symmetry" rather than "asymmetry" in thought about social and economic matters. Mandeville, even if he was not acquainted with the inanities of positive thinking as we know it today, had, as we have surely sufficiently noted by now, grasped firmly the point that, in the working of things social, asymmetry is often a prominent element. According to F.B. Kaye, "The general idea . . . of the possible usefulness of vice was frequently anticipated in the numerous seventeenth-century discourses on the passions." Kaye contends, however, that such anticipation "usually put little stress on the social implications of the value of vice."[46] And here again we do *not* confront cynicism or the like. In two of the pithiest sentences in the *Fable,* Mandeville observes: "To search into the real Causes of Things imports no ill Design, nor has any Tendency to do harm. A Man may write on Poisons and be an excellent Physician."[47] If "vice" be taken as a poison, an entirely serious Mandeville may be conceived to be speaking here: there is no reason not to take these words at face value. Sociology would be a far more powerful science than it is if it had thorough knowledge of a large variety of "poisons" and of their power of transformation, if it could say with great assurance which poisons must always remain such and which are convertible, and so on.

Our insistence that there is an extremely important realistic, non-cynical strain in Mandeville's thought about low passions and high outcomes thereof does not imply a denial that he ever sought to depreciate the high by revealing its sources or presumptive sources in the low. To some extent he did unquestionably put asymmetry to the uses of depreciation. But did it never occur to him that one might reverse the thinking of the "high" having its sources in the "low" and proceed, rather, to ennoble the "low" by celebrating its outcome in the "high"? After all, if vanity should act as a powerful counter-motive to suicidal impulse and if private economic lust (always under appropriate conditions) may be transformed into general economic welfare, why are not the lowly motivational foundations purified by the elevated outcomes? Kaye quotes from Mandeville's *Modest Defense of Publick Stews* to the effect that "it is the grossest Absurdity, and a perfect Contradiction in Terms, to assert, that a *Government* may not commit Evil that good may come of it." To this, Mandeville added at once: "for, if a Publick Act, taking in all its Consequences, really produces a greater Quantity of Good, it must, and ought to be termed a good Act."[48] Here, at any rate, is an obvious penchant toward a utilitarian view, there is no talk of "rotten foundations" in human nature, and once more there is evidently no intrusion of cynicism. And here Mandeville may be allowed to have a certain affinity, that has in fact often been noted,[49] with those philosophically inclined speculators who have been disposed to look upon men's ordinary, everyday acts of no great intellectual or moral inspiration as instrumentalities of "higher ends" never contemplated by ordinary actors. Mandeville does not conceive of a cunning of reason nor even of an invisible hand. But if such concepts are lacking in his work, his notion of private vices-public benefits bears some likenesses to them. The very idea of asymmetry intensifies the sense of resemblance here.

Quite possibly, Mandeville would not have been intrigued by the affinity of certain aspects of his thought with notions at the heart of various philosophies of history. There is a side of his intellect and temperament that might well have reacted negatively to those notions. One might readily conceive that with Hegel, at any rate, he would have felt little sympathy; and it is probably easiest to believe that he would have felt some kinship, after all, with Adam Smith, whose invisible hand is indeed a kind of philosophical construction, but one, if the matter may be so put, that is relatively at no great metaphysical remove from certain economic and social realities. The impression persists that Mandeville's origin as a physician deeply formed him. He could be a fine psychologist. He had an obvious taste for empirical phenomena. He could even be a most capable sociologist. If, however, there is an element in this thought that brings him in a way close to philosophy of history, despite himself, it does not harm but rather enriches his views on human nature and society. And thereby, he becomes an even more interesting figure somewhere near the beginnings of modern sociological thought. The future careful and thorough historians of that thought would be foolish to neglect him.

Notes

1. See, e.g., F. Gregoire, *Bernard de Mandeville et la "Fable des Abeilles"* (Nancy: George Thomas, 1947), pp. 43-55, on "Mandeville et la Sociologie." More important for our purposes is Joseph J. Spengler, "Veblen and Mandeville Contrasted," *Weltwirtschaftliches Archiv* 82 (1959):35-65. Spengler, p. 55, suggests that "Mandeville's approach may be looked upon as that of an anticipator of contemporary social scientists who make use of the so-called 'structural-functional' approach." M. M. Goldsmith more recently writes of "Mandeville's functional analysis of social institutions," in his article on Mandeville in *International Encyclopedia of the Social Sciences,* 17 vols. (New York: Macmillan and Free Press, 1968), 9:555. Reference will also be made in due course to structural-functional (or, elliptically, "functional") analysis, and the writer regards Spengler's statement well justified. It may be added that Spengler's excellent item, in its primary concern with contrasts between Veblen and Mandeville, actually devotes only a small amount of attention to the adumbrations in Mandeville of modern sociological analysis. These adumbrations are here considered more extensively and in wider contexts than Spengler could allow himself.

2. It is interesting to contrast present-day sociology and the sister discipline of economics in point of recent attention to Mandeville. Heinz Maus, *A Short History of Sociology* (New York: Philosophical Library, 1962), indexes the names of Adam Ferguson, Hume, and Adam Smith but not that of Mandeville. Raymond Aron, *Main Currents in Sociological Thought,* 2 vols. (New York: Doubleday, 1965, 1967), does not index Mandeville (or the Scots), although volume 1 has a chapter on Montesquieu. Robert Nisbet, *The Sociological Tradition* (New York: Basic Books, 1967), shows references to Ferguson, Hume, and Smith but not to Mandeville. G. Duncan Mitchell's *A Hundred Years of Sociology* (Chicago: Aldine, 1968) refers to Hume and Smith but not to Mandeville. For contrast, Joseph A. Schumpeter's *History of Economic Analysis* (New York: Oxford University Press, 1954) has two references to Mandeville, while Overton H. Taylor's *A History of Economic Thought* (New York: McGraw-Hill, 1960) contains a concise essay on Mandeville, at pp. 37-39, and the index of William Letwin's *The Origins of Scientific Economics* (Garden City, N.Y.: Doubleday, 1965) shows three references to Mandeville. It would be a very unusual article in a present-day journal of sociology or by a present-day sociologist that would contain the barest reference to Mandeville, while economists might come upon such papers as that of Spengler already mentioned, or Nathan Rosenberg, "Mandeville and Laissez-Faire," *Journal of the History of Ideas* 24 (1963):183-96; or Alfred Chalk, "Mandeville's *Fable of the Bees:* A Reappraisal," *Southern Economic Journal* 32 (1966); or Friedrich A. Hayek, "Dr. Bernard Mandeville," *Proceedings of the British Academy* 7 (1966): 125-41. A rare instance of mention of Mandeville by a sociologist in recent years is afforded by Robert K. Merton in his *On Theoretical Sociology* (New York: Free Press, 1967), p. 20, where he refers to Spengler's paper. This reference can now also be found in Merton's *Social Theory and Social Structure* (New York: Free Press, 1968), q.v. at pp. 20-21 (and also at p. 475 for a much earlier reference to Mandeville).

3.   One significant opinion may be noted in this connection. Hayek writes: "Though Mandeville may have contributed little to the answers to particular questions of social and economic theory, he did, by asking the right questions, show that there was an object for a theory in this field. Perhaps in no case did he precisely show *how* an order formed itself without design, but he made it abundantly clear that it did, and thereby raised the questions to which theoretical analysis, first in the social sciences and later in biology, could address itself." Hayek, "Mandeville," pp. 126-27.

4.   The origins of sociology in the contemporary sense are not infrequently traced to the work of Adam Smith and Adam Ferguson. See, e.g., Hans Proesler, *Die Anfange der Gesellschaftslehre* (Erlangen: Palm & Enke, 1935), p. 169. Numerous commentators have, of course, been engaged with the question of Mandeville's influence on Smith in particular. Note, e.g., the comments of F. B. Kaye, editor of *The Fable of the Bees* (hereafter *Fable*), 2 vols. (Oxford: Clarendon Press, 1924), in 1:cxxxiv, cxxv, cxli. Smith's critique of Mandeville in *The Theory of Moral Sentiments* (London: George Bell, 1907), pp. 451-60, is very well known, and it is at any rate difficult to see how anyone could resist Kaye's suggestion that Smith was thoroughly acquainted with the *Fable*. Hume, it may be contended, is also a figure not without some significance for the beginnings of sociology. For one instance of argument that he was considerably preoccupied with Mandeville, see Paul Sakmann's still valuable *Bernard de Mandeville und die Bienenfabel-Controversie* (Freiburg: Mohr [Paul Siebeck], 1897), p. 206. The paucity of explicit references to Mandeville by name in the entire body of Hume's work, however, is one of the circumstances that still makes Mandeville's relation to the Scots and to the origins of sociological thought a somewhat puzzling matter.

5.   We shall not be concerned here with the antecedents of Mandeville's own thought and will take his views as given. The interested reader will find in Wilhelm Deckelmann's *Untersuchungen zur Bienenfabel Mandevilles* (Hamburg: Friederichsen, de Gruyter, 1933) one of the ablest discussions of Mandeville's intellectual antecedents, with special reference to Pierre Bayle.

6.   *Fable,* 2:189. [That is, Mandeville speaks for himself through Cleomenes. Ed.]

7.   Ibid., 2:191.

8.   Ibid., 2:189.

9.   Ibid., 2:190.

10.   See the statements of Spengler, who argues ("Veblen and Mandeville," p. 39) that Veblen "was influenced little if at all by Mandeville," and of Arthur O. Lovejoy, who contends (in *Fable* 1: 452; personal letter to Kaye) that "nearly all of the fundamental ideas of Mr. Thorstein Veblen's *Theory of the Leisure Class* can be found in Mandeville." (In this form, these two statements are obviously not necessarily incompatible.)

11.   Ibid., 1:127-28. Cf. the whole of Remark M, in 1:124-34.

12.   Ibid., 1:206.

13.   Bernard Mandeville, *Free Thoughts on Religion, the Church, and National Happiness,* 2d ed. (London: Brotherton, 1729).

14.   On Cromwell and Puritanism, see Bernard Mandeville, *An Enquiry into the Origin of Honour and the Usefulness of Christianity in War* (London:

Brotherton, 1732), pp. 130-202, 207-208, 217-18, 230-32, 239. (Hereafter referred to as *Enquiry into Honour.)*

15. Even when Mandeville's limitations are most in evidence, some valid insight is likely to be lurking not far away. And we must qualify the stringency of our criticism of Mandeville as a kind of sociologist of religion insofar as he exhibits an incipient functional orientation. To note this gets ahead of our story, but it may be merely *loosely* remarked here that functionalism in social science is attentive to the social consequences of human actions. In the fourth dialogue of *Enquiry into Honour,* Horatio and Cleomenes discuss fast-days among the military. In a typical interchange, Horatio remarks that the object of fast-days is to gain divine favor and aid, but confesses that he cannot see how one can be sure that this will be their actual effect. Cleomenes-Mandeville responds that the politician does not think of things divine. The point of the fast-days has to do with their effects *upon the soldiery that fasts* (as on the line of inspiring that soldiery with "fresh hopes" that God will be on their side). The ostensible divine object of fast-days is not sociologically relevant. Perhaps a touch of the sardonic helps in its way to launch sociology into the world, even though, once it is launched, the sardonic impulse may hinder more than it helps.

16. He can write that "no Man fights heartily that thinks himself in the wrong," *Fable* 1:210, but this kind of observation does not lead him on to the presumption of the existence of a conscience not reducible to such things as pride.

17. See *Enquiry into Honour,* p. 41.

18. *Fable,* 2:287.

19. Ibid., 2:287-89; and note Kaye's editorial footnotes, 2:288.

20. Ibid., 2:319.

21. *Enquiry into Honour,* p. 64.

22. *Fable,* 2:179.

23. Ibid., 2:141.

24. Ibid., 2:142. It is a striking circumstance that whereas Mandeville referred to erroneous ascription to human genius of what is in reality owing to time and circumstance, Adam Ferguson held that "without the intervention of uncommon genius, mankind, in a succession of ages, qualified to accomplish in detail this amazing fabric of language, which, when raised to its height, appears so much above what could be ascribed to any simultaneous effort of the most sublime and comprehensive abilities." Ferguson, *Principles of Moral and Political Science* (Edinburgh: Printed for A. Strahan and T. Cadell, London; and W. Creech, Edinburgh, 1792), 1:43. Since we note that, it is also worth noting some lines of Friedrich Meinecke's with reference to Ferguson: "The institutions of a society, he said, are of dim and remote origin and arise out of natural drives, not out of men's speculation. As if in the dark, men grope toward institutions which are not intended but the result of their activity. And thus he recalls to us Cromwell's saying that man never ascends higher than when he does not know whither he is going." Meinecke, *Die Entstehung des Historismus* (Munich: Oldenbourg, 1936), 1:283. The words would apply to Mandeville with all the aptness with which they apply to Ferguson except for the quite accidental point that Mandeville did not cite Cromwell's particular saying.

25. *Fable,* 2:143. Mandeville adds that there are thousands of sailors "that

were first handl'd on board and detain'd against their Wills, and yet in less than three Years time knew every Rope and every Pully in the Ship, and without the least Scrap of Mathematics had learned the Management as well as the Use of them, much better than the greatest Mathematician could have done in all his Life-time, if he had never been at Sea." Ibid. Thus men of modest abilities can profit from what might be called accumulated and built-in sagacity. Leslie Stephen recognized the force of Mandeville's views in these premises, and the wording in which Stephen summarized some of Hume's argument in the latter's work on natural religion is of interest: "We admire a ship which has really been the gradual product of a system struck out by much botching and bungling; the world may have been made after the same fashion, or have been constructed by an infantile or superannuated or incapable deity." Stephen, *History of English Thought in the Eighteenth Century* (New York: Harcourt, Brace & World, 1962), 1:276. But this is succinct paraphrasing and Hume's own language in the dialogues is, if anything, even more strikingly reminiscent of Mandeville: "If we survey a ship, what an exalted idea must we form of the ingenuity of the carpentr, who framed so complicated, useful, and beautiful a machine? And what surprise must we entertain when we find him a stupid mechanic, who imitated others, and copied an art, which, through a long succession of ages, after multiplied trials, mistakes, corrections, deliberations, and controversies, had been gradually improving?" David Hume, *Dialogues Concerning Natural Religion* (Indianapolis: Bobbs-Merrill, 1947; originally 1779), p. 167.

26. Hayek, "Mandeville," p. 129.
27. Note Spengler's reference to the "primitive character" of Mandeville's view of social system, "Veblen and Mandeville," p. 43.
28. The reader seeking relatively full indications of the character of functional analysis will find illuminating Merton, *Social Theory,* "Manifest and Latent Functions," ch. 3; and Talcott Parsons, "An Outline of the Social System," in Parsons et al., eds., *Theories of Society* (New York: Free Press of Glencoe, 1961), 1:30-79.
29. Merton, *Social Theory,* p. 50; Parsons, "Outline," for example at p. 36.
30. Merton, *Social Theory,* p. 78.
31. *Fable,* 2:228.
32. Thus, Horatio avers that "the Design of Speech is to make our Thoughts known to others." And now Cleomenes takes advantage of Horatio's too quick use of the definite article. Cleomenes does not deny that, when men speak, "they desire that the Purport of the Sounds they utter should be known and apprehended by others." But he is almost excessively aware of the interested uses of speech and adds: "The first Sign or Sound that ever Man made . . . was made in Behalf, and intended for the use of him who made it, and I am of Opinion, that the first Design of Speech was to persuade others, either to give Credit to what the speaking Person would have them believe, or else to act or suffer such Things, as he would compel them to act or suffer, if they were entirely in his Power." *Fable,* 2:289.
33. Merton, *Social Theory,* pp. 100-101. See also Dorothy Emmet, *Function, Purpose and Power* (London: Macmillan, 1958), p. 46, for a pertinent statement.

34. *Fable,* 1:292. See also *Fable* 1:194, 248, 288, 289. Cf. Spengler, "Veblen and Mandeville," p. 51, n. 3.
35. *Fable,* 1:95-100.
36. Ibid., 2:102.
37. In view of the interest that has attached to comparing Mandeville with Veblen, it may be observed incidentally that the Veblen of *The Theory of the Leisure Class* would undoubtedly have enjoyed an endeavor to demonstrate that if there are any merits in good breeding (and for his part he would not have let that phenomenon itself escape jaundiced scrutiny), they are more than offset by an indiscriminate destruction of men's peaceable dispositions and by a general diffusion of dubious values associated with extreme touchiness about social status. See *The Theory of the Leisure Class* (New York: Vanguard Press, 1928), pp. 249-50, 397.
38. *The Wealth of Nations* (New York: Modern Library, 1937), p. 423.
39. See *Fable,* 1:231, 407-8; Bernard Mandeville, *A Letter to Dion* (Los Angeles: Augustan Reprint Society Publication No. 41, 1953), p. 34.
40. *Fable,* 1:366.
41. Ibid., 2;64.
42. Ibid., 1:191.
43. Ibid., 1:138-39.
44. One of the most brilliant passages in *The Fable,* in 2:129-36, on self-liking and self-love, seems to the writer to come close to suggesting that some rather "low" motives may inhibit or prevent suicide more effectively than "higher" ones.
45. The writer is not seeking to absolve Mandeville of cynicism or misanthropy in a general way. Even such a commentator as Hayek ("Mandeville," p. 128), who is most friendly toward him, refers to his "somewhat cynical mind." Leslie Stephen could write of him as both "cynical" and "brutal," and aver that he had "contempt for the human race." See Stephen's *Essays on Freethinking and Plainspeaking* (London: Smith, Elder, 1907), pp. 279, 280. Reaching a valid conclusion on this matter is made difficult, to be sure, by the circumstances that Mandeville often makes an important point which remains important regardless of possible cynical motivation and that he is undoubtedly often having fun by way of exaggeration. Perhaps one of the most unalloyed, convincing suggestions of misanthropy on his part is afforded by Mandeville's *The Virgin Unmask'd* (London: G. Strahan, 1724), which so dwells on the horrible things that may happen to women in marriage that one could conceive women's reacting to it by arguing marriage should not be undertaken and reproduction of the species is not worthwhile.
46. See the verso of the title page of *The Fable* reprinted after Kaye's "Introduction" to volume 1.
47. *Fable,* 1:408.
48. See *Fable,* 1:lx, "Introduction" by Kaye.
49. See, for example, Max H. Fisch's "Introduction" to Vico's *Autobiography* (Ithaca, N.Y.: Cornell University Press, 1944), at pp. 54-55.

2

Adam Smith on Human Nature and Social Circumstance

(1979)

Two centuries have elapsed since the publication of *The Wealth of Nations* and somehwat longer since the appearance of Adam Smith's other central work, *The Theory of Moral Sentiments*. During this time Smith has been pondered and repondered, and one might think that virtually every line of these major writings and his several minor ones had been weighed and in some sense tested. It is a witness to Smith's stature and significant place in the history of thought that we constantly come back to him, and it is always possible that a new time will discover in him new and engaging perspectives. But we must also be prepared for inevitable review of much that has been said about him previously. This chapter is designed to achieve a relative comprehensiveness (although we do not focus on the subject of sympathy) on the matter of Smith's views on human nature and its social and economic outcomes, the social constraints within which it operates, and the wider social contexts by which it is influenced (to all of which we mean to allude with the title phrase "human nature and social circumstance"). It is further hoped that this essay may usefully bring together cogent statements on Smith's work from major modern commentaries.

Of concern here will be rationality and its limitations and the meaning of these for a wider social order. Then, in relation to rationality, a certain incompleteness in Smith's thought will be considered. Thereafter, the concern will be with social and economic harmony, and, finally, with the shaping of motives by situations.

It is well to add two comments before proceeding with Smith on rationality. First, I hold firmly to the thesis (shared with numerous modern commentators, although not undisputed by others) that there is no serious discrepancy between the basic outlook of *The Wealth of Nations* and that of *The Theory of Moral Sentiments*. One modern student remarks, "The view that the central doctrine of one is inconsistent with that of the other is without foundation."[1] Since this chapter highlights

The Wealth of Nations, copious citation will be made from that work,[2] but certainly not to the neglect of what I regard as complementary statements from *Moral Sentiments.*

Second, I refuse to be inhibited by what seems to be a widespread horror of reading an author in terms that depart from what he presumably had in mind. If we want to know how Adam Smith conceived things, it is important to try to discover just that. We must not read present-day economic or sociological analysis into him. But it may be that, as Paul Samuelson has remarked, there is a worse sin than reading present-day analysis into earlier writers.[3] This is the sin of "not recognizing the equivalent content in older writers because they do not use the terminology and symbols of the present."[4] Adam Smith says much that may be translated into later language conveniently and without distortion, and the position taken here is that it is historicist foolishness to deny this. I do not wish to do violence to Smith's views nor to inflate the significance of something of present-day interest he may have referred to in passing, but a spade is surely a spade still, even if Germans call it a *Spaten.*[5]

From Rationality and Its Limitations to Social and Economic Order

The theme or matter of human rationality in Adam Smith's work has a certain complexity, and we must approach it with some patience. It has often been observed that Smith did not place great reliance on man's rationality and did not count on reason as a human faculty (here referred to as "rationality") that would serve in a major way to organize social and economic life. But this is a very broad, loose statement.

Granted that human rationality is for Smith a frail reed, it is still well not to forget that he conceded something to it. Human beings do have some rational faculty. They have capacity to comprehend, intelligence, insight, and foresight. Self-interest is after all a most significant reality for Smith and intimately associated with a certain endowment of human rationality. Economic agents have at least a commonsense sort of rationality about their interests. They are also likely to possess a modicum of relevant knowledge. They know which side their bread is buttered on —within limits but genuinely, nevertheless. This sometimes becomes quite explicit. Slave labor is ultimately "the dearest of any," for "a person who can acquire no property, can have no other interest but to eat as much, and to labour as little as possible." Whatever work such a person does in excess to what will buy his own maintenance "can be squeezed out of him by violence only, and not by any interest of his own" (*The Wealth of Nations,* p. 365). Smith contrasts metayers (sharecroppers) and slaves:

[Metayers,] being freemen, are capable of acquiring property, and having a certain proportion of the produce of the land, they have a plain interest that the whole produce should be as great as possible, in order that their own proportion may be so. A slave, on the contrary, who can acquire nothing but his maintenance, consults his own ease by making the land produce as little as possible over and above that maintenance [p. 366].

Only the obvious imputation of rationality by Smith is important for present purposes. He would undoubtedly have thought that he and even the least sensible of those he knew would have acted in the ways indicated had they been slaves or metayers.

It would seem also that individuals can be trusted to possess insight into what is in their interest better than others who might be tempted to be insightful for them. Smith tells us that the individual in his local situation can judge better than the statesman or lawgiver what is economically to his advantage or how he should employ his capital.[6] For his part, the statesman or lawgiver would evidently be the more inadequate, the larger the number and variety of individuals whose economic activity he might seek to direct to the end of general economic welfare. The statesman tempted to be thus oversupervisory would assume an authority with which no person and no organization could be trusted and which would "nowhere be so dangerous as in the hands of a man who had folly and presumption enough to fancy himself fit to exercise it" (p. 423). The aspiration to superintending the industry of private people with a view of effecting general welfare, indeed, "must always be exposed to innumerable delusions" and "no human wisdom or knowledge could ever be sufficient" for it (p. 651).

This plainly bears on the subject of laissez faire, but that would be a distraction; instead we note the curious character of these arguments as they relate to human rationality. What Smith concedes with one hand he withdraws with the other. Broadly, men have a commonsense rationality and perceptiveness about their own interests; but at the same time, a strong limitation on the scope of rationality in economic affairs is imposed: for the sovereign's rationality in economic matters is severely restricted, and any presumptions he might exhibit in this sphere would be mistrusted by Smith.

We already confront a transition. If we begin by emphasizing a limited but real rationality, we soon will emphasize, following Smith, a real but limited rationality. Men generally tend to act with very narrow ends in view. Their reason (that is, their rationality as a faculty) ordinarily operates within strict limits even within the economic sphere, in regard to what they envisage as aims. The owner of capital seeks his own welfare, and considerations appertaining to the economy as a whole "never enter into his thoughts'' (p. 355) as he does so. They never (or rarely) enter his thoughts partly because he is powerfully motivated to think in terms of his own interests and partly because his insight and penetration do not in any case extend to a comprehension of the economy as a whole.

Let us consider four related points. (1) We will look more closely into the matter of man acting with limited ends in view. (2) Then we may attend to the point that deliberately undertaken actions often have outcomes that transcend any calculation man may have made or any foresight he may have had. (3) Thereafter, we consider the operation of the cunning of reason in Smith's work. (When we speak of this, the sense of ''reason'' no longer has to do with rationality as faculty.) (4) And finally, in the present framework it will be appropriate to say something about unanticipated order or system as the outcome of human purposive action. These four matters are so closely connected that their separation may even seem a bit forced, but it is nevertheless helpful in comprehending Adam Smith.

What is involved in the matter of acting with limited ends in view was beautifully suggested in what might be called ''the watch passage'' in *The Theory of Moral Sentiments:*

> The wheels of the watch are all admirably adjusted to the end for which it was made, the pointing of the hour. All their various motions conspire in the nicest manner to produce this effect. If they were endowed with a desire to produce it, they could not do it better. Yet we never ascribe any such desire or intention to them . . .[7]

The wheels of the watch of course have no purposes at all; an analogy with men with their quite narrow purposes is clearly intended. If the wheels of the watch succeed in a ''pointing of the hour'' (what one might call the ''great end'' of the watch in Smith's teleological style), so too men will often in societies and economies inadvertently achieve or bring about ''great ends,'' although they deliberately pursue only decidedly limited ones. (Inevitably we begin to move toward the second of the four matters mentioned above.)

Even when Smith does allow (as he does just before the watch passage) that men may actually have certain ''great ends'' deliberately in view, he stresses human concentration on action that works immediately toward those great ends:

> With regard to all those ends which, upon account of their peculiar importance, may be regarded . . . as the favorite ends of nature, she has . . . not only endowed mankind with an appetite for the end which she proposes, but likewise with an appetite for the means by which alone this end

can be brought about, for their own sakes, and independent of their tendency to produce it. . . . [Reference is now made to "the great ends" of
self-preservation and the propagation of the species.] But though we are in
this matter endowed with a very strong desire of those ends, it has not been
entrusted to the slow and uncertain determinations of our reason, to find
out the proper means of bringing them about. Nature has directed us to the
greater part of these by original and immediate instincts.[8]

A sentence then immediately follows that, in its denial of human reflection upon the tendency of actions undertaken in very limited perspective
to work toward "beneficent" larger outcomes, is entirely in the spirit of
the later watch passage:

Hunger, thirst, the passion which unites the two sexes, the love of pleasure,
and the dread of pain, prompt us to apply those means [which actually lead
to the "favorite ends"] for their own sakes, and without any consideration
of their tendency to those beneficent ends which the great Director of
nature intended to produce by them.[9]

The impulses associated with self-interest clearly work in the same way
in the economic sphere. Human rationality, once more, at least ordinarily, does not extend to a comprehension of very important larger social
and economic "ends" or outcomes of action. If in *The Theory of Moral
Sentiments* we are told that the wheels of the watch could not succeed
better than they do in the pointing of the hour were they endowed with a
desire to effect that pointing, what could be closer to this than the well-
known statement in *The Wealth of Nations* that "by pursuing his own interest he [the individual] frequently promotes that of the society more effectually than when he really intends to promote it" (p. 432).

But if men act with limited aims or ends in view, it is a certainty that
their purposive social and economic action will often bring results they
never contemplated, as Smith was obviously well aware. A contemporary
sociologist has made familiar to social scientists the rather long but
useful phrase, "the unanticipated consequences of purposive social action."[10] Adam Smith never employs just this phrase, but what it points
to interests him again and again. It also interested other members of the
eighteenth-century Scottish school of social scientists doing work
stimulated by older moral philosophy, for example, Adam Ferguson and
John Millar. More or less in Smith's time alone it was a great interest to
Vico, Bernard Mandeville, and the Joseph Priestly who delivered *Lectures on History and General Policy* at the nonconformist academy of
Warrington. Indeed, so salient a matter as "unanticipated consequences
of purposive social action," which has played so large a role in the philosophy of history and social science, has expectedly attracted much at-

tention before and must again. Adam Smith's preoccupation with the idea is too large for us to handle casually; it plays far too significant a role in theoretical constructions in his main works.

It needs to be kept clearly in view that Smith's notion of human nature is inseparable from his social and economic thought. They belong together in such intimacy as to suggest the virtual inevitability of the conjunction of the components of "human nature and social circumstance." Man's endowment with rational faculty is such as to allow him only limited foresight of the effects of carrying out within social (or economic or political) frameworks his various aims. For Smith, the limitation is clearly unavoidable. It is inseparable from the nature of men and women. If they were different in this respect, human society and economy would certainly be different. In this sense the character of society and economy is of course deeply connected with human nature.

How then does the matter of unanticipated consequences come up in Smith? Near the very beginning of *The Wealth of Nations* we find the avowal that the division of labor is not initially the outcome of "any human wisdom, which foresees and intends that general opulence to which it gives occasion." Rather the division of labor grows out of a human propensity to truck, barter, and exchange "which has in view no such extensive utility" (p. 13).[11] (It is possible to distinguish unanticipated from unintended or even unrecognized consequences, but our usage here in this respect will be deliberately loose.)

There is so much to be noted in this connection, even with the limitations we must impose, that abrupt shifts of illustration may be allowed. In the sphere of banking the operations of the Ayr bank "seem to have produced effects quite opposite to those which were intended by the particular persons who planned and directed it." Indeed, ironically, in the long run it would seem "the operations of this bank increased the real distress of the country which it meant to relieve; and effectively relieved from a very great distress those rivals whom it meant to supplant" (pp. 299, 300). In connection with his discussion of the manner in which the commerce of the towns "contributed to the improvement of the country," Smith observes that "a revolution of the greatest importance to the public happiness was . . . brought about by two different orders of people, who had not the least intention to serve the public." Neither of these orders "had either knowledge or foresight of that great revolution which the folly of the one, and the industry of the other, was gradually bringing about" (pp. 391-92).

Another example of the same general phenomenon may suggest how pervasive the notion of unanticipated consequences was in Smith's outlook: "The tendency of some . . . regulations to raise the value of timber in America, and thereby to facilitate the clearing of the land, was neither, perhaps, intended nor understood by the legislature. Though their beneficial effects, however, have been in this respect accidental, they have not on that account been less real'' (p. 547). An example outside the economic sphere will suggest the same pervasiveness. The sect called Independents (Smith writes), "a sect no doubt of very wild enthusiasts," proposed to establish, at the end of the civil war in England, free sectarian competition without governmental or political commitment to any particular sect.

From Smith's point of view this would have been an admirable parallel in religion to competitive conditions he wished to see obtained in the economy. Had this happy scheme prevailed in the religious sphere, "though of a very unphilosophical origin, it would probably by this time have been productive of the most philosophical good temper and moderation with regard to every sort of religious principle" (p. 745). This is a speculative projection of unintended consequences, but it is clearly quite seriously set forth. It throws in an interesting paradox by suggesting that "a sect of very wild enthusiasts" might have brought about most "philosophical" and rationally desirable results. (The paradox is incidentally strongly reminiscent of Mandeville's whole style of thought.) Given the animus he reveals in the passage devoted to this matter, Smith may be said to be arguing roughly on the line that the juxtaposition and the interaction of numerous particular fanaticisms would result in diminution of fanaticism for the community as a whole (as the juxtaposition of self-interests on the market might have another kind of felicitous outcome). "The teachers of each little sect, finding themselves almost alone, would be obliged to respect those of almost every other sect . . ." (p. 745). Religious "monopoly" is as harmful as the economic kind.

It is well to remind ourselves lastly of a famous instance of unanticipated consequences in *The Theory of Moral Sentiments:*

> *They* [the rich] are led by an invisible hand to make nearly the same distribution of necessaries of life which would have been made had the earth been divided into equal portions among all its inhabitants; and thus, without intending, without knowing it, advance the interest of the society, and afford means to the multiplication of the species.[12]

Having seen that men act with limited ends in view and having considered unanticipated consequences, we turn to the third of our four related points, which has to do with the cunning of reason. This is closely connected with the invisible hand but helps to make the meaning of the latter more graphic, and to speak in terms of the cunning of reason is to sharpen our apprehension of Smith's position in intellectual history. We turn first to *The Theory of Moral Sentiments.*

We know that men are with some frequency, in Smith's view, led to realize "larger ends" indirectly, through being attracted to something that itself simply leads to larger ends. Smith contended that riches bring the rich only a very modest increment of satisfaction beyond what might be had without them. But the economy and the society have great need for the energy and industry of the rich or of those who have distinctive traits that in time will make them rich. How are the rich enticed to engage their energies in the interest of general warfare? The general answer Smith gives is that men are intrigued by the spectacle of the order and beauty of the complex operations set in motion to attend to the requisites of the rich. Thus:

> We are . . . charmed with the beauty of that accommodation which reigns in the palaces and economy of the great; and admire how every thing is adapted to promote their ease, to prevent their wants, to gratify their wishes, and to amuse and entertain their most frivolous desires. If we consider the real satisfaction which all these things are capable of affording, by itself and separated from the beauty of that arrangement which is fitted to promote it, it will always appear in the highest degree contemptible and trifling. But we rarely view it in that abstract and philosophical light. We naturally confound it in our imagination with the order, the regular and harmonious movement of the system, the machine or economy by means of which it is produced.[13]

"It is well," Smith adds, "that nature imposes upon us in this manner." For "it is this deception which rouses and keeps in continual motion the industry of mankind."[14] The invisible hand is at work. The rich are "usefully" induced to advance the interest of the society, precisely by an illusion, a seduction, an enticement. It may just as well be said that the cunning of reason is at work. For that cunning consists in alluring humans to work toward objects that have a mediating function and (with dim human knowledge, at best, that this is occurring) actually subserve "larger ends" or "the favourite ends of nature" (in the language of Smith's early work). Men follow their own passions and interests, in the limiting case wholly unaware that these find their place in a chain that stretches to points never imagined in a limited human envisagement of "links" (which in turn were not recognized by humans as being links in a chain at all). If we drop the teleological and theological vocabulary from all this, we are left with what many scholars have regarded as one of the most fundamental insights or perspectives in the social sciences.[15]

It bears stress that the cunning of reason clearly could not operate as presumed and would not "need" (!) to do so if man's own rationality were not so limited in the first place. We know that it would not have been uncharacteristic for Adam Smith to observe that all around it is better that it should be so. But in any case the cunning of reason underlines once more the narrow scope of human rationality.

Able modern commentators have suggested the affinity of Smith's thought to the notion of the cunning of reason. Thus one of Wilhelm Hasbach's notable treatises on the development of economic thought has this to say:

> Man produces and saves, in order to acquire wealth for himself, but without his knowledge or will he indirectly advances the material condition of the whole society. He is a tool in God's hand.

> To clarify Smith's meaning, I remind the reader of the intention of nature, of the cunning of reason, which plays so prominent a role in German philosophy, most grandiosely since Hegel.[16]

Overton H. Taylor takes up the invisible hand passage in *The Theory of Moral Sentiments* and rehearses Smith's view that the desire of an able and ambitious person for riches makes him inadvertently do things that are economically most useful. Taylor paraphrases Smith thus: "The goal of his selfish ambition is a chimera with which cunning 'nature' lures him into serving others better than he serves himself."[17] If Taylor did not have a Hegelian model in view, his language at any rate is sufficiently suggestive of one.

We may adduce a final and longer relevant statement that will appropriately indicate the fourth matter that we wish to discuss. In his monograph on the state of nature and the natural history of civil society, Hans Medick comments:

> Smith reveals society as an objective context of activity which not only guides the comportment of the individual by way of moral and aesthetic standards of conduct but lays down the consequences of this comportment beyond the subjectively oriented intentions of the individual, which are dictated by self-interest. This happens as if behind men's backs. The individual striving after wealth in a society differentiated according to status and property appears as "cunning of reason," through which socially interconnected action shows itself as economically productive in a measure that was in no way intended by the actor. Through social stimulation of the artificial need for wealth the individual is incited to economic actions which in their results in terms of productivity exceed all his consumption capacities and therefore finally lead to a higher level of need for the totality of the members of the society. This grounding of the Smithian "philosophy of wealth" in a theory of society as an objective, self-directing context of activity was described by Smith by the image of the "invisible hand."[18]

Medick's statement plainly intimates an unanticipated order or system resulting from human purposive action. Society becomes "an objective context of activity." It constitutes an order or system that constrains the individual, and it is at the same time one that comes out of individual actions (whether they are by individuals or groups or organizations). And certainly what is true of society is true of economy. This recognition of social or economic order or system on Smith's part has been noted by numerous students. Viner goes so far as to say that "Smith's major claim to originality, in English economic thought, at least, was his detailed and elaborate application to the wilderness of economic phenomena of the unifying concept of a coordinated and mutually independent system of cause-and-effect relationships. . . ."[19] Glen R. Morrow correctly discerned in Smith's work what he called "an effort to think of the social order as a genuine organic unity, with principles of structure and functioning which maintain themselves independently of the wills of individuals."[20] Schumpeter proposes concisely that Smith held that "free interaction of individuals produces not chaos but an orderly pattern."[21]

It has also been noticed that Smith's work has some strong affinities with modern functional analysis in sociology. Smith was obviously clear on the distinction between subjective intent of action and its objective effect within a larger context or system, as he was aware of unintended "beneficent" contributions of individual actions to larger orders or systems and of sheer systemic interdependencies in social and economic phenomena. To note Smith's cognizance of these "functionalist" points is not to do violence to his thought, nor to deny he was a moral philosopher with a normative outlook on society, economy, and policy. It is not to suggest that being in his own way alert to order or system, he was thereby blind to change.[22] It is not to neglect or thrust aside the circumstance that various social arrangements could in some respects work excellently toward general welfare and in others work very deleteriously—a notable example being the division of labor, with its simultaneous enhancement of productivity and degradation of the labor force.[23]

In connection with the argument, stretching from limitations of rationality through unanticipated consequences and the cunning of reason to order or system, we would unequivocally affirm that the representation given of Smith's thought holds for each of his two main works —*The Wealth of Nations* and *The Theory of Moral Sentiments*.

It is rather curious that Medick should observe that "one must certainly acknowledge the correctness of A. L. Macfie's view that the importance of the 'invisible hand' principle for the total intention of Smith's social philosophy has been overestimated." Medick himself adds at once that Macfie's view "should not mislead us into denying altogether the . . . value of Smith's metaphor."[24] The importance of this arises from what we perceive as the crucial role of the notion of the invisible hand in *The Wealth of Nations* (as well as in the earlier work). In the model of society and economy, involving limited rationality and so on through order or system, the importance of the invisible hand "principle" would be hard to overestimate. We contend that the relative paucity of invisible hand phrasing in *The Wealth of Nations* is of minor importance. In any case, that volume contains at least three relevant references. There is the central invisible hand passage, where Smith writes of the individual's being "led by an invisible hand to promote an end which was no part of his intention" (p. 423). There is the prior, cognate statement:

> Every individual is continually exerting himself to find out the most advantageous employment for whatever capital he can command. It is his own advantage, indeed, and not that of the society, which he has in view. But the study of his own advantage naturally, or rather necessarily leads him to prefer that employment which is most advantageous to the society [p. 421].

If Smith does not actually say "invisible hand" here, it is of purely verbal significance that he does not; and the same is true of the following assertion that appears later:

> Without any intervention of law . . . the private interests and passions of men naturally lead them to divide and distribute the stock of every society, among all the different employments carried on in it, as nearly as possible in the proportion which is most agreeable to the interest of the whole society [pp. 594-95].

The invisible hand thus intervenes or mediates between limited self-interest and general welfare. It effects an *Ausgleich,* a balancing or smoothing out, as it works within an economic or social scheme to coordinate human actions and make them come out a certain way without human intention. Smith was not so naive as to think that the invisible hand is omnipresent and omnipotent or that it is at work under any social or economic circumstances at all. What is central here is that it refers to what one may call conversion mechanisms—which operate precisely (with particular reference to the economic sphere) to convert private interest into public welfare and which have an indispensable place in the model, stretching from limitations of rationality to order or system (on which we have been insistent). Hollander illustrates well enough what is meant by a conversion mechanism and at the same time gives special credit to Smith for his treatment of the particular mechanism illustrated.

> The crucial mechanism in the process of adjustment which assures that the prices of commodities will in fact be "continually gravitating" or "constantly tending towards" their respective cost prices is the tendency toward an equality of the returns to labour, capital and land respectively in different activities. The harshest critics of Smithian value theory concede that his treatment in this regard represents a substantial achievement. For Smith explicitly recognized that resources are transferred individually from less to more remunerative uses until an equality across the board is achieved. . . .[25]

This mechanism has its evident starting point in the striving for advantage on the market. Smith could not foresee various theoretical refinements and highly sophisticated questions bearing on what Hollander thus suggests. His awareness of conversion mechanisms nevertheless provides a powerful constituent in the theoretical structure of *The Wealth of Nations*. In the sense of our interpretation, as the invisible hand refers to conversion mechanisms and fits as it does into the model from limited rationality on, it becomes utterly inadequate to conceive the invisible hand (as some economists have done)[26] as being equivalent to self-interest. Aside from being inadequate or simply wrong, such an equating obscures fundamental theoretical similarities between *The Wealth of Nations* and *The Theory of Moral Sentiments*. (It is still possible that Smith was too optimistic about the invisible hand, even if he was not hopelessly naive about it.)

Limitations of Rationality and a Certain Incompleteness in Smith's Thought

Near the beginning of this essay reference was made to a certain incompleteness in Smith's thought, which has to do with the matter of rationality. Attention to this will bring us a little closer to a rounded treatment of Smith on human nature and social circumstance.

Not only does man (for Smith) have limited rationality in the sense of an intrinsically limited insight and foresight, but further constraints on his rationality are created by the pressure of various motivations that diminish economic rationality in particular. This actually raises some problems of analysis of rationality in its economic contexts that cannot be faced here in their full complexity. But we note some relevant tendencies in Smith's thought. That he himself thought he discerned constraints on economic rationality arising from motivational sources other than inherent limitations of human capacity to see and foresee is beyond question. Among the most important of these motivational sources is that represented by vanity.

Vanity had caught Smith's attention early, and he evidently devoted considerable thought to it. He asks, in *The Theory of Moral Sentiments,* whence arises "that emulation which runs through all the different ranks of men, and what are the advantages which we propose by that great purpose of human life which we call bettering our condition?" He answers, "To be observed, to be attended to, to be taken notice of with sympathy, complacency, and approbation, are all the advantages which we can propose to derive from it. It is the vanity, not the ease, or the pleasure, which interests us. . . ."[27] That this point struck Smith forcibly is suggested by the repetition we find in *The Wealth of Nations:*

> With the great part of rich people, the chief enjoyment of riches consists in the parade of riches, which in their eye is never so complete as when they appear to possess those decisive marks of opulence which nobody can possess but themselves. In their eyes the merit of an object which is in any degree either useful or beautiful, is greatly enhanced by its scarcity, or by the great labour which it requires to collect any considerable quantity of it, a labour which nobody can afford to pay but themselves (p. 172).

Smith sees numerous social and economic phenomena he did not particularly admire or approve, but his peculiar outlook often allows them a sort of redemption because, even if they do not appear admirable, they perform some beneficent or useful "function" within a larger social or economic order, as we know. This is the sort of outlook with which he may approach vanity, riches, or the like. This was plain in *The Theory of Moral Sentiments* in any case. We recall how Smith there derives a general beneficence from a sort of aestheticism that makes attractive to one aspiring to riches the elaborate and idle machinery that caters to the desires of those who are actually rich. One may suspect from Smith's tone that he himself regarded this aestheticism as rather imbecilic. One might then think that this is the end of the matter and perhaps enjoy the contemplation of the ironic contrast (for Smith), whereby a vanity or an ostentation (or a "pointlessly" elaborate apparatus of want satisfaction) has useful social or economic effects. But we are not really at the end of the matter, for there is a strong hint that Smith also discerns a more powerful economically irrational element in vanity in particular and in the propensity of the rich to conspicuous consumption than this would suggest. Vanity and luxury may be economically damaging immediately and at the same time fail of a redeeming function in a larger economic context. A certain inconsistency or at any rate incompleteness in Smith's thought thus appears.

It is argued in *The Wealth of Nations* that "the high rate of profit seems every where to destroy that parsimony which in other circumstances is natural to the character of the merchant. When profits are high, that sober virtue seems to be superfluous, and expensive luxury to suit better the affluence of his situation" (p. 578). We are then told that the lapse of sober parsimony and attentiveness on the part of the members of higher economic strata affects the workman also, with further consequent economic damage. "If his employer is attentive and parsimonious, the workman is very likely to be so too; but if the master is dissolute and disorderly, the servant who shapes his work according to the pattern which his master prescribes to him, will shape his life too according to the example which he sets him" (p. 578).

All this occurs in the midst of one of Smith's critiques of monopoly and when he is not concerned with a general assessment of the functions of riches or affluence. Yet it seems fair to recognize a tendency on Smith's part to see luxury as "expensive," as breaking down "economic virtues" of parsimony and attentiveness, and thereby of ultimately diminishing wealth. The tone about "luxury" is now not the same as when it was conceived (as evidently it was in *The Theory of Moral Sentiments*) to redound to the general benefit. Assuming the rationality of productivity and accumulation of goals, high profits can apparently have an economically irrational effect by way of their destruction or mitigation of "economic virtues." And it also seems clear that high profits need not spread general economic benefit. "Have the exorbitant profits of the merchants of Cadiz and Lisbon augmented the capital of Spain and Portugal? Have they alleviated the poverty, have they promoted the industry of those two beggarly countries?" (p. 578). Apparently, for Smith, to ask these questions was to answer them. On the motivational side, the desire for wealth can actually interfere with the thrust of the "economic virtues." Man's rationality would then appear to be mitigated not only because his vision and foresight and grasp of social or economic wholes or systems are limited but also because "properly" productive and "soberly" accumulative propensities are blocked and inhibited by vanity and the attraction of "luxury."

Is there perhaps a radical disjunction between *The Theory of Moral Sentiments* and *The Wealth of Nations*? And was Smith indeed grievously inconsistent? It seems more sensible to contend that his scheme of thought was incompletely worked out. There is something to be said for both his perspectives on vanity, riches, and luxury. But a really thoroughgoing analysis of human rationality and its limitations, together with its social and economic effects and correlates, Smith did not in the end give us, despite his ingenious work on this line.

It is possible that Smith did not give the ideally full analysis he might have partly because he was torn between two inclinations. On the one hand, there was an aversion to conspicuous consumption and "luxury" and the impairment of the "economic virtues," which provoked a negative inclination. On the other hand, there was Smith's perception of the possibility of a rich economic development of what psychologists have called functional autonomy, which provoked a more positive inclination (although Smith still had his suspicions of wealth and the wealthy).

Where functional autonomy of motives comes about, one pursues an object for one set of motives but produces a result that brings into play another new set of motives, which are then followed.[28] If men strive for gain or wealth with a view to employing it for originally quite delimited wants, it is still nevertheless true that wants can strongly expand once accumulation is sufficient to permit it (and when cultural barriers are removed). One strives for gain for one use or reason, but once gain is present in sufficient quantity it occasions new strivings for different uses or reasons. This may result in highly creative endeavors and the generation of remarkable new commodities and services (although it may also get entangled with vanity or conspicuous consumption and corrupt industry, frugality, and the like).

This is not really a very airy speculation. It remains close to things we can read in Smith's two main books. But it is true that Smith is no great friend of personal wealth or its appurtenances (except of course as he may treat it in terms of the invisible hand). He writes readily of "the sober and industrious poor" (p. 823), but he has no parallel phrase suggestive of sympathy or compassion for the rich. Even when he writes of what we would today call social status or rank, which so easily attaches to wealth, his tone is not especially amiable. "Place," meaning status, is described by him as "that great object which divides the wives of aldermen." The language strikes one as at least mildly sardonic; then Smith goes on to say of "place" that it is "the end of half the labours of human life; and is the cause of all the tumult and bustle, all the rapine and injustice, which avarice and ambition have introduced into this world."[29]

Human Nature and Social and Economic Harmony

With this somewhat larger view of Smith on the subject of rationality achieved, it is appropriate to consider him on the subject of human nature and social circumstance on another front—that of harmony in social and economic matters.

There is appreciable optimism in Adam Smith (particularly in the first of his two major books), but it is by no means unmixed with a certain pessimism. One need not penetrate far beneath the surface of those books to ascertain that in both Adam Smith is much concerned with the matter of processing and training or domesticating a creature about whom one cannot be unqualifiedly optimistic. Overton H. Taylor was struck by the contrast between Smith's view of humanity as set out in *The Theory of Moral Sentiments* and Freud's more somber one—if somber is not too euphemistic a term.[30] Yet even if one grants the relatively optimistic nature of *The Theory of Moral Sentiments,* there is still the patent suggestion that, after all, humans are potentially rather unruly creatures whom societies must hold within bounds.

How, then, are humans to be held within bounds so that a harmonious or orderly society may be possible? The use of the term "orderly" as a synonym for "harmonious" at this juncture has to do not immediately with systemic interdependencies or the like but with standards and arrangements whereby aggression is restrained or conflict and outright murder and the like are kept within strict limits. On the problem of harmony or order suggested in this sense, Smith addresses what has sometimes been called the Hobbesian problem.[31]

Man might be a volatile, extremely passionate, unreservedly self-interested being, puffed up with notions of his own importance. But the impartial spectator is present to control these tendencies. This is one of the great themes of *The Theory of Moral Sentiments.* The impartial spectator of one's actions and reflections exercises a crucial moderating influence. The story is familiar to the most casual reader of Smith. One wants to punish cruelly the relatively minor dereliction of another who has done a small damage to one's self. The spectator is there to indicate that social approbation of one's punitive tendency is likely only when it is very much softened. The really great triumph of the spectator is that he does not remain "external." He is very likely to be made part of the self. In language now often used, he is "internalized." Man carries "society" within himself, constitutes as part of his own self the broad generalized standards, judgments, and sentiments of others. The impartial spectator, Adam Smith's own treatment encourages us to say, has as his inner counterpart "the man within the breast."[32]

Here the connection of human nature with social circumstance is very evident. Human nature is not even conceivable in the terms in which it is actually encountered without the existence of the impartial spectator. Smith's social psychology already shows much sophistication. What we call conscience has important foundations in the impartial spectator. And it must at times go back to such foundations: "The man within the breast, the abstract and ideal spectator of our sentiments and conduct, requires often to be awakened and put in mind of his duty by the presence of the real spectator."[33] In important ways human nature is evoked by society, and it is sustained by society. One may even argue reasonably that, granted that conscience can exhibit highly individual elements and operate with its own distinctive norms (as Smith granted), the individuality and individual norms are still likely to have social roots or references. This seems to be the burden of the statement by a student of Adam Smith who remarks that "the love of self-approbation, which is in fact the same as the love of virtue, is still founded on an implied reference to the verdict of persons external to ourselves, and thus the 'still small voice' of conscience resolves into the acclamations of mankind."[34] If this statement should be judged too strong (and much depends on how one interprets it), it still makes a useful point.

It is neither necessary nor feasible to go into detail here on the relation of the impartial spectator and conscience. Does the impartial spectator stand precisely for "the common consensus of the attitudes of the group," as Bitterman averred?[35] Does the spectator embody a norm "only in the sense of an average standard that emerges from the interplay of ordinary spectators and agents," as Campbell asserts?[36] How then does ideality, or ideal ethical judgment that in some sense transcends group norms, arise? These questions are beyond our present scope; it suffices to recognize the forthright contribution to the problem of harmony or order that Smith makes on the sociopsychological side, whatever we may decide about various particulars of his relevant conceptions.

In regard to what is necessary for social harmony or order, again, Smith does hold in *The Theory of Moral Sentiments* that society may subsist "from a sense of its utility" and without mutual love and affection. "Society may subsist, though not in the most comfortable state, without beneficence," but justice it must have, for "the prevalance of injustice must utterly destroy it."[37] Certainly, various social arrangements are possible on a basis of justice alone, but it is probably best not to press Smith too far on the matter and ask whether "a whole society" such as that of a large nation could really subsist with justice alone. Let us not strain his meaning, which is perhaps clear enough for his purposes at the point in *The Theory of Moral Sentiments* where he introduces these observations. What is important is that it seems unlikely, on Smith's general analysis, that powerful foundations for justice without support from the impartial spectator could exist.

But what about *The Wealth of Nations?* It may seem true that the impartial spectator is not in the premises of that book. Bitterman observes, "In the *Wealth of Nations* the impartial spectator puts in no appearance, unless perhaps Smith cast himself in that role."[38] Bitterman adds that the ethical assumptions are essentially the same in Smith's two main works. And again Bitterman writes that "the disinterested spectator does not put in an appearance in the economic treatise" (although he now comments that "there is the same regard for common sentiment").[39]

In *The Wealth of Nations* the specific job of social psychology that Smith undertook in *The Theory of Moral Sentiments,* in the sense of seeking to trace group influences on the morality and conscience of the individual, is not continued. How then does he handle the matter of harmony, order, or control? Plainly, Smith did not favor unimpeded play for self-interest. A problem of harmony or order is just as much confronted in *The Wealth of Nations* as it is in *The Theory of Moral Sentiments.* A by no means altogether promising human nature must be subjected to social controls. That Smith did not favor unrestricted play of self-interest is one of the best known features of his work in *The Wealth of Nations.* Three things may be considered in this connection.

First, Bitterman's qualification to his own contention that the impartial spectator does not appear in the economic treatise has been noted ("unless perhaps Smith cast himself in that role"). This is not an unreasonable qualification or suggestion. And in this sense there certainly are echoes of the impartial spectator in *The Wealth of Nations.* Essential evidence for the point is given in Smith's numerous strong reservations about merchants and manufacturers. These men complain about the high wages that elevate prices, but not about the untoward effects of high profits. "They are silent with regard to the pernicious effects of their own gains." Who has not read or heard Smith's observation that "People of the same trade seldom meet together, even for merriment and diversion, but the conversation ends in a conspiracy against the public, or in some contrivance to raise prices"? Again, the dealers in any branch of manufacture in effect wish "to levy, for their own benefit, an absurd tax upon the rest of their fellow-citizens" (pp. 98, 128, 250). This is a mere sampling of such statements, for they recur frequently in *The Wealth of Nations* (e.g., pp. 428-29, 434, 460-61, 565, 578). We may take it as a certainty that when Smith made the statement, "All for ourselves, and nothing for other people, seems in every age of the world to have been the vile maxim of the masters of mankind" (pp. 388-89), the more dubious ways of merchants and manufacturers were not far from his thought.[40]

Whether or not we wish to say in view of all these critical remarks that Smith himself is the impartial spectator in *The Wealth of Nations,* it seems fair to assert that he envisaged the possible results of social criticism of those who sought to disadvantage the public by monopoly or restraint of trade. Smith was entirely willing to make normative judgments on the economic order. No one with excessive scruples about such judgments could have written as he did about "pernicious effects of their own gains" or "an absurd tax" or "the vile maxim of the masters of mankind." If he is critical of these "masters," he is also capable of asking what he conceives to be justice for the "lower ranks of the people"— "It is but equity . . . that they who feed, cloath and lodge the whole body of the people, should have such a share of the produce of their own labour as to be themselves tolerably well fed, cloathed and lodged" (p. 79).

If the phrase "impartial spectator" is not used in *The Wealth of Nations,* the spectator is still on the premises. (Perhaps the largest concession one could make to Smith's failure to use the phrase in his later work is to speak of the implicit spectator there.)[41] It is simply not to be expected that the moral philosopher would cease to be at work in Smith when he turned to economic matters.[42]

It is quite accurate to contend that it is indeed control of economic appetite which Smith seeks. He wants restraint, not repression. There is justice in Macfie's observation, "To Mandeville, passions are evil. To Smith, they are natural, but to be duly restrained."[43] Mandeville's moral rigorism (assuming he really adheres to it) is not acceptable to Smith, nor is an older disposition to threaten with hell and damnation the desire to make a buck. The enterprise of buying and selling is not in itself an ineffable danger to the soul. The implicit spectator is critical only of certain kinds of excesses.

Second, there is the control of restraint exercised because the operations of the market economy are to take place within a government framework that establishes justice. "Every man, as long as he does not violate the laws of justice, is left perfectly free to pursue his own interest his own way . . ." (p. 651). According to what Smith called "the system of natural liberty," the sovereign had three duties to perform—to protect a society from violence and invasion from other societies; to build and maintain certain public works; to provide "an exact administration of justice" or to protect all from injustice and oppression, as far as possible (p. 651). Unbridled assertion of self-interest would evidently be checked; and the checking could combine with social criticism, so that properly hedged and bounded self-interest might work toward general benefit.

Third, we come again to the invisible hand. Government administration of justice, aided by the force of social criticism, modifies the power of deep impulses of human nature that carry a large potential of selfishness and scorn for mankind. (We accept here Smith's premises and raise no question about the "real sources" of selfishness.) With movement away from monopoly, we must move toward perfect competition and equilibrium prices. The ordinary material of self-interest changes into the golden metal of general welfare by the familiar paradoxical action of the invisible hand. Moreover, intimate connection of two senses of "order" is suggested. For the order that is synonymous with harmony and the result of legal and other norms or standards also produces a "factual" order. It does so in the sense of creating uniformities and predictabilities in conduct insofar as there is actual conformity to standards. It does so in the sense of preparing the way for emergence of a scheme that takes up minuscule human intentions and actions, shaping them by a kind of juxtaposition and synthesis into a larger systemic whole.

All this unquestionably has an "ideal" aspect. Smith knew very well that things do not always work thus. To say that he envisaged problems of harmony does not entail the preposterous view that he saw no social or economic conflict or disorder. His preoccupation with harmony or order arose out of a clear perception of disharmonies and a sense for potential disturbances. Certainly, the notion of class conflict was not foreign to him. Some also may be embarrassed by the evidence he would appear to give of partiality toward what he called "the martial spirit" (see, e.g., p. 738).

Social Situation and Motive

These remarks were begun with observations of Smith's need to be understood in a larger context than that of his economics alone; indeed, his economics is not properly understandable without considering a larger context. A final look at certain of Smith's sociological views will be in accordance with the spirit of the prior observations and will once again connect human nature and social circumstance, as we consider relations between situation and motive.

Man's intimate involvement in society and the inseparability of human nature therefrom are certainly indicated in the theory of the impartial spectator, but in Smith's view involvement in society runs further. For Smith sees motivation in the broadest terms (and much of habit and perception) as bound up with social circumstance.

For present purposes we utilize somewhat loose terms like "institution" or indeed the convenient broad term "social situation" to refer generally to social circumstances "surrounding" the individual and shaping his motivations, habits, or perceptions. Economists have been partial to "institutions," and this is understandable in view of the "sociological" bias of so-called institutionalists in economics. Nathan Rosenberg touches on the major theme of this portion of our remarks on Smith on human nature and social circumstance when he refers to Smith's concern with whether human institutions were so contrived or structured as to move self-interest to work for the general welfare.[44] Rosenberg recognized Smith's perception of the nexus between situation and motive and referred to the aptly illustrative passage in *The Wealth of Nations* where Smith, after criticizing self-aggrandizing behavior on the part of servants of the East India Company, comments:

> I mean not . . . to throw any odious imputation upon the general character . . . of the East India Company, and much less upon that of any particular persons. It is the system of government, *the situation in which they are placed,* that I mean to censure; not the character of those who have acted in it. *They acted as their situation naturally directed,* and they who have clamoured the loudest against them would, probably, not have acted better themselves [pp. 605-6; emphasis added].

Human beings have their potentials, and potentials of one kind or another are made actual by surrounding circumstances, saliently including social circumstance. Men may be encouraged to seek their self-interest in a way comfortable to general welfare, or they may not. It is not that there is indefinite or unrestricted malleability, and we believe Smith assumes strong common components of human nature for all mankind. Discussing certain demographic phenomena, he writes, "The laws of nature are the same everywhere, the laws of gravity and attraction the same, and why not the laws of generation?"[45] Had it not been for his particular preoccupation of the moment, he might as well have said, "and why not the laws whereby motives are evoked, habits formed, and perception influenced?" But within a common framework of human nature, variations are certainly possible, and social situations influence them profoundly. The influence of custom alone on mankind is great.

One pertinent set of observations in *The Theory of Moral Sentiments* may be noted before we return to *The Wealth of Nations.* Contrasting the civilized with those he called savages and barbarians, Smith remarks, "The general security and happiness which prevail in ages of civility and politeness afford little exercise to the contempt of danger, to patience in enduring labour, hunger, and pain." And a little farther on: "Among savages and barbarians it is quite otherwise."[46] The discussion that follows shows Smith's sensitivity to the connection of the situation of the "civilized" person and the "savage" or "barbarian" with the character and propensities of each. Smith even writes, "The different *situations* of different ages and countries are apt . . . to give different characters to the generality of those who live in them. . . ."[47] (Emphasis added.)

Consider something from a quite different context. Smith observes:

> To improve land with profit, like all other commercial projects, requires an exact attention to small savings and small gains, of which a man born to a great fortune, even though naturally frugal, is very seldom capable. The *situation* of such a person naturally disposes him to attend rather to ornament

which pleases his fancy, than to profit for which he has so little occasion. [p. 364; emphasis added].

Or we may once more refer to Smith on the subject of slavery. It is the slave's social and economic situation that explains his motivation as a worker. As stressed before, in Smith's conception the slave reacts rationally to his situation; but it is precisely to his situation that he so reacts. Referring to a pertinent passage in which Smith speaks of habits in relation to social situation, we find him comparing merchants with country gentlemen in respect to improving land—when merchants develop an interest on these lines. As we might expect, Smith argues that the merchant concerned with land improvement is the better improver: "The habits . . of order, economy and attention, *to which mercantile business naturally forms a merchant,* render him much fitter to execute, with profit and success, any project of improvement" (p. 385; emphasis added).

Consider perhaps the most strikingly relevant example of all. Now we deal with situational constraints that shape perception, consciousness, or understanding. We come in this context to Smith's famous conception of the adverse side of the division of labor—its effects upon the common people.

> In the progress of the division of labour, the employment of the far greater part of those who live by labour, that is, of the great body of the people, comes to be confined to a few very simple operations, frequently to one or two. *But the understandings of the greater part of men are necessarily formed by their ordinary employments.* The man whose whole life is spent in performing a few simple operations, of which the effects too are, perhaps, always the same, or very nearly the same, has no occasion to exert his understanding. [p. 734; emphasis added].[48]

It is hoped that it will not be anticlimactic, in view of the importance of Smith's speculations on the unhappy side of the division of labor, to allude briefly, in this array of cases, to a last item—that represented by professors, for they also act responsively to their situations. This was the clear conviction of a one-time professor of moral philosophy at the University of Glasgow, who observed that "in every profession, the exertion of the greater part of those who exercise it is always in proportion to the necessity they are under of making that exertion" (p. 717).

The nexus of social situation and motivation holds for Adam Smith's early occupation too, and he does not hesitate to say so. Greater integrity hath no man. Or was Adam Smith highly motivated to give expression to a disgruntlement with the teaching he had received as a youth at Oxford, which indeed he suggests in *The Wealth of Nations?*

Conclusion

Much of the considerable work that Adam Smith accomplished can be glimpsed through a view of his notions regarding human nature and social circumstance. What we see is not invariably satisfying; we must be particularly wary in Smith's case lest his appearance be distorted. It is notorious that he has been too readily twisted by many eager to apologize for a status quo, just as (in my view) he has been too readily seen by others as having strong affinities with Marxism. But if one tries to see Smith in as honest and unprejudiced a fashion as possible, perhaps it is well to say something like this: Of course he has his limitations. His is not the most powerful analytical mind that has appeared in economics or social science at large. It would be futile to turn back to him on the notion that one would thereby find shining remedies for the numerous shortcomings of the social sciences now sharply (even too sharply) proposed by their critics. "New and engaging perspectives" (as said in beginning) one might find in him, but resounding answers to the problems of the social sciences today: hardly. Yet when this is acknowledged, much about Smith still suggests the master builder. He still stands up as a figure eminently worth revisiting, for his achievement is such as to kindle or rekindle in those who return a faith in the social science enterprise itself.

Notes

1. Overton H. Taylor, *Economics and Liberalism* (Cambridge: Harvard University Press, 1955), p. 92. In connection with arguments about the mutual consistency of Smith's two major works, it is worth having Mossner's reminder: "Let us not forget that Adam Smith had seen through the press the Fourth edition of the *Theory of Moral Sentiments* in 1774 and, after the publication of the *Wealth of Nations* in 1776, the Fifth in 1781 and the Sixth, that greatly revised and enlarged edition, in 1790. Clearly, the ethical values of the first book were in his mind until the very end." (Only the ethical values?) See Ernest C. Mossner, *Adam Smith: The Biographical Approach* (Glasgow: University of Glasgow Press, 1969), p. 17. Our approach to Smith and our bias that *The Wealth of Nations* and *The Theory of Moral Sentiments* are basically quite consistent rest also on the easily supported notion that these books are portions of a larger work of social science that Adam Smith never completed and that would have had something of a unitary character. That the relationship of the two actually completed portions to one another is expressed thus by Meek. "The more narrow economic views of the *Wealth of Nations* have usually been emphasized at the expense of the general sociological system of which they were essentially a part. The elements of that sociological system can, in-

deed, be easily enough detected in the *Wealth of Nations* . . . but for a complete outline of it we have to go to Smith's *Glasgow Lectures* and to his *Theory of Moral Sentiments.*" See Ronald L. Meek, *Economics and Ideology and Other Essays* (London: Chapman & Hall, 1967), p. 35. (Smith's *Lectures* are given only incidental attention in this essay but we would still subscribe to Meek's statement by and large.) Or one may say that the ultimately unitary character of Smith's main works would be suggested by their emergence from the common matrix of moral philosophy and natural law. Among older writings on this subject, Hasbach remains outstanding. See Wilhelm Hasbach, *Untersuchungen über Adam Smith und die Entwicklung der Politischen Oekonomie* (Leipzig: Duncker & Humblot, 1891). Somewhat closer to our own day, Small is characterized by his special insistence that political economy for Smith was to be approached and understood against a background of moral philosophy and general sociological thought. See Albion W. Small, *Adam Smith and Modern Sociology* (Chicago: University of Chicago Press, 1907). A sense of the larger philosophical and social-science contexts of Smith's views in such areas as the economic has again been conveyed by Hans Medick, *Naturzustand und Naturgeschichte der bürgerlichen Gesellschaft* (Göttingen: Vandenhoeck & Ruprecht, 1973).

2. Edwin Cannan, ed., *The Wealth of Nations* (New York: Modern Library, 1938).

3. Paul Samuelson, Review of Hla Myint, *Theories of Welfare Economics, Economica* 16 (November 1949):371-74.

4. I am indebted for the reference to Samuelson's review made by Samuel Hollander in his *The Economics of Adam Smith* (Toronto: University of Toronto Press, 1973), p. 14.

5. In intellectual history, also, it would be arbitrary to overlook the sometimes very significant consequences of men's ideas, which they did not themselves anticipate.

6. Grampp observes that "if he [Smith] was at all optimistic, it was only in thinking that the economic man—as frail as he was in understanding and frailer still in execution—still knew his interests better than his governor could know them, and in thinking that the economy would be better off if each individual looked after his interests in his own way." This policy attributes too much "pessimism" to Smith, but that is incidental here. William Grampp, "Adam Smith and the Economic Man," *Journal of Political Economics* 56 (August 1948):336.

7. Adam Smith, *The Theory of Moral Sentiments* (New York: Kelly, 1966), p. 126.

8. Ibid., p. 110.

9. Ibid. German writers in the nineteenth century were keenly aware and appreciative of Smith's views as indicated in these quotations from the *Theory of Moral Sentiments*. Note the very pertinent and apt lines, quoted from Schiller and Goethe in Richard Zeyss, *Adam Smith und der Eigennutz* (Tübingen: H. Laupp'schen Buchhandlung, 1889), p. 115; and in Hasbach, *Untersuchungen,* p. 3. Schiller celebrates natural impulses (hunger and love) that maintain the mechanism of the world "before" philosophy can do so; Goethe affirms or approves "innocent drives,"

given by nature, which often irresistibly lead man to happy circumstances where "understanding and reason" cannot.

10. Robert K. Merton, "The Unanticipated Consequences of Purposive Social Action," *American Sociological Review* 1 (December 1936):894-904.

11. Note the parallel statement that "we cannot imagine" the division of labor to be "an effect of human prudence," in Adam Smith, *Lectures on Justice, Police, Revenue and Arms,* ed. E. Cannan (Oxford: Clarendon Press, 1896) p. 168. The matter of interest to us is just the having "in view" of "no such extensive utility," while to derive the division of labor from the "propensity" Smith appeals to is much too simple. See Robert M. MacIver, *Social Causation* (Boston: Ginn, 1942), pp. 315-16.

12. Smith, *Sentiments,* pp. 264-65.

13. Ibid., p. 263.

14. Ibid.

15. Just how important the teleological and, particularly, theological element here was to Adam Smith is notoriously a vexed question. One significant example of a statement on the matter that clearly seems to lean toward the view that Smith took the teleological and theological overtones of "the invisible hand" seriously is provided by Jacob Viner, *The Role of Providence in the Social Order* (Philadelphia: American Philosophical Society, 1972), pp. 81-82. An example of a quite different statement is provided by J. Ralph Lindgren, *The Social Philosophy of Adam Smith* (The Hague: Martinus Nijhoff, 1973), p. 148. Lindgren argues that Smith "embellished" *The Theory of Moral Sentiments* with phrases such as "the Director of Nature" by way of a "rhetorical stratagem" designed to enlist assent for his views or "to obscure the unorthodoxy of his religious convictions." Bitterman argues that there is no direct evidence to connect the term, "invisible hand," in *The Wealth of Nations,* with the deity "since the preceding and following discussion proceed in purely economic terms." But in *The Theory of Moral Sentiments* the invisible hand reference is immediately followed by a sentence that refers to Providence. See Henry J. Bitterman, "Adam Smith's Empiricism and the Law of Nature: II," *Journal of Political Economics* 48 (October 1940):719. Our best guess is that Adam Smith of *The Theory of Moral Sentiments* was only mildly pious and the Smith of *The Wealth of Nations* even less so. One must concede, however, that Smith did use pious language in *Sentiments.* We can often say justifiably that the core of his argument could be restated without the apparatus of piety, but it does not necessarily follow that the possibility of doing this would have appealed to Adam Smith.

16. Wilhelm Hasbach, *Die Allgemeinen Philosophischen Grundlagen der von François Quesnay und Adam Smith begründeten Politischen Oekonomie* (Leipzig: Duncker & Humblot, 1890), p. 153.

17. Overton H. Taylor, *A History of Economic Thought* (New York: McGraw-Hill, 1960), p. 70.

18. Medick, *Naturzustand,* p. 229.

19. *Jacob Viner, The Long View and the Short* (Glencoe, Ill.: Free Press, 1958), p. 213.

20. J. M. Clark et al., *Adam Smith, 1776-1926* (New York: Kelly, 1966), pp. 171-72. Cf. also Glen R. Morrow, *The Ethical and Economic Theories of*

Adam Smith (New York: Kelly, 1969), pp. 41-43.

21. Joseph A. Schumpeter, *History of Economic Analysis* (Oxford: Oxford University Press, 1954), p. 185. We have deliberately avoided use of the term *natural* or *natural order* in the present context. It is notorious that Adam Smith's own use of the word *natural* could be confusing. Thus: "Adam Smith misused the word 'natural.' Sometimes it meant in accordance with reason, sometimes in the natural course of things, sometimes corresponding to human nature, sometimes obvious, sometimes customary —and with this the task of a Smithian philosophy is still not exhausted." See Hasbach, *Grundlagen der Politischen Oekonomie*, p. 87.

22. He had much interest in social change, as indicated by his presentation of the rudiments of a theory of social evolution in *The Wealth of Nations*, p. 653f. and in his *Lectures*, p. 14f. That our representation of Smith's work is entirely compatible with the interest in social evolution and "progress" he also had is well indicated by Duncan Forbes, " 'Scientific Whiggism': Adam Smith and John Millar," *Cambridge Journal* 7 (August 1954):643-70, esp. 651.

23. See page 63. On the affinity of Smith's work with functional analysis, see Louis Schneider, ed, *The Scottish Moralists on Human Nature and Society* (Chicago: University of Chicago Press, 1967), Introduction; and T. D. Campbell, *Adam Smith's Science of Morals* (Totowa, N.J.: Rowan & Littlefield, 1971), esp. pp. 69-79.

24. Medick, *Naturzustand*, p. 231.

25. Hollander, *Economics of Smith*, p. 120. We must not be understood to wish to confine the meaning of conversion mechanisms to mechanisms that convert self-interest into public good within an economic context, but this point will not be discussed further.

26. For example, Bitterman, "Adam Smith's Empiricism: II," p. 219.

27. Smith, *Sentiments*, pp. 70-71.

28. Smith's sense of functional autonomy is pointed out by Lindgren, *Social Philosophy*, pp. 40, 75. Note the suggestiveness in this connection of those comments in *The Theory of Moral Sentiments:* "Bring him [man] into society, and all his own passions will immediately become the causes of new passions. He will observe that mankind approve of some of them, and are disgusted by others. He will be elevated in the one case, and cast down in the other; his desires and aversions, his joys and sorrows, will now often become the causes of new desires and new aversions, new joys and new sorrows: they will now, therefore, interest him deeply, and often call upon his most attentive consideration" (pp. 162-63).

29. Ibid., p. 80.

30. Taylor, *History*, p. 72.

31. See Talcott Parsons, *The Structure of Social Action* (New York: McGraw-Hill, 1937), p. 89f. Given the concern of this essay with the problem, it is worth remarking, whatever the merits of the recent argument by Giddens that Parsons's stress on the high importance of the problem in the work of outstanding modern sociologists (especially Durkheim) is unjustified and actually nourishes a "myth." I do not see how there can be any doubt whatever about the centrality of the problem for the thought of Adam Smith. See Anthony Giddens, "Classical Social Theory and the Origins of

Modern Sociology," *American Journal of Sociology* 81 (January 1976): 703-29.

32. Thus: "The *representative* of the impartial spectator, the man within the breast" (emphasis added). Smith, *Sentiments,* p. 314. Smith's social psychology has aroused interest far outside the ranks of economists and philosophers. For a significant comparison of Smith with Freud on certain points, and going beyond the noting of a general contrast such as that by Overton H. Taylor, see R. F. Brissenden, "Authority, Guilt and Anxiety in *The Theory of Moral Sentiments,*" *Texas Studies in Language and Literature* 2 (Summer 1969):945-62. A comparison of Smith's work with that of others, such as the social psychologist George Herbert Mead, can be equally illuminating.

33. Smith, *Sentiments,* p. 216.

34. J. A. Farrar, *Adam Smith* (New York: Putnam's, 1881), p. 77.

35. Bitterman, "Adam Smith's Empiricism: I," pp. 487-520.

36. Campbell, *Science of Morals,* p. 137.

37. Smith, *Sentiments,* pp. 124-25.

38. Bitterman, "Smith's Empiricism: I," p. 520.

39. Ibid., II, p. 728.

40. One should still not be misled about Smith's judgments on merchants and manufacturers, granted all the passion of his criticism of them. Smith *can* stress, as in his *Lectures,* that commerce and probity have certain connections. "A dealer," he observes, "is afraid of losing his character and is scrupulous in observing every engagement. When a person makes perhaps twenty contracts a day, he cannot gain so much by endeavouring to impose on his neighbours, as the very appearance of a cheat could make him lose." Again: "When the greater part of people are merchants, they always bring probity and punctuality into fashion, and these, therefore, are the principle virtues of a commercial nature." See Smith, *Lectures,* pp. 253-55.

41. Zeyss suggests that one might summarize Smith's views on the morality of conduct in the "practical" imperative: "So act that the impartial spectator is able to sympathize with the motive and with the tendency of your action." See Zeyss, *Adam Smith,* p. 52. Our argument would be that this imperative is, at the least, clearly implied even in *The Wealth of Nations.*

42. For example, see August Oncken, *Adam Smith und Immanuel Kant* (Leipzig: Duncker & Humblot, 1877), pp. 35-36.

43. A. L. Macfie, *The Individual in Society: Papers on Adam Smith* (London: Allen & Unwin, 1967), p. 81.

44. Nathan Rosenberg, "Some Institutional Aspects of *The Wealth of Nations,*" *Journal of Political Economics* 68 (December 1960):557-70.

45. Smith, *Lectures,* p. 83.

46. Smith, *Sentiments,* p. 297.

47. Ibid., p. 296.

48. Cf. Smith, *Wealth,* pp. 734-36, 127; and *Lectures*, pp. 255-57. For all the interest in Smith's views on the sociopsychological effects of the division of labor, they are only briefly developed by him. Smith's student John Millar offers some elaboration in *An Historical View of the English Government* (London: Mawman, 1818), 4:138-61.

3
Adam Ferguson: An Introduction
(1979)

Adam Ferguson is one of a number of men who won renown for eighteenth-century Scotland in philosophy and social science.[1] Ferguson's name is easily associated with those of others of his time whose endeavors were related to his. The names of Adam Smith and David Hume are the most salient. Considerably less prominent, but certainly worthy of mention, is John Millar, holder of the chair of civil law at Glasgow from 1761. Another man of the law who is not intellectually far from Ferguson is the jurist Henry Home, Lord Kames. In the background is the figure of Francis Hutcheson, the philosopher and disciple of Shaftesbury, who (although himself of Irish birth) was an important early thinker among these Scots and also the teacher of Adam Smith. William Robertson, the historian, also has his plain affinities with these men. Somewhat aside from the social-science current is the philosopher Thomas Reid. And pursuing his own eccentric way is the anthropologist James Burnett, Lord Monboddo, who with all his bizarre notions about men with tails and "sea men" and mermaids, had something of an authentic sense for problems of human evolution. Late in the Scottish development comes Dugald Stewart, who, at considerable length and sometimes a bit dully, summarizes much that came before him.

The Scottish Enlightenment includes more than philosophy and social science. It is also marked by notable achievements in science, technology, and literature. But this local enlightenment as a whole runs its course within rather less than a century. A fairly good point at which to mark the termination of a remarkable Scottish development of ideas that began to gather real force around the middle of the eighteenth century is the death of Dugald Stewart in 1828. In round figures, it lasted from 1750 to 1830. David Hume's *Treatise of Human Nature* appeared as early as 1739, but Hume was then only twenty-eight and he lived to publish significant work well beyond 1750. Even the early Francis Hutcheson's *System of Moral Philosophy* was published (posthumously: Hutcheson died in 1746) in 1755. Adam Smith's *Theory of Moral Sentiments* appeared originally in 1759 and his *Wealth of Nations* in 1776. Ferguson's main books came out between 1767 and 1792. When Ferguson died in 1816 at the age of ninety-two, the stream in which he had been included was close to its end.

We have here, in the persons of the Scottish philosophers and scientists, one of those striking clusters of very able men working out the possibilities of philosophical, scientific or artistic ideas that so intrigued the anthropologist Kroeber in his *Configurations of Culture Growth.* Kroeber notes how with the union of Scotland and England in 1707, a change in the relative cultural contributions of the two countries occurs. Scotland becomes more productive, and, writes Kroeber, "Scotch births of genius show a definite constellation. There are Hume . . . Adam Smith."[2] When the Scottish achievements attain their peak, they are outstanding by any reasonable criterion. There were gifted economists before Adam Smith, but there are some good reasons to regard his *Wealth of Nations* as marking the foundation of economic science in its modern form. Not the least of the achievements is the making of an early sociology, not yet so named of course but still sufficiently close in its concerns to the modern subject to allow it the same label in retrospect; and here Adam Ferguson is one of the most significant figures. The economics and the sociology are not unconnected by any means. Adam Smith was unequivocally a sociologist as well as an economist, as much of the content of the *Wealth of Nations* indicates, and there was a broad Scottish persuasion of the crucial importance of economic factors in social life.

It is often asked what there was about Scotland in the eighteenth century that might have occasioned its striking production of leading social scientists. One answer was suggested by Meek some twenty years ago when he pointed to the possible stimulation to social thought coming from a combination of rapid economic development in some places in Scotland with retention of older economic patterns of forms of organization in the Scottish Highlands.[3] But much remains to be done in comparing great creative periods in different times and places, and it is perhaps easier to explain how the potential of important cultural patterns carried by human clusters is ultimately exhausted as the problem-possibilities of the patterns are worked out than it is to explain the rise of the patterns themselves.

In any case, Adam Ferguson, with his participation in the eighteenth-century Scottish cluster with a special contribution to sociological thought, was born in 1723 (the same year as Adam Smith), in the manse of Logierait at Perthshire. He studied at the University of Saint Andrews and subsequently at Edinburgh. He saw service as an army chaplain, acquiring acquaintanceship with military matters that stood him in good stead when he came later to write his history of the Roman Republic, just as the historian Edward Gibbon's experience as a militiaman helped him in the composition of his own great history of the decline and fall of the Roman Empire. Although Ferguson had been educated for the ministry, his qualifications for being a Scottish clergyman were evidently rather less than ideal, for, as his biographer John Small tells us, "he was deficient in the gifts necessary for the popular preacher" and "his sermons were elaborate disquisitions showing more acquaintance with systems of philosophy than with the wants of common hearers."[4]

It was no doubt well for Ferguson and those who might have been his parishioners that he turned elsewhere for a life's vocation. He was appointed successor to David Hume as keeper of the Advocates Library at the beginning of 1757. But he quit this office abruptly and in 1759 succeeded John Stewart in the chair of natural philosophy at Edinburgh. It is a bit curious to think of Ferguson, preeminently the moral philosopher and historian, as a teacher of physical science subjects, but he continued in the natural philosophy post for some five years until in 1764 he was appointed to the chair at Edinburgh that enabled him to teach moral philosophy. He had found his métier and he had a distinguished career. If he has not the caliber of men like David Hume and Adam Smith, he is still a sturdy figure in his own right.

The scope of moral philosophy taught in Ferguson's day is worth recalling. Ferguson wrote, "for the use of students in the College of Edinburgh," a small volume entitled *Institutes of Moral Philosophy,* published in 1769, which gives a notion of the range of his teaching. But this little book was only the forerunner of a far more extensive, richer production published at Edinburgh in 1792, a two-volume affair entitled *Principles of Moral and Political Science.* Like the *Institutes,* this carried a subtitle indicating that it was designed for student use ("chiefly a retrospect of lectures delivered in the College of Edinburgh"). But it was not a "textbook," at least not in the often pejorative sense of that term. Rather, it was on the order of an authentic treatise. What does Ferguson take up in it? Simply a huge variety of subjects. Volume One of the *Principles* presents us with one chapter entitled "Of Man's Description and Place in the Scale of Being," with another entitled "Of Mind or the Characteristics of Intelligence," and with a third called "Of Man's Progressive Nature." The third chapter alone includes discussions of habit, ambition, the commercial and political arts, science and the fine arts, and "the progress of moral apprehension"; it concludes grandly, and most optimistically, with a disquisition on human immortality ("of a future state"). But we still face Volume Two (considerably longer than

Volume One), which in its first chapter deals with pleasure and pain, beauty and deformity, prosperity and adversity, virtue and vice, and more. Later chapters take up morality and politics again and deal with jurisprudence and with the virtuous life.

Given this range, inevitably not everything could be covered in depth. But the reader alert to the outlines of Ferguson's incipient sociology will find much that is far from superficial. There are shrewd passages that stress unintended, or unanticipated (or unrecognized), consequences of social action, a well-known and significant theme in many sociological works (although not occurring in sociological works alone in the social sciences), tracing back in its modern form for a number of centuries to some of the historical work of Niccolò Machiavelli. The theme of unintended, or unanticipated, consequences has been very much part of so-called functional analysis; it is well to observe that some of its most salient components antedate certain formulations in contemporary biology or the productions of sociology departments at Harvard or Columbia a generation or so ago. In the *Principles,* Ferguson will tell us that "the barons of England, in time of high feudal aristocracy, knew not that the charters which they extorted from their sovereign were to become foundations of freedom to the people over whom they themselves wished to tyrannize" (1:314). The theme also figures eloquently in the *Essay on the History of Civil Society.* "Nations," Ferguson tells us here, "stumble upon establishments which are indeed the result of human action but not the execution of any human design" (Part 3, Section 2). Friedrich Hayek, who has been profoundly influenced by the Scottish moral philosophers and by the themes often set out by them, follows deliberately in Ferguson's track, entitling one of his papers "The Results of Human Action but Not of Human Design."[5]

Ferguson also exhibits in his *Principles* a powerful sense of what may be called the nonrational foundations of society. (Indeed, this ties in with the theme just mentioned.) Societies are not created wholecloth out of processes of reasoning. "Laws and institutions, in every community, contain articles of agreements entered into by the parties with whom they originated, and by their posterity who accede to them; but such agreements are all of them posterior to the existence of society, and not the foundations upon which society was erected" (2:220). The observation is a fundamental one for Ferguson. It, too, had been anticipated in the *Essay,* where he writes, "Like the winds that come we know not whence and blow withersoever they list, the forces of society are derived from an obscure and distant origin. They arise long before the date of philosophy, from the instincts, not the speculations of men" (Part 3, Section 2). We may not now especially favor the term "instincts" in such a context, but Ferguson is broadly referring to impulse and emotion deeply grounded in and intertwined with custom and tradition. He urges us in the *Essay* to be cautious about stories of oldtime legislators and founders of states, for these often attribute large deliberate plans to such figures where there was probably little or no plan or "design."

Various other Scottish writers, like John Millar in his *Historical View of the English Government* or the less well known Gilbert Stuart, in his *View of Society in Europe,* also expressed strong skepticism of the supposed sagacity and all-foreseeing ability of ancient legislators. Lycurgus and Solon were often designated as men to whom far too much responsibility for the formation of society of constitutions, by philosophy and by speculation, had been imputed. Overattribution of rational design ties in again with the sense of the Scots that much that occurs in human societies was never intended or deliberately wrought. Society, at any time of which we can imagine an account of it, is already, "there," already present with its "establishments," with their grounding in custom, sentiments, values, interests, and conflicts. Reason may work upon these things, but then it works with given materials that are certainly not themselves outright products of "reason." Even where there are explicit contracts, there are, in Ferguson's view, precontractual realities that environ and influence contract itself. Human beings are in society together before they enter upon contracts. Contract rests on a base of a noncontractual character. It does not start from scratch. It is hedged and limited (although it may also be sustained) by noncontractual, nonrational elements. Ferguson conducts in his *Principles* a sharp polemic against Hobbes in the matter of a supposed original compact. He shadows forth ideas on contract set out by Durkheim in the *Division of Labor.*

Ferguson's theoretical views are not unconnected with his practical attitudes. Thus, the sense of substance of society existent prior to rational deliberations and plans for society as a whole could induce in him, and other Scottish thinkers of his time, a considerable reverence for the forms of the past. Near the end of his *Principles,* Ferguson commented that "it may be safely assumed as a maxim under every establishment whatever, that the present [political] order, if tolerable, is to be preferred to innovation, of which, even in very small matters, it may be difficult, and is often above the reach of human wisdom, to foresee all the consequences or effects" (2:498). He adds at once that under the fairest government grievances may come up and "must be redressed." But he was not disposed to subvert the social order and shared with other Scottish students of society a suspicion of political "projectors," persons with ready schemes to change society and policy for the better, incognizant, in the view of men like Ferguson, of the value and viability of established forms and vain of their own hare-brained schemes. It is a question whether a realistic view of nonrational elements in society must induce a conservative position. John Millar's sociology was not very different from Ferguson's and he too was critical of "projectors," but he sustained a more unambiguously "liberal" position than Ferguson did. And Ferguson himself is by no means passively affirmative of all he sees in the way of major social arrangements. The skeptical stance toward wealth and competition that appears in the *Essay,* on which we shall comment later, is also maintained in the *Principles.*

The persuasion that society is, and always has been, man's habitat is set out forcefully in Ferguson's early sociology. "The atmosphere of society . . . is the element in which the human mind must draw the first breath of intelligence itself," he tells us in the *Principles,* as at an earlier point he had assured us that "man is made for society" (1:268, 199). And in the *Essay* the statements bearing on man's sociality present the same general message. With man, "society appears to be as old as the individual," and if there was a time when "he had his acquaintance with his own species to make," when he supposedly lived in a nonsocial state, then that is "a time of which we have no record" and about which Ferguson suggests it is useless to speculate (Part 1, Section 3). The further notion that theorists may project their image of human nature in the present into the past lurks just beneath the surface. Ferguson might well have agreed with Rousseau in his dissertation on the origin of inequality of mankind, when the latter argued that philosophers inquiring into the nature of society had transferred to the "savage" in the state of nature ideas that had taken form only after that state had ended.

These and numerous other notions of a sociological character occur in the midst of Ferguson's moral philosophy. Ferguson was not a sociologist in a strict modern sense if only because he conducted no sociological inquiry conceived as separate from moral philosophy. But this calls for additional comment. There is widespread appreciation today of the historical integrity of past writings. Ferguson had his purposes and his intellectual environment, and we must not read him in terms that divest him of his historical place and significance if we wish to understand him. This is entirely just. But we must not carry it to the point where we fail to see that at times past writers are talking about precisely the things we are talking about, even if in somewhat different language, or allow it to induce us to find differences that do not exist.

In her fine book on Ferguson, Jogland has argued for a view of Scottish moral philosophy, including that of Ferguson, that would stimulate "a critical stance toward the present day state of sociological thought."[6]

This would require that we consider that moral philosophy again in its historical integrity, allow it to speak for itself, with at least an initial reserve about invading it with present-day sociological notions. The past has to be permitted its proper confrontation with the present. This is granted. Yet must not the present also be permitted its confrontation with the past? We may well "listen" to Ferguson by letting him tell his own story, but we may hear just what he himself has to say more acutely and even understand some of his own gropings better than he did if we also "listen" with a set of ideas deriving from a time subsequent to his own.

At the same time, as we "listen" to the old moral philosophy it is decidedly worth noting that one of its looming components is an ethical concern. We can clearly see processes of differentiation at work as modern social-science subject matters emerge from the matrix of moral philosophy. The history of the social sciences is varied and not everything in it is traceable to moral philosophy, but some differentiation of particular social-science subject matters did indeed take place as moral philosophy lost its original scope or fullness. In the differentiation a great deal of ethical concern was lost. Virtue and vice, justice and goodness, and benevolence are topics discussed in the works of men like Hume, Smith, and Ferguson. While the discussion is often of high analytical quality, it does not suggest anything like a refusal to make value commitments.

This points to matters about which there is considerable argument in sociology, as well as other social-science areas, today. This is not the place to carry on the argument. But it may still be suggested that in this area of ethical concern and value commitment we deal with matters on which Jogland's view of relevant Scottish work in the eighteenth century —as something that may induce "a critical stance toward the present day state of sociological thought"—is particularly apt. Perhaps one may be indulged if he says flatly that we have seen enough of absurdities and vicious notions stemming from a brand of "cultural relativism" that would in the end, if consistently pursued, exhort us to embrace something on the order of, say, Nazism as a "way of life" equally valid with others, no matter how nauseating the exhortation. There has been too much squirming away by sociologists (and others) from forthright consideration of moral questions of justice, of right and wrong, with resultant "answers" (for answers of some sort are repeatedly unavoidable) that are not one whit better for being surreptitious or self-concealing. Social science, sociology included, can still learn from the eighteenth-century Scots in these premises (although we may surely learn from other and later sources too). When the Scots wrote of justice, they really meant to refer to justice, not to some pleasant sounding but deceptive or meaningless noise produced by a glandular quirk, or an "interest" refusing to come into the open.

If the sheer range of moral philosophy is worth remarking upon, and the shrewd development of a number of significant sociological ideas within that range is notable, another significant feature of the endeavor of the Scottish moral philosophers is their large preoccupation with history. David Hume wrote a substantial, multivolume history of England. Adam Smith and Lord Kames (author of several volumes of *Sketches of the History of Man)* had unmistakable historical interests. William Robertson, so often associated with these men, was "purely" an historian, with histories of Scotland, the emperor Charles V, and America to his credit. Even that "minor" figure, Gilbert Stuart, was interested in European history and wrote extensively on the history of Scotland. Ferguson presents no exception to the broad Scottish interest in history. In 1783 he published his large *History of the Progress and Termination of the Roman Republic,* which is not a work to be overlooked if we are interested in his achievement in social science.[7] While much of this work is straightforward history, it also has a general tone and various passages that establish its close connection with Ferguson's other work, especially the *Essay.*

The political moralist in Ferguson, evident in the *Essay,* also comes out very clearly in the work on Rome. In the first century B.C. in Rome, Ferguson proposes that men became "glutted with material prosperity; they thought that they were born to enjoy what their fathers had won, and saw not the use of those austere and arduous virtues by which the state had increased to its present greatness" (pp. 169-70). Ferguson writes of Lutatius Catulus, in Caesar's day, as one of "great integrity, moderation, fortitude, and ability; a model of what the Romans in this age should have been, in order to have preserved their own republic" (p. 179). He writes also of the "paltry ambition" of Pompey and Caesar, an ambition which, "some ages before, might have been held in contempt by the meanest of the people, or must have shrunk before that noble elevation of mind by which the statesman conceived no eminence besides that of high personal qualities employed in public services, or before the austere virtue which confined the public esteem to acts of public utility, supported by unblemisheed reputation in private life" (p. 207). In the *Essay,* there is repeated reference to "corruption" and in the Roman history Ferguson refers to "the worst and most corrupting part" of the republic privileges of the Roman people as "that of receiving gratuities in money and corn, as well as that of being frequently amused with expensive shows" (p. 413). It is generally evident from the Roman history that the whole business of "bread and circuses" strikes Ferguson as a particularly unhappy species of corruption, wooing people away from their propensity to act as responsible members of a public.

There is in the Roman history also the suggestion of a kind of dialectical theme that had been intimated in the *Essay*. In the latter, Ferguson remarks, for example, "the virtues of men have shone most during their struggles, not after the attainment of their ends. Those ends themselves, though attained by virtue, are frequently the causes of corruption and vice" (Part 5, Section 1). Thus, wealth, once it has been amassed, may induce much greater "corruption and vice" than ever led to its acquisition. It may even have been acquired to begin with by "virtuous" enough impulses. Then a product of virtue tempts to, and induces, vices. This sort of dialectic of wealth has of course also been suggested in modern sociology, as in the view coming from Max Weber's work that "virtues" like industry, thrift, and frugality may help produce a wealth that acts in disintegrating fashion on the very virtues mentioned, to which it owes so much, presenting an irresistible temptation to idleness, waste, and lavishness. The triumph of wealth in this sense entails the defeat of what made wealth initially.

Again Ferguson proposes a dialectical theme in the *Essay* when he writes:

> The Romans only meant by their armies to encroach on the freedom of other nations, while they preserved their own. They forgot that, in assembling soldiers of fortune, and in suffering any leader to be master of a disciplined army, they actually resigned political rights, and suffered a master to arise for the state. This people, in short, whose ruling passion was depredation and conquest, perished by the recoil of an engine which they themselves had erected against mankind [Part 5, Section 4].

The dialectic whereby the instrumentality of "success" turns on those who employ it and brings them "failure" is thus touched upon. (And this is not greatly remote from what we just noted in the case of wealth.) The "victory" the Romans achieved by their peculiar military devices contained the seeds of defeat marked by the emergence of a "master for the state." In the Roman history, Ferguson tries to show how the enlargement of the territory of the Romans and the success of their arms abroad "become the sources of a ruinous corruption at home," as if again to emphasize the recoil of an engine (p. 83). But the dialectical notion that success can bring failure in its turn, or carry the seed thereof, is yet more widely suggested. Thus, in a passage in the Roman history that might have been written only yesteryear, we find this:

> The Romans, by the continual labors of seven centuries had made their way from the Tiber to the Rhine and the Danube through the territory of warlike hordes who opposed them, and over forests and rugged ways that were everywhere to be cleared at the expense of their labour and their blood; but the ways they had made to reach their enemies were now open, in their turns, for enemies to reach them. The ample resources which they had formed by their cultivation increased the temptation to invade them, and facilitated all the means of making war upon their country. By reducing the inhabitants of their provinces, in every part, to pacific subjects, they brought the defense of the empire to depend on a few professional soldiers who composed the legions [p. 432]. [Ferguson writes this under date U.C. 760, that is, 760 years after the supposed founding of Rome in 753 B.C.]

It will be noted that this sort of description again intimates the operation of unintended, or unanticipated, effects of social action. The Romans presumably never intended to rear an engine against mankind by whose recoil they themselves would perish. They presumably never intended, or foresaw, that the very ways they had cleared to reach their enemies would later serve their enemies to reach them. But it was remarked above that the sentences just quoted might have been written only yesteryear. In the very recent one-volume edition of his *Study of History,* Arnold Toynbee writes of the imperial Roman roads quite as if he had taken his cue from Ferguson. The resemblance is indeed striking enough to demand quotation from Toynbee:

> If the makers and panegyrists of the Roman imperial system of communications could have foreseen the future they would have found it intolerable, no doubt, but not unintelligible in a world in which "all roads" led "to Rome," that the thoroughfares which in their time were bringing prisoners, petitioners and sightseers to the imperial city should one day convey barbarian war-bands or the armies of rival empires. These imperial highways certainly enabled, and possibly inspired, the barbarian invaders to make straight for the heart of the Hellenic world.[8]

Thus does Ferguson appear to be peculiarly up-to-date in a book whose "day" is long gone. And it is evident that his history enriches his sociology—or that his sociology enriches his history.

The Roman history, like the *Essay,* strikes some somber notes. The strong theological optimism evident in Ferguson's *Principles,* which could lead him to write that "to those who are qualified with intelligence and grateful mind, every circumstance in the order of nature may serve to manifest and extol the supreme wisdom and goodness of God" (1:187), did not prevent him from noting the reality of decadence in the history of nations, which can become weak and obscure as "naturally" as they can rise to the very heights. Gibbon had presented in the third chapter of his *Decline and Fall* the famous view that if one were asked to indicate the period of the happiest and most prosperous condition of humanity, he would unhesitatingly name the period between the death of Domitian and the accession of Commodus (98-180 A.D.). On just about the same period, Ferguson's bias is that "if a people could be happy by any other virtue than their own," this was indeed a time in which human happiness might be supposed "complete." But a people cannot really be happy "by any other virtue than their own." They may receive protection from the justice and humanity of single men; but can receive "independence, vigour, and peace of mind only from their own" (p. 468). The opinion is clearly more "pessimistic" than Gibbon's, and the tone of the political moralist is again like that of the *Essay*.

One gets the powerful impression from the Roman history as a whole that Ferguson feels himself to be chronicling a great decline in political morality (as well as portraying a situation in which the Romans are defeated by their very successes). The decline is not entirely uniform or constant. Thus, Tiberius, Caligula, Claudius, and Nero do go, and are in time succeeded by rulers like the Antonines. (Ferguson does touch somewhat on the Empire too.) But the general picture of decline remains. (The germ of recovery may be in decline, as the *Essay* suggests, but that is something else.) Perhaps above all one gets the impression that the political moralist Ferguson is revolted by what he sees as the sheer decline in Roman virtue. The continuities with the *Essay* are marked indeed.

It is certainly fair to call Ferguson a "historical sociologist." His historical and comparative interests are evident from the *Essay,* even if one puts the Roman history aside. For Ferguson and his contemporaries the classical world was still a great subject for study and a great source of instruction.

For us, the last bit of instruction may now be drawn from the Roman history. Ferguson writes with Olympian calm: "The distinctions of poor and rich are as necessary in states of considerable extent as labour and good government. The poor are destined to labour, and the rich, by the advantages of education, independence, and leisure, are qualified for superior stations" (p. 85). It is once more quite clear that whatever else he may have been, Adam Ferguson was no revolutionary, no anarchist, no intransigent opponent of the status quo.

There are two other features, aside from the great range of moral philosophy (an important component of which is a sociology in process of formation) and keen interest in history, of the work of Ferguson and a number of his contemporaries that may be noted much more briefly. One is an interest in human nature that the Scots so strongly manifest. Human nature constitutes a preoccupation for Ferguson in both the

Essay and the *Principles*. Adam Smith's *Theory of Moral Sentiments* deals extensively with human nature. Hume's great early *Treatise of Human Nature* has a title that speaks for itself. The Scots were indeed "psychologists," being especially concerned with psychology as it bore on moral issues. One of the outstanding contributions of Scottish social psychology was Adam Smith's treatment of the impartial spectator in the *Moral Sentiments*. Ferguson has nothing comparable to show, but he made adroit use of stoic ideas to lay the foundations of a theory of human nature; and he constantly relates human nature to the circumstances of society.

The remaining feature to be noted is the empirical bias of Ferguson and others. The Scottish philosophers certainly had abstract interests, but in the midst of these they had a powerful tendency to rely on experience and observation. Their interest in human nature led them to, and was guided by, the view that human nature was rather universally the same, and their empirical-observational bias inclined them to take into account such information as was available from early anthropological reports and comparative materials. The combination of the interest in, and universalistic bias about, human nature with the empirical-observational bent often induced a sagacity of comment that anthropologists may still admire. Ferguson was not easily fooled by divergences in social or cultural forms that in the end amounted to little. He saw a constancy of motive and an incidental difference in form in phenomena which might have induced less sagacious observers to spin out dubious theories on a ground of questionable presumptions of basic divergence. Thus, he writes in his *Principles*, "It is the form of respect in Europe to uncover the head. In Japan, we are told, the corresponding form is to drop the slipper, or to uncover the foot. The physical action in these instances is different, but the moral action is the same" (2:142). No distraction is allowed to be created here by a "physical difference" that in relation to the "moral" meaning is quite insignificant. Possibly, Ferguson was inspired to make this comment by Bernard Mandeville, whose spokesman in the second volume of the *Fable of the Bees* observes that "to show respect, a man as well might have pulled off one of his shoes as his hat."[9] It is noteworthy that Mandeville (whom Ferguson refers to more than once in his works) insisted again and again that human nature is universally the same.

The concern with human nature (together with the emphasis on its constancy) and the empirical bias lend eighteenth-century Scottish social science a certain realistic, almost earthy quality. Social science does allow for "evolutionary" differences. Ferguson thus writes of "savages" and "barbarians," as Adam Smith writes of "the lowest and rudest state of society" or "a more advanced state of society." While such phrases inevitably imply some human differences, the general anthropological thrust is not toward vivid representation of, and great stress on, differences but rather toward noting common features beneath variations. Ferguson and others like Smith provide an approach to human behavior and human societies that, one might argue even today, makes a strategic beginning with all-important commonalities. (Even the important evolutionary differences do not destroy the commonalities.)

Let us turn now more particularly to the *Essay*. The book's reputation has not been an altogether consistent one. Its value has been questioned by some eminent men. David Hume did not care for it, although we do not know why.[10] Leslie Stephen, a century after Hume, found it superficial, also remarking, however, that "here and there we come across an argument or an illustration which seems to indicate greater acuteness."[11] The economist Schumpeter commented something over two decades ago that the considerable reputation the *Essay* enjoyed in Germany (partly through the influence of Marx) appeared to him to be "unmerited."[12] These are considerable critics and something must be granted to them. The drift of a certain amount of the adverse criticism (for instance as coming from Leslie Stephen) suggests that one clear shortcoming of the *Essay* is a declamatory tendency: declamatory rather than explanatory, oratorical rather then analytical. But this does not always hold and there are passages that exhibit depth (as indeed Stephen himself half acknowledged). Also, it is again merely accurate to note that the book has received decidedly favorable notice from other thinkers of stature. Karl Marx quoted (approvingly) from it at some length in his *Povery of Philosophy*.[13] The able Austrian sociologist Ludwig Gumplowicz regarded it as "the first natural history of society" and the man who composed it as "the first sociologist."[14]

The *Essay* has shown considerable stamina and has again come into some prominence in the world of recent scholarship. It presents a number of themes, or emphases, that various present-day scholars evidently find compelling. One of these is already referred to as the evolution of society, and Part 2 of the *Essay*, on this theme, is one of the better realized portions of the book.

When Ferguson suggests that Thucydides understood that he would find in the ways of barbarous nations in his own day indications of what the ancient manners of the Greeks themselves had been, and affirms, more generally, that if "in advanced years" we would know about the earlier social conditions from which we came, we must look to "the example of those who are still in the period of life we mean to describe" (Part 2, Section 1), he is now less likely to meet with the unfriendly criticism he once might have met. He is not saying that all particular societies must necessarily go through the same states precisely and down to the least detail. Ferguson's contemporary, John Millar, did write that "the smilarity of his (viz. man's) wants, as well as of the faculties by which those wants are supplied, has everywhere produced a remarkable uniformity in the several states of his progression."[15] But just what does "uniformity" mean? Millar was too knowledgeable historically to allow himself belief in an inflexible evolutionary scheme. An "original similarity in all the governments of modern Europe" did not prevent him from seeing certain divergences in the development of the European states.[16] There is no reason to think that Ferguson was more naive, or ignorant, in such matters generally than Millar. It seems quite plausible to suggest that Ferguson is telling us that there is likely to be some sort of pattern, or order, in major social sequences, at least when there are no potent special influences from "outside." (Given the actual chances of "outside" influence, we must say today, "laws" or evolutionary stages, or sequences, are to be regarded with utmost caution.)

There are scholars who continue to be interested in social evolution in terms of a broad view of societal "steps," or "stages," as Ferguson was, and there is some looking back with interest to what Ferguson, or his contemporaries, did in this regard.[17] But the more general idea of evolution has also been evoking a measure of interest and Ferguson's pages that are explicitly on evolution in the *Essay* might elicit intellectual sympathy even from scholars whose particular orientation in respect to evolution is not very much like that set out in the *Essay*. It must also be remarked, however, that the *Essay* is suggestive of an "evolutionary" sense in more than one way. Through long development and "successive improvement," human institutions may develop to a point of usefulness for meeting a variety of social necessities that could never have been provided for by a deliberate, conscious facing up to these necessities. Social establishments thereby carry a notable freight of gradually evolved "wisdom." This is Ferguson's bias, as when he writes "those [human] establishments arose from successive improvements that were made, without any sense of their general effect; and they bring human affairs to a state of complication, which the greatest reach of capacity with which human nature was ever adorned, could not have projected" (Part 4, Section 1). This is an aspect of Ferguson's evolutionary outlook that ties him to the earlier theories of Bernard Mandeville and the much later ones of Friedrich Hayek rather than to "step" or "stage" theorists.

Another feature of the *Essay* that attracts attention today is the place it makes for conflict in human social life. One contemporary commentator observes, "Ferguson's analysis of the nature and function of conflict is well known; it deserves to be, for its cool detachment is as impressive as it is chilling."[18] Ferguson himself writes at the end of Section 4 of Part 1 that "it is vain to expect that we can give to the multitude of a people a sense of union among themselves without admitting hostility to those who oppose them." Or he will tell us that "the frequent practice of war tends to strengthen the bands of society, and the practice of depredation itself engages men in trials of mutual attachment and courage" (Part 1, Section 9). Or again he will say that "Athens was necessary to Sparta, in the exercise of her virtue, as steel is to flint in the production of fire" (adding that "if the cities of Greece had been united under one head, we should never have heard of Epaminondas or Thrasybulus, of Lycurgus or Solon"; Part 1, Section 9). Conflict, for Ferguson, clearly has its social uses and civic value. We may not share his tendency toward enthusiasm for conflict, but we must discern here something of the effect of that empirical-observational bias we have noted—a bias that would in any case make him stress the sheer reality of conflict whether one happens to like that reality or not.

The treatment of conflict in the *Essay* intersects with its treatment of the division of labor. Ferguson has misgivings, in respect to the latter, as did Adam Smith and John Millar. One of the significant statements in the *Essay* presents, with reference to the division of labor, a situation in which "society is made to consist of parts, of which none is animated with the spirit of society itself" (Part 5, Section 3). Adam Smith thought that as the division of labor advanced, the great body of laborers, coming to work as they did on a few simple operations, suffered in their understanding and experienced "torpor" of mind, while the strictly confined skills they acquired were accompanied by loss not only of intellectual but also of social and martial virtues.[19] Millar sees the common workman of England as nearly "stripped of his mental powers" and "converted into the mere instrument of labor"[20] much more than the Scottish workman who was less subjected to the division of labor. Ferguson is no more blind to the advantageous side of the division of labor than Smith or Millar. He is well aware of the enhancement of productivity emergent with division of tasks. "By having separated the arts of the clothier and the tanner, we are the better supplied with shoes and with cloth." But then we are told that "to separate the arts which form the citizen and the statesman, the arts of policy, and war, is an attempt to dismember the human character, and to destroy those very arts we mean to improve." This separation deprives a free people of "what is necessary to their safety," prepares "a [purchased] defence against invasions from abroad which gives a prospect of usurpation, and threatens the establishment of military government at home" (Part 5, Section 4).

It is here that we see the intersection of the conflict and division of labor themes. Ferguson's concern over the removal from the citizen of all features of the soldier is expressed as a revulsion from what he evidently regarded as a diminution of full civic humanity, or full civic participation. He plainly indicates the fear of an inability of a people without soldierly experience to resist an enemy and an apprehension lest a citizenry deprived of all military engagement be subordinated by the agents it may procure to do its military work. (We have already noted similar intimations in the Roman history.) Adam Smith, for his part, favored the notion that "the security of every society must always depend, more or less, upon the martial spirit of the great body of the people."[21] This might be construed as a statement whose intent is purely empirical. But whether pertinent statements about the citizen's participation in military conflict are in the realm of political sociology, or of political ethics or morality, Ferguson, and Smith, are saying some things to us that are still important to consider.

Aside from its reflection on evolution, conflict, and the division of labor, perhaps the aspect of the *Essay* that accounts more for present-day attention to it than any other is its particular focus on wealth, or commerce, and civic life. We recall Ferguson's previously recorded sharp assertions that men's virtues have been most shining while they have struggled for their ends, not after they have attained them, and that "those ends themselves, though attained by virtue, are frequently the causes of corruption and vice." Ferguson very soon then refers suggestively to "neglects which prosperity itself had encouraged" (Part 5, Section 1). He is exercised above all over the pursuit of security, property, gain (and pleasure) while men lose their very political concerns and interests. To take advantage of the safety ostensibly rendered by certain political conditions merely in order to enjoy or advance fortune, is not to deserve the safety referred to, and is to decline into corruption. Wealth and commerce unreservedly pursued work insidiously to alienate humans from their own civic propensities.

Two recent commentators may be drawn upon to indicate something of the impression that these views of Ferguson's currently make upon scholars. The historian Pocock writes, precisely in context of discussion of Ferguson:

> The paradigm of commerce presented the movement of history as being toward the indefinite multiplication of goods, and brought the whole progress of material, cultural, and moral civilization under this head. But so long as it did not contain any equivalent to the concept of the *zoon*

politikon, of the individual as an autonomous, morally and politically choosing being, progress must appear to move away from something essential to human personality. And this corruption was self-generating; society as an engine for the production and multiplication of goods was inherently hostile to society as the moral foundation of personality. The history of commerce revealed once again that the republic had not solved the problem of existing as a universal value in particular and contingent time.[22]

The economist Hirschman also follows Ferguson on wealth, or commerce, and corruption. Ferguson, Hirschman notes, saw why preoccupation with individual wealth can lead to "despotical government," by way of corruption through luxury and prodigality. Hirschman observes that Ferguson added to that traditional argument and he alludes to Ferguson's touching upon fear of downward mobility, seen, in Hirschman's words, as "intimately bound up with the acquisitive society and its tumultuous ways" and as generating feelings of "relative deprivation and *ressentiment,*" which afford "a breeding ground for the ready acceptance of whatever 'strong' government promises to stave off such real or imagined dangers [of downward mobility]." Also, commerce, writes Hirschman, still expounding Ferguson, "creates a desire for tranquility and efficiency, and this may be another source of despotism."[23] Whatever the detailed mechanisms, the argument runs on the main line that wealth and commerce, once more, woo humans away from a civic disposition that would inhibit the inclination to despotism and constrain the people of possessions, the *"beati possidentes,"* to put public concerns and involvement before those same possessions.

The loss of human political and civic essence thus stressed is spelled out by Ferguson in large generalizations that are less than ideally exemplified and systematically developed. The declamatory tendency in Ferguson unfortunately does not nourish his much more impressive empirical-observational bent. There are, moreover, tensions in his thought with regard to the "liberal" and toward the "conservative" side that he never resolves. But once more he has been provocative on some crucial matters in political sociology and political morality. His stature is a larger stature than the *Essay on the History of Civil Society* alone might indicate. No one interested in Ferguson and early modern social science can afford to neglect the *Essay.* Its considerable actual influence in social science would in itself demand attention to it. No work by a man who figures in the background of Hegel, Marx, Lessing, J. S. Mill, and Friedrich Schiller, among others, can possibly fail to appeal to us as culturally significant.

Notes

1. Ferguson's main works are *An Essay on the Hisitory of Civil Society* (1767), *Institutes of Moral Philosophy* (1769), *History of the Progress and Termination of the Roman Republic* (1783; subsequent editions), and *Principles of Moral and Political Science* (1792; reprinted Hildesheim, Germany: Olms, 1975, with an introduction by Jean Hecht). Significant commentaries on Ferguson's work include William C. Lehmann, *Adam Ferguson and the Beginnings of Modern Sociology* (New York: Columbia University Press, 1930); Herta H. Jogland, *Ursprünge und Grundlagen der Soziologie bei Adam Ferguson* (Berlin: Duncker & Humblot, 1959); David Kettler, *The Social and Political Philosophy of Adam Ferguson* (Columbus: Ohio University Press, 1965). An older work, now in danger of being completely overlooked although it should not be, is Hermann Huth, *Soziale und Individualistische Auffassung, vornehmlich bei Adam Smith und Adam Ferguson* (Leipzig: Duncker & Humblot, 1907). The most comprehensive book on Ferguson is Pasquale Salvucci, *Adam Ferguson: Sociologia e Philosophia Politica* (Urbino, Italy: Argàlia, 1972).
    A very brief but informative account of Ferguson is presented by William C. Lehmann in "Adam Ferguson," *International Encyclopedia of the Social Sciences* (New York: Macmillan and Free Press, 1968), 5:369-71. Still important for Ferguson's life is the very readable but unfortunately not highly accessible account by John Small, *Biographical Sketch of Adam Ferguson* (Edinburgh: Neill, 1864). Statements on eighteenth-century Scottish thought, for those interested in social science in particular, may be found in Gladys Bryson, *Man and Society: The Scottish Inquiry of the Eighteenth Century* (Princeton: Princeton University Press, 1945; reprinted New York: Kelly, 1968), and in William C. Lehmann, *John Millar of Glasgow* (Cambridge: Cambridge University Press, 1960). Both these books have things to say about Ferguson among others. Ferguson's writings may be seen in relation to the writings of fellow Scots preoccupied with like subjects in the selected readings in Louis Schneider, ed., *The Scottish Moralists on Human Nature and Society* (Chicago: University of Chicago Press, 1967). There is an additional literature that continues to appear dealing with Scottish contemporaries other than Ferguson but containing references to him. Examples include Andrew S. Skinner and Thomas Wilson, eds., *Essays on Adam Smith* (Oxford: Clarendon Press, 1975); David A. Reisman, *Adam Smith's Sociological Economics* (New York: Barnes & Noble, 1976); William C. Lehmann, *Henry Home, Lord Kames, and the Scottish Enlightenment* (The Hague: Martinus Nijhoff, 1971); Ian S. Ross, *Lord Kames and the Scotland of His Day* (Oxford: Clarendon Press, 1972). A very detailed Ferguson bibliography appears in the Italian version of the *Essay, Saggio sulla Storia della Società Civile* (Florence: Vallecchi, 1972, under the editorship of Pasquale Salvucci), pp. 351-74.
2. A. L. Kroeber, *Configurations of Culture Growth* (Berkeley and Los Angeles: University of California Press, 1944), p. 713.
3. Ronald L. Meek, "The Scottish Contribution to Marxist Sociology," in John Saville, ed., *Democracy and the Labour Movement* (London: Lawrence & Wishart, 1954), pp. 84-102.

4. John Small, *Biographical Sketch of Adam Ferguson* (Edinburgh: Neill, 1964), pp. 4-5.

5. See F. A. Hayek, *Studies in Philosophy, Politics and Economics* (Chicago: University of Chicago Press, 1967), ch. 6.

6. Jogland, *Ursprünge und Grundlagen der Sociologie bei Adam Ferguson,* p. 164.

7. Of the numerous editions, we use here the one published in London by Jones and Co., in 1825. The book is very little read today but is described as that by which Ferguson was "best known in his own day," by James McGosh, *The Scottish Philosophy* (New York: Carter, 1874), p. 258.

8. Arnold Toynbee, *A Study of History,* new edition revised and abridged by the author and June Caplan (New York: Weathervane Books, 1972), p. 292.

9. *The Fable of the Bees* (Oxford: Clarendon Press, 1924), 2:150.

10. For Hume's opinion, see Ernest C. Mossner, *The Left of David Hume* (Austin: University of Texas Press, 1954), pp. 542-43. Mossner writes (p. 543), "Hume nowhere specifies his disapproval of Ferguson's reasonings, which were no little indebted to his own."

11. Leslie Stephen, *History of English Thought in the Eighteenth Century* (New York: Harcourt, Brace & World, 1962), 2:182.

12. Joseph A. Schumpeter, *History of Economic Analysis* (New York: Oxford University Press, 1954), p. 184, n. 16.

13. Karl Marx, *The Poverty of Philosophy* (Moscow: Foreign Languages Publishing House, n.d.), p. 124. In both this work and in *Capital* (New York: Modern Library, 1936), 1:139n. Marx, curiously, harbors the notion that Ferguson was Adam Smith's teacher.

14. As quoted by Lehmann, "Adam Ferguson," p. 369, from Ludwig Gumplowicz, *Die Soziologische Straatzidee* (Graz: Leuschner & Lubensky, 1892), p. 67.

15. John Millar, *The Origin of the Distinction of Ranks,* Part 3 in William C. Lehmann, *John Millar of Glasgow* (Cambridge: Cambridge University Press, 1960), p. 176.

16. John Millar, *An Historical View of the English Government* (London: Mawman, 1818), 3:10-11.

17 See Ronald L. Meek, *Social Science and the Ignoble Savage* (London: Cambridge University Press, 1976).

18. Peter Gay, *The Enlightenment* (New York: Knopf, 1969), 2:339-40.

19. Adam Smith, *The Wealth of Nations* (Oxford: Clarendon Press, 1976), 2:781.

20. *An Historical View of the English Government* (London: Mawman, 1818), 4:152.

21. *Wealth of Nations,* 1976, 2:787.

22. J. G. A. Pocock, *The Machiavellian Moment* (Princeton: Princeton University Press, 1975), p. 501.

23. Albert O. Hirschman, *The Passions and the Interests* (Princeton: Princeton University Press, 1977), p. 121.

4

Tension in the Thought of John Millar

(1971)

John Millar, the holder of the chair of civil law at Glasgow from 1761, was a notable historical sociologist in the manner of a number of his eighteenth-century countrymen. Sombart's estimation of his book *The Origin of the Distinction of Ranks*[1] as "astonishing" and his assertion that the book "contains one of the best and most complete sociologies that we have"[2] certainly is exaggerated, but at least the exaggeration, if not eliminated, is lessened if we think rather of the other and much more substantial work for which Millar is best known, namely, *An Historical View of the English Government*.[3] But it is no longer necessary to stress Millar's merits. They are by now sufficiently established. It does not detract from those merits to observe that the elements of originality in Millar's views are limited by his very clear intellectual affiliation with his countrymen and contemporaries and his very deep indebtedness to them.[4]

There is an obvious indebtedness to Adam Smith, for example, and Millar was in fact "one of Smith's favourite pupils."[5] For two years, Millar lived with Lord Kames and tutored his son, George Drummond-Home, and Kames undoubtedly influenced Millar also.[6] It is possible to view Millar's affiliations in more than one way. Meek writes of a Scottish historical school and considers as its four main members Adam Smith, Adam Ferguson, William Robertson, and Millar.[7] It is suggestive of possible influences, in a general way, that Robertson's birth year is 1721, that of Smith and Ferguson, 1723, while Millar was born in 1735. It is of interest that Meek also refers to Kames, Gilbert Stuart, Lord Monboddo, Hugh Blair, and James Dunbar as men who, if not properly members of the historical school, "at least worked on its fringes." Others than Meek might be disinclined to set Robertson in precisely the same contexts as Smith, Ferguson, and Millar, and would profess to see, rather, an emergent Scottish sociological school,[8] quite possibly with credit for pertinent work assigned in particular to David Hume. In any case, the different ways in which Millar's affiliations may sensibly be viewed are not really very divergent, and it is evident that he is solidly implanted among his Scottish contemporaries. He is very much a member of his "school," and, if our own bias is to regard that school as "sociological," there is some warrant for doing so, but there is also, at any rate in this case, a danger of getting quickly into trivial verbal issues if we worry overmuch about "sociological" versus "historical."

Like others of the Scots, Millar is conspicuously a man of intellectual tensions. It is proposed here to exhibit and comment on some of the most important of those tensions. Ultimately, Millar's whole school may very profitably be examined, I believe, precisely from the point of view of its tensions, and Millar's tensions are often much like those of the others. But it will not be feasible to document resemblances and points of differences, in this regard, between Millar and the others. At the same time, Millar's affiliations cannot entirely be thrust aside. They obtrude themselves far too strongly. A compromise in the strategy of the present discussion is accordingly adopted. The discussion of tension will be limited to Millar, but in an initial background sketch some notice will be given to crucial resemblances between him and his contemporaries.

There was a general sensitivity among the Scots to the phenomenon of "social evolution," understood in a broad sense. Human establishments or institutions develop and otherwise change. They are not initially present in the forms they assume late in their development. They are likely to develop rather slowly and as unforced, unplanned ways of men: they are "natural." Millar's overview of the history of the English constitution induced him to think of that history as involving three main "parts" or periods—from the Norman conquest to the end of Henry III's reign, from the beginning of Edward I's reign to the accession of Henry VII, and the age of the Tudors. "In each of these parts we shall meet with progressive changes";[9] and the whole context of Millar's treatment tends to lend the word *progressive* at least something of the connotation of *gradual*. Moreover, these changes are "analogous to such as were introduced, about the same time, in the other European governments."[10] Millar's gradualism is accompanied by a certain parallelism. Societies tend to go through the same phases or stages. In his *Origin,* Millar stated that "the similarity of man's wants, as well as of the faculties by which those wants are supplied, has everywhere produced a remarkable uniformity in the several stages of his progression."[11] And in the same sentence in the *Historical View* in which we note the gradualism and parallelism just mentioned, Millar writes of the changes he discusses that they "may be regarded as the natural growth and development of the original system" produced in Europe.[12]

Millar was too knowledgeable historically to indulge himself in any rigid evolutionary scheme. While there was an "original similarity in all the governments of modern Europe," they also exhibit differences; and Millar makes a simple division into two classes, of "such as were founded upon the ruins of the Roman provinces" and "such as arose in the countries which had never been subject to the Roman Empire."[13] The "materialist" in Millar will induce him to think that similar property forms will everywhere induce similar forms of government.[14] But the realist is aware that accident can play an important role in historical events. The Reformation was affected by "the existence of such a person as Luther in Germany," by "the dispute that arose in England between Henry the Eighth and his wife," by "the policy of particular princes"— by these "and other such casual occurrences."[15]

Again, "accidental circumstances frequently concur, in particular countries, to retard or accelerate the operation of particular causes,"[16] and the constitution established in the reign of William of Orange became what it was "through many accidental changes" (and—be it noted—"by a course of gradual improvements upon the primitive system of the European nations").[17] But there is one theme in connection with Millar's evolutionary views that requires powerful stress, perhaps stress above all others. It is a theme that Millar himself seemingly never tires of stressing in the first two volumes of his *Historical View*. This is the theme of the unintended consequences of social action.

The theme is one of the great preoccupations of the eighteenth-century Scots. It is taken up again and again by Smith, Ferguson, and others.[18] Let us attend to a few of its manifestations in Millar himself. It is the more pertinent to do so since the theme is quite basic to the understanding of intellectual tension in Millar. Whoever inquires into the circumstances in which those great charters of which the best known is Magna Charta were procured, argues Millar, "will easily see that the parties concerned in them were not actuated by the most liberal principles; and that it was not so much their intention to serve the liberties of the people at large as to establish the privileges of a few individuals." Originally, in this same connection, limitations of arbitrary power "had been calculated chiefly to promote the interest of the nobles," but, with changed circumstances, these limitations were "rendered equally advantageous to the whole community, as if they had originally proceeded from the most exalted spirit of patriotism."[19] A court of justice, for Millar, will typically have arisen "from no preconceived plan of altering the constitution" (even if it will have had that effect) but rather "from a natural and obvious accommodation to the circumstances of the community."[20] Indeed, much in the British mode of government "arose from the views of immediate conveniency," while "its distant consequences were neither foreseen nor intended."[21] The "great benefit arising to society from the interposition of the grand jury is not only totally different but even diametrically opposite to that which was originally intended by it." Both slow evolution and absence of sharp intention are suggested in the reference to the origin of juries in general that Millar makes when he writes that "the precise date" of their establishment is "uncertain," because they "probably arose from no general or public regulations, but from the gradual and almost imperceptible change authorized by common usage in the several districts of the kingdom."[22]

To trace out in detail Millar's connection with the other Scots with regard to unintended consequences alone, even though these are, as suggested, crucially important in the social thought of the Scottish Enlightenment, is too large a task to undertake here. But a modest portion of it must be undertaken. Given his view that human institutions are generally the products of steady evolution, not of deliberate design, Millar also holds, as he puts it in his *Origin,* that "the greater part of the political system of any country" will "be derived from the combined influence of the whole people." He concedes that some influence may be exercised by "particular persons" but doubts "whether the effects of their interpositions has ever been so extensive as is generally supposed." He specifically mentions—and his skepticism on this head is quite obvious—that "Brama is supposed to have introduced the peculiar customs of Indostan; that Lycurgus is believed to have formed the singular character of the Lacedemonians; and that Solon is looked upon as the author of that very different style of manners which prevailed at Athens." He adds: "It is thus, also, that the English constitution is understood to have arisen from the uncommon genius and patriotic spirit of King Alfred."[23]

It is instructive to turn now to Adam Ferguson and Gilbert Stuart and allow them a measure of space. First, then, Ferguson:

> We are . . . to receive with caution the traditionary histories of ancient legislators and founders of states. Their names have long been celebrated; their supposed plans have been admired; and what were probably the consequences of an early situation is, in every instance, considered as an effect of design. An author and a work, like cause and effect, are perpetually coupled together. This is the simplest form under which we can consider the establishment of nations; and we ascribe to a previous design what came to be known only by experience, what no human wisdom could foresee, and what, without the concurring humor and disposition of this age, no authority could enable an individual to execute.
>
> If men, during ages of extensive reflection and employed in the search of improvement, are wedded to their institutions; and, laboring under many acknowledged inconveniences, cannot break loose from the trammels of custom, what shall we suppose their humor to have been in the times of

Romulus and Lycurgus? They were not surely more disposed to embrace the schemes of innovators or to shake off the impressions of habit.[24]

Gilbert Stuart, like Millar, a lawyer, has something strikingly similar to say:

> It is to those only who apply to rude societies the ideas of a cultivated era that the institutions of chivalry seem the production of an enlightened policy. They remember not the inexperience of dark ages and the attachment of nations to their ancient usages. They consider not, that if an individual, in such times, were to arise of a capacity to frame schemes of legislation and government, he could not reduce them to execution. He could not mould the conceptions of states to correspond to his own. It is from no preconceived plan, but from circumstances that exist in real life and affairs, that legislators and politicians acquire an ascendency among men. It was the actual condition of their times, not projects suggested by philosophy and speculation, that directed the conduct of Lycurgus and Solon.[25]

Whatever modern scholarship may specifically say about Lycurgus and Solon, and the beginnings of law in India, it is evident that Millar and his fellow Scots are expressing a shrewd and generally useful skepticism of the imputation of rationality to either clear or dim historical figures when such imputation goes beyond certain limits. And this ties in with the theme of unintended consequences, which are frequently supposed to show an excellence or beneficence of social effect or function. In this sort of reflection there soon comes clear a certain *strain* of thought that Millar shows with others of the Scots (and, indeed, with others *than* the Scots). In referring to it as a *strain,* the intention is precisely to suggest that it does not hold exclusive sway and that other and quite different strains are copresent with it. It may be described as follows: Men's actions, as already suggested, often have unintended beneficent consequences, and it is these, rather than maleficent ones, that need primary emphasis. Excellence in institutions is characteristically achieved when men are not planning for it. Old institutions are likely to incorporate wisdom. (A view such as this, I would aver, however contravened it may be by others, is actually suggested in Millar.) Deliberate social planning is likely to have pernicious results. "System" is particularly to be regarded with wariness. Millar insists, somewhat irritably, it would seem, that "no system, be it ever so perfect in itself, can be expected to acquire stability, or to produce good order and submission, unless it coincides with the general voice of the community."[26] "System" would appear to involve comprehensiveness, large overview, conscious balancing and weighing of "parts," disposition to impose a symmetrical scheme without regard to human asymmetries. Social utility is achieved empirically and by small steps; and, at that, the small steps are most effective when they, too, are somewhat undeliberate. An incrementalist attitude toward change or reform is implied. Change is to be made by modest increments.[27]

Let us now follow Millar alone, leaving untouched any resemblance he may have to the other Scots. The above strain or tendency in his thought may be said to suggest a "model" of society whereby it works well if left essentially untouched and paradoxically flourishes when men do not concern themselves about its welfare. The model is plainly "low" on rationality. Men need not (and do not) reflect much on social objects. Unintended consequences of action are likely to provide necessary social forms and changes. It has already been amply indicated that projection, speculation, and system are to be looked at askance. The model is accordingly also "high" on laissez faire. But all this, as previously noted, is in tension with other very significant aspects of Millar's thought. In particular, the low-rationality feature is in conflict with Millar's animadversions on the Catholic Church, which, in his view, simply as a matter of fact, does not exhibit low rationality. And the laissez-faire feature quite fails to fall into easy congruity with the criticisms he makes of the society and culture of his day and place.[28]

When he deals with the Roman Catholic Church in particular, Millar tends to entertain a curiously "pragmatistic" or rationalistic outlook. Other human enterprises typically achieve a variety of important effects unintentionally, but the Church is given a very strong allowance to connive in the light of her interests and to attain what she aims at. Thus the Church "availed herself to the prevailing superstition, in order to propagate such opinions as were most subservient to her interests"; and Millar continues at once: "Hence the doctrines relating to purgatory, to the imposition of penances, to auricular confession, to the power of granting a remission of sin . . . with such other tenets and practices as contributed to increase the influence of the clergy, were introduced and established."[29] Again in a tone differing from the low-rationality tone in which he so often discusses human action, Millar argues that in the "dark ages" an interested clergy, "uniting in a system of deep-laid fraud and deception," persuaded the simple, ordinary people to yield them possession and an obedience to their behests—to the point where an ecclesiastical tyranny was established.[30] What could be more pragmatistic? Millar can refer almost casually to "that pomp and pageantry of worship which is manifestly calculated to promote superstition, to create in the people a blind veneration for their spiritual directors."[31]

It is not that one must force out an utterly stark contrast between a limited rationality that Millar ordinarily supposes, on the one hand, and a maximum of rationality that he presumes for the Catholic Church, on the other. He is inevitably aware that men possess rationality and act upon it in some degree; and at times he realistically allows the degree to be considerable. (The simple "model" above exhibits certain emphases in the interest of theoretical clarity, but, as I have indicated, its force is modified by that of contravening elements in Millar's thought.) But the contrast remains. It cannot be argued or qualified away. The difference in tone is there, though Millar may not have been aware of it. Certainly, he does not face up to it. It creates a tension in his thought that he never resolved. We seem to face a characteristic eighteenth-century case of "double truth"—truth for propaganda versus truth for science.[32] The Church must be given hard knocks by a Millar who repeatedly characterized it as a "superstition" ("the Roman Catholic superstition"). But what then of the wisdom putatively embodied in old institutions? Effectively, Millar may be said still to insist on some such wisdom, even in the case of the Church and in the presence of "superstition." For Millar's view of the Church is by no means completely simplistic. Thus, the Catholic clergy, once well established in Western Europe, whatever censure it might deserve for "the interested policy . . . pursued in other respects, still had the singular merit of endeavoring everywhere to repress the disorder and injustice arising from the anarchy of the feudal times."[33] The Church protected the weak and defenseless, widows and orphans. The clergy, indeed, "by the influence of religious motives, endeavored, as far as possible, to induce mankind to the observance of good faith in their various transactions."[34]

If Millar's general attitude toward the "Roman Catholic superstition" remains one of mistrust and suspicion,[35] he is still willing to allow the Church some "functional" aspects, some definite social utilities. The sheer persistence of the Church thereby does become somewhat more intelligible, and Millar thus saves a crucial element in that model of society which has been outlined above. But the model is still irretrievably damaged or violated by the presumption of the powerful component of manipulative self-interest in the Church's behavior. There are certainly important questions of historical fact involved in all this. My view is that Millar exaggerated the element of conniving and manipulative self-interest in churchly action. Yet even if he did not, there was still clearly a challenge to the terms of the model we have delineated, after all necessary reservations have been made.

The laissez-faire *tendency* in Millar is plain and carries over a wide range. He will observe that the mercantile people judge their own interest best and that, "by pursuing those lines of trade which they find most beneficial to themselves, they are likely to produce, in most cases, the greatest benefit to the public." Government interference with the mercantile people is likely to be inept and harmful. The "ingenious and profound author" of *The Wealth of Nations* is then invoked.[36] A certain pessimism, and perhaps the usual doubt about political projection and a laissez-faire bias, may be reasonably argued to be involved in this significant general statement: "The good which we can do to mankind at large is commonly inconsiderable; but the benefits which may result from our acting with propriety in the exercise of domestic affections are above all calculation."[37] But the entire laissez-faire tendency, unmistakable though it be, is by no means unqualified, and it is really quite evident that it is in tension with different tendencies.

Certainly, Millar was not a complacent man about his society and its culture. He supported the American War of Independence. He was a defender of the French Revolution, which, in Meikle's words, excited in him "the fondest hopes,"[38] even if he had some serious reservations about it. According to Meek, he was active in the effort to abolish slavery at home and abroad.[39] He was forthrightly against what he regarded as royal tyranny and pretensions to absolute power, as the volumes of the *Historical View* amply attest. He had little use for "the greater part of the wars in which nations are engaged," tracing these to the avarice of ambition of princes or their ministers and regarding them as based on "frivolous and groundless disputes" and eventuating in waste of blood and treasure.[40] We are not to imagine, he admonishes us, that "a government can be so contrived as, for ages, to remain equally suited to a nation whose conditions and circumstances are perpetually changing," but rather the legislature must adjust regulations to changes in the situation of the people and to new economic and cultural realities.[41]

Readers of Millar may recall readily that there are three spheres in which his doubts about the social or cultural life of his day are particularly conspicuous in the *Historical View*—the spheres of division of labor, of commercialization of life, and to the power of the crown. Of course, Millar is not displeased with all things in his time. He is obviously pleased with the removal or abolition of monopolies, with the extent and freedom of commercial enterprise, and with increased elaboration and diffusion of literary and scientific culture. But some of the very things he approves have obverse sides that occasion in him much unease. He observes that the common people everywhere are acute and sagacious while they remain in a condition of "rudeness and simplicity," but that as commerce and manufactures develop, they become "ignorant, narrow-minded, and stupid."[42] He contends that the farm workman has a certain variety of occupational experience and is accordingly much superior in "real intelligence and acuteness" to a typical town-dwelling pinmaker, although the latter may be better acquainted with books.[43] In nations, wealth and knowledge appear to go hand in hand, but the matter is not thus as far as individuals are concerned. As a nature advances in commerce and industry, a dulled class of laborers emerges. England is industrially and commercially more advanced than Scotland, and the common workman of the former country is accordingly the more surely "stripped" of his "mental powers" and the more certainly "converted into the mere instrument of labor." If, on the other hand, the same individual follows a greater variety of occupations, as in Scotland, "his understanding is more exercised, and his wits are more sharpened, by such different attentions."[44] Millar is sensitive to the welfare of the common people and concerned lest they become the "dupes" of their superiors. He takes a strongly anti-Mandevillian stance against any doctrine that would exploit the ignorance of the working people.[45]

Modern economy and society, true, have their complexities. If the division of labor dulls men and narrows their horizons, the advances of science and literature in the higher social strata contribute even to the enlightenment of the common people. Manufacture, commerce, and liberty go together. But on balance Millar is not at all sure that the modern sources of the improvements of the common people compensate for "the disadvantages of their natural situation." Indeed, he believes there should be reason to doubt this.[46] He does not marshal anything like thoroughly convincing evidence in these matters of the division of labor and the welfare of the common people, but his misgivings are very plain. At the least, it is evident that society and economy are not inevitably self-adjusting machines grinding out prosperity, unqualified freedom, and general excellence. Millar is even quite capable of reservations or second thoughts about the coincidence of the interest of merchants and of the public with whom they trade.[47]

In the matter of commercialization, it is clear that Millar also has some deep-seated misgivings. His views, once more, have a certain complexity. He is aware that there are some important connections between trade and manufacture, on the one side, and probity on the other. Succinctly: "According as the intercourse of society is extended, it requires more and more a mutual trust and confidence which cannot be maintained without the uniform profession and rigid practice of honesty and fair-dealing."[48] But he also knows well that businessmen are entirely capable of plunder and other abuses. He has his doubts about "a country where nobody is idle and where every person is eager to augment his fortune," for in such a place there are likely to occur "innumerable competitions and rival-ships, which contract the heart and set mankind at variance." Envy, resentment, and "other malignant passions" emerge. He can only remind one of many before and after his time when he observes: "The pursuit of riches becomes a scramble, in which the hand of every man is against every other"; or "That there is no friendship in trade is an established maxim of traders. Every man for himself, and God Almighty for us all, is their fundamental doctrine."[49] He can refer, in a phrase interestingly adumbrative of the Marxian style, to high-placed men acting unjustly and inhumanly while they are "inflamed with the rage of accumulation."[50] If keeping one's word, good faith, and honesty, as above intimated, are likely to prevail in "opulent and trading nations," yet the domestic affections, on the line of warmth and love, are "not likely to be improved by the peculiar manners of a mercantile and luxurious age."[51] In such an age, even "marriage becomes . . . almost always an interested connexion," in which pecuniary considerations are powerfully operative. And the commercial spirit is inimical to the peculiar and intimate attachment of friends—and now Millar has reference to friendship outside the context of business as such. The friendships of a "luxurious and mercantile country" are "cool and sober, breathing no ardor of enthusiasm, producing no unreserved confidence, requiring no sacrifice either of life or fortune."[52] A certain "justice" may supervene with opulence and trade, but little in the way of "generosity."

Again, Millar is not especially impressive for rigorous presentation and handling of evidence on all these matters. But his observations have been wide and his views are forcefully stated. He writes at one point of the "pleasing speculation" that man's "faculties and virtues" are everywhere improved by artistic and scientific progress and that human nature is led, "by culture and education," to "endless degrees of perfection."[53] Millar is of his time and place in being incapable of a profound pessimism, but he refers to the "pleasing speculation" as "this flattering, *perhaps generally well-founded* hypothesis."[54] The hesitation is noteworthy, and small wonder that it is there.

Nor is Millar's optimism enhanced by his observations on the Crown in his day. He writes retrospectively in the third volume of his *Historical View* of Crown and church as both being "the offspring of ignorance and prejudice" and of a kind of family compact between the two which "proved no less advantageous to either party than it was inimical to the interest of the whole community."[55] There is little suggested here of the presumptive wisdom deposited in old institutions. In the conflict between James I and Charles I, and Parliament and people, obviously Millar's sympathies would be with the latter. Hume is clearly regarded by him as an apologist for Charles I.[56] In his own time, the power he felt the Crown could exercise by patronage was an evident source of concern to him, and he felt that the Crown had gained greatly in this regard since 1688. Law has remained in many places in the world in a state of gross imperfection, and Millar is partial to the view that the world has altogether too much of despotism.

The pressure exercised upon the low-rationality, laissez-faire model finally, inevitably, becomes far too much. Millar opposes the principle of "utility" to that of "authority" and is patently in favor of the former. There is indeed a passage that sounds nearly like an outburst:

> The blind respect and reverence paid to ancient institutions has given place to a desire of examining their uses, of criticizing their defects, and of appreciating their true merits. The fashion of scrutinizing public measures, according to the standard of their utility, has now become very universal; it pervades the literary circles, together with a great part of the middling ranks, and is visibly descending to the lower orders of the people.[57]

Old institutions, on this view, *might* still in principle incorporate wisdom or have social utility or functionality, but they could surely no longer be justified by their mere support by those in authority. It is quite in line with this that Millar should say, apparently with the French Revolution in view, that "philosophy . . . triumphed at length over ancient customs" and that he should refer to "those corrupt institutions which had been the work of ages."[58] We are now far indeed from the historical image of a meritorious constitution, built bit by bit, by limited and often selfish actions that unintentionally but effectively redounded to the general welfare, finally reaching an outcome or status that no one would, or could, have contemplated initially. But even here the older views and the older model, it may be argued, have not entirely lapsed. Government, it would now seem, requires a combination of utility and authority. Millar's old animus against "projection" appears again even while he supports the principle of utility. He writes of restraints against "those rash and visionary projects which proceed from the ambition of statesmen, or the wanton desire of innovation, and by which nations are exposed to the most dreadful calamities."[59] He is as dubious as ever about "enthusiasm." He evidently regards rank as inseparable from the condition of a multitudinous society.[60] The French Revolution in the end overthrew too much, too much that might have valuably contributed to the direction and regulation of the new establishment.

The tensions in Millar's thought that we have sought to make plain are, as suggested, never satisfactorily resolved in a theoretical sense. One might describe them in a merely common sense way and even say perfunctorily that Millar had something of both "Whig" and "Tory" in him. But this would be most perfunctory and most inadequate indeed. Although Millar does not present himself as a great theorist, his work has definite theoretical interest. Not the least part of that interest has to do with how the grand theme of unintended consequences and related themes fare within a larger framework of historical-sociological analysis such as Millar undertook. What happens with Millar, in this regard, is not without relevance for what happens with the work of his fellow Scots, but this is a matter from which I have deliberately turned aside in this chapter. If he himself never lifted into clear and full awareness the tensions I have sought to describe, then, of course, he would not cleanly resolve them. Had he done so, he might have been an even more significant transitional figure in the history of social thought such as Macfie sagely perceives him to be.[61] But he had the defects of his virtues. Perhaps no man so jealous as he of the "empirical" character of law and so wary of speculation and system could have wrought out the monumental sociology that might ideally have emerged from his peculiar intellectual tensions. Bagehot thought, rightly or wrongly, that Adam Smith's work at the customhouse happily prevented him from writing in his later life, for what Smith might have produced then would have been overspeculative.[62] Had Millar lived to give finishing touches to the *Historical View,* one may venture the guess that the resultant work would have been underspeculative. His defects were nevertheless, as I have said, the defects of virtues. His empirical bent still commands respect, even if he cannot meet (how, after all, could one expect him to?) the highest present standards for presenting and organizing evidence. In failing of a mighty work of synthesis he is disarmingly like other and greater sociologists and other and greater men generally, while he still remains a sturdy and engaging representative of historical sociology in its earlier forms.

Notes

1. Reprinted in William C. Lehmann's fundamental work, *John Millar of Glasgow* (Cambridge: Cambridge University Press, 1960), pp. 173-322. The edition of *The Origin* printed in 1806 (Edinburgh: Blackwood) contains John Craig's valuable account of Millar's life and writings. The recent German edition, *Vom Ursprung des Unterschieds in den Rangordnungen und Standen der Gesellschaft* (Frankfurt: Suhrkamp, 1967), includes an extensive introduction by Lehmann.
2. Werner Sombart, "Die Anfänge der Soziologie," in Melchoir Palyi, ed., *Erinnerungsgabe für Max Weber* (Munich: Duncker & Humblot, 1923), pp. 5-19. See also pp. 13-14 for his further praise of *The Origin*.

3. Vols. 1 and 2 (London: Mawman, 1812); vols. 3 and 4 (London: Mawman, 1818).
4. Lehmann suggests with regard to Ferguson that he was neither an isolated nor an especially independent figure but was rather "part of a movement," especially in England and Scotland, toward emancipation from an a priori (or "metaphysical") mode of thought on problems of human social life. This applies just as aptly to Millar. See William C. Lehmann, *Adam Ferguson and the Beginnings of Modern Sociology* (New York: Columbia University Press, 1930); p. 257.
5. John Rae, *Life of Adam Smith* (New York: Kelly, 1965), p. 53.
6. Lehmann, *John Millar,* pp. 17-18.
7. Ronald L. Meek, "The Scottish Contribution to Marxist Sociology," in John Saville, ed., *Democracy and the Labour Movement* (London: Lawrence & Wishart, 1954), pp. 85-86.
8. The 1967 German edition of Millar's *Origin* contains (on its unnumbered terminal page) the simple assertion that John Millar, with Smith and Ferguson, was "one of the three great Scots of the second half of the eighteenth century who founded sociology."
9. Millar, *Historical View,* 2:1.
10. Ibid., 2:2.
11. Millar, *Origin,* in Lehmann, *John Millar,* p. 176.
12. Millar, *Historical View,* 2:2.
13. Ibid., 3:10-11. He adds that the feudal system "was more completely and rapidly-established in the former than in the latter." Ibid., 3:11.
14. Cf., ibid., 3:18.
15. Ibid., 2:432.
16. Ibid., 2:28.
17. Ibid., 4:77.
18. In this connection, see, for example, Duncan Forbes, " 'Scientific' Whiggism: Adam Smith and John Millar," *Cambridge Journal* 7 (1954):643-70. See also Louis Schneider, ed., *The Scottish Moralists* (Chicago: University of Chicago Press, 1967), "Introduction," particularly pp. xxix-xlvii.
19. Millar, *Historical View,* 2:80-81.
20. Ibid., 2:109.
21. Ibid., 2:232. These and other observations of Millar's suggest a whole world of allied commentary by other Scots, as in the case of Hume's references to the "great mixture of accident which commonly occurs with a small ingredient of wisdom and foresight in erecting the complicated fabric of the most perfect government" and to "the remote and commonly faint and disfigured originals of the most finished and most noble institutions." David Hume, *History of England* (New York: Harper, 1879), 2:50. See also the further course of the present remarks. Incidentally, when Millar writes "neither foreseen or intended," he properly suggests a distinction between the unanticipated and the unintended, but for the Scots either will ordinarily also imply the other.
22. Millar, *Historical View,* 1:187.
23. Millar, *Origin,* in Lehmann, *John Millar,* p. 177. Brama, Lycurgus, and Alfred appear also in *Historical View.* In a very characteristic rejection of the notion of Alfred as a kind of all-foreseeing father of a great deal of

English government, Millar observes: "Alfred, in a word, has become the English Lycurgus; and his interposition is the great engine which politicians have employed for explaining the origin of such particulars, in the English government, as have excited uncommon attention and are too remote in their beginnings to fall within the limits of authentic history." Millar, *Historical View*, 1:270-71. A similarly skeptical statement regarding Brama occurs at 1:325-26. Lycurgus, at least in Millar, makes a final bow in the following: "He who frames a political constitution upon a model of ideal perfection and attempts to introduce it into any country without consulting the inclinations of the inhabitants is a most pernicious projector, who instead of being applauded as a Lycurgus, ought to be chained and confined as a madman." Ibid., p. 329. It may be noted by the way that when John Craig observes that "general systems of Law have rarely, if ever, been formed by the projective wisdom of legislators" (Craig, in 1806 edition of *Origin*, p. xxxiv; cf. also p. lxxix) he is merely echoing Millar.

24.   Adam Ferguson, *As Essay on the History of Civil Society* (Philadelphia: Finley, 1819), pp. 223-24.

25.   Gilbert Stuart, *A View of Society in Europe* (Dublin: Whitestone, or Edinburgh: Bell & Murray, 1778), pp. 54-55. Relevant publication dates may be noted without further comment. Millar's *Origin* appeared in its original form in 1771 and the first edition of *Historical View* in 1787. Ferguson's *Essay* was first published in 1766 and Stuart's book in 1778. The common theme of unintended consequences, with its subthemes, is very likely to clothe itself in similar, and freely borrowed, language. The remark may be allowed in passing that while resemblances of language and analogy are obviously not central for the present paper, they appear to be outstandingly significant clues to the historical connections of the works of the eighteenth-century Scots and, for that matter, to the connections of those works with work by the Scots' intellectual descendents. In the same general area of unintended consequences, Thomas Reid (d. 1796), the philosopher, observed that bees "work most geometrically" but of course without knowing that they do so. Their cells are regular hexagons which men could never produce except via mathematics. Their little "intentions" add up to honeycombs none of them ever "intended." Reid, *Works* (Edinburgh: MacLachlan & Stewart, 1863), 2:545-47. A century after Reid's death, Robert Flint, in his *History of the Philosophy of History: Historical Philosophy in France and French Belgium and Switzerland* (New York: Scribner's, 1894), pp. 225-26, wrote of men's pursuit of "narrow and mean schemes merely for personal good," out of which "order, progress, plan" inadvertently arose—for men "have been as ignorant of the laws of the vast scheme they were realizing as the bees are of the mathematical principles on which they construct their honeycombs." A half-century after Flint, Robert M. MacIver observed in his *Social Causation* (Boston: Ginn, 1942), p. 314: "The purposive actions of man . . . bring unpurposed results that are no less remarkable than, say, the hexagons of the hive of the honey bee." Flint was a professor at Edinburgh. MacIver was born in Stornoway, Scotland.

26.   Millar, *Historical View*, 3:329. *Historical View*, one inclines to say, almost endlessly exhibits mistrust of "projection," "speculation," and system. Millar will write with unmistakable disapproval of "a political projector,

neglecting for the sake of a finical regularity, to avail himself of the usual sources of authority in a rude nation." Again: "Of all the sciences, law seems to be that which depends the most upon experience, and in which mere speculative reasoning is of the least consequence." There is the statement quoted above, note 23, about him "who frames a political constitution upon a model of ideal perfection." Millar further observes that in Cromwell's day "there was opened a boundless field to political projectors, in which they might range at pleasure, and declaim without end or measure upon their different speculative improvements." "The intrigues of any political projector," finally, is a wholly characteristic phrase. See Millar, *Historical View,* 1:18, 2:339, 3:329, 4:160.

27.   Incrementalism as here understood in opposed to utopianism. Millar, in regard to projection and system, thinks of utopianism in a pejorative sense. There is also the theoretical possibility of a valid utopianism. The essentially very old opposition of incrementalism and utopianism is cogently discussed in modern form in Amitai Etzioni, *The Active Society* (New York: Free Press, 1968), chs. 11-12. A vigorous advocacy of utopianism with an interesting historico-sociological underpinning is afforded by Fred L. Polak, *The Image of the Future* (New York: Oceana Publications, 1961). It is instructive to note not only how hoary the incrementalism-utopianism opposition is but how slippery, still, are some of the issues it poses and how hard it can be to get away from a purely verbal resolution of them even today.

28.   The model could easily be expanded on the basis of what has already been intimated. It is here kept simple for reasons of economy of space, but one could obviously add to it "indirection," for example. High indirection would be intimately connected with low rationality and high laissez-faire. In indirection, social theory postulates that a variety of socially significant conditions are attained indirectly and are often *best* attained indirectly— best in the sense of "most effectively" and in the sense of involving "highest social utility." Limited and even "mean" motives may thus work out indirectly to beneficent social outcomes. The brief observation is unavoidable that indirection had been profoundly expounded in Adam Smith's *Theory of Moral Sentiments* (Oxford: Clarendon Press, 1976).

29.   Millar, *Historical View,* 2:458.

30.   Ibid., 4:157.

31.   Ibid., 3:131.

32.   Cf. Forbes, " 'Scientific' Whiggism," p. 652.

33.   Millar, *Historical View,* 2:117.

34.   Ibid., 2:135.

35.   He is not necessarily more friendly toward Anglicanism or Protestantism; for example, see Millar, *Historical View,* 3:138, 144.

36.   Ibid., 4:109-10.

37.   Ibid., 4:217.

38.   Henry W. Meikle, *Scotland and the French Revolution* (Glasgow: J. Maclehose, 1912), p. 49.

39.   Meek, "Scottish Contributions," p. 97. Jacob Viner presents a well documented commentary on "slavery" in the Scottish mines, with some reference to Millar, in his "Guide" to Rae's *Life of Adam Smith,* pp. 109-16.

40. Millar, *Historical View,* 4:193-94.
41. Ibid., 4:78.
42. Ibid., 3:91.
43. Ibid., 4:154-55.
44. Ibid., 4:152.
45. Cf. ibid., 4:159-60. Lehmann quotes relevant lines in *John Millar.*
46. Ibid., 1:149.
47. See his letter to "David Hume" (whether the philosopher or his nephew is not clear) in Lehmann, *John Millar,* pp. 398-99.
48. Millar, *Historical View,* 4:237.
49. See ibid., 4:248-49.
50. Ibid., 4:262. Compare Marx: "Accumulate! Accumulate! That is Moses and the prophets." Karl Marx, *Capital* (New York: Modern Library, 1936), 1:652.
51. Ibid., 4:256.
52. Ibid., 4:258-59.
53. Ibid., 4:232-33.
54. Ibid., 4:233; italics added.
55. Ibid., 3:137.
56. Ibid., 3:313f.
57. Ibid., 4:305.
58. Ibid., 4:308.
59. Ibid., 4:310.
60. Ibid., 4:293.
61. A L. Macfie, "John Millar: A Bridge between Adam Smith and Nineteenth Century Social Thinkers?" in Macfie, *The Individual in Society: Papers on Adam Smith* (London: Allen & Unwin, 1967), pp. 141-51.
62. Walter Bagehot, *Historical Essays* (New York: New York University Press, 1965), p. 104.

Part II
Elements of the
Sociological Way

Introduction

The six chapters in this section range over a diverse set of themes in contemporary social science: freedom and social structure, the writings of P. A. Sorokin, common concerns in history and sociology, the category of ignorance, dialectical orientations, and the ironic perspective. These explorations cohere in several interesting ways that neatly underscore the argument in Part 1 that the insights of Mandeville and the Scots continue to inform social research today.

Chapter 5 is an early article written when Schneider was at Colgate University and first published in *Psychiatry*. It contains all the elements, discerned in the review of eighteenth-century moral philosophy, that distinguish his sociological way of looking at the world: interdisciplinarity, ethical concern, an interest in the limits of freedom, and the characteristic fascination with unintended consequences. Here, too, we get at least a glimpse into Schneider's interest in psychiatric views on human nature. Revealing some strong but ambivalent feelings about Freud and psychoanalysis generally, his aim is to establish, first, that the concept of freedom lies properly within a domain shared by the fields of psychiatry and sociology (and economics, history, and anthropology as well). On this basis, he sets up an opposition between the commentary on the subject by, e.g., Freud, Jung, Erich Fromm, and Karen Horney, and that by sociologists who have dealt with freedom in their studies of socialization and social structure—especially Talcott Parsons.

It is commendable to Schneider that psychiatrists have taken a special interest in freedom in order to contribute to the causes of "peace," "prosperity," and "well-being." This endeavor is clearly continuous with that of the founders of social science. For instance, Jung's concern about the trivialization (or de*person*alization) caused by increasing division of labor is substantially the same as that voiced by Smith and his colleagues some one hundred fifty years earlier. Nevertheless, Jung and psychiatrists in general have, in their desire to liberate man from his "bondage to others," typically evidenced more goodwill than thoughtfulness. For various reasons, among which the tendency to generalize inappropriately "from clinic to culture" is prominent, psychiatric uses of "freedom" lack precision. Most seriously, in search of the free man, the psychiatrist has attempted to *separate* human nature from social circumstance.

Schneider's stated purpose here is to show that psychiatric views on freedom are sociologically naive, that they posit (or seek) a situation in which the individual is so "free" that he is no longer a social—i.e., human—being. But in addition, and without so labeling it, in his criticisms of Fromm and G. B. Chisholm he identifies the main vulnerability in Marxist psychology specifically (which was explored and, to an extent, corrected by Georges Sorel and the "Franco-Italian" line of Marxists, but which did not enter in any significant way into the work of Fromm and his Frankfurt School colleagues). In response to the proposition that self-realization, as a goal, will inspire socialist revolution and, as a resource, will build a new, "free" social order, he poses a question—to Chisholm in particular—that highlights the importance of what is for psychiatry a seriously underestimated element in the human equation, social structure: What, he asks, are the social conditions (that is, the limitations or disciplines) that would be supportive of "free" people? He thereby reintroduces what is by now a familiar project—or, in any case, a new application of a familiar project—of dissociating the individual psychological level of explanation from the sociological one. And, again, integral to this is a reminder of the prominent role played by unintended outcomes in motivated human activity.

Schneider begins his critique with the identification of what sociologists refer to as functional requisites, that is, needs (e.g., reproduction) upon whose adequate satisfaction the survival (or well-being) of social systems depends. He then considers how such needs actually get satisfied, noting that "there is a certain indirection in the meeting of the requisites of a social system." From the point of view of the motivated individual, acts intended to serve certain limited and personal ends nevertheless *indirectly* contribute to the satisfaction of functional requisites. Schneider's favorite example is, in fact, reproduction. A system surely requires it at a certain minimal level (which demographers define as N [et] R [eproduction] R [ate] ≈ 1.0); and in an ongoing system people do act in ways that assure it. But their motivation in so acting is rarely that of contributing to system survival (or of keeping the NRR above 1.0).

Among the several interesting paths that Schneider often explored from this central point, one that is key in this section, and especially in Chapters 5 and 8, is the notion of "attractiveness of intermediates." In the fourfold ($\pm$) table in Chapter 5, for example, it is shown how functional requisites are frequently, if not typically, satisfied because people are attracted to certain ends (sexual gratification, the advantages of having one's own sons and daughters, etc.), which entail acts that serve as means to the ends of the system. When the further possibility is added that direct, rather than the more usual indirect, pursuit of functional requisites can be a *less* effective procedure from the point of view of the system, we come to the crux of the argument of Chapter 8 on the functions of ignorance.

This is developed most extensively in connection with the distinction between "motivational" and "synergic" phases in the operation of social systems.[1] This distinction, in turn, reveals some of the details of the psychiatrists' oversight in their treatment of freedom. It is of interest to note, as Schneider does emphatically, that the idea of synergic phase—the phase of collective outcomes relatively independent of individual motives—has its roots in Adam Smith's "invisible hand," and apposite concepts (Hegel's "the cunning of reason," etc.). That psychiatry has overlooked this factor is serious, especially because those armed with the distinction between motivations and synergy—from Mandeville to Parsons—have also known the importance of socialization, the learning of the "right" motives and the "proper" goals for the maintenance of a social system. Thus, in brief, the psychiatrist who has an interest in freedom would do well to consider the stress given by social scientists to such matters as social structure, functional requisites, unintended consequences, indirection, synergy, and all that these imply for the very necessity of (some type of) socialization. Social planning of the kind undertaken by Freud, Jung, and Fromm—the planning of an improved human being—must depend upon socialization; and socialization means that some norms or rules must be internalized and applied. In this sense, and for specific sociological reasons, the "free man" of psychiatric theory will never exist.

A subsidiary, but still significant, argument put forth in Chapter 5 and throughout this section is developed as Schneider's refutation of vulgar sociologism and/or functionalism. That the sociologist is prone to excesses in the direction of collective cause and effect as the psychiatrist is prone in the direction of individual will is a distinct possibility, one to which Schneider believes we should be alert and correct when discerned. In note 24, for example, he accuses Fromm of "outright individual anarchism," but balances this with a reference to the alleged "agelicism" of Durkheim. At other points, too, he is attentive to the tendency of many —users of the functionalist perspective especially—to formulate circular, teleological, and empirically barren explanations.

In Schneider's discussion of the work of P.A. Sorokin, principally in Chapter 6, the tendency to mystify the social level in this way as well as many of the specific points of criticism raised against psychiatric theory are brought to bear again. Chapter 6 first appeared as a memorial to

Sorokin in *Social Science Quarterly* and is included here, in part, because it typifies the high intellectual plane at which Schneider and Sorokin carried on an exchange that extended over the last decade of the latter's life. Sorokin was a giant in twentieth-century sociology, but he was also a controversial—one could say embattled—scholar: While he had some staunch defenders within and outside of the profession, his research was also subjected to criticism, even scorn, from many quarters, and not all of it was as fair or as thoughtful as it might have been. In addition, he found the time, during the course of producing uncounted thousands of pages reporting his own research, to author several works—including the widely read and discussed *Fads and Foibles of Modern Sociology*—in which the research methods and theoretical orientations of his contemporaries are literally torn apart.

All of this fascinated Schneider considerably, and it inspired him to undertake a careful study of Sorokin's work, during the course of which he probably read more of him than most of the other critics combined. Out of this there emerged in Schneider a deep respect for—even wonderment at—Sorokin's enormous output and his breadth of vision.

Consequently, Sorokin took quite seriously the types of objections raised in Chapter 6. It is beyond the scope of these introductory remarks to consider Sorokin's response in any degree of detail. (See Sorokin's "reply" in Zollschan and Hirsch.[2]) But it must be pointed out that he, also with deep respect, believed that Schneider had failed to understand him adequately and that, after all, he had still not read quite enough Sorokin to justify his criticisms. Yet, Schneider did have the last word, and he appears not to have retreated, not at least from the main objections raised when Sorokin was alive.

Schneider sees much strength in Sorokin's work, principally in his stress on the importance of culture (a major interest in Schneider's own research) and in his use—or discovery—of dialectical themes in the study of social change. As is especially noted in Chapter 9 of this volume, Schneider believes dialectic to be a member of the family of concepts that also includes latent functions, irony, and the like. Here, Sorokin is credited with a very able and often illuminating grasp of these relationships. Schneider also has some, guardedly, favorable things to say about Sorokin's handling of empirical data. He believes that the attempt to quantify and correlate information about phenomena as diverse as industrial productivity, culture heroes, and styles of painting and architecture is bold and commendable; though, like Sorokin's other critics, he finds this work to be, in other respects, naive and simplistic.

The central aim of these remarks, however, is to chide Sorokin for his neglect of social structure and related phenomena, just as Fromm is chided in Chapter 5. Here, even more than in the preceding chapter, functionalism and specifically the work of Talcott Parsons figure prominently as correctives to overly ambitious social theorizing. Of course, in view of the personal relationship between Sorokin and Parsons it is obvious that at least a small barb accompanies Schneider's calling attention to Sorokin's omission of Parsons in his text on contemporary theory. But the implications are more than personal. For, Schneider indicates, in overlooking or in not taking seriously enough Parsons's work on social systems and evolution, Sorokin gives too large a role to culture as a cause of social change. In this respect and in connection with what Schneider terms Sorokin's "emanationist" bias, *Social and Cultural Dynamics* and related works—which Schneider takes to be the core of his writings—are burdened with a peculiar cultural determinism. No doubt, cultural values and styles can and do affect the patterned ways in which people relate to one another, but, as Parsons shows, patterns of social relationships also operate in part by their own logic—and, at the very least, the determinism between culture and society operates in both directions. Moreover, not just in relation to Sorokin's treatment of culture but in his dialectical style as well, the introduction of underused structural concepts exposes the vulgarization of an otherwise useful approach (this is taken up at length in Chapter 9).

The matter of interdisciplinarity is the major focus of Chapter 7. Here we find a strong plea for a critical reconciliation between sociology and history, particularly in relation to two key themes: evolutionism and latent functions. In his characteristic tracing of these themes back to Mandeville and Smith (and in this case to David Hume and Hegel as well) and forward to structural-functional sociology, Schneider takes the opportunity to reiterate a prescription that arose in discussion of the foundation works of eighteenth-century social philosophy: Though a drawing together of sociological and historical insights on evolution, indirection, etc. may appear "ambitious," this is not to deter such efforts, for social science ought to be an ambitious sort of undertaking.

As he does throughout this section, Schneider shows a special interest in psychoanalysis, in Parsons's views on evolution—here as a corrective to certain types of historicism—and in socialization. With these in view, he illustrates the advantages of an interdisciplinary perspective on evolution with a familiar irony of socialization: the penalty of leadership. This is best known to sociologists and economists through Veblen's study, *Imperial Germany and the Industrial Revolution*. The penalty of leadership is paid by those who, like England in the early eighteenth century, take the lead by making an early commitment to certain economic goals, modes of organizing, types of technology, etc., but who eventually become inflexible or otherwise incapable of adapting to later goals and modes. This works to the disadvantage of the leader in competition with those who, like Germany in the late nineteenth century, had made no such commitment and are thus flexible enough to catch up with and even surpass the leader in a relatively short time.

This reference to Veblen introduces a long section on unintended consequences in history, in social philosophy, and in social science. In the course of this discussion Schneider brings to bear a substantial amount of material from contemporary sociology as well: a very brief, but brilliant analysis of scapegoating (i.e., as an "explanation" of outcomes no one intended); an illustration from his research on the sociology of religion in the Roman Catholic Archdiocese of San Antonio, Texas— which is also discussed at several points in Part 3 of this volume—where he discovered a liberal archbishop victimized by a "backfire" reaction by his own newly liberated priests; and a strong reassertion that dialectic is best understood in the light of intended versus unintended consequences.

In order to make the proposal for a better articulated sociology and history more concrete, Schneider devotes a large part of this chapter to an analysis of what he refers to in his work on Mandeville and the Scots as "conversion mechanisms" (here, simply "mechanisms"). Though the narrative is laced with Schneider's usual cautions and qualifications about "heuristics" and "suggestiveness," there is a clear intent to render the concept of mechanism a precise tool that can serve the student of social change—historian, sociologist, or other—in an immediate sense. As he is, often painfully, aware, it is unlikely that he achieved this purpose, here or anywhere in his work. But it is equally clear that he has made a useful beginning and that there is significance and ingenuity—not to mention relevance on other grounds—in using Freud's concepts of projection and displacement to illustrate the operation of mechanisms.

At several points in the discussion of the conversation of motivated acts of individuals into collective outcomes it is noted that a lack of knowledge about final ends on the part of actors can accompany or even appear to be conducive to the satisfaction of the needs of larger social systems. In Chapter 8 this phenomenon is analyzed at length. Though it may seem a virtual *non sequitur,* Schneider undertakes here to explore ignorance as a category in the sociology of *knowledge,* that is, to view it in relation to its social antecedents and consequences as others have looked at political ideologies and movements in science. The key to such an approach lies in what he terms "the ignorance-knowledge compound," a notion that is introduced—though not so labeled—in earlier comments on eighteenth-century views of evolution. The ignorance-knowledge compound reveals itself at many strategic junctures in the operation of social institutions (such as the economy in Smith's classic model), wherein it is evident that institutions incorporate "wisdom" that the individual characteristically lacks. It is this *compounding* of collective knowledge and individual ignorance that distinguishes social dynamics—and, in interesting cases, is clearly "eufunctional."

Ignorance, in this sense, is an entity that, like any other object of sociological inquiry, can have consequences in society—good, bad, and indifferent, manifest and latent, individual and collective. It is thus likely to be susceptible to functional, dialectic, and related modes of analysis. Indeed, one need not search too far in the works of major social theorists such as Marx, Weber, and—more recently—Sorokin, to find this orientation.

A very special, and for Schneider especially intriguing, application of functionalist approaches to ignorance is in the study of magic and religion. Drawing on Malinowski and Durkheim, Schneider indicates how these sacred institutions so often operate to meet some essential but altogether secular needs such as social solidarity, tension management, and the like—not because individual participants in magic or religious ritual intend to meet these needs but, significantly, because in attending to other matters their acts have this effect. As in the discussion of psychiatric views on freedom, it is a small step from this observation to an exploration of the possibility that it is somehow "better" that actors proceed in religious and other contexts in ignorance, that if the latent functions of these practices were to become manifest (known and/or intended) essential needs would be met less effectively: For instance, would religion continue to contribute to group cohesion if participants explicitly sought group cohesion rather than the usual, transcendent, ends?

This line of questioning reintroduces the concepts of indirection and intermediacy, and the related idea of the attractiveness of intermediates. In religion, as in other realms, intrinsic satisfaction is derived by actors through their pursuit of what are in fact intermediate ends—e.g., the sense of communion with God, spirituality, etc.—in a larger set of causes and effects. The attractiveness of such intermediates acts as a conversion (here "transmutation") mechanism that turns private motives into collectively beneficial outcomes.

Although Schneider's purpose here, as in the preceding chapter, is to help sharpen the conceptual tools of the social scientist, he again finds it necessary to pause to consider actual and potential abuses to which such tools are subject. In the case of ignorance, and particularly with regard to its eufunctions, there is in addition to the usual pitfalls of vulgarization and overgeneralization ample opportunity for analysis to shade into ideological partisanship. Eufunction is, after all, a value judgment: To so label an outcome is to take a stand concerning what is "good" for the individual, the institution, or society at large. As useful and as necessary as this may be, it can serve and often has served to mask the personal or political biases of the social theorist. For this reason, Schneider is especially careful to stipulate at several points that ignorance may (or may not, as the case may be) prove eufunctional *"from a liberal democratic,* [etc.] perspective." Without such care and attentiveness to the specific and typically several value orientations that may come into play in the presence of the ignorance-knowledge compound, the whole notion can dissolve into the trivial proposition that any type of ignorance is always "good" for someone.[3]

In offering these cautions, Schneider also takes the opportunity to direct some critical remarks at "the power of positive thinking"—à la Norman Vincent Peale and, here, Comte as well. In a related but more serious vein, consideration of how the category of ignorance can be misused introduces a superb discussion of ideology in social theory— specifically organic theory. Though this discussion is tangential to the main thesis of this chapter—and is carried on largely in the notes (especially note 19)—it is in fact one of the strongest statements on the philosophy of social science in all of Schneider's work.

Schneider's sensitivity to the appropriate uses and potential abuses of sociological concepts is perhaps most pronounced in the analysis of dialectic in Chapter 9. Here he takes on the truly difficult but most valuable task of separating the legitimate productive uses of the dialectical approach in sociology (following Gurvitch, Schneider is emphatic that "there is no dialectical 'method' to propound") from its all-too-common mystification and employment in the service of polemic—such as is found in "the lower reaches of Marxist literature." For those not so well versed as Schneider in Hegelian philosophy and related dialectical thought, these disclaimers may appear belabored, but his basic point is simple and important: Dialectic has a worthwhile role to play in social research, but "the pathology of the dialectic" detracts seriously from effective performance of this role.

As suggested earlier, dialectical styles can readily be traced back to the Scottish Moralists and particularly to Smith's, Ferguson's, and Millar's interest in the kinds of unintended consequences that differ in dramatic ways from the motivation of actors (as when the despotic intentions of the nobles who pressed for the Magna Carta aid in the spread of democratic rights to the masses). It is with more than mere symmetry in mind that Schneider reasserts, at this juncture, the position of the eighteenth-century philosophers as founders of social science. In showing, through reference to their work, the similarity among the presumably distinct concepts of dialectic, unintended consequences, and —in Chapter 10 at greater length—irony, he is able to bring dialectic "back to earth," precisely to render it more mundane and thus, it is hoped, to make it more useful. Moreover, as Schneider indicates, to see Adam Smith—a philosopher clearly *not* "nurtured in the tradition of German idealism"—as a dialectician, is to apply and judge the approach without the impediments of a Hegelian theodicy of history. As in the preceding chapter, attention is also given here to Herbert Spencer's evolutionary sociology. Spencer is credited as an able user of dialectic, in general and especially in his commentary on evolutionary *mal*adaption. According to Spencer, there is tendency for once-progressive institutions to become entrenched and overstructured, and thus to act to block the development of new institutions that are, in other respects, better adapted. As noted, Schneider believes this idea to be pivotal in the history of social science; and to emphasize this, he demonstrates once more how it comes into play in such major works as Marx's analysis of capitalism, Weber's discussion of charisma, the entire social systems approach to freedom—as discussed in Chapter 5, and (not least) Veblen's "penalty of leadership." Also, reference is made in this regard to Sorokin as dialectician and to the Schneider-Sorokin dialogue (e.g., Chapter 9, note 13).

A large portion of Chapter 9 is devoted to an analytical exercise, similar to that employed in the discussion of ignorance, in which seven "clusters of meaning" of dialectic are identified and described. While—as Schneider readily (too readily) admits—there is much that is tentative about this classification scheme, it also helps to give some precision to the concept and orderliness to its use in social science—thus also to free it from some of the, understandably, unpleasant connotations that it has for many scholars.

It is noteworthy, too, that Schneider reaches for illustration into the realm of literary criticism and specifically to the book *Language and Silence* by George Steiner. Steiner, who is generally unknown to sociologists, is an exceptionally skillful (and an exceptionally sociological) student of the dialectic. Schneider quotes him here on the affinity of love and hate in connection with the dialectical "principle" of contradiction. But, as he was undoubtedly aware (though I know of no other reference to Steiner in Schneider's writings), there is much in Steiner's work that illuminates the various "clusters of meanings" as well as or better than this. But the reference to Steiner effectively underscores what is arguably the most important reason for retaining "dialectic" in the social science vocabulary, despite its many misappropriations: the utility of the dialectical "bent" in forging closer ties between humanistic and scientific approaches to the study of social relations.

Irony, the last member of the family of themes in this section, has for a very long time been a prime source of fascination for writers and critics of drama and fiction. In establishing that irony is also "intimately bound up with a great deal of sociological thought," Schneider seeks to illuminate an especially powerful and authentic point of contact between sociological, literary, historical, and philosophical analysis.

As a literary device, irony is typically employed (by an author) to induce in an audience such emotional states as surprise, relief, outrage, and sorrow.[4] In this context and, Schneider proposes, in social science as well, irony is effective because it draws attention to shocking (or even "mocking") discrepancies between results and the intentions of actors. Viewed in this light, the similarities between irony, dialectic, and latent functions and dysfunctions are obvious—as, perhaps, are some of the differences as well.

In exploring these connections, the writings of Mandeville and the Scots are once more brought to bear. The purpose here is to show that coincident with their interest in collective outcomes, indirection, the attractiveness of intermediates, and related mechanisms the originators of social science were also laying the foundations for a distinctively modern *perspective* on social relations, one that they believed would be especially productive of insight into such matters. As the substantive concerns of Smith and the others were developed through the nineteenth and early twentieth centuries, this perspective came to be incorporated in the role of sociologist-as-ironist.

In a sense the ironist *is* the impartial spectator of eighteenth-century social philosophy; and he continues as the detached "objective" analyst of twentieth-century sociology. Involvement in, or *lack* of detachment from, social relations commits actors to taking seriously their own motives and intentions, so seriously that they are "blind" to a range of outcomes of their acts—especially those that approach outright contradiction or opposition to intentions. To an Oedipus or a Calvin, for example, certain results of their acts such as self-destruction or the spread of materialism are virtually inconceivable, beyond reason, for they could not have acted as they did had they "known" what would result. The protosociology of Mandeville and, Schneider insists, the effective social science of any era are superior to commonsense understanding because they help us to see beyond the limited outlook of actors, to be—as Schneider prefers—"in on things." The sociological ironist, because he is willing and able to entertain the hypothesis that Oedipus' plan both to destroy his father's assassin *and* to save his own life and honor will prove to be impossible, or that Calvin's program to promote other-worldly spiritualism will be a cause of industrial revolution, has a very special standpoint among "diversely located observers."

To illustrate how ironic perspective serves the contemporary social scientist, Schneider points to applications in structural-functional analysis, in the general study of the (ironic) vulnerability of experts, and —of special interest—in the labeling "theory" approach to deviant behavior and the related study of iatrogenesis. Here and in *The Sociological Way of Looking at the World* considerable attention is given to the last two; and the last-named, iatrogenesis, was the subject of Schneider's most intense research at the time of his death.

The discussion of labeling is especially clarifying. Indeed, it is a largely successful attempt to use the ironic focus to salvage our understanding of labeling from its (by now familiar) excesses. In outline, Schneider's argument runs this way: Acts on the part of public authorities of labeling and subsequently treating a person or group as "deviant" have been shown, in many well-documented instances, to amplify, intensify, or even in some cases initiate the tendency for the person or group to behave in deviant ways. This is patently true, it is revealing, and—not incidentally—it is ironic in authentic literary and sociological senses. But to observe this is in no way to prove that labeling is a sole or principal cause of deviancy. There are ironies in our *expert* treatment of alleged deviants; this is beyond question. But it is a different, and far more controversial, matter to conclude from available evidence that deviancy is merely the construction of expert "handling."

Once our focus on deviancy is realigned to its proper objects—experts, laymen, and their definitions of "therapeutic" situations—we can see that labeling in the treatment of deviants can produce what is known in medicine as iatrogenic disease—a disorder caused in the course of cure: "the cure that kills." Here and throughout his writings Schneider uses the example of physician-induced puerperal fever, a discovery by Semmelweis that led to modern antisepsis. Another ready source of examples, drug-induced illness, has in common usage become a virtual synonym for iatrogenesis. In such cases, an expert is given often very broad discretion in his treatment of the layman (-patient)—while, not so incidentally, the layman is sufficiently *ignorant* that he cooperates or is easily forced to cooperate in giving free rein to the expert. These actions eventuate, clearly unintentionally, in what the expert would himself recognize as harm to the layman. In understanding labeling-induced deviancy as an iatrogenic disorder, as a pathology—an, often tragic, irony—of interaction between patient and practitioner, the irony is clear and the virtues of the ironic focus are evident. At the same time, there are explicit limits to such a focus, for not all disorders are iatrogenic, nor is all deviant behavior caused by police and psychiatrists.

The ironic focus, like the other elements of the sociological way discussed in this section, has its appropriate uses as a spark to insight (in the context of *discovery* of hypotheses), but always with very real and noteworthy limitations. This should detract neither from its obvious utility as a central and enduring perspective in social science nor from its value as a bridge between scientific and humanistic approaches. To the contrary, much of the value of the ironic focus, dialectic, the category of ignorance, etc. comes from the fact that they are, when properly understood and applied, substantial aids to sociological understanding but certainly not substitutes for it.

Notes

1.   Synergy is an important concept for Schneider's sociological approach as a whole and is brought to bear in his discussions of Durkheim's *Elementary Forms of the Religious Life,* the theories of Sorokin, and elsewhere. It is close to the idea of conversion or transmutation mechanism, pointing as it does to the fact that, as the German organic theorist Savigny put it, "the outcome of the general will is no one's will in particular." Note 31 of Chapter 5 contains what is perhaps Schneider's best and most concise discourse of synergy.

2.   George K. Zollschan and Walter Hirsch, eds., *Explorations in Social Change* (Boston: Houghton Mifflin, 1964), pp. 401-31, or Zollschan and Hirsch, eds., *Social Change: Explorations, Diagnoses, and Conjectures* (Cambridge, Mass.: Schenkman, 1976), pp. 583-613.

3.   See note 33 of Chapter 8 for an extended discussion of this point.

4.   There is much that could be said, and that Schneider does say—here and elsewhere in his writings—about such refinements as types of irony, degrees of irony, and whether irony is a characteristic of events themselves or only of our perceptions (or reports) of events. For the sake of discussion as general as that in this section it may be sufficient to view irony, narrowly, as a characteristic of reports—e.g., sentences—about events. Thus, sociological description or explanation can be said to be ironic to the extent that it contains ironic statements, and the sociologist can be said to be employing an ironic focus to the extent that he produces such statements. In view of Schneider's frequent cautions to this effect, it should not be necessary to add—but it may still deserve reiteration—that a report, sentence, etc. may be ironic but also false, nonironic but also true. In such cases, the sociologist is obviously constrained to support a nonironic interpretation; such are the limits of the ironic focus as a "sensitizer" or heuristic. For additional comments see our article "Irony and Technology," *Social Science Quarterly* 63 (June 1982):293-311.

5

Some Psychiatric Views on Freedom and the Theory of Social Systems

(1949)

The existing collaboration between psychiatry and social science is regarded by numerous practitioners of each as highly desirable. As this collaboration continues it is to be expected that psychiatrists and social scientists will come to scrutinize more carefully some of the basic suppositions emanating from each side. While this will undoubtedly be mutually clarifying, it is also to be anticipated that many difficulties will appear on the way, as indeed, they have done already. To cite a well-known instance, sociologists and anthropologists—and a number of psychiatrists also, for that matter—could scarcely be satisfied with the various pseudo-sociological pronouncements delivered by Freud in *Totem and Taboo, The Future of an Illusion, Civilization and Its Discontents,* or *Moses and Monotheism.* It would be unfortunate to allow any avoidable accumulation of such difficulties. The collaborative enterprises on which social scientists and psychiatrists engage are in any case sufficiently intrinsically demanding. This chapter is designed to suggest a few difficulties that appear in the areas of convergence of psychiatry and social science and that seem particularly to need airing. Our procedure will be to outline a strain of thinking about social systems that has been manifested in a considerable amount of psychiatric literature and that clearly calls for criticism. To help in understanding this strain, some preliminary exposition of selected psychiatric views on "culture" is necessary. To put the strain in better perspective, some general comments will subsequently be made on the operation of social systems. Consideration will have to be given to the socialization process as this procedure is carried out. The intent is friendly but serious.

Psychiatrists, along with many others, have become deeply concerned about the trend in world affairs. They often experience a feeling of responsibility which makes them eager to assess their own possible contributions to the causes of peace, prosperity, and well-being. If it would require a curious insensitivity not to be rejoiced over this, it may nevertheless be suggested that there has sometimes been more of commendable good will than of thoughtfulness in the relevant statements psychiatrists have made. From a certain limited—and, within specific limits, legitimate—point of view there is perhaps little to dispute in the quoted words that follow, but from certain other points of view, as will be shown, they will seem to strike a strident note:

> Man's freedom to observe and to think . . . present in all children and known as innocence, has been destroyed or crippled by local certainties, by gods of local moralities, of local loyalty, of personal salvation, of prejudice and hate and intolerance—frequently masquerading as love—gods of everything that would destroy freedom to observe and to think and would keep each generation under the control of the old people, the elders, the shamans, and the priests.[1]

Various criticisms, implicit or explicit, of the social order are quite in the tradition of psychiatry. There are six to which special attention may be given.

Socialization, the very process of "humanizing" the human being by way of internalization of norms, is a crude and rough affair accompanied by many "failures." Even so loose and general a typological division of individuals as that suggested by the categories, "under-socialized," "over-socialized," and "adequately socialized"[2] evidently emphasizes this. The apparent incidence in most diverse cultures as well as in our own of neuroses and psychoses—insofar as not constitutional—would on the whole indicate that the roughnesses and crudenesses that are dealt with here might be extremely difficult to eradicate. Perhaps this even puts the matter too conservatively. There is no necessary dispute here between psychiatrists and social scientists. "Certainly the social science approach has nowhere revealed an easy process by which the individual is assimilated to the cultural norm; the process involves constant struggle," remarks Gardner Murphy.[3]

Closely allied with this emphasis is another which draws attention to the emotional *costs* incident to the socialization process. Here the intent is not so much to stress such relatively gross phenomena as "failures" of the process but rather to call attention to the burdens borne in connection with it even by those who may be said to be more or less "adequate" or "successful" products. This emphasis is an entirely familiar one. Freud made it upon any number of occasions, and it is quite characteristic of him, for example, to "raise the question whether our 'civilized' sexual morality is worth the sacrifice which it imposes upon us."[4] "Civilization" in broad fashion itself demands countless "sacrifices," hurts man grievously, and indeed sits upon him much less securely than popular illusions on this matter would indicate.[5] Moreover, Freud considers all this inevitable. While it is true that man has also a "higher nature" in the form of an ego-ideal or super-ego which represents the moral precipitate of his relations to his parents; while it is true that "social feelings" resting on the "foundation of identification with others" exist; and while it may be contended that man is a much more "moral"—as well as much more "immoral"—creature than he inclines to think himself[6]—still, there is a strong stress in Freud on the view that ultimately "civilization" is confronted with the extremely difficult and always uncertain task of coping with a terrible "savage." "Civilization" may touch upon the "savage" lightly; it may induce in him an external, merely expedient conformity; and—most to the point for present purposes—if by its oppressions it does not succeed in making him ill, there is always a good chance that it will make him acutely uncomfortable. It is unnecessary to agree with many of Freud's particular views in order to agree on the very general point that "civilization" is emotionally costly.

The third point, again, is quite closely allied with the first two. It is in fact differentiated from the first two only in that it shifts attention from the particulars of the socialization process to "culture" or "civilization" as such. "Culture" itself shows varying degrees of "expensiveness" and exhibits numerous distressing "contradictions." The matter of how individual psychiatrists react to this general orientation, whether "pessimistically," or with hope for the future, and so on, may be for the moment left aside. Also, it is impossible to give a complete catalogue of, say, the "contradictions" that have been pointed to even within the limits of our own "Western" society. A few random choices of relevant statements that psychiatrists are likely to make or to sympathize with will reveal contentions: that there continually occur certain not atypical but very onerous shifts in social demand, such as the shift from an insistence on a consistently peaceable disposition to the abrupt requirement that pugnacity be shown to enemies in war, or the shift from a prohibitive or inhibitive attitude toward sexuality to the expectation that it shall express itself easily in marital relations; that economic misfortunes still tend to be more or less exclusively construed as the outcome of personal shortcomings, thereby generating a strong sense of guilt, although the responsible factors may well be altogether outside the person's control; that there is emphasis upon Christian kindliness but a person frequently confronts the necessity of being rather considerably less than kindly; that there occurs within particular strata the building up and encouragement of character constellations that conduce to frugality, thrift, and a wary caution, while inspection of the newer economic realities shows that these traits no longer "pay off"; that general goals on the lines of "success" and "eminence" are held out to all, and all are effectively bombarded by media of communication that diffuse the conviction of the excellence of these goals, while at the same time there exists a monopoly on the legitimate, limited means to their attainment.

There is once more, on this third point, no reason for serious disagreements. These and other "contradictions" might certainly be more carefully formulated; nearly all are now rather impressionistic and casual statements, although the brilliance of some is undeniable. But if more rigor is desirable in these premises, they nevertheless constitute a field in which it may be anticipated that some of the most fruitful collaboration is yet to come.

The fourth point is that the mass of men in any culture are likely to be more or less standardized cultural products lacking keen insight into the limitations and arbitrariness of the norms they follow or adhere to; only a favored few constitute something like an emancipated (psychological) elite. Some of Jung's views bring this point out incisively enough. The division of labor in modern society, he contends, following certain hints of Schiller's, demands that man develop to a high pitch certain special and highly specialized functions to the neglect of others. The system of division of labor, indeed, once it exists full blown, demands further specialization, further adaptation to narrow and meticulous tasks that exhaust the whole of the working life and inevitably affect the character of living itself. Men tend to get stamped in a common mold that may be economically valuable, say, but which deprives them of "individuality." Jung in fact hints that any particular culture is likely to show a special normative organization, or selection and structuring of values, making a claim to universal validity and thereby exhibiting the presence of a "power principle." When there occurs renunciation of this power principle—that is, in Jung's language, "of the claim to a generally valid standpoint on the strength of one differentiated and generally adapted function,"—then "the direct outcome of this renunciation is *individualism,* i.e., the necessity for a realization of individuality, a realization of man as he is."[7] It is peculiarly true of the "neurotic" that he shows high potentialities for becoming "man as he is." If the "natural" or "archaic" man—and this is a distinctively Jungian phrase—can be made to emerge beneath the confusions of the "neurotic," those confusions can be dissolved along with the inappropriate and badly assimilated trappings of the "collectively orientated consciousness." For the mass of men, there is little hope: They are doomed to live their lives in the ruts of convention, which represents indeed a "collective necessity" but is nevertheless "a makeshift and not an ideal";[8] for the "neurotic" there is a real chance that with proper psychiatric aid he may become "free," "himself," and throw off the trammels imposed by the "gods of local moralities, of local loyalty," and so on.

I wish at this point to note only two matters that will be considered more fully later. First, the close relationship of this line of thinking with the *clinical experience* of the psychiatrist should never be overlooked. Difficulties arise precisely when this is forgotten and ambitious generalization from clinic to culture is attempted. Second, the phrase "man as he is" bristles with complexities that exemplify well just the problems the psychiatrist faces in making the transition from clinic to culture. For the rest, and for our purposes, Jung's view may be regarded as quite legitimate. There is no intention of seriously denying the close involvement of masses of men in the terms, definitions, and prescriptions of their culture, nor is the contention denied that the "neurotic" may be peculiarly capable, at least potentially, of a large degree of emancipation from "convention."

Jung, however far he may be from many contemporary psychiatrists on a large number of points, is also close to many in this particular matter. Thus, Erich Fromm, who on a variety of other matters is far removed indeed from Jung, states:

> The problem of selfishness has a particular bearing on psychotherapy. The neurotic individual often is *selfish* in the sense that he is blocked in his relationship to others or overanxious about himself. This is to be expected since to be neurotic means that the integration of a strong self has not been achieved successfully. It means, for the majority of *well-adapted* individuals, that they have lost their own self at an early age and replaced it completely by a *social self* offered to them by society. . . . If the *neurotic* becomes well, he does not become *normal* in the sense of the conforming *social self*. He succeeds in realizing his self, which never had been completely lost and for the preservation of which he was stuggling by his neurotic symptoms.[9]

It appears again that the "normal" person is rather thoroughly "conventionalized"—not "himself," a kind of cultural automaton—whereas the "neurotic" may with proper help find a genuine rather than a merely "social self." Again, we will bear in mind the thus far very meagerly indicated difficulties that have been noted just above for Jung's similar views.

A fifth point of criticism may be stated by way of a paraphrase of what are in effect psychiatric commonplaces: All of the above involves men in great difficulties in their enterprise of living together. Especially may it be noted by the psychiatrist that men tend to be emotionally wedded to antique modes of conduct that prove utterly inappropriate to the necessities of survival and "health" in a changing social scene. "Though He slay me yet will I trust in Him." The convention which Jung character-ized as a "makeshift" rather than an "ideal" reveals its makeshift character most plainly in critical times. And great penalties may be paid and may still have to be paid for the luxury of holding to familiar and established ways when responsible and mature persons would realize the necessity for more "adaptive" behavior. Again Jung anticipates later comment well enough: "The mechanism of convention keeps people *un-conscious* and then, like wild game, they can follow their customary run-ways without the necessity of conscious choice. This unintentional effect of even the best conventions is unavoidable, and it is also a terrible danger" since "new conditions not provided for by the old conventions" may arise.[10]

There is no occasion for quarrel with these views which, except as they may be distinctively colored by the psychiatrist's special insights into the emotional aspects of adherence to conventional ways, are shared by a good many others who are not psychiatrists.[11] It will be a part of the subsequent task of this paper in dealing with social systems to give this particular point a somewhat wider context.

It will be economical to illustrate the sixth point of criticism by reference to some of Jung's views once more. This criticism is perhaps necessarily a rather vague and unsatisfactory one. It consists in an in-timation that the "burden of culture" or of a particular culture may become so great, so radically uncongenial with man's basic "needs" that he may somehow revolt against it. Jung, it may be recalled, distinguished between "inferior" and "superior" functions. Roughly, the "inferior" functions—Jung is as far as possible from intending an imputation of in-trinsic inferiority when he calls them this[12]—are human functions that re-main in arrears in a process of development and differentiation. Thus under the modern system of division of labor, the function of working as a kind of highly specialized machine-appendage making an economically valuable contribution—the "superior" function—may be very well elaborated while other human potentialities, possible developments of other, "inferior" functions, are neglected. And Jung then states somewhat obscurely, but nevertheless with a hint that he is discussing something which will ultimately prove intolerable:

> But this one-sided development must inevitably lead to a reaction since the repressed inferior functions cannot be indefinitely excluded from common life and development. The time will come when "the cleavage in the inner man must again be resolved," that the undeveloped may be granted an op-portunity to live.[13]

It is extremely difficult to evaluate this. It must remain in the sphere of vague intimations. An implicit appeal to human "needs" is bound to be imprecise in the degree in which the "needs" fail to be specified. The idea involved may have value, and it is possible to conceive of limiting cases—for example, the case of a society that demanded complete abstention from food on the part of its members and would thereby either perish or provoke revolt against its prescriptions—which would at least illustrate it well, but it would require considerable refinement and investigation before it could be profitably used by psychiatrists or social scientists.[14]

With qualifications, there is warrant for these criticisms. The reactions to them have been fairly sharp and distinctive. Freud's, for example, was in many respects quite "pessimistic." One must not expect too much, generally, from this uncertain animal man, filled as he is with illusions and endowed as he is with dangerous and difficult-to-process drives. In view of the nature of "civilization" and of man, attempts at basic reforms do not appear particularly likely to be profitable. Conceivably, Erich Fromm's characterization of Freud as *"ein klassischer Vertreter des patrizentischen Charaktertype"*[15] may be overdrawn, but it is still a thesis for which a reasonable amount of evidence can be assembled that Freud was very far from hostile to the values current in the civilization he knew and, more especially, that he would have looked askance at reformist efforts.[16] Jung ended on a note of great approval for the "free" man, the man who has been rid of the trammels of "convention"—and at times the distinction between the man who is "free" in the clinically significant sense or the man who has with psychiatric aid worked out an "original" standpoint, on the one hand, and, on the other hand, the man who is in any way "exceptional" or a "leader" tends to blur—while expressing contempt, perhaps even hatred, for more ordinary, convention-filled beings. The masses, he says, "as we know too well—are blind beasts." He refers to "the historical fact that the great, liberating deeds of world history have come from leading personalities," but "never from the inert mass that is secondary at all times and needs the demagogue if it is to move at all."[17] These two types of reactions are here merely mentioned. A type of reaction of more immediate interest—with the qualification that it still incorporates *some* of Jung's notions—is expressed by Erich Fromm, who, also against a background of criticisms of the general character of those outlined above, would recommend that man now be "himself," or "for himself," and that he exercise his "freedom to."[18] Some of Fromm's relevant ideas are chosen precisely because they are not idiosyncratic, as the most casual inspection of pertinent literature will reveal.

From the time of some of Freud's original discussions of the nature of man, a wraith has haunted psychoanalytical writing: the figure of a human being somehow distinctively *human* and yet somehow also appearing as "spontaneous man" or "natural man" or, in Jung's phrasing, "archaic man." The reference in the appeals made to this figure is not to a set of distinctive biological potentialities proper to man, but to something that is in some unspecified fashion concrete, a good deal more "already realized," so to put it. The burden of proof and of clarification is, of course, on those who hold to the validity of referring to such a figure, although their language will seldom run on these lines. But that such a figure persists in contemporary psychoanalytical thought cannot be doubted. Thus, a good deal of what is currently spoken of as "freedom" covertly implies the image of the "archaic" or "natural" man. Nothing is more impossible humanly than to be "free" in other than a relative sense. "Freedom" *qua* word is a general descriptive term covering cases of concrete "freedom" which are always relative to specific conditions of environment and circumstances. That the psychoanalyst, say, should be concerned with "freedom" is entirely understandable and entirely legitimate in view of his peculiar business. That he should be concerned, at least from certain special points of view, with the fortunes of the social world and of "freedom" within it and that he should take seriously and examine the implications of criticism of the type we have outlined—this again is entirely understandable. But it is of great importance to recall the particular clinical sources of the psychoanalyst's devotion to the idea of "freedom."

Upon completion of a highly successful psychoanalytical therapy a person who has greatly suffered from, say, "ridigity," who sharply manifests "discrepancy between potentialities and accomplishments,"[19] and so on, manages to attain considerable "flexibilty," to realize his potentialities, to develop considerable self-confidence, to function harmoniously, without serious or incapacitating self-conflicts. It is certainly then justifiable to say that he is in some sense "free," whereas previously he was not. But in just what sense? He has been freed from certain devastating conflicts, he is "happier," he can expend energies on "externals" that were before expended in fruitless "internal" self-engagements. But is he perfectly "free" to act like a Roman centurion or a Trobriand Islander? Would he even want to? He still exists necessarily as a being, relative to time, place, the hopes and expectations of relatives and friends—many of which he probably wants to fulfill—and even the circumstances of his upbringing. Whereas previously he was "neurotic" restaurateur on a main avenue in a big city, he is now perhaps a "free" or non- "neurotic" restauranteur on a main avenue in a big city. It is impossible to be "free" in any absolute sense even if one grants that the restaurateur might become a playwright or indeed a psychiatrist. He would always have to be somebody or something in particular, and thereby he would have a specific self and specific roles. Is freedom originality? Then it is always a specific kind of originality. It is not possible to be "original" *in abstracto*. The very pre-condition of "freedom" —or originality, and so on—is a *set of limitations*. To emerge into human-ness and in fact to envisage the problems of "freedom," man must be a particular, and particularly, specifically socialized being.[20]

If the "freedom" that the "neurotic" may attain is therefore a concrete, particular, culturally conditioned, and culturally relevant "freedom," how shall he become a man "as he is" or "man himself"? How reach down to the very roots of human-ness and become simply "man"? Is there a being with highly specific presocial traits, whatever they might be, for whom the psychiatrist would probe and whom he would release? Some such being, however vaguely, is postulated by implication. He is still after all a "natural man" even when he has repented the old cannibalistic and homicidal traits which Freud imputed to him and now appears as "innocent" and "free." One may recall the contention by Fromm with regard to those he calls "well-adapted" individuals that "they have lost their own self at an early age and replaced it completely by a *social self* offered to them by society." This really has two aspects. With the first there is no quarrel. It follows on the lines of the fourth criticism noted above. Insofar as it may be shown that men have merely unoriginally taken the stamp of current and local social norms and are highly conventionalized creatures, perhaps unimaginatively, dully, and at least without undue protest, psychic or otherwise—"without the noise of a neurosis," as Fromm puts it—going through their daily routines, it may be legitimately claimed that, for a number of them at any rate, certain possibilities or potentialities in the way of "freedom" and "independence," as the analyst understands those terms, remain unrealized. But there is a second aspect. *Everyone* must in degree possess a "social self." It is only when that is regarded as a *pure imposition* on something natively and intrinsically "good" and "unspoiled" and somehow *existent apart from the incidents of the social process* that it seems reasonable to say without qualification that the "own self" has been lost early in life and completely replaced by a "social self." Is the "neurotic" actually helped to the realization of an "own self" that is in no manner a "social self"? (When the question is asked in this bald and extreme form, everyone will of course answer in the negative; but it is just because this line of thinking appears as a kind of sleeping, quiescent element that it can exercise the influence it does.) Then indeed does the psychiatrist plumb abysmal depths and come up with "man himself," perhaps "man as he *really* is," whatever he may then be. The same psychiatrists who have made excellent contributions to understanding of the socialization process, which makes man "human," paradoxically tend to forget that he does not become "human" except in society. The individual "neurotic," when he becomes well with help, does not individually attain the status of "man." Rather, the "noise of the neurosis" has been abated, and he is mentally well but still, and again, a very particular kind of man.

It may be granted that some social systems may more readily generate mental illness than others or that "freedom" may be generally easier to achieve in some societies than in others, but that is an altogether different matter. The projection of concepts and descriptive terms elaborated in the clinic onto the social structure is provocative and frequently stimulating, but it carries definite dangers. Thus, Fromm's concepts of "freedom from" and "freedom to," which have an unmistakable clinical flavor, are employed in reference to mass conditions in a fashion that is no doubt to some extent illuminating. But when we say that a person who has reached a certain point in psychoanalytical treatment is afraid of his own "freedom to," the meaning is clear enough. The image of himself that a convalescing "neurotic" has had may have involved the presumption that to make free, independent, and congenial decisions about various matters was incredible audacity, and perhaps he still looks timidly back to a self-inhibition that at least did not involve the burden of responsibility for himself. But if all this is defensible, the "leap of faith" that now comes is not. Fromm states:

> Man has built his world, he has built factories and houses, he produces cars and clothes, he grows grain and fruit. But he has become estranged from the product of his own hands, he is not really the master any more of the world he has built; on the contrary, this man-made world has become his master, before whom he bows down, whom he tries to placate, or to manipulate as best he can.[21]

Accordingly, Fromm ends *Escape from Freedom* with the following words:

> Only if man masters society and subordinates the economic machine to the purposes of human happiness and only if he actively participates in the social process, can he overcome what now drives him into despair—his aloneness and his feeling of powerlessness. Man does not suffer so much from poverty today as he suffers from the fact that he has become a cog in a large machine, an automaton. . . . [Democracy] will triumph over the forces of nihilism only if it can imbue people with a faith that is the strongest the human mind is capable of, the faith in life and in truth, and in freedom as the active and spontaneous realization of the individual self.[22]

None of this, of course, is intended to pass for concrete prescription. But is it unfair to ask just what is meant by man's "mastering society" and how he is to do it? How can a start be made unless man emerges and develops in an already established concrete social context? Man's "freedom to" must be a *norm* or *value* fostered and cherished by some kind of consensus if it is going to achieve any wide realization. It may actually help to obscure this important circumstance to say that "inasmuch as social and parental authority tend to break his will, spontaneity, and independence, the child, not being born to be broken, fights against the authority represented by his parents; he fights for his freedom not only from, but also for his freedom to be himself—a full-fledged human being, not an automaton."[23] Or, at any rate, in making this kind of statement it is crucial not to confuse psychological and sociological levels of discourse. Otherwise, it once more becomes only too easy to envisage, in effect, a "good," "natural" man from whose "spontaneous" interactions with others a "good society" will emerge.[24] But this is of course quite impossible. A social system will not arise out of nothing. Fromm indeed has an occasional saving awareness of this.[25] But the *strain* of thought I have noted remains nevertheless.

Even if one accepts for the most part the six criticisms of the social order that have been set out, it scarcely follows that anyone would seriously suggest that that order be entirely "scrapped." It is in fact difficult to determine what such a suggestion would mean. Unless the sixth point of criticism in regard to the utterly radical uncongeniality of social institutions has larger merits than would now appear, and a kind of holistic revolt against those institutions is due—with perhaps an added presumption that man's frustrated basic "needs" are somehow going to build a new order—evidently all that could be suggested is a concrete set of changes. However, on the suspicion that some serious confusions about social systems persist, and in order to clarify the statement that it appears to us that there is a strident note in Dr. Chisholm's previously quoted strictures on local certainties, and so on, I would like to undertake such an outline of some important aspects of social systems as is feasible within the compass of a brief paper. Would the "innocence" of which Dr. Chisholm speaks flower in the absence of local certainties and local moralities? Would it appear spontaneously, without need for social arrangements of any kind? Or would it require the emergence of distinctive types of groups that have scarcely appeared before and that would call for new and special expedients to be fostered on a large scale? Once more, it is necessary to separate issues that are at separate levels. It cannot be at all doubted that in a defensible psychoanalytical sense release from local certainties, from "the control of the old people, the elders, the shamans, and the priests," may help to produce "freedom." But the issue involved with this is not identical, and is all too readily confused, with relevant sociological issues.

In connection with the model of social systems that I wish to set out briefly, an initial pertinent proposition is that such systems must meet certain conditions or realize definable "functional prerequisites" if they are to survive and continue.[26] Among the more obvious of these requisites are the self-maintenance of the personnel or agents of the system through an adequate food supply, their continuation either through biological self-reproduction or some other means,[27] and the management of their aggressions and hostilities within the margin of disruption of the system through slaughter or complete alienation. Certain limits are imposed by these requisites or conditions. Thus, to carry to "extremes" a practice of having old men marry young women and boys old women would not comport with survival necessities. A second pertinent proposition is that the functional requisites, although indispensable, are not necessarily made objects of conscious endeavor. However, the agents of the social system must be stimulated, or "motivated," in such fashion that they will act to bring about, as the conjoint effect of their individual actions, the functional requisites.

The manner in which the agents of a system are motivated to act in accordance with requisites the system must subserve is well illustrated by the case of the birth rate. In his private capacity one is not ordinarily interested in "reproducing the race." It takes a somewhat special set of circumstances for a substantial portion of a nation to become concerned about such a matter. For example, in the case of the Swedes in the 1930s, there was an awareness of a low national birth rate, some anxiety about possible extinction as a distinct national entity since others might be tempted to press in upon the land and resources of a declining population, wide popularization of relevant facts, and so on.[28] But under our older "rural-familistic" system the individual, although scarcely preoccupied with reproducing the race *qua* race, was provided with adequate motivation for marrying and having children. The individual was subject to constraints and afforded inducements—for instance, on economic lines—that "pushed" him in the direction of appropriate reproductive behavior. Alternative behavior would have appeared quaint or foolish. If, on the other hand, the older constraints and inducements impinging on individuals begin to fail, as mechanisms designed,[29] precisely in their working through numerous particular individuals to bring about the general effect of reproduction at, say, a rate sufficient to maintain a numerically stable population, then relevant motivation is no longer adequate. Of course, the assumption is made that "other things are equal"; situations may, plainly, arise in which a reduction rather than maintenance of the birth rate would comport well with "survival necessities." Under the older circumstances the requirement of survival or continuance was met not by a deliberate and widespread facing up to the requirement itself but through mechanisms which in their total effect guaranteed the requirement. There is a certain indirection in the meeting of the requisites of a social system. Since the requisites specified are as broad as they are, it may readily be seen that theoretically there might be a number of alternative ways of realizing them, although here also there would be some limitations.

There is a third set of considerations. Motivated individual actions have results—in the case of the birth rate, say, the result of fulfilling the requisite for survival—that are beyond the intentions of the individuals. It will be convenient accordingly to distinguish two phases of the operation of social systems: the *motivational* and the *synergic*. The former has just been briefly discussed; the latter refers precisely to the conjoint effects of motivated actions, looked at from the point of view of an observer not directly interested in motivation nor in its effects or results for an *individual*, but rather in its effects or results for a *social system*. In the case of the birth rate, given the very simple consideration of it that has been afforded, the synergic phase operates with utmost simplicity. It operates additively: if individual pair after individual pair produces a sufficient number of children, or if the reproduction rates are suffuciently high—under given conditions of age composition, hygiene, disease control, and so on—survival or continuance is automatically the result. But the synergic phase does not always operate so simply and "beneficently"—nor is it the case that there are never problems with regard to adequacy of motivation in the first place. Adam Smith's famous observation that the individual "intends only his own gain, and he is in this, as in many other cases, led by an invisible hand to promote an end which was no part of his intention,"[30] the end being of course the general welfare, is scarcely self-evident and appropriately evokes considerable skepticism today.[31]

It may be granted that situations are conceivable in which no "problems," no "troubles" need arise at either the motivational or synergic levels, virtually regardless of what the motivation might be. Thus, from the point of view of food supply, an environment for a very simply organized society might be positively paradisiac, and the impulse to pick up and ingest food to be had quite freely and plentifully might be all the motivation necessary for the agents of the society to survive. The question whether so uncomplicated a situation would ever actually be found is something else, as is also the question as to what conditions might prevail in other spheres than that of the commissariat. But it is clear that within the limits indicated neither the motivational nor the synergic levels would occasion serious "problems." It will, however, be useful to note the following possible combinations, in which the plus signs refer either to adequate motivation or beneficent results—"beneficent results" always in the sense of beneficent from the point of view of survival of a system, "health" of its agents, and so on—and the minus signs to their opposites:

	A	B	C	D
Motivational Level.	+	+	−	−
Synergic Level.	+	−	−	+

In Case A, agents are adequately motivated to do certain things necessary to, or having the effect of making for, the survival of the social system. If it is granted that *in concrete cases* they may *simultaneously* be doing other things not making for, or contra-indicating, the survival of the system, this type of action (1) will necessarily be held within bounds as long as we make the assumption that the system survives, and (2) may in any case be disregarded for present purposes. In Case B, agents are still adequately motivated, still carrying on action that was *but lately adaptive*[32] from the point of view of the system, but is now no longer so. This may occasion surprise, elicit denial, evoke anger, initiate a research for adventitious "interferences," and so on. Case C may be conceived as a further extension of Case B. Adaptive results are no longer attained, and thereby the social system, as in B, is in precarious condition, but now with the added circumstance that individuals are no longer even adequately motivated as they were in B and also in A. By way of illustration, in Case A, let us say, individuals pursue their private gain, and "general welfare" in some rationally acceptable sense does supervene. In Case B, let us say, individuals continue exclusively to pursue their own gain, but no amount of optimistic construction can make it appear that "general welfare" supervenes. In Case C, let us say, neither the prospect of gain nor any other instrumentality that might be effective in initiating work is any longer (adequately) motivating; for the time being, men will not work and in no sense is there general welfare.

Such a situation as this would of course soon be destructive, and, *empirically,* would very often be likely to figure as only one strain or component in a larger total situation. Concretely, too, there may often be varying margins of safety or indifference—from the point of view, again, of survival of a system—dependent on specific conditions, within which what would otherwise be pressing survival requirements may for varying lengths of time be neglected. Thus, at least for a time and even if with not very satisfactory results from any other than a biological point of view, a society might recruit needed new personnel exclusively from other societies. Case D, finally, involves the set of circumstances of the paradisiac type which is of little interest here, or else is quite impossible in fact or actuality: When men are not adequately motivated to do those things which, conjointly considered, will effect survival, then, other things equal, there will simply not be survival. This case is included only for logical completeness.[33]

It is now pertinent to review some of the rather familiar conditions necessary to ensure effective or adequate motivation and relate these to social systems. As is well known, the human being may be molded in a variety of ways, but a particular type of training is required to ensure his responsiveness to the norms and goals set out in any particular society, in a word, his "motivatability." Thus, Fromm indicates that the family is an agency for the "production of the socially desired psychological structure"—that is, that the family is in effect an instrument for turning out individuals psychically conformable to the situation of their time and place.[34] No social system can possibly operate by the direct exhortation of neonate recruits to act in conformity with the abstract requisites for survival of the system itself. It has already been implied and may now be stated directly that even for many fully adult members the connection between daily routine action and those same abstract requisites will be quite obscure, and no particular problems need arise from this obscurity as long as plus signs appear at both motivational and synergic levels. The previously referred to indirection in meeting the requisites of a social system is especially clear in the process of socialization, in the course of which there is established a "culturally standarized system of organization of the instincts and emotions of individuals."[35] A child obviously can scarcely be responsive to the consideration: "A certain minimum of order must be preserved in the community." The socialization process is indeed *emotionally* indispensable, to say nothing else, since the child is not a mature social philosopher. By the use of punishment to train and to inhibit, the exhibition of approval or disapproval, the presentation of examples of parental behavior to serve as paradigms, the use of cajolery, persuasion, encouragement, sarcasm, and at times rational argument, and so on, members of different societies ultimately make the new individual an agent of a particular social system in his own right. He is trained in the light of, and in conformity with, the surrounding conventional schemes and in time "internalizes" the appropriate values.[36] It may be possible in a particular society to eliminate some of the particular techniques just mentioned on the ground that they are undesirable—for example, sarcasm—but it is clear that they cannot *all* be eliminated: they are on the whole necessary to the building-in of moral furniture, so to put it. The importance of the socialization process for the present purpose is just that it constitutes a matrix for the development of motivatability, which has at least three aspects: (1) by socialization, *acceptable* (motivated) behavior is produced; (2) in the ideal case—and always in degree, unless a social system is not to survive—the acceptable behaviors of individuals conduce also, at the synergic level, to fulfillment of the requisites of a social system; (3) by socialization, actions that contra-indicate or are irrelevant to survival necessities may also be motivated, but will "normally" be held within bounds.

There is a sense in which the more "successful" the socialization is the more dangerous it may become from the point of view of functional requisites realized at the synergic level. In a more or less "static" society, this danger may be minimal. Insofar as a going social scheme is achieving beneficent end-results and the socialization process turns out reasonably "conforming" individuals, no particular "trouble" need arise. But insofar as a social system begins to fail in the achievement of beneficent results—as when an economic scheme "breaks down" and falls short of certain minima in the provision of necessities of life[37]—and values and conduct which are designed to support that system continue in full force in their old form, a significant shift takes place. The situation changes from one in which the always indispensable socialization process effects "functionally useful" end-results to one in which the normative elements involved in socialization have become positively inhibitive and prevent support for social changes that would allow better realization of "functionally useful" end-results. In this type of situation, social belt lines, so to put it, still function well enough at the motivational level but falter at the synergic level. This only connects the socialization process with Case B in the table of cases, and one should therefore expect, again, that this type of situation will stimulate self-scrutiny and prompt the recasting of cultural ideals. If one recognizes the indispensability of the socialization process and is at the same time aware that "adequate" or "successful" socialization may pass into "over-socialization"—that is, in this *immediate* context, socialization that goes to the point of inhibiting changes called for by non-beneficent synergic effects—it is easy enough to make some very general appropriate comments to the effect that we must reconcile and combine "moral rules" with "flexibility."[38] But the concrete achievement of such a reconciliation is something else. No social system has yet worked out techniques for a foolproof or frictionless solution of this problem.

This is scarcely an occasion for extended discussion of the possibilities inherent in social planning. All that it is necessary to note for the present purpose is that even the most enlightened planning and the most enlightened socialization could still not dispense with the socialization process itself. Conscientious planning might conceivably change greatly many particular incidents of prior socialization processes, but the training of the neonate would still have to be undertaken to insure his minimum responsiveness to whatever goals and norms might be set out in a new social scheme. Even with the best will in the world toward planning, it would indeed appear that one of the "perversions" to which planning is subject is precisely the attempt to make the socialization process an extremely rigid affair. This is not to deny that our best resources may be needed when, say, synergically beneficent results are not attained. Society may even wish to plan carefully for a variety of beneficent results; it may also wish to plan "for freedom," either as the psychiatrist understands the term or in any case in senses closely connected with his manner of understanding it. This is perhaps concretely difficult, but there is no reason to deny in the abstract that it can be done.

However, "archaic man," "freeman," "man himself" can never emerge and come to triumph. Grant that some miracle, such as therapeutically effective and universal psychoanalysis, could take place, the beneficiaries of the miracle would still have to raise and train a new generation and thereby would have to train them in *norms* or *rules* of behavior. Either these would be such *general* norms that their utility as guidelines to action in numerous concrete social situations that children and adults must encounter would be in doubt, or they would be more *concrete, particularized* norms, and in that case they would very likely *in time* become useless or dangerous while some "misguided" individuals would continue to hold to them.[39] They would in fact appear as the "gods of local moralities" all over again. It may be suggested that these "gods"—that is, the conventions—cannot be eliminated and yet that there will continually be refusal to make obeisance to them. "There will always be a certain appeal in the doctrine that the spirit is not at home in this world," says the philosopher Santayana, and we may take this in the sense that whatever conventions may flourish—and *some* conventions will continually flourish—and however "fine" they may be, man will still be gratifyingly capable of discontents and visions that will make him critical of them. With these discontents the psychiatrist may have the highest sympathy. When either the effects at the synergic level of a social system are nonbeneficent or the costs on the way to them are very large— from, say, the point of view of the psychiatrist—personal values may again dictate the summoning of society's best efforts toward improvement; but it is always a matter precisely of continuing efforts and not conceivably one of a finished Utopian pattern realized because *"man"* has at last become "himself" or thrown off for good the yoke of local deities, local certainties, local moralities.

Notes

1. G.B. Chisholm, "the Psychiatry of Enduring Peace and Social Progress," *Psychiatry* 9 (1946):8.
2. Clyde Kluckhohn and H. A. Murray, eds., *Personality in Nature, Society and Culture* (New York: Knopf, 1948), p. 27.
3. Gardner Murphy, *Personality: A Bio-Social Approach to Origins and Structure* (New York: Harper, 1947), p. 903.
4. Sigmund Freud, *Collected Papers* (London: Hogarth Press, 1942), 2:99.
5. See, e.g., *Civilization and Its Discontents* (London: Hogarth Press, 1939) and "Thoughts for the Times on War and Death," in *Collected Papers* (London: Hogarth Press, 1934), 4:288-317.
6. See *The Ego and the Id* (London: Hogarth Press, 1935), pp. 47, 49, 75-76.
7. *Psychological Types* (New York: Harcourt, Brace, 1923), pp. 132-33. Virtually the whole of this work is useful for the understanding of Jung's opposition between "freedom" and "convention," which is set out with his characteristic combination of brilliance and bombast.
8. Carl G. Jung, *The Integration of the Personality* (New York: Farrar & Rinehart, 1939), p. 290.
9. Erich Fromm, "Selfishness and Self-Love," *Psychiatry* 2 (1939):522.
10. Jung, *Personality,* p. 295.
11. For one example out of a great number, compare Gunnar Myrdal's comment on "the tremendous social costs of keeping up the present irrational and legal caste system," in *An American Dilemma* (New York: Harper, 1944), p. 1009, especially in the context of ch. 45.
12. Jung, *Types,* pp. 100, 563-65.
13. Ibid., pp. 95-96.
14. Intimations substantially similar and similarly vague are sometimes set forth by social scientists: "A human social maze may be so constituted that the planned society can train its citizenry from infancy to learn to act as rational men in a rational social universe. But these same men and women are composed of muscle and bone, viscera and nerves, and animal impulses. As members of their species they possess a sub-cultural interaction system of behavior which is species behavior, which existed before culture and still lives within it. . . . No people can impose logical and rational action on its social order too far without experiencing serious and possibly disastrous results." W. L. Warner and J.O. Low, *The Social System of the Modern Factory* (New Haven: Yale University Press, 1947), p. 192.
15. "Die Gesellschaftliche Bedingthelt der Psychoanalytischen Therapie," in *Zeitschrift für Sozialforschung* 4 (1935):384.
16. Compare the interesting defense of Freud on this matter by Roland Dalbriez, in *Psychoanalytical Method and the Doctrine of Freud* (New York: Longmans, Green, 1941), 2:311.
17. Jung, *Personality,* pp. 274, 281.

18. See especially Fromm's *Escape from Freedom* (New York: Farrar & Rinehart, 1941) and *Man for Himself* (New York: Rinehart, 1947).
19. See Karen Horney, *The Neurotic Personality of Our Time* (New York: Norton, 1937), p. 22.
20. In analogous vein, Green appropriately comments on the statement that there is "only one meaning of life—the act of living itself." "No society of which we have any knowledge has ever resembled the Garden of Eden: men have lived and can live, only for various ends—the clan, the guild, the family; to kill, to succeed, to spread the Word of God, to renounce the world in monastic seclusion—but certainly not 'to live.' " A. W. Green, "Sociological Analysis of Horney and Fromm," *American Journal of Sociology* 51 (1946):538.
21. Fromm, *Freedom,* p. 117.
22. Ibid., p. 276.
23. Fromm, *Man for Himself,* p. 157.
24. Compare Green, "Horney and Fromm," for some further suggestive comments. There are some important points of resemblance between Fromm's conception of "freedom to" and what the sociologist Emile Durkheim discussed under the heading of *"égoisme."* The latter may be briefly defined as a type of relationship of individual to group (as in Protestantism, by contrast with Catholicism) in which the *group norm* is that the individual shall be "on his own," find his own way to God, etc. See E. Durkheim, *Le Suicide* (Paris: Alcan, 1930), pp. 149-232; and Talcott Parsons, *The Structure of Social Action* (New York: McGraw-Hill, 1937), pp. 332-34. The clear emphasis on the background by way of group norm is quite lacking in Fromm. Durkheim also demonstrated broadly that *égoisme* made for a high suicide rate, which is not incompatible with Fromm's emphasis that along with "freedom from" there has supervened considerable loneliness and a sense of isolation. A practical problem in this sphere, for one who values "freedom to," and yet regrets loneliness and isolation, would be how to preserve "freedom" while maintaining a certain level of relatedness. On the *sociological* level, there is not the faintest suggestion of a genuine answer to this on Fromm's part. If Durkheim could be guilty of "agelicism" (a term of E. Benoit-Smullyan's to describe "group-ism" or that bent in sociological thinking that seeks to attribute to "the group" all values, categories of thought, and important contents of thought; compare Benoit-Smullyan's "The Development of French Sociologism and Its Critics in France" [Ph.D. dissertation, Harvard University, 1937]), writers like Fromm are in an important part of their thought capable of a close approach to individualistic anarchism.
25. He states, for example, in contrasting the "humanistic" and "authoritarian" conscience: "It needs to be emphasized that the difference between humanistic and authoritarian conscience is not that the latter is molded by the cultural tradition, while the former develops independently. On the contrary, it is similar in this respect to our capacities of speech and thought, which, though intrinsic human potentialities, develop only in a social and cultural context." Green, "Horney and Fromm," pp. 171-72. Or, elsewhere, "I believe that *in a cultural situation in which respect for the individuality* and integrity of every person—hence of every child—*is realized,*

the Oedipus complex will belong to the past. . . ." "The Oedipus Myth," *Scientific American* 180 (1948):27 (italics added).
26.   For a recent clear statement of this line of theory and some of its implications, see A. K. Cohen, "On the Place of 'Themes' and Kindred Concepts in Social Theory," *American Anthropologist* 50 (1948):436-43. Compare also Talcott Parsons, "The Present Position and Prospects of Systematic Theory in Sociology," in Georges Gurvitch and W. E. Moore, eds., *Twentieth Century Sociology* (New York: Philosophical Library, 1945) pp. 42-69; and J. W. Bennett and M. M. Tumin, *Social Life: Structure and Function* (New York: Knopf, 1948), chs. 2, 4.
27.   As Cohen succinctly states, "Any given system is viable only if it includes adequate arrangements of *procuring, maintaining and motivating* the human material of which it is made." " 'Themes' and Kindred Concepts," p. 436. The "motivating" of human material will be considered immediately.
28.   See Alva Myrdal, *Nation and Family* (New York: Harper, 1941).
29.   The language employed is consciously metaphorical. In the absence of an appropriate vocabulary one is constrained in these premises to metaphor, which can, it must be acknowledged, lead astray, as sharply indicated by D. Gregg and E. Williams, in "The Dismal Science of Functionalism," *American Anthropologist* 50 (1948):594-611; these writers, however, in criticizing functionalism, wish to throw out the baby with the bath.
30.   Edwin Cannan, ed., *The Wealth of Nations* (New York: Modern Library, 1938), p. 423. One learns from Smith, states J. M. Clark, that "nature implants impulses in man's breast which are wiser than his reason since nature intends always the good of the species and endows man with social sentiments . . . the pursuit of happiness through wealth is elusive, but justified, by its results, through this same wisdom of nature." *A Preface to Social Economics* (New York: Farrar & Rinehart, 1936), p. 188. Smith's view thus appears to be that a somewhat "shabby" motivation terminates synergically in a beneficent result.
31.   The term "synergic" may seem confusing and an affected substitute for such phrases as "unanticipated consequences." Thus, compare Robert K. Merton, "The Unanticipated Consequences of Purposive Social Action," *American Sociological Review* 1 (1936):894-904; also Karl Popper's contention that "only a minority of social institutions are consciously designed while the vast majority have just 'grown' as the undesigned results of human action . . . undersigned social institutions may develop as *unintended consequences of rational actions;* just as a road may be formed without any special intention by people who find it convenient to use a track already existing." In "The Poverty of Historicism, II," *Economica,* N.S., 11(1944):122, 122, n. 3; and Morris R. Cohen's contrast between "the little drops of human volition" and "the general social streams which result from them," in *Reason and Nature* (New York: Harcourt, Brace, 1931), p. 342. (Compare also C. I. Barnard's use of the phrase "unsought consequences" in *The Functions of the Executive* [Cambridge: Harvard University Press, 1948], pp. 19, 20, 44-45.) But while I wish also to emphasize absence of anticipation, I am equally interested in the sheer nature of the phenomena precipitated without anticipation of intention: Precisely *what* do we see when we view in some comprehensive fashion "unanticipated

consequences" of action? The word *synergic* has appeared a convenient one to carry economically the burden of this double stress. It should definitely not carry the implication of some mystical strain or pressure attributable to "Society." It will aid greatly to avoid such a suggestion if we remind ourselves constantly that the sources of the synergic effect are perfectly "natural," whether desired or not, foreseen or not, etc. If large numbers of men independently make and implement decisions to come to a given place, in ignorance of one another's decisions, the place will in time contain large numbers of men, which may occasion surprise and may or may not evoke discomforts. Thus, the urbanization of a country, the price system, or the business cycle all have crucial synergic aspects, but to understand them it is in no case necessary to invoke transcendental entities.

32. This usage of "adaptive" in the sense, "making for survival," is suggested by Kluckhohn and Murray, *Personality*, p. 15; compare also O. H. Mowrer and Clyde Kluckhohn, "Dynamic Theory of Personality," in J. McV. Hunt, ed., *Personality and the Behavior Disorders* (New York: Ronald Press, 1944), 1:171; and Clyde Kluckhohn, *Navaho Witchcraft* (Cambridge: Peabody Museum, 1944).

33. A highly relevant and acute discussion of the matters just presented is given by F. A. von Hayek in his "Scientism and the Study of Society," *Economica*, N.S., 9 (1942):267-91; 10 (1943):34-63; 11 (1944):27-39. What appears to me to be unfortunately missing from Hayek's analysis of what I call the synergic level is a genuine attention to nonbeneficent effects. This seems to me to be quite in accord with the bias of "liberal" economic thought in these matters. [Not to detract from the validity of the tangential claim concerning this "liberal" bias, Schneider appears to have made two mistakes in the corresponding section of the text. The first, which may be the result of a conscious decision made for the sake of economy of argument, is the unfortunate lumping together of the survival of a system and the "health" of its agents—which also includes "welfare"—as a single functional requisite. These are arguably two distinct (or even two distinct levels of) requisites, and their confutation here weakens the examples to the point of incomprehensibility. The second mistake is in the interpretation of Situation D. The " − + " configuration should be interpreted as a truly "paradisiac" state in which men are not motivated to work yet social "health" (and/or survival) still obtains. In overlooking this, Schneider also misses the opportunity to move to perhaps more meaningful gray areas (in which he is clearly interested) in which "indirect" motivation—say, to toil not for material gains but for enjoyment—may be viewed as the most desirable type. Ed.]

34. See the "Sozialpsychologischer Teil" in Max Horkheimer, ed., *Studien Über Autorität und Familie* (Paris: Alcan, 1936), pp. 77-135, esp. p. 87.

35. For some keen comments on the conditions necessary for the development of the superego, compare Margaret Mead, *And Keep Your Powder Dry* (New York: Morrow, 1943), pp. 126-36. For simplicity of treatment, I am omitting consideration of cases noted by Mead, Kardiner, and others in which only "shame" rather than a "true superego" appears.

37. This is deliberately stated in this very general form. Our whole construction of social systems has necessarily been quite abstract. Some indication of the concrete problems that would have to be wrestled with in connection with

talking about the "breakdown" of an economic scheme and the failure to provide minimum necessities of life is conveniently supplied by Kenneth Boulding's statement: "It must be pointed out that in one sense, if we look at the economic life of the world with a truly world-view, the depressions of western capitalism are of secondary importance. Even at the depth of depression, the standard of life of the industrial nations of the west is so far above that of the rest of the world, that a Hindu or a Chinese peasant might well be amazed at our concern over the problem." *The Economics of Peace* (Englewood Cliffs, N.J.: Prentice-Hall, 1945), pp. 124-25.

38.   The following is a good example: "The more complex societies become, the harder it is for morality to function through purely automatic mechanisms. Circumstances are never the same, and moral rules must consequently be applied intelligently. The character of society is in perpetual evolution; morality must therefore be sufficiently flexible to allow change as soon as change is necessary. But in order for us to have such a situation, morality cannot be inculcated in such fashion that it is beyond the reach of those primary agents of change: criticism and reflection. What is needed is that individuals shall, while conforming to moral rule, understand what they are doing and that their conformity shall not go to the point of completely shackling intelligence. Thus, it does not follow from belief in the necessity of discipline that it must be blind and enslaving. Moral rules must be invested with an authority without which they would be inefficacious, but from a certain historical point onward, this authority should not safeguard them from discussion and make of them idols upon which, so to put it, man dare not lift his eyes." Emile Durkheim, *L'Education Morale* (Paris, Alcan, 1925), p. 60.

39.   Perhaps as important as this, even again assuming the miracle referred to, is the circumstance that it is impossible for man to foresee all the consequences of his actions and interactions: he would have to be not merely "himself" but very much more—indeed, superhuman.

6
Pitirim A. Sorokin: Social Science
in the "Grand Manner"
(1968)

Pitirim Alexandrovitch Sorokin was born, as he writes in his auto-biography, in northern Russia, in Yerensky County of Vologda Province, in Turya village, on January 21, 1889.[1] He was secretary to Kerensky before the Bolsheviks came to power, and his personal encounter with the Russian Revolution was dramatic and intense. He arrived in the United States in 1923 and came to Harvard as professor of sociology in 1930. He relinquished professional duties at Harvard in 1955 and became free of residual duties at the Research Center in Creative Altruism at the end of 1959. On February 10, 1968, he died in Winchester, Massachusetts. The last event occasions the present statement.

Sorokin was certainly one of the most productive social scientists of his time and perhaps of all time. There will come a day, no doubt, when some scholar enamored of library dust will try a complete listing of his books and papers, including such items as British, French, German, Turkish, Spanish, Portuguese, Dutch, Norwegian, Finnish, Japanese, Chinese, and Indian editions of the books. Translations aside, there are roughly three dozen books, a number of these being very sizable contributions and only a few of the total being coauthored. The bibliography published in 1963 in the symposium on Sorokin, edited by Philip J. Allen, refers to several hundred, presumably rather ephemeral, editorials and essays and to about two hundred papers in scientific journals.[2] Nor did Sorokin stop publishing in 1963. This chapter is perforce designed to consider his work only briefly and selectively. Considerable detailed commentary is bound to be added, in time, to what already exists, but Sorokin's death prompts some immediate reflections about the value of what he did.

The work to be considered may be divided into six categories. Sorokin's first book in English, published in 1924 and issued in an enlarged edition in 1950, was *Leaves from a Russian Diary*.[3] It recounts his experiences under the Bolsheviks and in its second edition contains an evaluation of the Revolution. It may be considered as roughly autobiographical and may be joined with the later formal autobiography, *A Long Journey*. These are still readable, useful books for anyone interested in the personal experiences of their author. No more need be said of them here.

A second category may be labeled, a bit arbitrarily, but certainly with no pejorative intent, conventional sociological works. These include such volumes as *Sociology of Revolution*,[4] *Social Mobility*,[5] *Principles of Rural-Urban Sociology*,[6] and *A Systematic Source Book in Rural Sociology*.[7] Partly falling into this category and partly into the fourth category to be mentioned below is the book entitled *Society, Culture, and Personality*.[8] There are some substantial performances here. *Social Mobility* was particularly notable for its time. It gave American sociologists largely cut off from European sources of analysis and data some sense of the value of what they might find abroad and it exhibited genuine sturdiness in its effort to combine theoretical analysis with historical materials and such pertinent statistics as were then available. The work on rural-urban sociology was deservedly an educative influence in the American field. The source book still strikes one as gratifyingly rich, and the treatment of such a subject as migration in these rural-urban studies of the late twenties and early thirties still suggests an impressive mastery of relevant European and American materials. Some of the most respectable work in this area, for instance T. Lynn Smith's superior text, markedly shows the Sorokin influence.[9] The numerous chapters in *Society, Culture, and Personality* that deal in "conventional" sociology—chapters on groups, group bonds, mobility, stratification— are definitely worth reading today. Sorokin summarized much of what was known up to his time, and his own distinctive formulations are often sharp and striking, not least when he deals with what he calls group vehicles (briefly, instrumentalities that externalize or "objectify" and "socialize" or diffuse a group's meanings, values, and norms).

A third category comprises the central work on culture. In this category belongs, above all, the four-volume *Social and Cultural Dynamics*.[10] One may also include the portions of *Society, Culture, and Personality* that deal with culture and *Sociocultural Causality, Space, Time*,[11] which adds little to other items but clearly belongs here. Since the *Dynamics*, which dominates the category and is indeed the culmination of Sorokin's work, will be discussed below, the category may be left aside for the moment.

Sorokin wrote a good deal about social theories other than his own and exhibited a constant interest in the relation of his own views to those of others. Probably the best known of his works in the category of commentary on, and critique of, theory (and method) is his *Contemporary Sociological Theories*.[12] He again performed a service by suggesting to American sociologists the wealth of resources they might draw upon in the form of European materials. But authentic as some of the contributions of the book were, its discussions of a number of leading figures in sociology were not always so illuminating as they might have been. Sorokin was a scholar of very considerable range, but he was a "romantic," in the terminology of Wilhelm Ostwald, a fast productive writer who did not invariably turn out the most finished, most careful, or most tidy piece of work conceivable. Within this fourth category also belong *Social Philosophies of an Age of Crisis*,[13] not one of its author's most significant publications, and *Fads and Foibles in Modern Sociology*,[14] a short (short for Sorokin, that is) treatise on the positivistic vagaries of psychology and sociology in which Sorokin obviously had a great deal of fun discoursing on testomania and testocracy and quantophrenia and metrophrenia and numerology. He had his points to make, but they were at times couched in a rather exuberant style, not calculated to make friends. Sorokin is revealed here in one of his most bellicose intellectual moods, not only antagonizing the whole species of "numbers" men, genuine and spurious, but also taking care to annoy incidental audiences, such as those that were inclined to think that he had always taken an unjust one-sided view of the work of Freud. Finally to be placed under the present rubric is Sorokin's last voluminous work, *Sociological Theories of Today*.[15] This study plainly suffers from failure to keep up with some important developments. A notable example is the neglect of the development in structural-functional analysis represented by Parsons's hierarchical ordering—and treatment in cybernetic fashion—of the structural categories of values, norms, collectivities, and roles. It could reasonably be argued that in this book Sorokin expended too much space on weak contributions, and he did not take into account a good deal of high-level research carried out during the preceding two decades, from which one might have expected an able sociologist doing a large-scale job of critical and constructive review to extract material relevant for theory. Yet the book still suggests occasionally something of the sweep of the old-time Sorokin and his capacity for revealing and pungent commentary.

The publicist and popular commentator is the author of still another, fifth, set of items that include *Crisis of Our Age*,[16] *Man and Society in Calamity*,[17] *Russia and the United States*,[18] *The Reconstruction of Humanity*,[19] *S.O.S.: The Meaning of Our Crisis*,[20] and *The Basic Trends of Our Times*.[21] These writings tend to have much of their grounding in the central work Sorokin had done on culture. (*Russia and the United*

States stands rather apart from the others.) Some of the titles suggest a certain gaudiness of style and substance, but the Sorokin of this genre is not altogether incapable of shrewd observations. Two or three items that apparently belong in this general category, including *The American Sex Revolution*[22] and *Power and Morality,*[23] have not been examined by the writer.

There is finally a category of works on love, including among others, a study of "good neighbors and Christian saints," under the title of *Altruistic Love,*[24] and *The Ways and Power of Love.*[25] Of the works in this vein, the latter is the best known to the writer. It is spun out at considerable length, but it contains points of sociological and psychological interest and reveals rather more than the familiar fact that Sorokin had become convinced that love was a kind of cure-all for the most serious afflictions of mankind. The devotion to love and the preoccupation therewith that the Sorokin of this line reveals are inevitably reminiscent of the later Auguste Comte, although Sorokin, for all his intensity about love, did not perhaps become quite so intense about it as Comte did, and presumably did not have so deep and stirring a set of personal experiences as the latter to afford background to the great concern with altruism.

On Culture

The six categories listed do not capture everything Sorokin wrote, without qualification. Thus, his early works in Russian include an item of science fiction, to baffle the categorist. But the categories are useful, certainly, for most purposes. And Sorokin the analyst of culture, the social scientist of the third category, stands forth most prominently, if only because the four-volume *Social and Cultural Dynamics* outdoes anything else its writer accomplished.

It may serve to jog the memory to record again that Sorokin distinguished Sensate, Ideational, and Idealistic types of cultures. In Sensate culture, ultimate reality is taken as a set of phenomena that can be grasped by the senses, while Ideational culture rests on the premise that "true reality" transcends the sensible or material world, and Idealistic culture makes an uneasy (if in its concrete manifestations often aesthetically, and otherwise, most pleasing) and short-lived synthesis of the Sensate and Ideational premises. In Sensate culture, it is presumed that this palpable world and its goods are most eminently worthy of concern, while in Ideational culture the preoccupation is with the goods pertaining to a higher reality, and Idealistic culture again represents a combinative formation. Sensate culture has several forms and is seen at its most vigorous in the onslaughts of the world by such men as conquerors of disease and great organizers of human effort to advance industry and technology. This sort of activity is characteristic of Active Sensate culture. In the case of Passive Sensate culture, the world is exploited for the resources it may offer to enhance sensual pleasure, while, under the Cynical Sensate form, hypocrisy, interested conformity, and a "yen for the payoff" are all likely to be powerful.

Within Ideationalism, an Ascetic form holds itself resolutely aloof from the world and an Active form seeks to remold the world in line with the demands of the spirit. The (intermediate) Idealistic and the Pseudo-Ideational forms represent a sixth and a seventh type, respectively. But Sorokin's overriding concern is the Sensate and Ideational types in the large, although he is attentive to the Idealistic type also. His main data relate to Western history, in which two cycles of the sequences, Sensate-to-Ideational-to-Idealistic, have been completed since early Greek times, and in which there has latterly been reached a phase of Sensate decline, evidently to be followed by an Ideational (or Idealistic) upswing. It is worth noting incidentally that Sorokin's terms and ideas appear in some measure to have become part of popular culture. *Newsweek* for November 13, 1967, carried an article on "the permissive society," in which Max Lerner was quoted as saying that we live in "a Babylonian society," a "late sensate period," in which emphasis is "on the senses and the release of the sensual."

An immense amount of evidence and argument was adduced for Sorokin's various theses about the character and development of the main cultural types. The argument was far from flawless. The data were uneven and at times of quite poor quality. They did not invariably support Sorokin's contentions. But Sorokin did obtain data. He often sought empirical and statistical knowledge about matters which most American (and indeed non-American) sociologists would not dream of being empirical and statistical, such as the movement of nominalist, conceptualist, and realist currents of thought over a period of twenty centuries.[26] The application even of the simplest statistical techniques (as nearly as the writer can recall, there is nothing more complicated than a geometric mean in the four volumes of the *Dynamics*) to what might initially appear to be recalcitrant spiritual or philosophical phenomena is an enterprising thing. Its effect is often provocative and it is something of a "trademark" of Sorokin's work. Yet at the same time the data he had at his disposal were not adequately handled. If they had been better handled, with less concentration of purpose on the effort to find differences among cultural types, Sorokin might have been healthily prompted to find considerably more than he did in the way of similarities. It may be suggested that he never saw the extent to which even his own materials and arguments implicitly constrained one to the outlook that there are indeed very substantial cross-cultural similarities and that large numbers of concrete cultures, if not nearly all, are simultaneously Sensate and Ideational and Idealistic or compromising in very significant ways. He was aware that even the most aloof ascetic must make concessions to the body and that this fact had cultural implications. He was aware that more generally, in many areas of actual conduct, there is great resemblance between participants in ostensibly different cultures, despite Sorokinian presumptions that different premises and norms prevail which might be expected to induce different conduct.

Such a brief critical statement as this must, admittedly, conceal much that should ideally be made explicit and it may in its brevity even appear to accept an "emanationism" of which Sorokin has with at least some justification been accused.[27] But brief as the statement must be, it should not be construed to mean something as flat and foolish as an assertion to the effect that there simply are "no differences" across cultures. Rather, the suggestion is that Sorokin's analysis would definitely have fared better had he been more alert to cultural similarities and more willing to penetrate "differences" that are not authentic differences. Not every discrepancy in cultural styles must be taken with utmost seriousness as a manifestation of fundamental divergence. "A handmaiden of the Lord," "a very fine girl," and "quite a kid" may all "mean" much the same, in at least some contexts. This *sameness* of meaning could be far more significant than the differences the variant phrasings suggest.

Related Endeavors

It is interesting to compare with Sorokin's work on culture that of two of his outstanding contemporaries in America, the anthropologist Alfred L. Kroeber and the sociologist Talcott Parsons. Kroeber, as is well known, was an imposingly erudite scholar, and a very careful one. He gave considerable richness to the general notion of culture as understood by the anthropologist. He was apparently willing to work extremely hard in order to come to most modest conclusions. He would review nine or ten major historical growths of philosophy and inquire about what common features they showed "in the forms of their growths or in their relations to the cultures of which they were part." The response to his own inquiry?—"The answer must be mainly, None."[28] Or (in the same volume from which this "answer" is taken) he would undertake to summarize observations based on a great deal of material on culture growth with the aid of an extremely simple conceptual apparatus, featuring hardly anything more abstruse than the circumstance that culture patterns or forms tend to develop to the limits of their potentialities, at which point "pressures" arise under which the patterns are likely to be dissolved or expanded or otherwise changed, unless a bias sets in toward repetition and something on the order of "retrogression."[29] Kroeber was skeptical about ambitious theses on the flowering of culture patterns as he was also skeptical about the notion that Western culture was in decline.[30] In the great second edition of his *Anthropology* he added to the richness of his descriptive materials on culture and again made use of quite simple concepts—universal pattern, systemic pattern, stimulus diffusion, reduction-segregation—to illumine the materials.[31] By comparison with Sorokin, Kroeber appears nearly colorless. But he has an impressive solidity and soundness. He is less likely to mislead the unwary.

A more direct and fuller challenge to Sorokin's work is represented by the work of Parsons. In one important piece, the latter has taken issue with some critical views of Sorokin's, with particular reference to the development of religion and the case of Protestantism.[32] Parsons has approached the study of culture generally with distinctively different preoccupations from those of Sorokin. He is a neater, tighter, more rigorous theorist, and his presentation of cultural dimensions in terms of cognition, evaluation, expressiveness, and ultimate meaning achieves some things that Sorokin did not.[33] But of course allowance must be made for sheer difference of interests (although this is not to deny that it might be possible in principle to judge of the value of the overall approaches to culture of the two men). The work of the two may be compared, however, on the crucial point of how the relations of culture and society or social systems are analyzed, an inevitably significant matter for sociologists.

There is a plain tendency for Sorokin to treat the forms of social interaction as yet another expression or function of overall Sensate or Ideational cultural trends, so that "contractual," "familistic," and "coercive" relationships among men, for example, appreciably reflect and depend upon the main cultural circumstances.[34] This leaves much to be desired. Parsons has engaged in some meticulous discriminations of culture and social system which, in conjunction with his thought on evolutionary lines, have been of help to him in developing more subtle conceptions of the relations of the cultural and the social. In the paradigm of evolutionary change he has worked out, for example, stress is put on processes of differentiation, integration, adaptive upgrading, and value-generalization.[35] The last process—value-generalization—refers to a development in which values (which are "top-level" in a structural hierarchy and which unequivocally originate in culture) become more abstract and "stretch" more in order to accommodate increased complexity and diversity in a society that features a greater range of goals and types of activities than previously prevailed. Thus, economic activity, let us say, gets separated from the household and assigned to factories, and thereby differentiation of household and factory occurs. But factory workers continue to have kin and live in households, and thereby integrative problems (by way of "putting together" factory and home) must be met, so that, for instance, the time it takes to go back and forth between factory and home has to be sharply limited. The now structurally segregated economic activity is more efficiently performed than before and there is some ground for asserting that the household-kin-family complex, freed of economic tasks, can perform residual tasks better. These emerging arrangements and the social interactions they involve are accommodated in a value pattern (eminently a cultural phenomenon that in cases of this kind comes to be incorporated within the social system, or "institutionalized") that tolerates them and makes them acceptable in the face of the criticism, perhaps, that the world is going to the dogs when a man can no longer direct daily the economic performance of his own son.

A less rough, less elliptical statement than this might explicitly stress that there is no simple opposition between social system and culture. Thus, technically, in Parsons's view the structure of the social system itself consists in institutionalized normative culture; any contrast between culture and social system, therefore, would involve an opposition between culture incorporated in the social system and a social system itself pervaded by certain cultural components. The statement above is limited in more than one way. It is conceivably somewhat forced and not quite fair to Sorokin. But the point is precisely that the rigidities of Sorokin's cultural theory do leave him vulnerable in the sphere of relating the cultural and the social. It should also be noted that Parsons and others, including some prominent anthropologists, are currently showing a renewed interest in evolutionary thought in general. They are making what to numerous social scientists today appears a convincing case for taking the hypothesis of social evolution most seriously. There are significant differences in the views of various writers and the whole matter cannot be gone into here, but Sorokin's bias toward a cyclical view of cultural development does not appear to get nourishment from this source. Some features of his views may theoretically be reconcilable with evolutionary thought, but many others may well be seriously impaired by it.

Heritage

Kroeber would appear, then, by the present argument, to be a sounder scholar (although not one of greater scope) than Sorokin, and Parsons a tidier theorist.[36] Moreover, it has at least been strongly intimated that Sorokin's thought, more especially in the *Dynamics,* has serious defects and limitations. And theories like Sorokin's that come close to philosophy of history are now (for some good reasons) hardly in fashion among leaders in the endeavor to enhance the achievements and stature of the field of sociology. Even Parsons's "grand theory" and Sorokin's performance in the "grand manner" are in many crucial respects very far apart, despite Sorokin's perception of major similarities between them.[37]

Is the *Dynamics* still worth reading? For this writer, at any rate, the answer can only be an emphatic affirmative. The *Dynamics* has considerable defects, true, but so also has many a book unequivocally recognized as a sociological "classic." One can hardly take up here the merits of reading and rereading classic works in sociology.[38] And no measure can be offered to ascertain precisely how defective the *Dynamics* is. The work—and this is the most cogent point to urge—also has its considerable virtues. In it Sorokin shows brilliance on numerous aspects of the history of thought. His views on immanent change, with their "dialectical" flavor, remain most provocative. Some of his cultural portraiture is vivid and powerful. Many of the concepts he employed, either his own or those which, in a peculiar sense, he made his own—the principle of limit, sociological singularism and universalism, fideism, vehicles, the "tragedy of culture" (cf. Simmel), and others—cast a clear light on extremely important ideas. He has a great wealth of insights to offer. The *Dynamics* has much to interest sociologists, anthropologists, theorists of culture, political scientists and historians. Sorokin was not strong on— or even, one suspects, especially concerned about—formal economic analysis. But this and other reservations aside, his main work holds out the prospect of an education in the social sciences to anyone who wishes to take advantage of it. No reasonable person would consider his education finished with Sorokin's work, but he well could find it palpably advanced by it.

The tumult and the shouting have died for Sorokin. He will not write any more furious lines to, or about, editors of prominent journals. His triumphs and his defeats as well as his angers, as personal experiences, are quite vanished. But obviously he left behind a considerable body of work. If the present chapter has been at all persuasive on the point that much of work (not the *Dynamics* alone, although it in particular) still eminently merits scrutiny, it will have served as an appropriate memorial for a very remarkable man.

Notes

1. *A Long Journey: The Autobiography of Pitirim A. Sorokin* (New Haven, Conn.: College and University Press, 1963), p. 11.
2. Philip J. Allen, ed., *Pitirim A. Sorokin in Review* (Durham, N.C.: Duke University Press, 1963), p. 501.
3. *Leaves,* enl. (Boston: Beacon Press, 1950).
4. Philadephia: Lippincott, 1925.
5. New York: Harper, 1927. *Social and Cultural Mobility* (Glencoe, Ill.: Free Press, 1959).
6. With Carle C. Zimmerman (New York: Holt, 1929).
7. With Carle C. Zimmerman and Charles J. Galpin, 3 vols. (Minneapolis: University of Minnesota Press, 1930-1932).
8. New York: Harper, 1947.
9. T. Lynn Smith, *The Sociology of Rural Life* (New York: Harper, 1947).
10. New York: American Book Company, 1937-1941. New York: Bedminster Press, 1962.
11. Durham, N.C.: Duke University Press, 1943.
12. New York, Harper, 1929.
13. Boston: Beacon Press, 1950. New York: Dover, 1963.
14. Chicago: Regnery, 1956.
15. New York: Harper & Row, 1966.
16. New York: Dutton, 1941.
17. New York: Dutton, 1942.
18. New York: Dutton, 1944.
19. Boston: Beacon Press, 1948.
20. Boston: Beacon Press, 1951.
21. New Haven, Conn.: College and University Press, 1964.
22. Boston: Sargent, 1957.
23. With Walter A Lunden (Boston: Sargent, 1959).
24. Boston: Beacon Press, 1950.
25. Boston: Beacon Press, 1954.
26. *Dynamics,* 2:ch. 6.
27. See Robert K. Merton, *Social Theory and Social Structure* (Glencoe, Ill.: Free Press, 1957), p. 466.
28. Alfred L. Kroeber, *Configurations of Culture Growth* (Berkeley and Los Angeles: University of California Press, 1944), p. 75.
29. See Kroeber, *Configurations,* pp. 320, 666.
30. See Kroeber, *Configurations,* p. 761; and Kroeber's *The Nature of Culture* (Chicago: University of Chicago Press, 1952), ch. 49.
31. See his *Anthropology,* 2d ed. (New York: Harcourt, Brace, 1948), chs. 8 and 9, and, more generally, chs. 8-15.
32. See Talcott Parsons, "Christianity and Modern Industrial Society," in Edward A. Tiryakian, ed., *Sociological Theory, Values, and Sociocultural Change* (New York: Free Press, 1963), pp. 33-70. Sorokin makes a spirited reply to this piece in "The Western Religion and Morality of

Today," in *Sociology and Religion: Theoretical Perspectives,* International Yearbook for the Sociology of Religion (Cologne: Westdeutscher Verlag, 1966), 2:9-43. See also his *Sociological Theories of Today,* pp. 438-39.

33.　See Talcott Parsons et al., eds., *Theories of Society* (New York: Free Press, 1961), pp. 963-93.

34.　See *Dynamics,* 3:Part 1.

35.　See Talcott Parsons, *Societies: Evolutionary and Comparative Perspectives* (Englewood Cliffs, N.J.: Prentice-Hall, 1966), pp. 21-24.

36.　It should not be overlooked, incidentally, that all three men carry on the general sociological-anthropological tradition of attributing enormous significance to culture in human life. Sorokin's emphasis on cognition, on ideas, on values is most pronounced. The three resemble one another greatly in *this* regard and it is of interest that Sorokin and Parsons perhaps particularly converge here.

37.　*Sociological Theories of Today,* pp. 420-31. Sorokin also sees some dissimilarities, ibid., pp. 432-40. The list of similarities draws on nothing by Parsons published later than 1951.

38.　Two interesting recent statements on this matter are provided by Edward A. Shils, in Parsons et al., *Theories of Society,* 2:1446-48, and by Robert K. Merton in *On Theoretical Sociology* (New York: Free Press, 1967), pp. 34-37.

7

On Frontiers of Sociology and History: Observations on Evolutionary Development and Unanticipated Consequences

(1969)

There are recent indications of renewed interest on the part of American sociologists in historically and comparatively oriented sociological endeavor. American historians, for their part, have clearly been stirred by the ideas, concepts, and methods that have been developing in the field of sociology.[1] If there is still something a little strange in encountering a term such as "multivariate analysis" in the writings of historians, the strangeness soon may well wear off—and one can even hope that before long it will be not uncommon to find, let us say, sociologists of religion in the United States as avidly preoccupied with the history of Jainism as they are with the contemporary character of Pentecostalism when they aspire to deal subtly with the phenomenon of the sect.

It is understandable that historians, from their side, should stress the stimulation to historical work received from sociological analysis of, say, occupations or stratification or social mobility, while sociologists ponder historical contributions to understanding of such phenomena and both sociologists and historians cautiously (but with a quiet joy) celebrate sociological methodology. This is all to the good and we do not even fairly indicate how good it is unless we add that the range of sociological fields by which historians feel stimulated is actually far wider than mention of occupations, stratifications, and mobility alone would suggest. Specific sociological concepts, as well as sociological preoccupations, modes of thought, and methodology in general have begun inroads into historical analysis. Stanley Elkins's notable study of slavery considers the meaning of Durkheim's strategic concept of anomie.[2] Lipset recommends to historians the use of a concept such as "reference group."[3] Elkins and McKittrick derive concepts from Robert K. Merton's work on public housing communities to apply to analysis of the American frontier.[4] These are interesting, even exciting developments that give a kind of vividness to Paul Barth's characterization of history as "concrete sociology"[5] (of course without involving that extremely large commitment, for sociologists, to historical concerns that Barth's old-fashioned view of sociology necessitated).

But all this, valuable though it may prove to be, does not immediately suggest certain orientations or themes that have been significant for sociological theory and that at the same time clearly border on historical concerns. Or we may put the matter in this way: It has indeed been noted that sociological "preoccupations" and "modes of thought" have made inroads into historical analysis. This is broadly true, but we wish to mark out some particular sociological preoccupations that seem to us especially to merit attention on the frontiers of sociology and history. These preoccupations—or, if one will, orientations or themes—have to do with (1) evolutionary development and (2) unanticipated consequences. We do not need to claim that the interrelating of sociology and history through consideration of subject matters (such as stratification), concepts, and methods on the lines on which this is going on today would fail to lead to the various particular issues to which we shall be referring. We wish only to suggest the utility of putting the matter of interrelations of sociology and history immediately, directly within the framework of certain intellectual traditions.

Evolutionary Development

Much of what follows draws upon familiar material, but there is also much that can now be stated only in inchoate, groping fashion. Thus, it will be noted in due course that our use of the term "mechanism" frankly falls short of ideally desirable precision. But this remains a term that we cannot here do without. There are other shortcomings, inevitable in an effort based, as this one is, on the notion that rapprochement between sociology and history should be properly ambitious and that in accordance with proper ambition it is permissible or even desirable to point to problems not allowing of easy resolution and sometimes hardly even allowing of sharp or systematic statement. We turn first to the theme of evolutionary development, which it is somewhat arbitrary but highly convenient to divide into the three subthemes of fitness of "grown" institutions, stages of evolution and inclusion, and the method of evolution.

The Fitness of "Grown" Institutions

Questions and issues bearing upon evolution in some plain sense of that term (even when it has not been used as such) have been posed and considered from the beginnings of sociology in the eighteenth century. Obviously, evolution could not be and was not approached with "Darwinian" preconceptions by men like Bernard Mandeville, David Hume, and Adam Ferguson.[6] But there were two closely related "evolutionary" ideas clearly present in the thought of these men and others. One was the idea—often expressed with great eloquence and power—that strategically important human institutions had "grown" or "evolved" over time and not been invented out of whole cloth in the minds of creators or legislators deliberately and at once setting up a system of society designed to achieve previously conceived ends. In particular with the three men already mentioned it was a great point to emphasize that much in human arrangements or establishments that looked as if it might well have been achieved by outright design had in fact been achieved gradually and by way of fumbling efforts in which the outcomes finally actually attained were never originally foreseen. A second "evolutionary" idea was that precisely men's unintended, uninvented, unforeseen establishments very often had a certain "fitness" and incorporated wisdom that had been come by in piecemeal, hard-won reflection and experience. A well-fashioned tool or a modern ship (to use a famous example of Mandeville's) will incorporate a very considerable experience and sagacity, now at the command of men who themselves may have contributed little to that experience and sagacity but still can enjoy their fruits. There is a kind of storing up of cultural gains here which is in the end really quite familiar to the present-day sociologist, although he does not approach these matters in the eighteenth-century terms. The cultural storing-up has its evident analogies to genetic storage of ancestral "wisdom" achieved in the course of biological events.

How comparable are human institutions with tools or machines? How does a ship compare with a system of marriage classes allowing and disallowing various marital relations? From the view that institutions cumulate the wisdom of the species, is it not easy to make a transition to a conservative ideology that makes grossly exaggerated claims to scientific foundations? These are evidently questions to give one pause. But this early "evolutionary" thought was important—and it is far from trivial even now. Some of the issues that arise in present-day so-called structural-functional analysis in sociology are already adumbrated in it. It challenges us to very serious consideration of some tantalizing ideas that are still not readily susceptible of thoroughly clean and clear statement. Just what role does accident play in the development of a ship on the one hand and of marital classes, say, on the other? To what extent is the history of technology exploitable for purposes of throwing light on various institutionalized schemes of marriage? This much is certain, as

Mandeville already very clearly saw and as has already been suggested: Technology, too, does not work simply deliberately or "rationally." This is almost a matter of common sense. Inventors and engineers start with one sort of notion and are likely enough to end up with something else, perhaps something much more intriguing.

What role does "error" play in the development of institutions? What role is played in the outmoding of various arrangements by unexpected eruptions from outside a social system that hasten the lapse of arrangements that might in other circumstances have lasted much longer? Ideally, we should have an apparatus for handling such questions as these that would carry us well beyond the realm of the obvious in which we now tend to be fixed. "Fitness" might ideally be as well judged for an institution as for a tool, where utilitarian considerations are the important ones. An institutional "mix" of the utilitarian and the purely "expressive" or aesthetic in a scheme of marital classes might ideally be described with a precise sense of the contribution of each of these major elements or functions. We may indeed concede that all this poses extremely large questions. But, by the testimony of what social scientists have done, these questions have by no means always been rejected as too overarching. In one form or another they occupy sociologists, anthropologists, and others into the present day.

It seems evident that sociology and history may fruitfully work together in these premises. In fact, the active introduction of a historical dimension in newer and more sophisticated terms might well be enormously useful here. Consider simply the matter of the form or organization of the Western family. The stimulating work that Malinowski did well over a generation ago on the Trobriand family form[7] suggests that in the West there has historically been a pronounced tendency to concentrate in the one male biological parent the roles of "father" and of "dad." "Father" is, briefly, a disciplinarian, anciently mother's ultimate appeal in a varity of things, an authoritarian figure, the one from whom one inherits if there is anything to inherit. (We must omit much and refer only in passing to class nuances.) Father is likely to show a certain sternness and austerity. "Dad" is friendly and chummy with his children, liberal in dispensing sundry good things to them.

The father-dad consolidation in the composite role of one person has obviously been important. It has had important psychological effects. How did it arise? (Is it indeed sensible to ask such a question?) In what ways and at what loci is it changing now? What is the significance of this consolidation or its breakup in relation to changing family functions? Can we document and fix with precision in time the appearance of various changes? The history of the contact of social classes (and, in a country like the United States, of White and Negro "castes") has evident bearing on these matters. Is it wholly naive to ask whether the role consolidation has indeed incorporated "wisdom"? Or has it incorporated a good deal of "foolishness"? It is perhaps too easy to persuade one's self that this particular role consolidation has been responsible for raging psychic conflicts. It would seem clear enough that it would be a source of ambivalent feeling, probably particularly for young males, but this is not enough to prove at once its general "inferiority" to alternative role arrangements.

We are certainly not *entirely* without light in these matters. Psychoanalysis and anthropology have been especially helpful in regard to them. But there is still considerable light to be thrown on them by historical and historical comparative work. History has been pecularily "out" of relation to formal family-kinship organization study in the sense intended. It may be high time for it to be "in," with its distinctive kind of contribution. Historians are already quite familiar with the sorts of family documents that may be illuminating on various particulars relevant in this special field. In a time when considerable interest attaches to the form of the American Negro family, with its tendency to distinctive role arrangements on matrifocal or matriarchal lines, we are bound in the end to question just how much "wisdom" traditional American upper- and middle-class family organization incorporates, whether certain structural alternatives to it may not be made to function equally satisfactorily, and so on. Is it the case that the Negro matrifocal bias has developed and involves no "wisdom" of its own? Is there nothing here but an unhappy story of such things as adult male feelings of inadequacy, male flight from responsibility, apathy about an uncontrollable future, and a non-White illegitimacy ratio eight times as high as the White? The older types of evolutionary thought to which we have pointed would tend to some skepticism about so unbelievably poor an account (because of a bias that the "grown" or old or traditional is likely to have some measure of fitness) but perhaps wrongly so. One can at least conceive a "new" social history that could make a fine contribution toward illuminating such matters.

Stages of Evolution and Inclusion

There is a second general type of concern with evolution that shows stress on evolutionary stages and on enhancement of adaptation to environment in the course of those stages, with an associated stress on increase of differentiation and of complexity of organization. The names of Comte, Spencer, and Durkheim are particularly likely to suggest themselves to sociologists in connection with this type of concern, and recently Parsons and his students and associates have been giving much attention to evolutionary development[8] in this sense. This kind of endeavor has always promised to throw light on fundamental problems in social and cultural change. It is well known, nevertheless, that it is a hazardous enterprise to set out evolutionary schemes in the social science field at large, whether in sociology proper or in historical economics or anthropology or political science. Here the individualizing skepticism of the historian is extremely valuable as a disturber of the peace of the stage-maker. In many areas of inquiry, we are still far from knowing securely what is comparable and what is not, what can be subsumed under useful generic categories and what cannot. The materials of the stage-maker obviously need the closest scrutiny of the historian intimately familiar with the historical and structural particulars, say, of various societies that are considered by the stage-maker as legitimately classifiable in certain ways. And of course older teleological biases, which presumed all history was constrained through "indispensable" stages to move to an era of bliss (marked, for example, by the inauguration of a Positive Regime in Comte's scheme of evolution) must be looked at askance by everyone. Nevertheless, with all due reservations, even some of the older schemes of evolution, such as Comte's, precisely, are in their way impressive readings of the historical record and not so far removed as might initially seem from a number of sophisticated modern efforts at stage construction. Work on evolution will unquestionably continue. It will also take on quantitative form that will audaciously classify and ambitiously and appropriately seek to find important common elements in social systems of whose difference in many particulars there can be no doubt.[9]

Of the plethora of problems on the frontiers of sociology and history that might be suggested here, we choose two that emerge from the recent effort of Parsons to conceive a modern evolutionary perspective on societies. One has to do with separation of culture and society. And society will generate and carry cultural components. Where we have to deal with the culture of a primitive society (with its distinctive social system), there is likely to be strong fusion of the cultural and the social. We deal with something, for instance, on the order of myths about ancestors emerging from water holes, which is not at all readily spread, not likely to appeal beyond a very small circle of primitive "customers." The myths in question do not travel. Who notes the particular society notes the particular culture and who notes the particular culture notes the particular society. But there do plainly exist societies in which elaborated cultural material can be and is released from its original social matrix and travels and finds acceptance far beyond its point of origin. There are myths or "stories" (and indeed other cultural items) that are diffusible and seem to make appeal to very considerable portions of mankind, to "speak to man's condition" in more or less universally persuasive terms.

Parsons characterizes ancient Israel and Greece as "seed-bed" societies, societies that generated cultural phenomena that were of enormous importance outside the particular Israelite and Greek communities of antiquity and greatly transcended the boundaries of the latter in time. Here there was marked differentiation of the cultural and the social. Cultural material proved eminently separable from its original social groundings. And Israel and Greece performed distinctive services in making their unique contributions to social evolution. Seed-bed societies are clearly in a special category (which is of course not to deny some degree of "seed-bedding" in societies not specifically classified as seed-bed) in a conception of evolution. Is there need for other special categories that have crucial significance in evolutionary process? This would not be the place for an effort to improve on Parsons, even if the writer could carry it through. But there is certainly no reason to think that Parsons's evolutionary scheme is conclusive, and the historian might well exercise his imagination and his knowledge of the detail of particular societies to help build an ultimately rich and genuinely well-ordered evolutionary edifice. The category of seed-bed societies for Israel and Greece may evidently be conceived as a response to the question: How treat Israel and Greece in a scheme of stages, when it is plain that they made extremely important evolutionary contributions, and yet at the same time, considered as the very small, limited socio-physical communities (or collectivities) they were, were in a plain sense simply not to be compared with Egypt or China or India or Rome—and thus do not "fit" easily into a stage sheme? Once again, in a developing evolutionary construction, will it be necessary to create other special boxes? It would indeed be surprising if the historian could not be helpfully imaginative here. Perhaps nothing more is needed in these premises than we already have, but our question surely appears worth asking.

The second problem that we choose to stress in the present context has to do with what Parsons, after T. H. Marshall, calls inclusion.[10] Inclusion may be defined as the incorporation (or condition of incorporation) into the civil community of elements, such as lower classes, that have previously been in various ways excluded. To extend the franchise to previously disfranchised groups is to enhance inclusion in the political dimension. To diffuse middle-class patterns of deferment of gratification among lower classes and thereby to "bourgeoisify" them is to enhance inclusion.[11] To diffuse a "higher" literary culture among lower classes is to enhance inclusion. (It can at least be noted broadly that the adaptation and viability of a social system may be seriously threatened by the existence of an unchided "low-class" mass that resents its condition of nonincorporation; hence, evolutionary or "adaptive" significance for inclusion and noninclusion.)

In the perspectives this suggests, particular interest will obviously attach to historical studies of mass culture, to studies of social mobility, to studies of the processes of democratization. Very significant questions of interpretation arise here for both sociologist and historian. Thus, historically, movements such as Methodism and organizations such as the Salvation Army have beyond any doubt played an important role in "upgrading" lower classes by dint of imbuing them with economic and moral values that effected their "civil-izing" and embourgeoisement.[12] In such cases, it would seem, "religion" is hardly the opium of the people. On the contrary, it has helped appreciably in their rise in this world. Was this ultimately "illusory" and contrary to the interests of the common people who were civil-ized or bourgeoisified? We may indicate our own view that only a doctrinaire and very strongly ideological social science could flatly maintain this, but this bare reference must suffice for indication of the significance for sociologists and historians of the problems of inclusion. It is hard to see how sharing of work on these problems could be other than profitable to representatives of both disciplines and both are in fact already well launched on relevant tasks.

The Method of Evolution

In a third general type of concern with social and cultural evolution, there is particular preoccupation with what may be called the method of evolution. It is true that in one way or another all who are concerned with evolution are likely to have something to say about its method. (One might even contend that inclusion has something to do with the method of evolution.) But what we shall attend to under the present heading is sufficiently distinct to warrant separate consideration from what has gone before. One of the best examples of approach to the method of evolution on the sociocultural scene is afforded by Elman R. Service, the anthropologist.[13] Service writes on "the law of evolutionary potential," which states that "the more specialized and adapted a form in a given evolutionary stage, the smaller is its potential for passing to the next stage." The fundamental idea involved here is that the greater the success of a particular form in adaptation the more it is likely to be lacking in that degree of relative amorphousness and diffuseness that allows flexibility and a kind of inventiveness in adapting to *new* circumstances. To be sure, as Service notes, "the evolution of species takes place *because* of adaptation," while it is still true that "the evolution of the total system of life takes place *in spite* of adaptation." Thorstein Veblen's notions of the merits of borrowing and of the penalty of taking the lead are among those particularly relevant in this connection.[14] Germany, industrializing far later than England, could profit from its backwardness. It was still "loose," so to put it, as it began its major spurt of industrialization in the last third of the nineteenth century. It was uncommitted to what Veblen regarded as wasteful inhibitions of technological development (of "pecuniary" or financial origin) and wasteful practices of conspicuous consumption that had developed in England from which it substantially took over the modern machine technology. In general, the important core idea (however it may be with respect to various details of Veblen's treatment of Germany and England) may be generalized in the form that, being "unstabilized" and relatively uncommitted in ways in which countries more advanced are stabilized and committed, the backward country can under appropriate circumstances move more rapidly ahead industrially, as Germany developed the machine technology tremendously in less than half a century before the First World War. Service accordingly writes on the "privilege of backwardness."

The privilege of backwardness certainly has its other economic illustrations. Japan, "once a poor cultural relative of China," as Service correctly notes,[15] moved into the technology of coal and oil energy while China remained behind; but now in its turn, China, "not nearly so adapted as Japan to the present and soon-to-be-outmoded complex of coal and oil energy" may well in its relative noncommitment forge rapidly ahead. In general, new and developing areas may be able to take over the latest and most advanced forms of technology. (The post-World War II *Wirtschaftswunder* or miracle of German economic recovery and development once more, it may also be noted, has shrewdly been attributed in part to the sheer wartime destruction of an older German technology, whose very destruction lifted a burden of commitment to obsolescent devices.) But the principle involved also extends beyond economic affairs, as is seen for instance in the circumstance mentioned by Service that in antiquity Levantine peoples without writing were able to make a fresh start in building a true phonetic alphabet out of the complex and cumbersome Egyptian system of writing.[16]

Here, then, is a significant element in the methodology of evolution to which sociologists and anthropologists have given attention. There is obviously a great deal here also to interest the historian. When McNeill writes in his "outline of history" for the 1960s that "Thorstein Veblen, *Imperial Germany and the Industrial Revolution* . . . did perhaps more to shape my conceptions of the peculiarities of German industrialism than any other book,"[17] there is ground for suspicion that notions on the line of the penalty of taking the lead or the privilege of backwardness or the penalties of success are likely to appeal to at least some historians. Toynbee contends forthrightly that the chances are against the favorite and on the side of the dark horse in the writing of new chapters and creativity. For him, too, success has its costs. The author has elsewhere summarized some of Toynbee's relevant thought by reference to "those 'fumbling and irresolute' animal adaptations which, just because they are indecisive, leave open possibilities of change and adjustment which are closed off for organisms that have worked out 'perfect' and detailed solutions to particular problems in evolutionary course."[18] The "law" that success leads to failure (or carries its penalties and costs) has human applications of major interest to Toynbee, to be sure.

The point of all this is of course not to celebrate McNeill and Toynbee. It is to indicate the existence of some awareness of the privilege of backwardness on the part of historians. Economic history, technological history, the history of a variety of discoveries in nontechnological fields such as the arts, scientific history—all can be profitably approached with an eye to the method of evolution that has been reviewed. We are not in the presence of unassailable principles that work with unmistakable effect and regardless of particular circumstances. But we are in the presence of some significant clues to the course of development in a large variety of historical fields. The talented historian will always, and inevitably, want to master his historical particulars but he will also be alert to profit from clues that will illuminate his particulars, and it is arbitrary to insist that he can make no contribution whatever when any question arises about the possible light that the particulars themselves may cast upon generally useful clues.

Unanticipated Consequences

In the above, we have sought to exploit traditions on the line of evolutionary thought in social science, and particularly in sociology, for the purpose of suggesting the character, and what we take to be the considerable significance, of a number of issues or questions on the frontiers or borderlines of sociology and history. We now turn to another intellectual tradition (not entirely unconnected with the first), with a similar purpose in view.

The tradition to which we now refer is one that has rested upon the insight that men frequently act in social context with certain objects in view but attain results that either fail to realize those objects or actually harm or destroy them. The contemporary sociologist stands in this tradition when, after Merton, he speaks of the unanticipated consequences of purposive social action.[19] In Merton's article under this title, a listing of some of the modern theorists who have (although not in equally significant ways) dealt with unanticipated consequences gives the names of Machiavelli, Vico, Adam Smith, Marx, Engels, Wundt, Pareto, Max Weber, Graham Wallas, Cooley, Sorokin, Gini, Chapin, and von Schelting. Merton also indicates that "some later classical economists" after Smith might be included and indeed he might have added numerous other names, such as those of Mandeville, David Hume, Adam Ferguson, and the economists Carl Menger and Friedrich Hayek. (It is no accident that names such as those of Mandeville and Ferguson crop up here again, for indeed in the thought of these men, as we have sought to make clear, much that evolved in human institutions redounded to men's benefit or advantage without there ever having been any intention that it should do so.)

The development of the entire idea of unanticipated consequences of purposive social action is itself a matter of tremendous interest in intellectual history.[20] The idea certainly reveals traces of origin in philosophy of history (although it may also have had other sources). Hegel was one of the many thinkers who grasped the idea firmly. Contrary to some silly popular notions on the matter, he was thoroughly well aware that "the actions of men proceed from their needs, their passions, their characters and talents."[21] But these actions inadvertently produced certain outcomes that had little directly to do with what men aimed at in carrying out their small, private purposes. Those outcomes fell into patterns that seemed to Hegel, as is well known, to reveal a kind of "process of development and . . . realization of Spirit" which constituted the true theodicy, the authentic "justification of God in History."[22] Men were surely motivated by everyday concerns and mundane needs but by ways of the "cunning of reason" their uninspired motives and actions led to large and important historical results. "Reason" was indeed "cunning" enough to ensnare men into producing certain grand results by enlisting their lowly impulses that unwittingly led thereto. When the philosophical and religious background of this kind of outlook is gone, the basic insight that men act purposively in society and achieve results not necessarily in accordance with their purposes remains. Now thoroughly secularized, it appears precisely in philosophically and theologically unadorned statements about "unanticipated consequences," in preoccupation with "latent functions" and the like.[23]

The fundamental insight bearing on unanticipated consequences has been well stated by the sociologist MacIver, among others. His statement may serve as a reminder of the insight to those thoroughly familiar with it and perhaps as something of a useful expository statement for those to whom it is less familiar:

> The purposive actions of men, expressive of a diversity of dynamic assessments, bring unpurposed results that are no less remarkable than, say, the hexagons of the hive of the honey bee. It is scarcely an exaggeration to claim that the larger framework of every society, its institutional complex, is a resultant of this type. It may be compared with the physical layout of a city every single edifice of which has been built according to someone's plan, whereas the total structure, whether it serves well or ill the purposes of those who inhabit it, has not come within the compass of any controlling design. So men build their social cells, form and re-form their associations, enter into changeful relations of one kind or another; and through this multitude of activities there comes into being a larger pattern to which also their traditions and habits become attached. Now and again a revolutionary spirit may be bred that seeks to control and to remake the entire fabric. However far it succeeds, along whatever new channels the multitudinous activities of men proceed, patterns other than those designed and superintended again emerge.[24]

The same point has actually very often been made by historians. One of the numerous statements of it, at least in broad form, is given in [E. H.] Carr's little volume on history: "Writers of many different schools of thought have concurred in remarking that the actions of individual human beings often have results which were not intended or designed by the actors or indeed by any one else."[25] Sociologists and historians (to say nothing of social scientists in other disciplines, such as economics) clearly share an insight here. But it is no ordinary "insight." Two ways of modern thought in which its larger significance becomes plain can be considered here. One has to do with the circumstance that the consequences of men's own actions may appear as alien things, even not things that men themselves have brought about. To this we turn first (to turn subsequently to "mechanisms" that are of interest in connection with unanticipated consequences).

Results of Human Action but Not of Human Design

If social actors (who are of course also always historical actors) constantly produce effects that transcend their own intentions (and at times baffle those very intentions)—or, in other words, if they bring about results that are indeed "the results of human action but not of human design" (Hayek, after Adam Ferguson)—then there are three possibilities to note that become actualities often enough to be quite interesting. One is that the social phenomena created unwittingly by men can give the impression of "getting away" from men themselves and of even constituting an alien world, a world "we" never made (although, to be sure, "we" made it without wanting to). A second is that these same phenomena are as it were endowed with a life of their own and become anthropomorphized and fetishized (in the sense in which Marx wrote of the fetishism of commodities). A third is that the phenomena fetishized are conceived as unfriendly or malevolent. For all the criticisms of Marxian theory developed in connection with the notion of the fetishism of commodities that may now justly be made, Marx still had a fine grasp of the matters here suggested. Men could act in socioeconomic context and determine the value-relations among commodities on the market by their actions (to put things in simplified form) while unaware that they were responsible for those relations, so that what was in the last analysis their own action took for them the form of the action of objects alienated from them, performing a kind of dance of commodities all on their own, quite autonomously, and often enough with results inimical to various human interests.[26] But it should at once be added that conservative and radical thought have profoundly different biases in these matters, although they *share* the basic insight of the transcendence of intention by purposive action. Radical thought has tended to emphasize the possible developments noted in this paragraph—on lines of alienation, fetishism, conception of the fetishized as inimical. Conservative thought is more apt to emphasize that men, in creating establishments or institutions that transcend their own intentions, create something good, something that works beneficently for them—a natural social growth, as it were, which it would be foolish to tamper with overmuch; after all, to repeat the point once again, hallowed social institutions are supposed to incorporate "wisdom."

These considerations will perhaps seem familiar enough to many. But how can they serve to bring sociology and history together? We would suggest that they greatly enhance our sensitivity to a variety of problems, again on the frontiers of the two. How does Marx fit the depression of 1929 and subsequent years? Was there in fact strong and widespread feeling that things economic and social had "gotten away" from men, had become alienated and were indeed in the saddle and riding mankind? Was such feeling particularly acute in pre-Nazi Germany? The phenomenon of scapegoating is interesting in this context. It has great psychic "advantages," as social psychologists well know. Instead of bothering about complex explanations (involving among other things, precisely, clarification of how phenomena arose that were the effect of human action but not of human design) it fixes on particular, presumed "villains." There is a marvelous, if perverse, intellectual economy in this. Even children can understand when someone says, "Johnny did it."

Scapegoating not only makes the world "understandable," however; it also makes it peculiarly actionable, for villains can be directly attacked and removed, say from a housing development, without waiting for answers to complex social, political, and economic questions that might suggest only disappointingly ambiguous and time-consuming devices for the impatient. Is scapegoating in any sense produced or encouraged by the sense of an alien and inimical "world we never made," while it seeks to deny such a world within its comprehension and within its power at the same time? How do historical and anthropological phenomena of witchcraft and demonology fare in this light?[27] The social psychology of all this has received some development, but it is susceptible of much more, and historians can certainly contribute to it, as indeed they have already done (although hardly even in quasi-formal terms and certainly not always against a background of full awareness of the intention-transcendence of various social phenomena).

It may also be noted that there do seem to be times or epochs when men feel the world to be peculiarly "open"—open to "reason," open to revision, open to efforts to sweep away irrelevant or noxious tradition. Here the social world has not "gotten away" in alienation, or at least there is a significant feeling that it can be recontrolled or repossessed. There are obviously other times or epochs when men seem oppressed by the dead hand of the past, virtually paralyzed thereby. Perhaps there are still others about which it is best to say that men are aware that they have created in the form of the social world more than they ever intended but that the results seem to them quite tolerable or even very good. The respective "mottoes" might be said to be, "We can change it," "We are weighed down by it," "We didn't intend at all but we rather like it." Obviously there is a great deal of simplification of difficult matters here.

A relevant and well-developed typology of historical attitudes toward the social world might introduce a multiplicity of terms and nuances not remotely hinted at here. But even now we may ask, in full consciousness of the crudeness of the question, whether sociologists and historians might not work together profitably in efforts to find out what produces one of the historical attitudes toward the social world rather than either of the others or others still not mentioned here. This is quite deliberately ambitious. It could well entail juxtaposition of findings from small-group research and findings from sociological and historical inquiries into vast organizations and societies. It represents the kind of ambition that the social sciences ultimately can hardly avoid.

Mechanisms

The second way of thought to which we turn exploits precisely the same insight we began with in a different direction. It draws attention to such things as "oppositeness," boomerang, self-destruction, and dialectical play connected with unanticipated consequences. In referring to Mandeville's paradox that private economic lusts or "vices" lead (under appropriate conditions) to public "virtues," Max Weber also referred aptly to "that power which constantly seeks the bad and constantly creates the good."[28] Men can seek personal economic welfare but inadvertently create public welfare, the "opposite" of what they had intended. Or one may easily invert Weber's statement and describe processes of social development that exhibit the working of a "power" that seeks the "good" and constantly creates the "bad." Moreover, in this line of thought there is likely to be emphasis on boomerang or negative boomerang or self-destructive effects. To give a well-worn example, one that is by now almost banal but still useful, Weber in his study of the Protestant ethic contended that the exercise of virtues such as industry, thrift, and frugality (encouraged in ascetic Protestantism) produced wealth, which then at times reacted destructively or in negative boomerang fashion upon the virtues which had created it, by way of holding forth temptations of pleasure to which numbers of the ascetic succumbed.

We may also attend briefly to dialectical play, with specific reference to the idea that dialectical movement occurs if some "element" in a system initially prospers the system or is a source of strength for it but subsequently disadvantages the system and becomes a source of its downfall or destruction. A rough, but for our purposes adequate, fit to this is given by the way in which ascetic Protestantism, once more, could gain a wealth that gave it the means to order the world more in accordance with God's glory, as it conceived it, but also a wealth that could corrupt the ascetic impulses out of which it was created. In this reading, industry, thrift, and frugality were a source of strength but could and did at times become sources of weakness or destruction. In a study of Catholicism in San Antonio that the writer is currently conducting, it appears that Archbishop Lucey (who has faced a kind of revolt on the part of some sixty-eight priests who are critical of him in a variety of ways and have requested formally that he resign) was long regarded by many of his clergy as a man of liberal social and political principles. But there is now considerable discontent with his liberalism, which is seen by dissatisfied clergy as not vigorous enough and as unduly restricted in the manner in which the archbishop relates himself to his priests. The archbishop himself initially seems to have encouraged and inspired with his liberalism numbers of young priests. They admired that liberalism and gave him much credit for it. But they have carried it forward—and a liberalism that he launched and that originally gave him strength among his clergy has now, in intensified form, come back to accuse him of inadequacies and thereby to hurt his standing among many of his clergy.[29] Again for our purposes we have a good enough dialectical fit. It should be carefully noted that we are still, in all this, in the realm of intended versus unintended consequences. The archbishop originally intended to manifest a certain liberal stance but certainly did not intend for relatively remote consequences of that stance to come back to challenge him.

But it is very important, in our view, to observe that we begin in these premises to verge upon "mechanisms." Precisely *how* does it come about that certain purposive actions have certain unintended consequences? It will be noted that different processes are at work in the two cases noticed above. In the ascetic Protestantism case something produced (wealth) reacts disintegratingly on the traits ("virtue") out of which it has come; its temptations become too powerful for the asceticism of some to resist. In the Lucey case, a trait (liberalism) becomes intensified in persons other than the one who showed it originally and in consequence of this intensification the original liberalism seems inadequate. In each of the cases a source of "strength" becomes a source of "weakness," true, but the negative boomerang effect is differently brought about in the two. If the boomerang effect is itself regarded as a mechanism, it may be taken as giving one kind of answer that is sometimes possible to the questions asked just above: *How* does it come about that certain purposive actions have certain unintended consequences? But clearly, *within* the boomerang context, as it were, we need to ask about more detailed "hows." The detail we discover may lead us to the specification of further mechanisms—or it may conceivably be too low-level for formulation of any mechanism, but what is important is for us to recognize that it is profitable to ask certain kinds of questions in these matters.

Although we do not attempt here to define mechanisms with rigor, some additional comment on them may be helpful. Mechanisms are clearly not at the level of "laws." The linguistic indicators of mechanisms are terms standing for certain concepts (such as the concept of "displacement," which points to a mechanism familiar to anyone even slightly acquainted with psychoanalysis). Moreover, mechanisms can be understood as actually or potentially contributing to the maintenance or breakdown of a system [which laws, as linguistic entities, cannot do. Ed.]. Thus, in Freudian terms, displacement of aggression from a greatly feared object to a less-feared one may help preserve a certain psychic system, although in a more *ultimate* sense or in the longer run this same displacement may undermine the system in which it is adopted as a device to express, with *immediately* lesser danger, an anger that demands some kind of outlet. In the Freudian mechanism of projection one attributes to others what holds of one's self, as in the imputation of virtually any motive, say jealousy. And here again the "security" and psychic system-sustainment purchased can be very precarious and projection can figure as an element in any ultimate system breakdown. The conceptualization and detailed exemplification of such mechanisms as displacement and projection are testimony to Freud's great talents.[30]

We wish to suggest that the whole field of social or socially significant mechanisms is one in which sociologists and historians can cooperate to their great mutual advantage. Was Weber right in seeing a negative boomerang effect in the Protestant ethic case? There is considerable controversy, as is very well known, about the whole Protestant ethic thesis. And with regard to essential facts and interpretations in the field, historians have a great deal to say and indeed have been saying a great deal for a considerable time. Merton argued in his own classic but now also much disputed work on seventeenth-century England[31] that Puritanism in particular exhibited a value-bias that aided in the development of science but that in time a developed and ambitious science reacted back upon the religious factors which had originally nourished it and challenged some of the essential foundations of those factors. Religion thus nourished a science that returned to devour it—and this had certainly never been intended by the pious men who had supposedly devoted themselves to science in the first place out of religious devotion. Gustav Mensching, the student of comparative religion, has argued repeatedly that the "high" religions are constantly involved in a kind of self-defeat. If they chose to remain elite religions this would not happen. But seeking to conquer the world they succeed merely in conquering masses who thoroughly vulgarize them, so that in the thrust toward greater strength and sway they achieve only an empty victory as they come to destruction or watering-down or cheapening of their own content.[32] This, too, was certainly never intended by those who launched widespread proselyting efforts in the first place.

Now, as we have indicated, Merton is currently disputed.[33] If Weber had a point, there is some uncertainty, at any rate, as to just how widespread and important the process he indicated was, although we are not suggesting that it was trivial. Mensching's dialectic is perhaps initially appealing, but it is possible to argue that in many cases he sees relevant phenomena the wrong way. Thus, "high" religions can often sensibly be argued to have "upgraded" populations that would otherwise not have changed. Did vulgar masses corrupt Islam or can it be argued with even greater cogency that Islam lifted large masses out of a very marked "vulgarity"? Perhaps the sociologist is too easily tempted to assume a dialectical play, too ready to make an effort to understand all in terms of some adroit paradox or intriguing mechanism—and perhaps especially so when he comes to that most tempting area of "unanticipated consequences of purposive social action." It will often be true that the historian can point to uncomfortable factual data that makes it clear that some presumed neat mechanism is not at work at all or only at work in a halting or lame way. With his knowledge of detail for particular societies the historian will often be able to indicate that some streamlined dialectical development postulated by a sociologist with a flair for theorizing simply does not do justice to the data which it is supposed to organize and clarify. All this is excellent and indispensable.

Conclusion

It is indispensable, but it is not enough. What is very much needed in this area is precisely close interaction between sociologist and historian. It will not do for the historian to dismantle some presumed mechanism and then be gleeful about the matter. His own chances for understanding in depth a caste system, an estate system, a class system, a feudal system,[34] the emergence of new cultural forms out of old can only be enhanced by a sure grasp of relevant mechanisms. (In emergence of new cultural forms from old, the process whereby historical actors start with certain ends in view but attain other, uncontemplated results which they *then* take up as new ends-in-view, abandoning the old ones—a process Wundt put under the heading of heterogony of ends—is not the least important to scrutinize.) The historian can do more than merely "cast doubt" here. By way of precise and thorough marshaling of detail he may help in a quite positive way. He may, for example, in the spirit of a previous comment we have made, elucidate a number of special ways in which an initially grossly discriminated boomerang effect operates. One may argue that it is broadly true that, as Joynt and Rescher say, the historian "is not a *producer* of general laws but a *consumer* of them."[35] But we already know that there is no question of general laws here. Knowledge of mechanisms as we have begun to understand them may help greatly in the formulation of laws, but that is something else. We suggest that mechanisms represent an area of really crucial convergence of the interests of sociologists and historians. Perhaps what we have already said is sufficiently persuasive on the point that the field of purposive action-unintended affect is an especially good one for the relevant collaboration on ferreting out and specifying mechanisms and enriching our comprehension of them. Both the sociological and the historical imaginations have a history of deep engagement in this field. Here, as elsewhere, too much would be lost to those imaginations by failure to take direct cognizance of the intellectual traditions that have been reviewed.

Notes

1. See Seymour M. Lipset and Richard Hofstadter, eds., *Sociology and History: Methods* (New York: Basic Books, 1968); also Hofstadter and Lipset, eds., *Turner and the Sociology of the Frontier* (New York: Basic Books, 1968). Note also the numerous references to "social sciences" and "sociology" indexed in John Higham et al., *History: The Development of Historical Studies in the United States* (Englewood Cliffs, N.J.: Prentice-Hall, 1965).

2. Stanley Elkins, *Slavery: A Problem in American Institutional and Intellectual Life* (Chicago: University of Chicago Press, 1959), p. 168.

3. Lipset and Hofstadter, *Methods*, p. 25.

4. Stanley Elkins and Eric McKittrick, "A Meaning for Turner's Frontier: Democracy in the Old Northwest," in Hofstadter and Lipset, *Turner*, pp. 120-51.

5. See Paul Barth, *Die Philosophie der Geschichte als Soziologie*, 3d and 4th eds. (Leipzig: Reisland, 1922), p. 124.

6. For Mandeville, the basic source is F.B. Kaye, ed., *The Fable of the Bees* (Oxford: Clarendon Press, 1924). For the Scots, in the present connection, see Louis Schneider, ed., *The Scottish Moralists* (Chicago: University of Chicago Press, 1967), "Introduction."

7. See especially *Sex and Repression in Savage Society* (London: Harcourt, Brace, 1927) and *The Sexual Life of Savages* (New York: Halcyon House, 1929).

8. See, e.g., Talcott Parsons, *Societies: Evolutionary and Comparative Perspectives* (Englewood Cliffs, N.J.: Prentice-Hall, 1966); Robert N. Bellah, "Religious Evolution," *American Sociological Review* 29 (June 1964): 358-74. Parsons gives more detailed indications of the sheer meaning of evolution at the level of societies than can possibly be given here. He stresses adaptive upgrading and inclusion in this entire connection. Inclusion is discussed below. Parsons's technical sense of social system and other matters (consideration of which would help in understanding the detail of his views on evolution) cannot here be taken up. As regards adaptive upgrading, evidently any discussion of this would have to take up once more the matter of "fitness" previously referred to. Such overlaps explain why our division of evolution into three subthemes was initially called somewhat arbitrary.

9. See Gary L. Buck and Alvin L. Jacobson, "Social Evolution and Structural-Functional Analysis: An Empirical Test," *American Sociological Review* 33 (June 1968):343-55.

10. See Parsons, *Societies,* passim. Cf. also Karl Mannheim, *Man and Society in an Age of Reconstruction* (New York: Harcourt, Brace, 1941), pp. 44-49.

11. [Here is an unacknowledged reference to the "Deferred Gratification" article. Ed.]

12. Note, for example, the work of Robert Wearmouth, as in the case of his *Methodism and the Common People of the Eighteenth Century* (London: Epworth, 1945). Still suggestive as background material in this entire connection is the treatment of Methodism in Lecky's great history of eighteenth-century England. See W. E. H. Lecky, *A History of England in the Eighteenth Century* (New York: Appleton, 1879), 2:567-699. Lecky writes of Whitefield that "he was filled with horror and compassion at finding in the heart of a Christian country, and in the immediate neighborhood of a great city, a population of many thousands sunk in the most brutal ignorance and vice, and *entirely excluded* from the ordinance of religion." *History of England*, 2:611, italics added. The reference is to the colliers of Kingswood in the neighborhood of the "great city" of Bristol.

13. See Marshall D. Sahlins and Elman R. Service, eds., *Evolution and Culture* (Ann Arbor: University of Michigan Press, 1960), ch. 5.

14. Cf. Veblen's *Imperial Germany and the Industrial Revolution* (New York: Viking Press, 1939). Cf. also Douglas F. Dowd, ed., *Thorstein Veblen: A Critical Reappraisal* (Ithaca, N.Y.: Cornell University Press, 1958), chs. 15, 16.

15. See George Sansom, *A History of Japan to 1334* (London: Cresset Press, 1958).

16. It should be entirely clear that the principle under discussion has biological as well as sociocultural applications. Chardin in effect suggests well what is involved in the principle when he remarks that "*para passu* with their physical development, horse, stag, and tiger become, like the insect, to some extent prisoners of the instruments of their swift-moving or predatory ways." See Teilhard de Chardin, *The Phenomenon of Man* (New York: Harper, 1959), p. 159. Chardin's point may be stated in the form that success brings its penalties and costs. Having, for example, made an "investment" in powerful jaws, the tiger has thereby made a commitment that cuts off certain possibilities of development as long as it lasts. The primates, and man in higher degree, feature a notable evolutionary strategy of avoiding various animal entrapments by "specializing" in the development of intelligence. Chardin, again, writes: "In itself, at its best, the differentiation of an organ is an immediate factor of superiority. But, because it is irreversible it thus imprisons the animal that undergoes it in a restricted path. . . . Specialisation paralyzes, ultra-specialisation kills. Paleontology is littered with such catastrophes. Because, right up to the Pliocene period, the primates remained the most 'primitive' of the mammals as regards their limbs, they remained also the most *free*. And what did they do with that freedom? They used it to lift themselves through successive upthrusts to the very frontiers of intelligence." *Phenomenon*, pp. 158-59.

17. William H. McNeill, *The Rise of the West* (Chicago: University of Chicago Press, 1963), p. 743, n. 13.

18. See George K. Zollschan and Walter Hirsch, eds., *Explorations in Social Change* (Boston: Houghton Mifflin, 1964), p. 384. Cf. Arnold Toynbee, *A Study of History* (London: Oxford University Press, 1939), 4:120, 260, 423f.

19. Cf. Robert K. Merton, "The Unanticipated Consequences of Purposive Social Action," *American Sociological Review* 1 (December 1936):894-904. Cf. also Merton's concern with unanticipated consequences in his *Social*

Theory and Social Structure (Glencoe: Free Press, 1957), passim.

20. A major relevant contribution is Friedrich Meinecke's remarkable book, *Die Entstehung des Historismus,* 2 vols. (Munich: Oldenbourg, 1936), which traces the idea through the works of a number of great historically oriented thinkers.

21. G. W. F. Hegel, *The Philosophy of History* (New York: Wiley, 1900), p. 20.

22. Ibid., p. 457.

23. Some good, germane remarks are made by Mazlish, who observes, for instance, that Hegel's major achievement was "to implement his insight by translating the intuitions of religion into philosophical statements, bearing within them the seeds of social science hypotheses." Again Mazlish notes more generally that "in its halting journey toward the precise cultural sciences, philosophy of history took sustenance from the vital waters of religious thought." Once more: "One of the strongest surviving elements of religion in much of the nineteenth-century philosophy of history and social science was the concept of Providence. Translated into more secular vocabularly, as the 'invisible hand' of Adam Smith, the 'cunning of Reason' of Hegel, or the 'historical materialism' of Marx, Providence became a sort of naturalistic Maxwell's 'demon,' regulating and controlling the behavior of human molecules." See Bruce Mazlish, *The Riddle of History* (New York: Harper, 1966), pp. 434-35, 436-37, 440; note, also, p. 441.

24. Robert M. MacIver, *Social Causation* (Boston: Ginn, 1942), p. 314.

25. Edward H. Carr, *What is History?* (New York: Knopf, 1962), p. 62. The great book, however, on this insight among historians is again Meinecke's *Die Entstehung des Historismus.*

26. Cf. Marx, *Capital* (New York: Modern Library, 1936), 1:81-96. Note also the thrust of the following: "In our description of the way, in which the conditions of production are converted into entities and into independent things as compared to the agents of production, we do not enter into a discussion of the manner, in which the interrelations of the world market, its constellations, the movements of market prices, the periods of credit, the cycles of industry and commerce, the changes from prosperity to crises, appear to these agents as overwhelming natural laws that rule them irresistibly and enforce their rule over them as blind necessities." Marx, *Capital* (Chicago: Kerr, 1909), 3:967-68. The connection of all this with "false consciousness" is quite plain.

27. One can make a *beginning* in these matters with Clyde Kluckhohn, *Navaho Witchcraft* (Boston: Beacon Press, 1962). (It is regrettable that Kluckhohn did not live to give this monograph the brilliant revision that the writer, on the basis of personal knowledge of the man, feels convinced he could have afforded.)

28. Weber, *Gesammelte Aufsätze zur Wissenschaftslehre* (Tübingen: Mohr, 1951), p. 33.

29. From the writer's field notes.

30. It should be added that we do not have to insist on tying the idea of mechanism exclusively to that of purposive action-unintended effect. Our discussion could too easily create an erroneous impression about this. But we do incline to the view that the purposive action-unintended effect area is a very

promising one for the discovery and analysis of mechanisms.

31. Robert K. Merton, "Science, Technology and Society in Seventeenth-Century England," in *Osiris* 4 (1938):360-632.

32. See, e.g., Mensching's *Soziologie der Religion* (Bonn: Röhrscheid, 1947), pp. 137-48.

33. See, e.g., T. K. Rabb, "Religion and the Rise of Modern Science," *Past and Present* 31 (July 1965):111-26.

34. How important have *consciously employed* mechanisms been in the sustenance of systems such as feudalism? How frequent the scheme whereby the great lord "invites" the lesser ones to his place of residence for a prolonged period (lest the lesser ones gain too much power in their own provinces) and then later delicately allows them to return when things threaten actually to get out of hand in their provinces because of *too long* an absence? And how often does this sort of consciously employed mechanism escape control and generate unforeseeable consequences?

35. C. B. Joynt and Nicholas Rescher, "The Problem of Uniqueness in History," *History and Theory* 1 (1961):154, as quoted and cited by William H. Dray, *Philosophy of History* (Englewood Cliffs, N.J.: Prentice-Hall, 1964), p. 6.

8
The Role of the Category of Ignorance in Sociological Theory: An Exploratory Statement
(1962)

Concern with the category of ignorance, whether implicit or explicit, has constantly appeared in the work of sociological theorists. Without attempting to be exhaustive, we may note the following examples. Marx's views on the fetishism of commodities "make sense" only on the presumption of ignorance on the part of laborers who do not know that their own actions in social context help to account for the relations of commodities to one another on the market. (In Marx's conception, "error," as well as "ignorance," plays a part in the fetishism.) Weber's treatment of formal and substantive rationality allows the significant presumption that economic agents engaged in formally rational action may be quite *unaware* of the failure of formal to coincide with substantive rationality. Mannheim, in making his own distinction between functional rationalization and substantial rationality, holds that, except for relatively few who have substantial rationality, men involved in the organizational processes of, say, factories and armies, tend to be ignorant and that systematic coordination of their own disparate activities which constitute functional rationalization. The sheer variety of concerns with ignorance on the part of sociological theorists is added to by Sorokin, who observes that "if empirical truth is . . . given an unlimited liberty for its development, it may prove exceedingly injurious to many 'illusions' which are necessary for the existence of values in a group."[1]

At least one contemporary theorist, namely, Merton, has built the category of ignorance into central terms of analysis. In making his familiar distinction between manifest and latent functions, he defines the former as "objective consequences contributing to the adjustment or adaptation of [a social] system which are intended and *recognized* by the participants in the system," while latent functions are "neither intended nor *recognized*."[2] Leaving aside "adjustment" or "adaptation," it is clearly no deviation from Merton's sense to say that latent functions are consequences of social actions and arrangements intended by no one and unknown to some (unspecified) proportion of actors. In the same year in which Merton's paper on manifest and latent functions appeared, Moore and Tumin published their valuable pioneering analysis of "functions of ignorance," with its provocative terminal suggestion that "ignorance must be viewed not simply as a passive or dysfunctional condition, but as an active and often positive element in operating structures and relations."[3]

Given this variety of concerns with ignorance, it is not possible to say that there is any unitary, highly self-consistent preoccupation with ignorance that points to "*the* problem of ignorance in sociological theory." However, the work of Merton, that of Moore and Tumin, and the few recent specifically sociological researches on ignorance that are available have placed concern with the category of ignorance within the framework of functional analysis, and it is also more or less within that framework that the present paper seeks to define its problem. Indeed, the paper proceeds from the contention that functional theory suggests a perspective on ignorance and a conceptual apparatus for its analysis *in institutional context* (a phrase which will be explained subsequently) that have not been made explicit. But it is also contended that so-called organic theory presents a significant complementary perspective and apparatus that need exhibition at the same time. This does not mean that there are no differences between functional and organic theory in the perspective on ignorance they afford. Differences do exist, but there is also a substantially shared perspective. It is the design of this paper: (1) to exhibit the perspective on ignorance in institutional context and present the conceptual apparatus for analysis of phenomena of ignorance that can be found in functional and organic theory; (2) to show the relevance of the perspective and apparatus to areas of sociological interest (organizational analysis and relations of "experts" and "laymen" being taken as examples) other than those in which they will have been initially exhibited; (3) to give a preliminary formulation of types of cases in which ignorance is "eufunctional,"[4] that is, influenced by the perspective and apparatus that will have been presented; (4) to comment very briefly on some problems of ignorance in relation to "reason." The stress that ignorance can be "eufunctional" pervades much of this paper. The motivation for this, however, is "heuristic," and it would be a gross misinterpretation of the paper to take it as a paean in praise of ignorance. In the carrying out of the objects indicated, an authentic sociological theory of ignorance is not achieved; it is the design of the paper to move *toward* an authentic theory through the presentation of a perspective, certain concepts, a number of tentative propositions about ignorance as "eufunctional," and a consideration of ignorance in relation to reason. In broader terms, the paper has the twofold object of setting out an analytical apparatus whose relevance to areas outside those in which it originates is explored and of presenting some particular conditions in which ignorance is "eufunctional."

Perspective on Ignorance: Pertinent Aspects of Functional and Organic Theory

Some recent studies focused on ignorance have been concerned with ignorance in *situational* rather than in *institutional* context. Stryker, in an analysis of role-taking accuracy and adjustment,[5] found that parents, more emotionally involved as they are with their adult offspring than the latter with them, are more likely than the offspring to resist and distort evidence of discrepancies between parental and filial attitudes and behavior. He also noted that when parents openly recognize the character of such evidence the problem of their adjustment to their offspring becomes intensified. Stryker's evidence is congruous with his hypothesis that parental vulnerability increases the likelihood of blocks to communication that would apprise parents of the outlook and comportment of their adult children. Ignorance, in this framework, appears to exercise a protective function, and, as Stryker puts the matter, "at least under certain circumstances," knowledge of others can be "maladjustive." Ignorance is thus a central concern in a context of immediate interaction, and its effects—or the effects of knowledge or enlightenment—are studied within the confines of a specific interaction net and not beyond these. Similarly, when Davis considers situations in which physicians must arrive at some decision about how much and what kind of information to convey to the parents of victims of paralytic poliomyelitis,[6] his focus is on the consequences of ignorance or knowledge for specific persons in a strictly delimited interaction context. There is no stress on ramifying consequences of ignorance or knowledge (on the part of specific persons), outside or beyond the interaction network which he studies. He and Stryker are thus both concerned with ignorance in situational context.

On the other hand, Clark's study of cooling-out in higher education[7] comes closer to consideration of ignorance in institutional context. Clark considers problems presented by junior college students who might desire to transfer to four-year institutions but lack necessary ability. These students "need" a reorientation which will draw them away from interest in four-year schools. However, the process of cooling them out "must be kept reasonably away from public scrutiny and not clearly understood by prospective clientele," since otherwise "the organization's ability to perform it" would be damaged. Cooling out is reinterpreted for its "positive" character as stress is placed on the junior college as a device to give high-school graduates additional opportunity; and Clark indicates that students themselves help to keep the cooling out function "concealed by wishful unawareness." But most significant for present purposes is this observation: "If high-school seniors and their families were to define the junior college as a place which diverts college-bound students, a probable consequence would be a turning-away from the junior college and increased pressure for admission to the four-year colleges and universities that are otherwise protected to some degree." Clark's construing of the functions of cooling out thus takes him beyond the consideration of ignorance in the context of interaction between, say, mediocre junior college student and benevolent but sage counselor who wishes to "guide" the student without unduly obtruding on him the fact of his limitations. It takes him into consideration of the ramifying consequences of ignorance for a wider social structure. This occasions concern with ignorance in institutional context, which is ignorance as it is involved in or accompanies actions that can be regarded by an informed outsider from the point of view of their contribution to a "large" social outcome. The following review of certain aspects of functional and organic theory should clarify the meaning of ignorance in institutional context, and it will also be clear that it is ignorance in this sense that has been the main concern of the theory reviewed; in fact, ignorance in situational context has often been without interest for functional and organic theorists.

Functional Theory

Some of the strongest intimations of the significance of the category of ignorance in the genesis or maintenance of magic. But there is also the analysis, particularly as that analysis has to do with religion and magic. It is accordingly worthwhile to revert briefly to the work of such functionalists as Durkheim and Malinowski. In Durkheim's work on religion,[8] the category of ignorance has a special kind of fortune. In the literature produced by Tylor, Spencer, and others, of which Durkheim was of course highly critical, primitive man is represented as building essentially false constructions of the world, constructions in which sheer ignorance plays a large role. Animism appears as a faulty construction, to be explained by ignorance—or by ignorance and error. But in repudiating the intellectualist or rationalist position on religion which depended so heavily on the presumption of ignorance on the part of primitives (who at the same time reasoned most competently), Durkheim in his own way continued to give considerable scope to ignorance. If the "reality" to which religion supposedly corresponds is "society itself," at the very least Australian primitives do not know this. Durkheim's analysis has repeatedly raised the question of how effectively religion would function, or how nearly it would still have the consequences he claims for it, if the "veil" were penetrated by the ordinary participants in religious exercises. By penetration of the veil is meant the acquisition by the participants in the exercises of the knowledge that feelings of awe and of the presence of the transcendent are simply occasioned by the attributes and constraints of society and that actions initially addressed in good faith to subjectively significant religious objects merely lead to outcomes like group solidarity.[9]

The role imputed to ignorance by Durkheim in his theory of religion is, thus, clearly a considerable one, and the same thing is generally true of functional theories of religion: Such theories insistently raise the question of what may happen when latent functions become manifest, surely one of the basic questions for sociological analysis of ignorance. But more than this: Durkheim's view was that the solidarity, cohesiveness, integration of the individual with the group, and the like, that religion brought about, were brought about indirectly. *Indirection* is the first in a set of terms bearing on ignorance that will be specified here. Social solidarity is not achieved in the religious context through a deliberate fixing of solidarity as an end to be achieved. It is achieved, in Durkheim's theory, through actions subjectively addressed to other ends, and "ends" such as solidarity are achieved in ignorance *and* indirectly.

In Malinowski's view of magic,[10] the category of ignorance is overtly stressed as an explanatory category at one point, but at another point its role becomes somewhat obscured and is not systematically considered. When Malinowski sets out his familiar thesis that magic comes into play at the margin of knowledge and control, where resources of a scientific-technical character are at an end (and where, also, men feel that vital interests of theirs are involved),[11] he imputes a plain and important role to ignorance in the genesis or maintenance of magic. But there is also the matter of the magician's ignorance of the ways of the functioning of his magic. There is an evident difference between the magician's claims for what his magic "does" and his apprehension of his own magical procedure, on the one hand, and what the magic may "do" in actuality and the manner of its interpretation by the analytical anthropologist, on the other. In this matter of the magician's unawareness of the way of working of his magic (a way the anthropologist believes himself able to grasp), Malinowski offers little. But this whole aspect of his theory plainly suggests questions similar to those raised by Durkheim's theory.

The anthropologist of Malinowskian persuasion goes on the hypothesis that the claims of the primitive magician for the effects of his magic (which claims typically refer to the external world) are incorrect and have little or nothing to do with the actual effects of the magic (which typically bear on the human psyche and human group). What if the magician should learn that his vaunted ability to avert storms, say, was not an ability to avert storms at all but an "ability" to avert a measure of desperation? Would the latter result be attained as effectively as before, or attained at all, once awareness that it, and not some putative influence on the external world, was in fact being brought about? Evidently, this again raises questions about the making manifest of latent functions. Durkheim and Malinowski both appear to place heavy reliance on ignorance as "preservative." Their views strongly suggest that, were knowledge to supervene at certain crucial junctures, religion and magic would not perform their "beneficent" functions. But at the same time these functions are attained indirectly. No more than Durkheim's Australian does Malinowski's Trobriander rationally and deliberately devolop magic as a "technology" instrumental to such ends as tension alleviation. Rather, he engages in actions that, according to Malinowski's hypothesis, terminate indirectly in tension alleviation. The actions are not oriented to tension alleviation.[12]

This feature of indirection is even more evident in a comment by Charles Bennett on Santayana's functional view of prayer. In broad and inevitably somewhat poetic terms, Santayana suggested: "Prayer . . . accomplishes nothing material. . . . It will not bring rain, but until rain comes it may cultivate hope and resignation and may prepare the heart for any issue." Bennett observes—and the observation is as pertinent for Durkheim or Malinowski as for Santayana—that "it is clear from this that if one is to gain these spiritual benefits *one must pray not for these benefits but for rain.* The very condition for getting them is that you be superstitious and unenlightened."[13] Thus, Bennett stresses, in these two brief sentences, first indirection and then ignorance.

If certain social effects are attained indirectly they are also attained *intermediately.* Actors in religious context engage in behavior that has, according to Durkheim, effects such as social solidarity; but such effects, when we look "back" from them, have antecedents which can be regarded as intermediates or intervening elements that lead to them. Indirection and intermediacy are substantially the same phenomenon, looked at in somewhat different ways. When it is simply emphasized that actors do not aim at "beneficent" outcomes at the remote level of such things as social solidarity but at far more limited personal goals, and that the latter are implicated in a process that leads to the remote outcomes, the focus is on indirection. But when perspective shifts and attention is particularly directed to the way in which individual actions (together with the consequences) "causally" construct the remote outcomes, the individual actions are looked upon as intermediates. *Intermediacy* is the second term in our set of terms bearing on ignorance in institutional context. It may be noted, incidentally, that the chain metaphor has sometimes been employed to suggest indirection and intermediacy, as, for example, by S. F. Nadel, when he remarks that "the actors can calculate only the adjacent links in the chain but not the end links, which, for them, are unexpected or at least unintended."[14] If the chain metaphor has some (limited) utility, the other terms suggested—*indirection* and *intermediacy*—will nevertheless be retained.

If actors do not anticipate or plan for those termini or consequences of their actions that are called end links in the chain metaphor, a question arises how it comes about that actors are motivated to "forge" the intermediate links. This question may be rephrased as a question bearing on the *attractiveness of intermediates*—which is a third term in our set. In illustration, the question of the attractiveness of intermediates is easily answered in a case in which actors are ignorant of the circumstances that sexual activity leads to reproduction. Reproduction is an end link, and the motivation to forge intermediate ones is explained by the intrinsic attractiveness of sexual activity itself. Durkheim and Malinowski may without violence to their theses by interpreted as saying that the immediate emotional "gain" from certain totemic and magical activities makes those activities intrinsically "attractive."

The sense of the three terms presented may be sharpened by a consideration of organic theory. In the course of our discussion two other terms will be added.

Organic Theory

Organic theory, [15] as here understood, is partial to the general notion that historically evolved institutions, as they stand at any particular time, are likely to incorporate considerable "wisdom" based on past experience and reflection. This wisdom is not necessarily present to the minds of those who act in the terms of the institutions; it is indeed more likely to be unknown to them, but that does not preclude its having "beneficent" effects. From Edmund Burke to Friedrich Hayek, law, polity, language, religion, the market, and other phenomena have been lauded by organic theorists for their supposed incorporation of a wisdom that was never direct and deliberate but, rather, indirect and inadvertent. The organic, spontaneously developed institutions are opposed to deliberate, rationally constructed social arrangements (whether projected in fancy or worked out in reality), and the organic theorists tend to stress the relative success of the former, their surer and socially less hazardous achievement of "results." This claim for the superiority of the organically evolved is associated with an insistence that the organically evolved institutions attain their efficacy precisely *because* they involve indirection and ignorance. As a kind of prime text for organic theorists, we may take Adam Smith's famous and familiar observation that the individual "neither intends to promote the public interest, *nor knows* [italics added] how much he promotes it" when he pursues his own gain, but that, nevertheless, "by pursuing his own interest he frequently promotes that of the society more effectually than when he really intends to promote it." This significantly represents the individual as ignorant of the circumstance that he promotes public interest, indicates that the pursuit of the individual's interest leads indirectly to public interest, and asserts that this combination of ignorance and indirection is "more effectual" than would be an alternative combination of knowledge of one's objects and effort to attain them. The locus of wisdom, one may say, is neither in the individual nor in any combination of individuals deliberately seeking to attain some large social end such as public welfare;[16] it is in a set of arrangements, well-worn and traditional paths of action, that older organic theorists were inclined to regard as providentially given.

But organic theory is not confined to the economic sphere, or to the political, or the legal or the religious, or the like. It has an unmistakably very wide relevance and scope, as indicated, for example, by Hayek's citation of Menger's comment that "perhaps the most significant problem of the social sciences" is raised by the question of "how it is possible that institutions which serve the common welfare and are most important for its advancement can arise without a common will aiming at their creation.[17] The question is thus raised in a form that clearly carries it beyond any particular sphere such as the economic. It becomes a general sociological question.

In sociological terms, then, organic theory rests on the view that there occur cases of action (which for organic theory are crucial and render a basic "model" for the understanding of social action at large) having the following characteristics: (1) As actors seek to achieve their goals and proceed accordingly, they produce some or all of the results at which they aim, but simultaneously produce other results, effects of their own action which they do not know about. (2) This ignorance on the part of the actors of "collateral" effects ("unanticipated consequences")[18] they produce is intimately connected with indirection, since through one object at which they aim they also bring about another or others. (3) The objects sought by the actors operate as intermediates or intermediary agencies instrumental in bringing about the effects which are not contemplated: as seeking individual gain independently by many individuals operates to bring about public prosperity; or as in Durkheim's functionalist view worship on the part of individuals terminates remotely in social solidarity. (4) The objects sought by the actors are intrinsically attractive and are presumed to give adequate motivation for their action. (5) The uncontemplated effects are "beneficent" or "eufunctional"; they advance the interests or values of the actors—and "more effectually" than would a procedure in which the actors initially knew the remote effects, projected them as goals, and deliberately strove to attain them.

The question whether this representation is ideologically influenced or has ideological consequences cannot be done justice here.[19] But the terms *indirection, intermediacy,* and *attractiveness of intermediates* as all (effectively) prominent in organic theory and as significant in it as in functional theory. The problem posed by the last term, *attractiveness of intermediates,* can be stated (as has already been noted) as the problem of the motivation of actors in their movement from one intermediate to another in the flow of intermediates that construct the social outcome that interests the theorist. When intermediates are in fact attractive to actors, at least some partial explanation of movement from one intermediate to another is achieved. In organic theory, it may be stressed again, actors cannot be presumed to be motivated by a contemplation of ultimate or remote social outcomes, but they must, to put it crudely, somehow "get" to those outcomes, and if they are to do so they must be given inducements from point to point on the way. In his very interesting endeavor to explain the rise of the institution of money, Menger in effect relied heavily on the conception of the attractiveness of intermediates, endeavoring to show that, as each intermediate in a sequence (chain) of intermediates that led to the fully developed institution was constructed, its construction was adequately motivated by the working of self-interest.[20] The attempt is thus made to answer Menger's own question of "how it is possible that institutions which serve the common welfare . . . can arise without a common will aiming at their creation." But there is one further line of emphasis in organic theory that is also designed to help answer this question. This rests on the conception of what will here be called the *ignorance-knowledge compound.* Only slight utilization will hereafter be made of this notion, but it clarifies relevant aspects of organic theory and is clearly a part of the conceptual apparatus which that theory brings to bear on ignorance.

In the view of social institutions held by organic theorists, there is an element of stress that knowledge plays a role compounded with that of ignorance. As, let us say, actors follow their self-interest, they apply such knowledge pertinent to problem-solution as they can discover. This knowledge becomes "built into" their behavior. Its background in original problem-solution is often forgotten, and the behavior founded on knowledge is then transmitted from one generation to another simply as normative: so one must do. As bits of wisdom are built into heritable biological modes of functioning, so bits of wisdom are represented as built into social institutions. Ignorance and knowledge become mixed or compounded. On such grounds, one may adhere to an "evolutionary" view, "based on the insight that the result of the experimentation of many genenerations may embody more experience than any one man possesses"; or one may contend: "Most of the advantages of social life, especially in its more advanced forms which we call 'civilization,' rest on the fact that the individual benefits from more knowledge than he is aware of. It might be said that civilization begins when the individual in pursuit of his ends can make use of more knowledge than he has himself acquired and when he can transcend the boundaries of this ignorance by profiting from knowledge he does not himself possess." The conception of the ignorance-knowledge compound helps in understanding why organic theorists repudiate the view that, as Hayek puts it, "all useful institutions" must be "deliberate contrivances."[21] Organic theorists hold that while actors may conjointly achieve important "beneficent" results, they do so in considerable ignorance *and* in ignorance that the (socially) transmitted behavior they are reproducing contains accumulations of "knowledge" now forgotten or no longer perceived as knowledge. If this is correct, the conception of the ignorance-knowledge compound presents another avenue whereby some explanation of the "beneficent" effects of action not oriented to those effects as goals may be attained. The actors do "better than they know" merely because they "know" better than they are aware of knowing. The notion of the ignorance-knowledge compound is at most rather vaguely suggested in functional theory, but much more plainly suggested in organic theory.

There is a final notion constantly hinted at in functional and organic theory and pertinent to the aspects of these theories here reviewed. It may be called the notion of *the transmutation mechanism*. Functional and organic theorists constantly touch on, although they often fail to solve satisfactorily, the problem of *the precise ways* in which individual purposive actions addressed to limited objects can lead on to uncontemplated social effects. The words "lead on," as just used, in fact (however hard they or like words may be to avoid) beg all the questions that need to be answered by knowledge of transmutation mechanisms. Just how do individual purposive actions "lead on"? Transmutation mechanisms operate in the area "between" individually realized goals and uncontemplated outcomes taken or defined as social effects. Thus, where individual couples desire and have children but there is no contemplation of "continuance of the personnel of the society" as a goal or desideratum, the conversion from individually realized object to social outcome or effect is contingent on simple additivity. As one female after another gives birth a certain level of births is reached and "continuance" ensured (other things being equal) by the sum of all individual births. In Adam Smith's classic effort to show how the desire for individual gain ignorantly and unintentionally brings about general economic welfare, transmutation mechanisms are already more complicated: they work through interaction of individuals on the market, through relations of supply and demand that are certainly not reducible to anything like simple additivity. It has been easier for sociologists to note the sheer existence of "unanticipated consequences of purposive social action" than to demonstrate why or how specific purposive social actions become transmuted into specific unanticipated consequences and thereby identify and describe transmutation mechanisms.

The above perspective and conceptual apparatus have been developed as they have in part because they bear on ignorance in institutional context, which is currently receiving very little attention from sociologists. But it is not the object of this paper to stress, and rest with, a simple distinction between ignorance in institutional context and ignorance in situational context, or to rest with presentation of any of the above. Actually, the outlook and conceptual apparatus presented, bearing on ignorance in institutional context, show clear continuity with, and relevance to, problems of current interest to sociologists. This continuity and relevance can be exemplified in organizational analysis and in the relations of experts and laymen. The heuristic stress on the "eufunctional" character of ignorance is maintained in the following exemplifications.

Organizations and Experts

Organizations

In his well-known analysis of a state employment agency, Blau found that nondiscriminatory action toward Negroes was more securely attained *indirectly*—through the motivation of employment interviewers to make placements, regardless of whether specific persons placed were White or Negro—than by the direct requirement not to discriminate. The interviewers could and did do certain things (such as not discriminating against Negroes) more effectively when they simply did *not* know that their action was bringing those things about. Blau comments: "The hypothesis may be advanced that a social pattern that has a latent function is more effective than a different pattern that has the same manifest function if conscious or unconscious resistance against attaining this objective can be expected.[22] There may also be other conditions in which "a social pattern that has a latent function is more effective than a different pattern that has the same manifest function," but that is not the essential point here. Rather, it needs stress that the notion of "gain through indirection"[23] and through ignorance is implicit in Blau's work. The emphasis on indirection itself is plain enough. Further, in the terms previously developed, the making of placements by the interviewers worked intermediately toward the terminus (not "goal") of nondiscrimination, and Blau also makes it clear that the making of placements was an "attractive" intermediate (while nondiscrimination as an overtly posed *goal* had only limited attractiveness).

That problems bearing on ignorance in institutional context constantly come up in organizational analysis is also strongly suggested by March and Simon's general study of organizations. March and Simon distinguish between "motivational" and "cognitive" identification with a "subgoal," and they ask: "What difference does it make whether subgoal identification is motivationally or cognitively produced— whether the attachment to the subgoal has been internalized or is only indirect, through a cognitive link to some other goal?"[24] Where the attachment is indirect, *in March and Simon's sense,* the link to a larger goal is "cognitively" produced, through knowledge of how subgoal leads to larger goal. Where attachment is "motivational," the subgoal is cherished for its own sake. Ideally, it should be shown how immersion in and involvement with the subgoal alone "leads," or fails to "lead," to the larger organizational goals (and what part supervision may play in this). Are intermediates demonstrably attractive? Precisely who has to keep the overall goals in view? The intrinsic superiority of cognitive links is by no means clear a priori. Do organizations present problems of strategic allocation of ignorance as well as of knowledge? Soldiers, on some of the evidence presented in *The American Soldier,*[25] appear to contribute quite effective links to the chain of military behavior leading to the overall object of defeating the enemy in time of war even when they quite "forget" the object.[26]

Barnard observed long ago that "understanding or acceptance of the general purpose of [organizations] is not . . . essential. . . . Complex organizations are characterized by obvious lack of complete understanding and acceptance of general purposes."[27] Does enlightenment of variously located participants in organizations "help" their functions or merely hinder the smooth working of indirection and intermediacy, and under what circumstances? The perspective here developed constrains one to ask such questions, even if March and Simon's own interests lead elsewhere. The perspective is particularly relevant to what Gouldner calls the natural-system "model" of organizations, in which, "in given situations, the ignorance of certain participants may not be considered injurious but functional to the maintenance of the system's equilibrium."[28]

It is evident, too, that organizations present a rich field for the analysis of transmutation mechanisms. The worker substantially ignorant or only dimly aware of various "high-level" factory goals (and potentially indifferent to them if he should become aware of them) may nevertheless be motivated to "help a buddy," just as the soldier in a somewhat analogous situation may be, while the limited motivation of each can be effectively built into a chain whose terminal link is just the "high-level" goals. Organizations undoubtedly present more complexities in the analysis of transmutation mechanisms than this bare indication can suggest.[29]

Experts and Laymen

The outlook on ignorance in institutional context and the associated concepts, derived from functional and organic theory, are also relevant to other areas of sociological concern, but only one other broad area can here be treated—very cursorily and incompletely: that of relations of experts and laymen in therapeutic situations.

The problems of the professional therapies are partly problems of allocation of knowledge. The question of the extent to which the professionally equipped expert lets the (patient-) layman "in" on what he seeks to do is a crucial one. The psychoanalyst's stress on the need for the layman to acquire peculiar kinds of knowledge is familiar. Cure or remission of symptoms is held to be appreciably contingent on insight, on the layman's acquisition of the kind of knowledge the expert-therapist is supposed to possess. With some reservations, the layman must become an "expert" himself. In medical practice at large, outside psychotherapy, cure or symptom remission is generally thought to be far less dependent on converting the layman into something like an expert. There are special circumstances in which the layman's knowledge has to be relatively large for his own protection, but knowledge is often not therapeutically important for him, he often lacks interest in it, and he might be disturbed by relatively precise knowledge of medical detail. In the first (psychotherapeutic) type of case, both expert and layman need to "know"; in the second (with exceptions), only the expert needs to "know" very much.

A third type may be exemplified by the situation of a social worker who wishes to convert youngsters away from delinquent behavior by involving them, say, in the acitivities of an athletic-social club. The social worker as expert has certain ends in view and regards the athletic-social activities as means to these. It would scarecely do to let the youngsters "in" on his purposes. That would require that they also take an instrumental attitude toward the activities and become enlisted in an endeavor to effect their own "reform"—a thing the more hazardous the more they are ambivalent or downright antagonistic toward the notion of their own reform.[30] In this kind of case, letting the layman "in" on what the expert has in view easily becomes dysfunctional: the announcement of the sheer "therapeutic" purpose could well jeopardize that purpose, and accordingly the layman had "better not know."

There are parallels to these cases elsewhere, as of course in organizations, but it needs main stress that the social worker confronts a problem of indirection, intermediacy, and the making attractive of intermediates. Success is dependent on the involvement of the delinquents in a behavioral chain that leads through links that have an intrinsic appeal to a terminus (not for the delinquents a "goal") unknown beforehand. The case has strategic points of resemblance to that presented by Blau, in which motivation to make placements functioned indirectly to effect nondisriminatory practice (putting aside the adventitious circumstance that there was no "planning" in Blau's situation). The perspective here developed enforces realization of the cognate character of such cases. It also indicates that the consideration of ignorance in situational context shades into concern with ignorance in institutional context, precisely as one would expect, as soon as there is readiness to consider the consequences of ignorance outside very particular frameworks. The social worker's problem gets beyond the bounds of ignorance in situational context within which the other types of problems (psychotherapeutic and general-medical) occur. It is still recognizably a problem in therapy but it also clearly points toward objects such as the mitigation of juvenile delinquence in the society at large. It is worth remembering that a sufficiently old-fashioned and single-minded organic theorist could well have been tempted to see the three types of cases presented as a "progression" suggesting a fourth term. In such a fourth term there would be neither expert nor layman in the human world, but a divine expert would have so disposed matters that a "beneficent" ignorance would prevail here below while all sorts of happy "purposes" (perhaps contingent on that very ignorance) were being realized.

These indications of the relevance of the perspective developed to areas of sociological concern beyond those in which it was initially presented still give no systematic answer to the problem of specification of conditions or types of cases in which, as Moore and Tumin have phrased the matter, ignorance functions as a "positive element in operating structures and relations." The next section represents an attempt at a listing of relevant types of cases. This attempt exploits and rests on the foregoing materials and is limited by them. It is neither "complete" nor designed to afford rigorously formulated and verified propositions, which are substantially unavailable in this field. It contains an inevitable speculative element. Its purpose is not to afford a broad taxonomy of functions of ignorance, as in the case of Moore and Tumin's work. Its purpose is rather to move toward a presentation of types of cases or conditions in which those with "liberal" or "democratic" values would agree ignorance is "eufunctional." The rationale of this purpose should be at least suggested. Where ignorance appears as an element in a crude "exploitation" situation and works at the same time to the interest of manipulators, against the interests of manipulated persons, and to the interests of no other parties, it is of little significance from the point of view now adopted. If physicians should manipulate ignorant laymen in such fashion as to make money and not to advance the laymen's health, ignorance on the part of the laymen might be said to be formally "eufunctional"—*if* the making of money by physicians is taken as the criterion in the light of which "eufunctionality" is judged. But the design of the following is to present a number of cases or conditions in which ignorance does *not* appear as an element in a crude and obvious "exploitation" phenomenon— where it appears to constitute a "real problem" in the light of "liberal" or "democratic" values and cannot easily be dismissed as a non-desideratum. Myrdal has attempted to develop more fully the logic of the procedure here involved in terms of what he speaks of as selection of "relevant and significant value premises."[31] The effort that follows must pay the price of the relative vagueness of the criteria rendered by values only generally described as "liberal" or "democratic." The propositions to be presented, then, are tentative in a number of ways. They are set out on the presumption that it is useful in moving toward a sociological theory of ignorance to make the kind of beginning that they afford. In the course of presenting them, advantage is taken of the opportunity to make some additional comments pertinent to the concerns of this paper.

Eufunctional Ignorance

1. Ignorance is eufunctional in cases or conditions in which knowledge would mean the revealing of information that would be directly and simply painful to have and no other significant consequences

would occur. Stryker's type of case fits well here, as do cases of the type considered by Davis, in which realization on the part of parents of the poor prospects of their poliomyelitis-afflicted children would be disturbing. This is the simplest kind of case here considered. It is the existence of this kind that underlies much of the crude force of the folkloristic "where ignorance is bliss, 'tis folly to be wise." Cases of this kind are from one point of view rather trivial. But from another point of view, they are of significance because of their clear-cut character. From this point of view, "interesting" cases bearing on ignorance arise when germane empirical points and value assumptions are widely agreed upon and those with a "liberal" or "democratic" outlook *still* are constrained to admit that ignorance is eufunctional. Cases of this first type, then, are significant *insofar as* it is hard to deny the painfulness, in fact, of obtaining certain kinds of knowledge, hard to relinquish the value stance that pain is not a desideratum, and hard to show that there are compensations for the pain brought by knowledge.[32]

2. Ignorance is eufunctional in cases or conditions in which some of the results of action, if they became known to the particular actors who brought them about, would be objects of indifference or even of distaste or antagonism, and in which the following also hold: there is no manipulation; the results to which there is indifference or hostility are taken by definition or value assumption as generally socially desirable; there are additional results of action which are in the interest of the actors. The situation described by Blau and noticed above is an example. The actor's "motto" upon enlightenment (insofar as he focused *mainly* on the "unwanted" results) would be: "If I had known what this would lead to, I would not have done it"—as interviewers inclined to discriminate against Negroes might regret that their placement-oriented action had inadvertently led to nondiscrimination (although they had still benefited insofar as they had in fact made placements) and seek to prevent this in the future. Nondiscrimination would be taken as "generally socially desirable." No one manipulated the interviewers into nondiscrimination. Variants of this type of case need not be pursued—such as the actually simpler variant in which all the conditions specified would hold except that there would not be results in the interest of the actors. (Also, in this type of case, questions of quantity are of evident importance, and may have to be given some rudimentary answer before statements such as the one with which this paragraph begins can become fully meaningful. In what "degree," for instance, are certain results social desiderata?)

3. Ignorance is eufunctional in cases or conditions in which a therapeutic or quasi-therapeutic situation prevails and therapeutic per-

sonnel exercise supportive manipulation. In supportive manipulation, therapeutic experts handle patients, clients, and the like, in such fashion as to reinforce the "positive" side of an ambivalent orientation on the part of the treated. This is not acknowledged to those under treatment, who are ambivalent about such matters as "getting well" or desisting from delinquent behavior. The whole procedure is undertaken on the presumption that the treated are "not yet ready" to affirm and pursue on their own resources a variety of "healthy goals." The situation may be seen as one of implicit contract between therapist and treated person that certain therapeutic goals shall not be revealed up to a certain point because of their probable alarming or disorganizing effect upon the treated if they are made known prematurely. (Ignorance thus becomes eufunctional virtually by definition of supportive manipulation.) A manipulative element is clearly present in the therapist's procedure. This type of case also differs from the first in that premature knowledge on the part of patient or client would not simply have painful results but would endanger an entire therapeutic enterprise.

4.   Ignorance is eufunctional in cases or conditions in which the acquisition of knowledge by the previously ignorant would have the distinctive results further indicated. Knowledge would bring awareness to the previously ignorant that they were being handled in such fashion as to bring about some end defined as socially necessary or desirable by manipulators and by others—an end such as the diversion of a surplus of students from regular four-year colleges which would otherwise be overburdened and suffer lowering of standards. At the same time, the acquisition of knowledge would hamper realization of the end because those becoming cognizant of the manipulation would react resentfully and resist the end on the ground that it failed to benefit *them*. The type thus specified plainly covers some of the more "delicate" kinds of cases. A variant form presumably more acceptable, more unequivocally eufunctional to the "democratically" inclined, would be one in which such an end as diversion of surplus students was still realized but in which it could also be reasonably argued that students cooled out were being benefited themselves. (Various questions of degree or quantity would again become important.) In some of its forms, this type of case would evidently show important points of similarity to the previous one. (The types of cases in the last three categories have been somewhat arbitrarily ordered on the dimension of manipulation, ranging from no manipulation through supportive manipulation to manipulation in which the supportive element is either absent or present only in special variants. The next type of case is of a different order.)

5.   Ignorance is eufunctional in cases or conditions in which knowl-

edge of functions of action, as of functions of religious action, would be taken by believers in the intrinsic value of the action as "irrevelant" or "insulting" and would initiate serious self-questioning. In Durkheim's and similar representations of religion, once more, religious activity indirectly and intermediately works toward consequences such as social solidarity. The religious actor's apprehension of the character and significance of what he is doing has nothing to do with social solidarity. As he sees the matter, he addresses himself to a god or a transcendent realm or the like. The notion that his activity produces consequences in this world ("functions of religion") is irrelevant to his intention and orientation. Since these consequences, in the sociological view, are mundane or secular, he readily looks upon them with suspicion, as functions that somehow challenge the validity of his subjective understanding and orientation. The believer certainly can, in principle, affirm that prayer, religious ritual, and the like have efficacy in a transcendent realm *no matter what* their mundane effects may be. But when he becomes informed about their mundane effects, there is at least a chance that he will begin to suspect, rightly or wrongly, that the mundane effects are the only ones. The result of this may be loss of faith. It may also be the initiation of an "instrumental" attitude toward religion, in which some knowledge of its functions and an acceptance of those functions as "valuable" leads to the effort to "make" religion do what it may once have been presumed to do "naturally." This reaction is seen in figures as diverse as Auguste Comte and Norman Vincent Peale. Finally, the believer cognizant of the sociological perspective may seek to *ignore* ("forget about") it in an attempt to preserve belief despite such tension as may be created by the knowledge that the belief has mundane effects. A basic hypothesis here is that the acquisition of knowledge of previously latent functions creates a good chance that religious transmutation mechanisms will be jeopardized.[33]

There are also cases or conditions looming large in the eyes of organic theorists, in which knowledge carries the danger that it will bring arrogance or *hubris* and initiate endeavors in planning that overlook or despise the "natural" mechanisms of society providing for automatic adjustments of difficulties, imbalances, disequilibria, or the like, and that will be more "costly" than "natural" adjustments. Stress upon this kind of case is connected, in organic theory, with a philosophical view, which may or may not have validity, that human agents are presumptuous to think that they can successfully revise the natural foundations of the society that sustains them. But whether this view is valid or not, a characteristic and major question for organic theory is whether it is even possible to collate and organize that diffuse, widely allocated knowledge that goes into the working of institutions (such as the market) in such a way that *centralized,* planned direction of the institutions shall be more effective in the attainment of beneficent social outcomes than spontaneous action.[34] The type of "suspicion" of knowledge that organic theory manifests is accordingly different from the suspicion implicit in much functional theory (as of religion) of the past. The latter is suspicious of knowledge as something which may damage significant functions by bringing a demoralizing enlightenment on the point that a variety of actions demonstrably produces not what actors have in view but something else (not, for example, closeness to the divine, but social cohesion). But organic theory is suspicious of knowledge because of its presumed tendency to be overweening. Organic theory in a sense opposes two kinds of knowledge: the knowledge that may be organized and applied in deliberate planning versus that (unsystematic but very considerable) knowledge, compounded with ignorance and unaware of itself as knowledge, which may be said roughly to be the possession of a population at large. Organic theory inclines, in general, to the notion of the superiority, or greater effectiveness in achieving eufunctions, of the latter kind of knowledge.

To put the contrast somewhat dramatically, there is a strain in functional theory toward distrust of the man of knowledge because of a fear that he will bring a demoralizing enlightenment to the plebs, while organic theory distrusts the man of knowledge because he so readily comes to think that he "knows better" than the knowledge that is incorporated in traditional institutions. We must again leave aside numerous ideological issues that all this suggests. But even if we grant that there are instances of the type of case in which intellectual *hubris* overlooks "the 'uncomprehended' wisdom embodied in organically developed social institutions,"[35] this type would differ from the others in that it focuses on the presumed untoward effects of the *application* of knowledge, not on the effects of knowledge itself.[36]

Ideally, the above type of effort should lead not to an uncontrolled sprawl of cases and conditions in which ignorance can be argued— always within given frameworks—to be eufunctional but to a sharp indication and comparison of conditions of sufficient generality to be useful for construction of significant theory.

A Note on Ignorance and Reason

The notion of the at times eufunctional character of ignorance may have had a popular origin. It can in any case still be found even in fairly disciplined popular writing. A psychotherapist and marriage counselor, writing in a popular medium, asks, "How much should you tell your mate?" and answers, "While many happenings and personal attitudes should be brought into the open between married folks, it's also a good idea to let some sleeping dogs lie."[37] In this connection, a remark by Schelling is worth noting: "It may not be an exaggeration to say that our sophistication sometimes suppresses sound intuitions, and one of the effects of an explicit theory may be to restore some intuitive notions that were only superficially 'irrational.' "[38] Sociologists who believe in reason[39] are nevertheless still likely to experience some qualms about even a heuristic stance toward the notion that ignorance can be eufunctional which does not dream of denying the obvious and enormous "positive" value of knowledge. It is difficult, thus, to overlook or forget the rather unqualifiedly manipulative attitude toward popular ignorance that Pareto expresses.[40] The remarks that follow are severely limited to an indication of several points about the analysis of ignorance in relation to reason.

If by reason is meant the scientific rationality of the sociologist, then reason clearly suggests the need for coming to some sort of assessment of the role and functions of ignorance in social life. Moreover, the analysis of ignorance can be looked upon as a member of an entire family of studies in which sociologists have very profitably come to explore the presence of the "good" in the "evil" (or of the "evil" in the "good," for that matter). A rough "liberal" common sense might suggest the unqualifiedly "evil" character of the political machine or of social conflict; yet, Merton and Coser have argued cogently that there are "good" elements in both.[41] Similarly, in a naively "liberal" outlook, ignorance may appear as an unqualified "evil." There is excellent ground for thinking that such an outlook is indeed naive. It is not necessary to engage in idle paradox hunting or dilettantism to recognize "good" in "evil" or "evil" in "good" and analyze whatever sociological issues may be involved in such conjunctures. Some of the sharpest and most distinctive sociological findings have come out of consideration of just such conjunctures.

If by reason is meant the rationality of those who are not social scientists and concern about reason in this sense carries with it concern about the "consensual" participation, as Shils calls it, of the former in the social science enterprise, then the problems presented are undoubtedly much more complicated. Shils himself asserts that "there are undoubtedly human situations that can be ameliorated only by manipulation" and that "not all manipulation is immoral—vide the education of children—and the sociology that serves this purpose is not immoral either," while, in general, he decries, "the manipulated improvement of society."[42] But the notion of "consensus" in this context suggests at least one possibility worth consideration. As the norm of individualism implies consensus that individuals shall be allowed to be "independent," so, analogously, in connection with ignorance it is conceivable that a citizenry may be helped to find areas in which it will give open-eyed acquiescence in the notion that certain things are "better left unknown." Much more needs to be said about this matter that cannot be said on this occasion.

The present explanatory statement suggests that the category of ignorance has a more considerable role to play in sociological theory than has yet been realized. To this writer it also suggests the possibility of a strategic sociological approach to ignorance. It is hoped that future work will bring the possibility closer to actuality.

Notes

I am indebted to Bennett Berger for a number of suggestions in connection with this paper.

1. See Karl Marx, *Capital* (New York: Modern Library, 1936), 1:81-86, and *Capital* (Chicago: Kerr, 1909), 3:962-68; Max Weber, *The Theory of Social and Economic Organization* (New York: Oxford University Press, 1947), e.g., pp. 184-86, 211-12; Karl Mannheim, *Man and Society in an Age of Reconstruction* (New York: Harcourt, Brace, 1941), p. 51f, Pitirim A. Sorokin, *Social and Cultural Dynamics* (New York: American Book Company, 1937), 2:120.
2. Robert K. Merton, *Social Theory and Social Structure* (Glencoe: Free Press, 1957), p. 51, italics added; also, p. 63.
3. Wilbert E. Moore and Melvin M. Tumin, "Some Social Functions of Ignorance," *American Sociological Review* 14 (December 1949):795. Some of the additional contemporary evidences of sociological concern with ignorance will be documented subsequently. Concern with ignorance, in a large variety of perspectives, is also evident in neighboring fields. It is discernible from psychoanalysis to game theory. Particular forms of the concern—and the selection again must be limited and arbitrary—may be seen in Floyd Allport's concept of "pluralistic ignorance"; in Simon's effort to throw light on the problem of the effect of the publication of predictions of behavior (and thereby of removal of ignorance) on the predicted behavior itself; in Stigler's recent attempt to develop the economics of information. On Allport's concept, see e.g., John W. Thibaut and Harold H. Kelley, *The Social Psychology of Groups* (New York: Wiley, 1959), pp. 66, 246; for Simon, Herbert A. Simon, *Models of Man* (New York: Wiley, 1957), ch. 5; for Stigler, George J. Stigler, "The Economics of Information," *Journal of Political Economy* 69 (June 1961):213-25.
4. Cf. the section on eufunctional ignorance, below.
5. Sheldon Stryker, "Role-Taking Accuracy and Adjustment," *Sociometry* 20 (December 1957):286-96.
6. Fred Davis, "Uncertainty in Medical Prognosis, Clinical and Functional," *American Journal of Sociology* 66 (July 1960):41-47.

7. Burton R. Clark, "The 'Cooling-Out' Function in Higher Education," *American Journal of Sociology* 65 (May 1960):569-76; also, Clark, *The Open Door College* (New York: McGraw-Hill, 1960), esp. pp. 160-65.

8. Emile Durkheim, *The Elementary Forms of the Religious Life* (New York: Macmillan, 1926).

9. Imogen Seger is one of those who have considered the question of "what would happen if Durkheim's theory became generally known and accepted," See her "Durkheim and His Critics on the Sociology of Religion" (New York: Columbia University Bureau of Applied Social Research, 1957), pp. 52-53. Cf. also Merton, *Social Theory,* pp. 51, 70, on the becoming manifest of latent functions.

10. See, e.g., his *Magic, Science and Religion* (New York: Doubleday, 1954).

11. The analyses of medicine and medical situations by Parsons and his students are also brought to bear where resources end, "vital" interests are involved, and doctors "face the unknown." See, e.g., Talcott Parsons, *The Social System* (Glencoe: Free Press, 1951), ch. 10; Renée Fox, "Training for Uncertainty," in Robert K. Merton, George Reader, and Patricia L. Kendall, eds., *The Student-Physician* (Cambridge: Harvard University Press, 1957); pp. 207-41; Fox, *Experiment Perilous* (Glencoe: Free Press, 1959).

12. Tension alleviation—which is indeed important for Malinowski's theory of magic—is alone mentioned here in order to conserve space. Additional space would allow the indication that there are elements in Malinowski's theory of magic which focus on ramifications into "large" social structures of "ignorantly" undertaken magical activity.

13. Charles A. Bennett, *The Dilemma of Religious Knowledge* (New Haven: Yale University Press, 1931), p. 68, italics added. The quoted matter is from George Santayana, *Reason in Religion* (New York: Scribner's, 1905), p. 47. In the light of the question Seger has considered (cf. n. 9, above), it is of interest that Bennett refers to "unfortunate theories which are in danger of being falsified as soon as they become public property" (ibid., p. 41). Cf. Simon, *Models,* ch. 5.

14. Siegfried F. Nadel, *The Foundations of Social Anthropology* (Glencoe: Free Press, 1951), p. 271.

15. In the following on organic theory, much help has been received from Friedrich A. Hayek's *The Counter-Revolution of Science* (Glencoe: Free Press, 1952), *The Constitution of Liberty* (Chicago: University of Chicago Press, 1960), and *Individualism and Economic Order* (Chicago: University of Chicago Press, 1948), particularly the first two; and from Carl Menger's brilliant book, *Untersuchungen über die Methode der Sozialwissenschaften* (Leipzig: Duncker & Humblot, 1883).

16. As a writer on the organic theorist Savigny says, Savigny put in the place of "the reason that belongs to the individual" another kind of reason—"the reason that belongs to history" (*"die Vernunft der Geschichte"*). Edouard Muller, *Freidrich Karl von Savigny* (Leipzig: Weicher, 1906), p. 4.

17. *The Counter-Revolution of Science,* p. 83; Menger, *Untersuchungen,* p. 163.

18. Part of the value of Menger's previously mentioned work comes from the acuteness of his comprehension of "unanticipated consequences of purposive social action." The very title of one of his chapters is revealing in

this connection: "On the theoretical understanding of those social phenomena which are the product neither of prior agreement nor of positive legislation but rather the uncontemplated results of historical development" (Bk. 3, ch. 2).

19. Organic theory has undoubtedly served ideological ends, and some of its propositions have been shaped by ideological purposes. A full handling of this problem is beyond the scope of the present treatment, but a few pertinent remarks may be made. While it may be recognized that many of the observations bearing on ignorance in institutional context which come from organic theory have value, this does not necessarily involve commitment to the political conclusions that some organic theorists claim must be drawn from those observations. Thus, one can agree with many of Hayek's shrewd comments on ignorance and knowledge but resist a number of the policy positions he reaches, ostensibly on the foundation of the comments. Also, it is time and again a crucial issue of *fact* whether various social results are most reliably attained through inadvertence, ignorance, and indirection, rather than through "planning," and there is perhaps some danger of too readily dismissing certain views as "merely ideological." The same sociologists who might be very critical of Hayek for what they would regard as overstress upon "that higher, superindividual wisdom which, in a certain sense, the products of spontaneous social growth may possess" *(The Constitution of Liberty,* p. 110; cf. also pp. 111, 291-92) and to whom the "marvels" of the spontaneous workings of the market constitute an overtold and dubious tale would, if they hold to the fairly common functional views of religion, be inclined to reject "planning" in the area of religion. They might well hold that religion gets such "eufunctional" effects as it does just through nonplanning and allowance of the "spontaneous" workings of the religious institution via inadvertence or ignorance, indirection, and intermediacy. Their outlook in this matter might well be unequivocally "laissez faire." The point is neither to suggest that such an outlook must be "reactionary" *nor to deny that there may be such things as "imbecile institutions"* (Veblen's phrase). It is to reinforce the notion that the question of the "eufunctional" character of ignorance and related questions having to do with the relative effectiveness of direct and indirect approaches to social problems in a large sense are questions that bear heavily on fact and appropriate analysis. (It may be added that it is not at all necessary to affirm that functional analysis, for its part, has been free of all ideological elements.)

20. *Untersuchungen,* pp. 172-78.

21. The quoted matter is from *The Constitution of Liberty,* pp. 62, 22, 21.

22. Peter M. Blau, *The Dynamics of Bureaucracy* (Chicago: University of Chicago Press, 1955), p. 81; cf. also pp. 92-93, 112.

23. The entire notion of "gain through indirection" merits amplification that also cannot be undertaken here. Neither in functional nor in organic theory nor in any sociological theory is there a genuinely systematic and thorough confrontation of the question of which social "goals" (understanding by these for the moment both objects of purposive activity and phenomena such as functional requisites that are not perceived as objects to be attained) may be attained "directly" and which "indirectly," and with what degree or amount of indirectness, and with what differential distribution of

consciousness of the "goals" according to location in the social structure of the human organization achieving the "goals." But, at any rate, the idea of "gain through indirection" in human phenomena at large is a fairly familiar one. Philosophers have stressed the hedonistic paradox that pleasure or happiness, deliberately and directly sought, is elusive, but, dismissed from the mind, "forgotten about" or ignored as one immerses one's self in other things, may be attained. It is a standard psychiatric recommendation to the psychically impotent that they "forget about" sexual prowess and become immersed in object-love. Students of insomnia (as Edmund Jacobson in his *Progressive Relaxation* [Chicago: University of Chicago Press, 1929]) develop approaches to sleep that depend heavily on indirection and intermediates that lead to the goal. (Even "truth," says Mr. Auden the poet, "like love and sleep, resents approaches that are too intense.") That Blau's interviewers did not happen to be concerned to bring about nondiscrimination, although they could "achieve" it indirectly, is here only of incidental importance. In economics, Böhm-Bawerk's demonstration of gain through indirection by first producing capital (produced goods used in further production) rather than making a "direct" effort to achieve certain ends remains classic. See Eugen von Böhm-Bawerk, *The Postive Theory of Capital* (New York: Stechert, 1923). Organizations obviously rely on the principle of gain through indirection and build indirection into their structures. But the whole phenomenon still awaits rigorous and wide-ranging sociological analysis.

24. James C. March and Hebert A. Simon, with the collaboration of Harold Guetzkow, *Organizations* (New York: Wiley, 1958), p. 157.

25. Samuel A. Stouffer et al., *The American Soldier* Princeton: Princeton University Press, 1949), 2:ch. 3.

26. The distinction between "not knowing" and "ignoring" ("forgetting about"), made by Moore and Tumin ("Social Functions," p. 788n.), is of course quite valid. But the illustration of "ignoring" (rather than of "ignorance") on the part of soldiers could be varied so that "ignorance" would be unequivocally featured.

27. Chester I. Barnard, *The Functions of the Executive* (Cambridge: Harvard University Press, 1938), p. 137.

28. Alvin W. Gouldner, in Robert K. Merton et al., eds., *Sociology Today* (New York: Basic Books, 1959), p. 406.

29. No reference has been made in these remarks on organizations to the ignorance-knowledge compound. Nevertheless, the notion might well be of some use for organizational analysis, as in the recurrent problem of "re-organization" of offices, in which one might raise the question of the extent to which widely diffused bits of unsystematic but useful knowledge (conceivably shrewder than their possessors realize) are taken into account in order to guide a conscious "re-organization." It should also be noted, to avoid misunderstanding, that to stress problems of ignorance in institutional context in organizations clearly is not to assert that problems of ignorance in situational context fail to occur in them.

30. There is not the space to treat this type of case circumstantially and indicate in precisely what ways it lies in the same dimension of "therapy" as the other two types, in just what sense the delinquent may be said to be a "patient," and so on.

31. Cf. Gunnar Myrdal, *An American Dilemma* (New York: Harper, 1944), Appendix 2.
32. It is of course still undeniable that "higher values" may dictate that pain be suffered on the ground that it is less important than enlightenment.
33. It is very clear that this last type of case is among the most highly "delicate" suggested. The contention that ignorance is eufunctional in this type of case is not only contingent on often difficult questions of empirical truth (for example, the question of when or under what circumstances, in fact, religion does contribute to such termini as solidarity) but on a number of value assumptions, such as the assumption that termini such as solidarity are desiderata, which they evidently need not always be for those adhering to "democratic" values. Furthermore, for those adhering to "democratic" values, "serious self-questioning" might at least in some cases seem preferable to continuation of sociologically unenlightened commitment. The tentative formulation of the eufunctional character of ignorance in this last type of case is retained mainly on the presumption that the "democratically" inclined will have an appreciable bias toward preservation of "sacred" values at the expense of some knowledge on the part of those who adhere to them. (At the expense of *how much* knowledge? At the expense of *whose* knowledge, precisely? Does this suggest complacent willingness on the part of a number of important things? If the formulation given reinforces the significance of such questions, it perhaps justifies itself on this ground alone.)
34. See, e.g., Hayek, *Individualism,* pp. 85-86.
35. Menger, *Untersuchungen,* p. 283.
36. Where functional theorists *are* tempted to reconstruct religion (as Comte was—and he most certainly had a functional view of religion), they too are likely to be severely criticized by organicists for trying to do better than established institutions do. It is no accident that Hayek, for example, has been exceedingly critical of Comte. See *Counter-Revolution.*
37. Harold E. Fink, in *St. Louis Post-Dispatch Parade,* October 30, 1960, p. 23.
38. Thomas C. Schelling, *The Strategy of Conflict* (Cambridge: Harvard University Press, 1960), p. 17.
39. Cf. Reinhard Bendix, "The Image of Man in the Social Sciences," in Seymour M. Lipset and Neil J. Smelser, eds., *Sociology: The Progress of a Decade* (Englewood Cliffs, N.J.: Prentice-Hall, 1961), pp. 30-37.
40. See, for example, his discussion of oracles in *Mind and Society* (New York: Harcourt, Brace, 1935), 4:1759-62. Consider the very different perspective on popular ignorance implied in the context of Shils's discussion of manipulation, in Talcott Parsons et al., *Theories of Society* (New York: Free Press, 1961), "The Calling of Sociology," 2:1405-48.
41. Merton, *Social Theory,* pp. 71-82, and Lewis A. Coser, *The Functions of Social Conflict* (Glencoe: Free Press, 1956).
42. Shils, "The Calling," pp. 1421-38.

9
Dialectic in Sociology
(1971)

From time to time sociologists concern themselves with "dialectic" (for example, in recent years, Gurvitch, van den Berghe, Blau, Schneider, Sorokin, Friedrichs).[1] But in so concerning themselves they are occupied with something likely to appear elusively varied and even indefinite. If they are prompted to look to philosophers for guidance about proper use of the term "dialectic," they may find Hook contending, a good generation ago, that "the term 'dialectic' is so infected with ambiguity"[2] that it would be best to drop it from rigorous discourse. Or they may find Kaufmann more recently remarking that the meaning of dialectic is "far from clear."[3] Or they may turn to an article by Hall to find that scholar indicating eight meanings of dialectic—which are only "among the more important."[4]

It is our contention that it is well to retain the term "dialectic" as of some use in sociology, at least until the clusters of meanings to which the term points are better arrayed and better understood than they are now. But a price has to be paid for the ambiguities of the term. We take it that there is no near prospect of consensus on the exact meaning of dialectic in sociological usage. The presentation of clusters of meanings, below, is bound to be tentative and crude (although it seeks to catch the intentions of sociologists as best it can).

It is well, also, to state some other cautions. There is no dialectical "method" to expound. Gurvitch writes easily—we would even say, glibly—of dialectical method, but his own dialectical categories of complementarity, mutual implication, polarization of antinomies and reciprocity of perspectives suggest little or nothing of method.[5] Kaufmann allows that Hegel's own dialectic is "at most a method of exposition . . . not a method of discovery."[6] Dialectical "bias" or "bent" or "perspective" is quite a different matter from method.

Again, on another front, words like *denial, negation,* and *contradiction* have been much featured in dialectical disquisitions. It is perhaps still useful to urge that, when such terms are taken out of the primary logical frame in which they have to do with the relations of propositions, the operation of displacement should be marked by care.[7] The lower reaches of Marxist literature have constantly and notoriously shown a careless "dialectical" wordmongering, a downright licentiousness of usage of "contradiction" and "negation" and "oppositeness" and the like. Verbal play is salient in what might be called the pathology of the dialectic. Also, it may be noted that dialectic need not be tied to any particular "system" or philosophy of history, as Gurvitch is well aware.[8]

A final observation is appropriate in this context. There has been so much devalued by able men—that is in one way or another associated with dialectic—that the reactions of those men to dialectic sometimes appear more antagonistic than they actually are. Thus, it does not seem to us arbitrary to use the term *dialectical* to describe the bias of much of Max Weber's thought. But of course there was a good deal in Hegel (in particular), including a theodicy of history, that Weber could never accept. It is even more obvious that he could not have embraced a proposition merely because it had a dialectical "look" or form and that he would have been strongly interested in evidence for it. Troeltsch was well aware of Weber's desire that social scientists should seek "strict and pure" causal connections and of Weber's explicit rejection of certain procedures as relapse into dialectic[9] or into an emanationist logic[10] or the like. Yet Troeltsch indicates that Weber did not reject the notion of dialectic out of hand and actually worked with it—"as every side of his [Weber's] sociology shows," in Troeltsch's own words.[11] This ambiguity of Weber's response to "dialectic" is understandable, but it complicates the task of a sociology with a dialectical bias. Within the general context of cautions about efforts to make authentic analytical use of dialectical notions, then, it is appropriate not merely to be wary of such things as Marxist vulgarizations but also about adverse reactions to dialectic that are modified by other more "positive" ones that may not be so immediately evident. As far as Weber is concerned, an effective dialectical bias on his part remains, as will be further suggested.[12]

With these cautions, an effort to probe the character of dialectic in sociology should be more profitable than it would otherwise be. The following effort will be worked out on three fronts, which may, for convenience, be labeled *historical, analytical,* and *estimative.* Dialectical bias, as we conceive it, has been profoundly involved in the entire history of modern sociological thought, dating back for two centuries or more. It is important to note, too, that strong dialectical bias appears in the work of many men, like the early Scottish moral philosophers and like Herbert Spencer, who cannot be suspected of having been nurtured in the tradition of German idealism. But we will "take" some relevant points from the history of sociological thought and not attempt an historical account of dialectic. The interest here is not in history of thought as such.[13] The analytical job will be simply one of discriminating and describing meaning-clusters that appear to us to be central to a dialectic in a sociological sense. (And we rely to a considerable extent on our own best understanding of what sociologists have groped for when they have felt themselves to be working on the line of dialectic.) Finally, a very short estimative statement will be designed to ascertain some likely sociological uses of the dialectical bent.

But what in fact is the dialectical bent or bias or perspective (with special reference to sociology)? The major aim of this paper is to answer the question. We have stated that there is no dialectical method for sociology to follow and have noted that Kaufmann, too, however, expands on the character of dialectic in the following statement made near the end of his discussion of Hegel's *Phenomenology:* "What do we find if not a usable dialectical method? We find a vision of the world, of man, and of history which emphasizes development through conflict, the moving power of human passions, which produce wholly unintended results, and the irony of sudden reversals. If that be called a dialectical world view, then Hegel's philosophy *was* dialectical—and there is a great deal to be said in its favor. This is certainly an immensely fruitful and interesting perspective. . . ."[14]

With the reservations that Kaufmann's suggestions will be followed below in a somewhat free way and that our interest in Hegel in particular is incidental, this statement gives invaluable hints for the performance of our main task. What follows should also be read in the light of the writer's bias (that the material adduced should help to vindicate) that dialectical points of view have been involved in some of the most fundamental insights of sociology and merit explanation at some length.

Some Pertinent Thought of the Past

We break into the midst of Kaufmann's quoted statement by taking up his reference to "wholly unintended results." A very important element in the Hegelian philosophy was Hegel's perception of unintended or unanticipated consequences—in particular, "unanticipated consequences of purposive social action" (to use a phrase of Merton's).[15] Hegel was sharply aware that men in society, acting with certain intentions, constantly produce effects that are not compassed by, or that transcend, those intentions. ("Unintended" is taken in this paper as usually implying also "unanticipated" and vice versa.) Hegel's small volume *Reason in History* contains a particularly compelling description of how "human actions in history produce additional results, beyond their immediate knowledge and desire."[16] Let us note how this conception occurs early in the development of sociology and then recurs, as we argue its relation to dialectic.

The well-known Scottish writers of the eighteenth century whom we readily think of as in whole or in part sociologists—men like Adam Smith, Adam Ferguson, and John Millar—were certainly early representative of sociological thought and certainly independent of Hegel.[17] Their perception of unintended consequences is to be found in a very large number of relevant statements. The first two of the four volumes of Millar's impressive book *An Historical View of the English Government,* for example, stress such consequences again and again.[18] Millar then writes of Magna Charta and other related charters in English history and indicates that the parties concerned in these charters were "not actuated by the most liberal principles"; that "it was not so much their intention to secure the liberties of the people at large as to establish the privileges of a few individuals." But if "the freedom of the common people" was not envisaged as an aim of the charters, that freedom was in time inadvertently realized with economic improvement of the condition of the peasantry and others of low rank as these came to share in the benefits of free government. Millar remarks accordingly: "The limitations of arbitrary power, which had been calculated chiefly to promote the interest of the nobles were thus, by a change of circumstances, rendered equally advantageous to the whole community, as if they had originally proceeded from the most exalted spirit of patriotism."[19]

Millar was dead some few years before Hegel's first major work on the phenomenology of the spirit appeared (and Adam Smith died before Millar by more than a decade). But the Scottish writers do sound a note that is of basic importance in Hegel. There is the sheer transcendence of purpose or intention (with the usual implication of nonanticipation). There is the strong suggestion of paradox. Men will strive for their own narrow advantage and achieve "the liberties of the people at large" (or, in the economic sphere, à la Smith, the community welfare). There is also already in this a hint of what Kaufmann calls "the irony of sudden reversals."[20] (Certainly, too, again to recall Kaufmann, we can discern in the ranges of phenomena that Millar, Smith, et al. refer to in connection with unintended consequences, "the moving power of human passions.")

But the Scots are hardly alone in all this. Herbert Spencer is another man acutely sensitive to unintended consequences of action. This appears, for instance, in his opposition to a certain kind of rationalism, however guilty he might be of rationalistic excesses of his own, in other ways. Thus, Spencer observes that "even" the historian George Grote "in his comparison between the institutions of ancient Greece and those of medieval Europe . . . tacitly implies that conceptions of the advantages of this or that arrangement furnished motives for establishing or maintaining it." (Spencer's adverse reaction to this mode of thought was, if anything, overdone.[21]) Spencer adds to this that "the facts show that as with the genesis of single political heads, so with the genesis of compound political heads, conditions and not intentions determine."[22] His sense of the strictly limited effect of intention is thus suggested. But the central matter of nonanticipation of consequences had already been attended to in his notion of the multiplication of effects. Who could have foreseen the ramifying social consequences of the human actions involved in inventing the locomotive engine and using it in a railway system?[23] It is characteristic of Spencer's style in these premises to write that "no prophecy is safer than that the results anticipated from a law will be greatly exceeded in amount by results not anticipated."[24] Abrams justly remarks of Spencer: "By extending his early notion of single causes having multiple effects he arrived at a brilliant sociology of unanticipated consequences."[25]

Beyond Spencer, one quickly reaches men whose work is well known even to those with little concern with the history of sociological thought. Unintended consequences were a familiar and significant matter to Pareto, who was also presumably largely uncontaminated by Hegelianism. Pareto observes: "When we say that at the present time our speculators are laying the foundations for a war . . . we in no sense mean that they are doing that deliberately"; and he adds: "Some day the war they have made way for but not wanted may break out; and then it will be a consequence of the past activities of the speculators, but not of any intent they have had either at that time or ever." And Pareto also adds a sentence that might easily have come from a Smith, a Ferguson, or a Millar: "So the speculators of ancient Rome brought on the fall of the Republic and the dictatorships of Caesar and Augustus, but without knowing that they were headed in those directions and without the slightest desire to reach those goals."[26] Among those importantly influenced by German philosophy, Max Weber looms as one to whom the matter of unintended consequences was of very considerable importance, but for the moment it is enough to recall a minimum statement of his to the effect that "the cultural consequences of the Reformation were to a great extent . . . unforeseen and even unwished-for results of the labors of the Reformers."[27] If one prefers Marx to Weber (or to Spencer or Pareto), the same point is developed in him, and so it comes down to contemporaries like MacIver, and, for that matter, appears constantly outside strictly sociological frameworks, in the work of anthropologists, economists, and philosophers.[28]

It is a short step from the noting of unintended consequences to the notion that man, in connection with the unintended precipitations of his own conduct, comes to confront a world he may think he never made but which he did make, if with a considerable degree of inadvertence. Here one can readily pass to the study of phenomena of reification and alienation as one observes that human agents, often *losing* all firm sense of connection between their own actions and the unexpected outcomes thereof, hypostatize those outcomes and feel apart from, perhaps even in a sense driven by, them. Interesting ideological notions have arisen in connection with this sort of study, as in the case of unqualified presumptions that unintended outcomes must work to the best possible social effect—or, indeed, that they must work to the worst possible social effect. Marx on the fetishism of commodities is particularly important here, with his argument that it is men's actions in economic context under capitalism which ultimately determine the value relations of commodities to one another on the market, while at the same time men do not recognize this but hypostatize and animate the commodities, so that to them "their own social action takes the form of the action of objects which rule the producers instead of being ruled by them."[29] To separate the wheat from the chaff in this would be a large job in itself.[30] But certain ideological differences between Marx and numerous other sociologists do not prevent sharing of some highly significant insights that, at least, are very congenial to a dialectical bias.

The dialectical bias itself, however, is further developed in past (and present) sociological thought. We turn to a second area of insight that has some overlap with what has already been noted. Again, we consider human agents and the consequences of their actions, but now the focus is on change of human aims, including change brought about because men become newly cognizant of results they have already unwittingly produced and now make them objects of conscious endeavor. It is pertinent to recall Wundt's heterogony of ends. This takes in three elements, the first (1) being the sheer process whereby the consequences of action become larger or more encompassing than those consequences that would arise from intention alone. As Barth puts the matter, "The end attained contains more than the motive one had proposed to one's self";[31] in construing Wundt, we have relied heavily on Barth.[32] Evidently, there is, in respect of this first element, an overlap with what we have dealt with before. (2) There is in the heterogony of ends a process whereby means become ends, as a state form may be initially valued for its protection of citizen life and later valued for itself simply as state form. (3) There is a process whereby originally derived or secondary effects of action become of primary significance. It is well to remind ourselves that (3) is allied to Allport's functional autonomy of motives, on the psychological side. I do x because of motive m, but I thereby happen to generate result r, which, originally a derived or secondary thing, now gets central motivational significance for me.[33] One works hard to "show the old man" but then discovers that one can make good money and henceforth works for that and not just to "show the old man." This whole area of things, at social and psychological levels, is rich with "unintended results" and "the irony of sudden reversals."

The ideas thus suggested have constituted a component of sociological analysis not always so explicitly recognized as it might be. In a time of renewed interest in social evolution, it is well to turn to some exemplification of these ideas, again in the work of Herbert Spencer. For Spencer, various social activities of the past had had their evolutionary value, now outlived. As is well known, he thought that war had been necessary "for forming great communities and developing their structures."[34] But now the communities are formed and the structures developed, and the energies once turned to the uses of war can be otherwise employed. Dubious motives and dispositions like bellicosity have had their socially useful effects. Indeed, many of the social structures that man has built and that are exceedingly "useful" were originally supported on the motivational side by greed, lust, spite, and the like. (The paradoxical character of this should not be missed, nor the fact that Spencer is here much like Millar deriving liberties for the people from the illiberally motivated actions of the few, or like Smith making economic selfishness the root of general welfare or for that matter, like Hegel, in his philosophy of history, making the mastery- or power-impulse of great men contribute to the uses of human freedom.)

It is worth noting how Troeltsch construes this aspect of Spencer's work. Troeltsch remarks that "social structures created by older tendencies may be put into the service of quite new goals, of whose origins one knows nothing and of which one only discovers that they have been unconsciously constructed under the cover of the older forms." And Troeltsch continues, remarking that thus is given "the clear principle of the heterogony of ends, as Wundt taught it later," and observing that "what cruelty, violence and superstition have wrought with a thousand horrors and terrors" can be subsequently utilized for its own different and distinctive ends by a "moralized" culture. (One cannot help adding parenthetically that such utilization could hardly have been "intended" or "foreseen" by cruelty, violence, and superstition.) Troeltsch ends with an observation suggesting that Spencer's views, despite Spencer himself, take on a strong "dialectical" flavor.[35] It is quite clear that Spencer does effectively suggest the elements of the heterogony of ends. He does so, moreover, in a very modern way. His statement—"by the histories or organizations of whatever kind we are shown that the purpose originally subserved by some arrangement is not always the purpose eventually subserved"[36]—is quite in line with some of his fundamental ideas.[37]

Another word may be said about element (2) in the heterogony of ends. It is the merest gesture toward noting this element and also toward bringing the heterogony of ends closer to the present to refer to Merton's particular treatment—in his analysis of bureaucracy and personality—of the process whereby means becomes ends.[38] Spencer's last quoted statement above sufficiently reminds us of organizational applications— and this again takes us toward the present. Means repeatedly become ends in organizational context, and the point is so well known that it requires no special comment.

To unintended consequences and the heterogony of ends we add a third set of insights that very often have been regarded as being dialectical. These again bear on social evolution—and we turn to Spencer once more. He presents a masterly exposition of the point that an already developed structure can stand in the way of or impede adaptively better structures. An "investment" is not always easily relinquished and can block the path of new forms, at both the biological and social levels. Spencer asks how far this "law" may hold for "the social organism." He inquires: "To what extent does it happen here, too, that the multiplying and elaborating of institutions, and the perfecting of arrangements for gaining immediate ends, raise impediments to the development of better institutions and to the future gaining of higher ends?" He goes on: "Socially, as well as individually, organization is indispensable to growth: beyond a certain point there cannot be further growth without further organization. Yet there is not a little reason for suspecting that beyond this point organization is indirectly repressive—increases the obstacles to those readjustments required for larger growth and more perfect structure."[39] He asks us to observe in an "insignificant" yet pertinent situation how the inconveniently narrow gauge of railways "has become an insuperable obstacle to a better gauge."[40]

This recalls one of Veblen's better pieces of sociological analysis in *Imperial Germany and the Industrial Revolution*.[41] Spencer's point is central for Veblen, and the latter could very well have been greatly stimulated by the former. England's "investment" in obsolete or obsolescent industrial equipment—an investment not simply to be pushed aside—constituted a handicap in late-nineteenth-century competition with a newly industrializing Germany which was already performing a kind of primitive or original *Wirtschaftwunder* from about 1870 on, as it enjoyed freedom from commitment to old industrial forms, and could begin with the new and the more efficient. Quite independently (presumably) of Spencer and Veblen, Weber sees the same basic point. He does not elaborate it, but he does mention it plainly twice in *Economy and Society*. Spencer and Veblen saw that "backwardness" could have certain advantages from a developmental point of view. There is the advantage of the latecomer, the one who has been backward, who in coming late need not take on the burden of forms that constrain and limit as much as or more than they help. So Weber for his part writes of "modes of thought of western medieval law that were in many respects 'backward' " and observes: "These very elements of 'backwardness' in the logical and governmental aspects of legal development enabled business to produce a far greater wealth of practically useful legal devices than had been available under the more logical and technically more highly rationalized Roman law."[42]

The second and last reference to the point in *Economy and Society* occurs when Weber remarks, in the course of discussion of bureaucracy, that the advance of bureaucracy depends on technical superiority. Where older pertinent structural forms are found and are "in their own way technically highly developed and functionally particularly well adapted to the requirements at hand," there bureaucracy will not easily win out. Weber writes: "This is the same general phenomenon as when areas which have highly developed gas illumination works or steam railroads, with large fixed capital, offer stronger obstacles to electrification than completely new areas which are opened up for electrification."[43] There can be "evolutionary" advantages in "backwardness," and important "adaptive steps" ahead may be made rather by structures that do not already have a good adaptation than by structures that have done relatively well and represent an "investment" already made. Not the well adapted a form in a given evolutionary stage, the smaller is its potential weak, will at least at times move ahead to the most effective new adaptations available at particular junctures. The paradoxical character of this is worth noting in passing. And there is also here more than a faint suggestion of "the irony of sudden reversals." An interesting latter-day taking up of the relevant ideas is seen in Service's reference to "the law of evolutionary potential," which states that "the more specialized and adapted a form in a given evolutionary stage, the smaller is its potential for passing to the next stage."[44]

Unintended consequences confront us once more. If Veblen's thesis about Germany and England has merit, England did not historically develop certain economically relevant structures and invest in certain kinds of equipment *in order to* bring about its own future relative industrial inhibition. Nor did Germany presumably quite foresee that its relative freedom to pick and choose among alternative structures and technical applications would (together with other things) enable it to rival England as an industrial power within an amazingly short time, indeed within a few decades at the most. Finally, there is an aspect of all this that may be put under the rubric "success leads to failure."[45] The very source of "failure" appears at least at times to lie in "success." An adaptation once effectively made can inhibit better ones. And "failure" conversely can lead to "success." The historian Renan remarked that institutions die by their victories—*"Les institutions périssent par leurs victoires"*;[46] and it is a fair presumption that his meaning was close to that indicated here.

The material covered above provides us with some foundation for setting out a number of meaning-clusters, clusters of meanings that we believe the term "dialectic" has tended to take on in sociology. But it will be necessary to add to what the above suggests, still drawing to some extent on historical sociological thought but not reviewing it in the relatively considerable detail in which it was reviewed above. While continuing, then, in an attenuated way with our roughly labeled "historical" job in the next section, we move also to the "analytical" task of discriminating and describing the meaning-clusters of the dialectic.

Meanings of the Dialectic

The outline of sociologically significant meanings of the dialectic now to be presented is intended to be suggestive rather than rigorously organized on some principle or principles. There will be overlaps in our enumeration (itself somewhat arbitrary) that will show the need for better systematizations. A ready objection will be that "too much" is included. Distinguished scholars *have* become reluctant to employ the term "dialectic." It is a bloated term. It *can* be reasonably contended that it tends to be used where its use is not necessary. That is all part of the problem sociologists face. But we hold to the position already affirmed that it is best to retain the term until the clusters of meanings to which it points are better arranged and understood than they are now.

1. A first meaning-cluster has to do with the much-mentioned discrepancy between aim or intention and outcome in social action. This is a circumstance that we suggest is "dialectical" or appeals strongly to a dialectical bias in sociology. The Hegelian background is to the point. The cunning of reason in Hegel's philosophy clearly features the

discrepancy between aim and outcome and always involves unintended consequences. We have argued that the feature of paradox quickly appears in these premises, as does the irony of abrupt reversals. And the notion of "a world I never made"—a sociocultural world unintentionally precipitated out of past human actions that human agents begin newly to confront at particular times—is also readily suggested. There is a rich cluster of meaning of dialectic here. The cluster is closely related to the first of the three areas of insight referred to previously.

2. Goal shifts and displacements—and we recall here the previous discussion of heterogony of ends—can also be considered dialectical events or congenial to a dialectical bias, provided that goals to which shifting is done have emerged in a process whereby means have become ends or whereby originally unintended or derived outcomes are taken up as new aims. Heterogony of ends, functional autonomy, and the connection with the prior (first) cluster of meanings via nonintention of consequences are suggestive of the richness of this second cluster. This cluster in turn is clearly related to the second area of insight referred to previously.

3. A third cluster of meanings of dialectic arises in connection with the third area of insight above reviewed. We have now to do with structures or forms that constitute relatively effective adaptations but that stand in the way of still more effective adaptations because of "investments" already made. Success again brings failure; strength, a kind of downfall (although our metaphors must not be allowed to become too enthusiastic). Perhaps sociologists would be somewhat readier to allow the dialectical character of phenomena under this third heading than that of phenomena under the previous two. Be that as it may, in this third cluster there are some significant nuances.

A nuance arises as one thinks of a "system" context in which some specific product that emerges from and marks "success" turns about, so to speak, and leads to failure or system breakdown. To take a familiar example from the history of socioeconomic thought, without commitment to the empirical value of the example: in the old Marxian view, the gathering of surplus value (in the technical sense of value produced by labor-power over and above the value required to sustain itself, and appropriated by the capitalists) emerges from the basic structure of the capitalist setup, with its restricted ownership of means of production to which nonpossessing laborers must come to apply their work.[47] Surplus value does in a sense emerge from the success of capitalism. It unequivocally marks or signalizes that success. And yet in time, for economic (and class-psychological) reasons, this very product of surplus value brings about the downfall of capitalism (although surplus in another sense was once a precondition of the modern capitalist order). It is the *form* of dialectical movement here indicated that has suggestive value, not the detail of the economic thesis.

A further nuance is suggested as one thinks again in terms of a system context in which a product emerges and marks success, then to turn about and occasion failure or breakdown, but by a different mechanism (mechanisms?) than the one (or ones) just outlined. In the Marxian example, as indicated, surplus value gets its effects through economic complications and ramifications leading to collapse of the capitalist economy (and in the very end through resentments aroused in the proletariat). The case now confronted is one in which the system product traces back or operates retroactively to destroy or corrupt the motivational "machinery" out of which it came. An example from Weber will complement a previous reference to the Protestant ethic. His wife notes in her biography that for Weber "in its earthly course, the idea, in the end, always and everywhere works against its original meaning and destroys itself." She evidently regards this as a kind of synopsis of Weber's work in the sociology of religion. She remarks the conception of Protestant obligation or duty in relation to one's possessions and observes that here begins "the tragedy of the idea," for "even Puritanism cannot resist the temptations of *acquired* wealth any more than the medieval communities of monks. The remarkable religious structuring of life gets destroyed in virtue of its own consequences."[48] Acquired wealth marks the success of the Puritan work-discipline (with its supposed appreciable religious sources), but then this wealth creates temptations that break down those very original religiously influenced motives and values that could produce it. The empirical issues involved have notoriously produced a vast literature.[49] But what is important is again the *form* of the argument. The argument itself is not only well known but in essential features was no doubt often anticipated (although it does *not* follow from this that Weber's specific work on Protestantism and in the sociology of religion was notably unoriginal).

Here we seem to be dealing with elements in a kind of dialectic of defeat or failure or breakdown. Are there still other phenomena of a dialectic of defeat which the above does not comprehend? One may now be touching on an entire dialectical family or entire families. Taking a different line from any of those just suggested, we recall the circumstance, often enough noted, that the means one employs can destroy the end (or ends) one pursues. (This of course has its affinities with means-becoming-ends.) A quaint but intriguing example may be adduced, subject to correction by those better informed historically. Max Weber, among others, knew well the Taoist interest in macrobiotics. Desiring to achieve immortality, a number of Taoist emperors apparently hopefully swallowed elixirs that ruined their health and shortened their lives. In the field of urban affairs, the relevant pattern evidently occurs with some frequency, as when, in a more commonplace example, a bridge or highway built to relieve traffic congestion operates to increase it. It is suggested that there has also been a sense on the part of numerous sociologists that this sort of phenomenon is dialectical and it might well be conceived as a fitting component of a dialectic of defeat.

If there is a dialectic of defeat, there is yet also a dialectic of triumph or build-up.[50] If there is such a notion as that of the tragedy of the idea, whereby the "idea" is defeated by the retroactive effect upon its original self of its own "products," we know very well that there is after all also, in Hegelian terms, such a notion as that of the cunning of reason. Unintended consequences are crucial in the cunning of reason, but they are consequences that are supposed to stand morally "higher" than the motivations that originally set them off. This is all connected with a theodicy of history that no one today would find acceptable. But we are here clearly pointed to matters that have an interest independent of any dubious or dead theodicy. And what is particularly of interest is precisely the possibility of mechanisms of build-up of "higher" or more "significant" development. Pertinent in this context, too, is the Hegelian notion of sublation, whereby there is a removal and at the same time a retention, within the framework of a selective elevating synthesis. Hegel's commentators never tire of pointing out that the German *"aufheben,"* meaning to "lift up," also means *both* to "negate" and to "preserve"—as, in a famous example, "being" and "nothing" are negated, but additionally taken up or preserved and synthesized in a new category of "becoming."[51] In the case of sublation, too, reference may be to practice or "reality," not merely to concepts or propositions.

4.   Kaufmann, in the strategic statement on dialectic that has served as a guiding text, refers to "development through conflict" even before he refers to unintended results and ironic reversals. Development through conflict calls for stress as constituting another cluster of meanings of dialectic. But there can be an excessive stress on "conflict" as such, as constituting virtually the whole of the dialectic. This may go to the point of overlooking the word *development* in the phrase "development through conflict." It may be recalled that Hegel did effectively stress *development* through conflict, as suggested in his aspiration, stated in the preface to his *Phenomenology,* "to recognize in what seems conflicting and inherently antagonistic the presence of mutually necessary moments"[52]—for developmentally in the history of thought for Hegel, ostensibly contradictory modes of thought have a way of revealing them-

selves as ultimately necessary to one another. But the idea of conflict does remain important as an idea that has been much featured in dialectic, and to sociologists, as to numerous others, it is probably most familiar in the class oppositions or antagonisms postulated by Marx and the Marxists. The particular mechanisms, whereby conflict achieves such outcomes as it does, are a matter of inevitable interest to sociologists.[53] A very recent indication of difficulties that can arise with too exclusive a stress on social conflict as central to dialectic is afforded by Boulding, who both associates dialectical thought very closely with conflict and at the same time devalues conflict.[54] He refers to "nondialectical philosophies such as Christianity, Buddhism, psychoanalysis, social democracy and social work," and he goes on to say of these "nondialectical" outlooks that they "emphasize love, empathy, resolution of conflict. . . ."[55] At the very least, in Buddhism and psychoanalysis there are powerful "dialectical" elements other than those suggested by conflict. Moreover, as will be noted in due course, "love" itself, ironically, has a markedly dialectical aspect.

5.   The last meaning-cluster may be said to be expanded by contradiction, oppositeness or opposition, paradox ("seeming contradiction"), negation, dilemma. These have been alluded to before, but they so thoroughly pervade what appears to be dialectical thought, and such thought has been so *sensitive* to them (in sociology as elsewhere) that they call for special and separate stress. (Clearly, however, one need not be a dialectician in any strongly distinctive sense simply to be aware of and appreciate contradiction, paradox, dilemma, or the like.) Perhaps the notion that Weber was a man with a strong dialectical bent by now carries some conviction. If so, there is some point in recalling here that his work presents a paradox of charisma—for charisma, to have social effect, must sheerly get involved in society, yet in getting involved in society it becomes attenuated and routinized. The price of its social effect is in a sense its own demise; and it is evident that all this has its dilemmatic side.[56] This brief and partial illustration of the meaning-cluster suggested will suffice, particularly as our further discussion will also have some relevance to the matters just touched upon.

6.   "Contradiction" has the emotions or passions as a highly important area of application. Kaufmann quotes Royce's phrase, "contradictory logic of passion"; and Royce evidently contended that "all the greater emotions are dialectical."[57] We may adapt this to our own sociological uses. An illustration from Myrdal will serve. In a brilliant statement in *An American Dilemma,* Myrdal averred that "the Negro people have to carry the burden not only of the white man's sins but also of their virtues. The virtues of the honest, democratic . . . white

Americans in the South are great, and the burden upon the Negroes becomes ponderous."[58] The White man's virtues produce guilt about exploitative action. A frankly predatory sexual attitude toward Negro women, without twinges of conscience (however morally reprehensible it might be judged to be), could in the past well have given *less* support to notions of Negro female "bestiality" and "lust" than such notions actually received. The Negro has suffered additionally for the White man's "decency." Unqualified adherents of the American Creed would not be exploitative. Unqualified predators, comfortable about sexual, economic, and other exploitation, would have no use for "justifications" and moralizations or perhaps even theories purporting to show Negro inferiority. But in-betweeners, partly given over to the American creed and partly inclined to exploit, will justify and moralize and find appeal in certain racist theories. Here virtue can produce some vicious results. Only unadulterated virtue would work otherwise. An unadulterated vice would at least spare the victims of its exploitation additional insults and burdens. A tiger needs no "philosophy" to prove its right to prey on lesser beasts. This effectively illustrates the "contradictory logic of passion," and in this connection Myrdal shows an unmistakable dialectical bent. Psychoanalysis generally features many similar turns of thought, and indeed this is a main reason for our previously asserting that there are powerful dialectical elements in it. But obviously sociologists cannot overlook lines of thought of the kind Myrdal presents. For sociologists as for others, they will suggest a significant meaning-cluster of dialectic, no matter how it may be best ordered in relation to others.

7.   Of the above, Item 4 addresses itself directly to conflict; Item 5 at least still strongly intimates certain forms of it; Item 6 clearly suggests conflict of emotions. In a final meaning-cluster, conflict is in a sense "dissolved" in a kind of coalescence of opposites. Tentatively, we may simply let this also stand as a meaning-cluster on its own, although it is connected with other portions of the whole dialectical edifice in ways that might well be given close inspection. What is involved here must be briefly exemplified. Again we wish to focus on the emotions, merely illustratively. Love and hatred are notoriously close. Love includes involvement, preoccupation with the beloved. Where hatred exists, this preoccupation remains: the other, now the hated one, is obviously important. Accordingly, it is often argued with considerable plausibility that "the true opposite" of love is not hatred but indifference. Perhaps no sociologist ever saw with greater clarity than Simmel how close love and hate can be. He notes that ancient Jewish law allowed bigamy, but not in the form of a man's marriage to two living sisters, "for this would

have been especially apt to arouse jealousy." "In other words," adds Simmel, "This law simply assumes as a fact of experience that antagonism on the basis of a common kinship tie is stronger than among strangers."[59] Those who are closely bonded and among whom love may be presumed to prevail with some frequency are also those (at least under certain sociocultural conditions) among whom hatred is especially likely to exist. Sociology, literature and psychology are impressively near to one another on such themes. It need not occasion surprise that it is an outstanding literary critic who makes the highly paradoxical remark that "as in marriage, or the bond between father and child, there are moments when love is changed to something very much like itself, pure hatred."[60]

The above attempt to set out meaning-clusters of dialectic in sociology is neither "complete" nor designed to refer to all pertinent literature. Generous documentation of the point that dialectical bias persists into contemporary sociology would be a formidable task in itself. Matza has recently provided a pertinent view of Merton on ambition and deviance, of Davis on prostitution, of Goffman on psychiatric redefinition of patients.[61] Much additional material might be drawn upon. But what has actually been provided above does allow a rough estimate of lines on which dialectic may be of use.

Toward Assessing the Value of Dialectic

From the three insights or areas of insight from which we started, important enough in themselves, the dialectical bent in sociology appears to go on to develop into a powerful bent indeed if our procedure is basically defensible. If we attend to what dialectic evidently has meant historically in sociology and carry on our attention to dialectical tendencies into the present day, we may achieve an array of major dialectical stresses and an elaboration of their meaning. Such an enterprise has been carried on in the above, in an incipient way. In this direction lies the possibility of a rather distinctive classification or ordering of certain crucial types of social change. There are indeed limits. The kinds of social change that dialectic has contemplated do not comprehend all social change. But a well-developed array of types—on a more inclusive and more carefully arranged basis than has yet been offered—might well be of help in getting at the character of change. It is already quite apparent that such an enterprise cannot be an entirely unique thing. What is called by some dialectical will overlap with phenomena that others would never bother to call dialectical. Yet there do seem to be in so-called dialectic reasonably distinctive concerns with special changes that feature paradox, the suggestion of the closeness of ostensible opposites, and so on and on. If the effort to gather up and consider seriously the possible analytical utility of the manifestations in sociological thought of the dialectical bias yielded no more than a shrewd taxonomy not quite achieved previously and enhanced awareness of a certain subtlety that attaches to particular kinds of social change, this would still constitute a valuable giving of point and direction to sociological inquiry.

A second utility of dialectic, closely related to the above, would work on the line of reinforcing awareness of the need to discriminate subtypes and particular mechanisms when we consider the meaning of various interesting folkloristic, philosophical, or scientific statements that bear on the sociological field. "Institutions die by their victories." "Success brings failure." "Failure brings success." "Virtue generates vice and vice, virtue." "The seed of death is in the thrust of life"—or, in a Spenglerian application of this, as oracular as usual but, for once, engagingly brief: "The birth of the City entails its death."[62] "They that take the sword shall perish by the sword." Evidently, those who take the sword can evoke resentments that bring the swords of others against them. But it is equally evident that another meaning of the statement may be that violent means ("the sword") may insidiously become ends and damage and destroy original or ideal ends. There is more than one "type" or mode of perishing by the sword. As regards mechanisms, it is clear that no dialectic would have any value that did not indicate precisely how, say, vice becomes virtue or virtue, vice. The obvious need not be elaborated. The dialectical bent here would, as intimated, serve to reinforce an already-present drive in sociology, although it might also encourage close relationships between sociology and special kinds of literary, historical, and philosophical analysis.

A third possible utility would be on the line of sharpening for sociologists the sense of various scientific notions that they have found helpful. The notion of feedback is one that immediately suggests itself. There are some evident overlaps between historical dialectical notions and the idea of feedback, but simple identifications of ideas on each side would clearly often be quite inept or downright wrong. Curiously, archaic notions of a kind of hierarchy of "results"—ranging from the results of the aim-oriented actions of historically even rather insignificant individual actors to the aggregate, unpurposed historical result-concretions of the type called "the Industrial Revolution"—suggest some possible relationship to Parsons's notions of hierarchy, of "cybernetic" flavor. We do not claim to know precisely how much profit there might be in conceptual juxtapositions or confrontations of the kind thus intimated, but there does exist a considerable conceptual heritage from dialectic that still invites comparison with some of the ranges of sociology's conceptual equipment today.[63] Even if dialectic does not lead us toward some very potent "logic" or "grammar" of social life or toward an impressive "chemistry" of social change, it may still offer enough of value for close rescrutiny of it to be justified. But let it be said once again and finally that the present item should ideally soon be superseded by more effective efforts to preserve the sociologically valuable in past dialectical conceptions while dropping the inhibitive or irrelevant.

Notes

1. Georges Gurvitch, *Dialectique et Sociologie* (Paris: Flammarion, 1962); Pierre L. van den Berghe, "Dialectic and Functionalism: Toward a Theoretical Synthesis," *American Sociological Review* 28 (October 1963):695-705; Peter M. Blau, *Exchange and Power in Social Life* (New York: Wiley, 1964), ch. 12; Louis Schneider, "Toward Assessment of Sorokin's View of Change," in George K. Zollschan and Walter Hirsch, ed., *Explorations in Social Change* (Boston: Houghton Mifflin, 1964), pp. 371-400; Pitirim A. Sorokin, *Sociological Theories of Today* (New York: Harper & Row, 1966), pp. 462-525; and Robert W. Friedrichs, *A Sociology of Sociology* (New York: Free Press, 1970), passim.
2. Sidney Hook, "Dialectic in Social and Historical Inquiry," *Journal of Philosophy* 36 (July 1939):378.
3. Walter A. Kaufmann, *Hegel* (New York: Doubleday, 1965), p. 167.
4. Roland Hall, "Dialectic," *Encyclopedia of Philosophy* (New York: Macmillan, 1967), 2:385.
5. For example, Gurvitch, *Dialectique,* p. 27.
6. Kaufmann, *Hegel,* p. 175.
7. Something of the character and function of this displacement in Hegel himself is neatly suggested by Soll in a comment on denial and negation. In the background of Soll's statement stands the circumstance that Hegel's volume on the phenomenology of the spirit treats not only forms of "consciousness," strictly, but also forms of "practice." Ivan Soll, *An Introduction to Hegel's Metaphysics* (Chicago: University of Chicago Press, 1969), pp. 12-13.
8. Gurvitch, *Dialectique,* pp. 14-15.
9. Ernst Troeltsch, *Der Historismus und Seine Probleme* (Tübingen: Mohr, 1922), p. 567.
10. Cf. the statement on emanationism in Max Weber, *Gesammelte Aufsätze zur Wissenschaftslehre* (Tübingen: Mohr, 1951), pp. 141-45.
11. Troeltsch, *Historismus,* pp. 657-58.
12. Several statements regarding Weber in the present paper draw on similar ones made in a different context in Louis Schneider, "Max Weber: Wisdom and Science in Sociology," *Sociological Quarterly* 12 (1971): 462-72.
13. Dialectical perspectives continue on into contemporary sociology and the notion of their intimate involvement in the field is thereby inevitably reinforced.

14. Kaufmann, *Hegel,* p. 174.

15. Robert K. Merton, "The Unanticipated Consequences of Purposive Social Action," *American Sociological Review* 1 (1936):894-904.

16. G. W. F. Hegel, *Reason in History* (New York: Liberal Arts Press, 1953), p. 35.

17. Merton lists in a footnote a number of modern theorists treating unanticipated consequences. He includes Adam Smith but does not mention Ferguson or Millar. Of the others he lists, those of most interest for purposes of this paper are Marx, Pareto, Max Weber, and Wundt. Merton, "Unanticipated Consequences," p. 894.

18. John Millar, *An Historical View of the English Government,* 4 vols. (London: Mawman, 1812), vols. 1 and 2.

19. Millar, *Historical View,* 2:109.

20. Differences between paradox and irony are suggestively treated by Bruyn and Matza. Severyn T. Bruyn, *The Human Perspective in Sociology* (Englewood Cliffs, N.J.: Prentice-Hall, 1966) and David Matza, *Becoming Deviant* (Englewood Cliffs, N.J.: Prentice-Hall, 1969).

21. He remarks, unqualifiedly: "Adhering tenaciously to all his elders taught him, the primitive man deviates into novelty *only* through untintended modifications." Spencer, *Principles of Sociology* (New York: Appleton, 1898), vol. 2.

22. Ibid., pp. 394-95.

23. Herbert Spencer, *First Principles* (New York: De Witt Revolving Fund, 1958), pp. 449-51.

24. Herbert Spencer, *The Study of Sociology* (New York: Appleton, 1896), p. 225; also, pp. 92-96.

25. Philip Abrams, *The Origins of British Sociology* (Chicago: University of Chicago Press, 1968), pp. 69-70.

26. Vilfredo Pareto, *The Mind and Society* (New York: Harcourt Brace, 1935), 4:1577-78.

27. Max Weber, *The Protestant Ethic* (London: Allen & Unwin, 1930), p. 90.

28. It is impossible to do justice here to the significance of the phenomenon of unintended consequences for sociology and the social sciences generally. But it has actually been argued by some that the phenomenon is *the* most important one the social sciences have to deal with. It is clearly basic to economics, and it is no wonder that economists (as well as sociologists) have been among those to attribute primary significance to it. It is also instructive to turn back to Edouard Feuter's still useful survey of modern historiography for its clarity on the point that a rational modern historiography could not arise until it came to be seen that unintended, cumulative changes —the results of human action but not of human design, in an Adam Ferguson-like phrase—were extremely significant in historical process (Feuter, *Geschichte der Neueren Historiographie,* 3d ed. [Munich: Oldenbourg, 1936], pp. 344-45, esp.). The results of human action in social context constantly build structures—as of language, custom, the market—that transcend anyone's intentions and can also be analyzed on their own terms, without reference to the motivations that contributed to their initial rise. The problems that this suggests for contemporary phenomenological orientations are beyond our scope.

29. Karl Marx, *Capital* (New York: Modern Library, 1936), 1:81-96.

30.   It would obviously be futile to try to present within the limits of one paper the empirical pros and cons of various views set out here for purposes of exhibiting relevant forms of argument.

31.   Paul Barth, *Die Philosophie der Geschichte als Soziologie* (Leipzig: Reisland, 1922), p. 337.

32.   Ibid., pp. 293, 337, 641, 744-45.

33.   Cf. Robert K. Merton, *Social Theory and Social Structure* (New York: Free Press, 1968), p. 253.

34.   Spencer, *Principles,* 2:241.

35.   Troeltsch, *Historismus,* pp. 428-29.

36.   Spencer, *Principles,* 2:429.

37.   One other observation of Troeltsch's is worth remarking, to the effect that "the clear principle of the heterogony of ends, as Wundt taught it later . . . is only another formula for Hegel's 'cunning of reason' " (Troeltsch, *Historismus,* p. 428). Historical actors are induced by their passions, as by the lust for mastery and power, to engage in action that contributes to larger historical "ends" that they, the actors, do not envisage—and thus reason exhibits its "cunning," for it does not reveal its own "ends" but entices hitorical actors via ends that appeal to them but actually lead to what is (abstractly) rationally apt. However one may judge Troeltsch's equating of Wundt and Hegel here, it is evident that unintended consequences are vitally important to both of them.

38.   Merton, *Social Theory,* p. 253.

39.   Spencer, *Study,* p. 59.

40.   Ibid.

41.   Thorstein Veblen, *Imperial Germany and the Industrial Revolution* (New York: Viking, 1939).

42.   Max Weber, *Economy and Society* (New York: Bedminster Press, 1968), 2:688.

43.   Weber, *Economy,* 3:987.

44.   Marshall D. Sahlins and Elman R. Service, eds., *Evolution and Culture* (Ann Arbor: University of Michigan Press, 1960), ch. 5.

45.   Cf. Schneider, "Assessment of Sorokin's View."

46.   As quoted by Helmut Schelsky, *Ortsbestimmung der Deutschen Soziologie* (Dusseldorf: Diederichs, 1959), p. 7.

47.   Cf. Marx, *Capital,* vol. 1.

48.   Marianne Weber, *Max Weber: Ein Lebensbild* (Heidelberg: Lambert Schneider, 1950), pp. 385, 390.

49.   Cf. Louis Schneider, *Sociological Approach to Religion* (New York: Wiley, 1970), ch. 6.

50.   Cf. Kenneth E. Boulding, *A Primer on Social Dynamics: History as Dialectics and Development* (New York: Free Press, 1970), pp. 49-53, on benign and malign dialectical processes.

51.   Cf. Soll, *Hegel's Metaphysics,* pp. 134, 139; H. B. Acton, "Hegel, G. W. F.," *Encyclopedia of Philosophy* (New York: Macmillan, 1967), 3:436; John P. Plamenatz, *Man and Society* (New York: McGraw-Hill, 1963), 2:134, cf. also Hegel himself, e.g., *The Phenomenology of Mind* (London: Allen & Unwin, 1966), p. 164.

52.   Hegel, *Phenomenology,* p. 68.

53.   Cf. Boulding, *Social Dynamics,* ch. 3.

54. See, e.g., ibid., pp. 52-53.

55. Ibid.

56. Cf. Weber, *Economy,* 2:ch. 14.

57. Kaufmann, *Hegel,* pp. 170, 171.

58. Gunnar Myrdal, *An American Dilemma* (New York: Harper, 1944), p. 591.

59. Georg Simmel, *Conflict and the Web of Group Affiliations* (Glencoe, Ill.: Free Press, 1955), p. 42.

60. George Steiner, *Language and Silence* (New York: Athenaenum, 1967), p. 142.

61. Matza, *Deviant,* ch. 4; cf. also Bruyn, *Human Perspective.*

62. Oswald Spengler, *The Decline of the West* (New York: Knopf, 1939), 2:102.

63. Walter F. Buckley affirms: "The modern systems perspective is providing conceptual tools that are taking the mysticism out of the notions of 'immanent change' and the harboring of 'seeds' of an institution's own destruction—or construction." Whether Buckley is right or not, he thus suggests significant questions. *Sociology and Modern Systems Theory* (Englewood Cliffs, N.J.: Prentice-Hall, 1967), p. 137.

10
Ironic Perspective and
Sociological Thought
(1975)

It is the aim of this chapter to support the view that irony is intimately bound up with a great deal of sociological thought and that ironic perspectives stimulate such thought profoundly. It would be quite absurd to go so far as to claim that thinking in ironic terms is the alpha and omega of the whole sociological enterprise. Thus, the most penetrating ironies, by themselves, could hardly yield a theory of social structure. But the sociological significance of ironic perspectives or terms is easily suggested, as we shall see, by efforts to specify the meaning of irony as soon as one gets away from a very limited conception of it as a figure of speech.

In a broad, general sense, social life is rife with ironies. One might make considerable ironic play with what Sutherland called "white-collar crime." The area of "race relations" is a most inviting one for the ironist. Modern technology in its social and cultural bearings is equally inviting and equally important. Bureaucracy is tried and true subject matter for irony.

Our reach, here at least, must be restricted. We shall be particularly concerned with irony as bearing first on structural-functional analysis (under the rubric "Ironic Perspectives") and second on labeling theory. Consideration will then be given to the idea of iatrogenesis or medically generated disease, for its suggestiveness in relation to labeling theory and to some broader matters. There will follow comment on the ironic vulnerability of experts in general and on the limitations of the ironic perspective and a concluding word on irony and humanistic and scientific values.

Where there is irony,[1] there is a sense that things are not the way they are "supposed to be." Ironic outcomes of action involve an element of the unintended and unexpected. (Thus, "Irony is seen in a depiction of human action the consequences of which are opposite to what is intended by the participants."[2]) But irony also suggests a "knowing" or wry smile

231

just because one witnesses the bafflement of mockery of the fitness of things, of their supposed-to-be character. This does not, however, preclude a certain affinity of the ironic with the tragic, coexistent with its affinity with the comic. There is certainly such a thing as tragic irony. Indeed, irony would appear to lend support to the contention of those students of laughter who claim that we laugh because if we didn't we would cry.

If irony suggests the existence of some persons who are capable of the "knowing" or wry smile because they were at least not taken completely by surprise by something that in fact was quite unintended and unexpected by others, and the former persons are "in the know," "wise," in on the secret, the latter, of course, are more innocent. Irony strongly hints also at a sense of incongruity going beyond nonexpectation or nonintention alone. The smile is "knowing" because one is, to be sure, "in" on things. It is, on the other hand, wry because one appreciates a special (incongruous) twist in the way things turn out. For instance, ostensibly powerful persons actually turn out to be weak, supposedly strengthless persons, strong. The effect of irony is in such cases enhanced when, say, the weakness of the powerful is traceable to some pretension of strength on their part or when the strength of the supposedly weak is achieved through the same qualities that were despised by others as the mark and confirmation of their weakness.[3]

For working out a minimum definition of irony as here conceived, one may propose the element of the unexpected or unintended in combination with the element of incongruity. Where an ironic sense prevails, let us say, one perceives in things the combination indicated. But the other elements indicated are also significant. Irony is emphatically not the same as cynicism or sarcasm or satire or a jaundiced view of the world. To allow a careless identification or coalescence of it with these things is to render it—and properly so—suspect for purposes of sociological analysis; and the present object is precisely to help rescue it for its uses for such analysis.

The element of the unintended or expected that irony happens to feature has caught the attention and challenged the reflection of numerous sociologists, including Robert K. Merton. The matter of different audiences or diversely socially located observers is bound to interest the sociologist. As well as incongruity, irony suggests ambiguity and paradox, which are indeed very close to it, and none but a simplistic sociology could fail to be alert to these things.[4] There is certainly enough here to intimate the sociological significance of irony. The effort will now be made to sustain in some detail the view stated in our opening sentence. The strategy we adopt is to build the case for the view cumulatively and somewhat discursively as we inquire into the several matters that have already been designated as concerning us.

Ironic Perspectives

"One of the basic results of [my] study," writes Merton in his main early work on science, "is the fact that the most significant influence of Puritanism upon science was largely *unintended* by the Puritan leaders. That Calvin himself deprecated science only enhances the paradox that from him stemmed a vigorous movement which furthered interest in this field."[5] There is a hint here that irony has played some role in Merton's sociological outlook. Despite our lack of concern with the detail of the relations or irony and paradox, since Merton does write "paradox" in the lines just quoted, it is worth noting an appropriate comment by another sociologist: "In the general meaning of paradox, something can be both paradox—a tenet contrary to received opinion—and irony—an outcome of events that mocks the fitness of things."[6]

This hint of irony in Merton's outlook is supported elsewhere in his work. In his paper on social structure and anomie, it would appear that a prime American virtue—ambition—curiously fosters a prime American vice—deviant behavior.[7] But there is rather more than this bare reference would suggest. It would also appear from Merton's paper that that "good thing"—democracy—generates a number of very uncomfortable consequences for many who under less democratic circumstances would be unhurt (at least, in some special, important ways), for the deviance in which Merton was interested, it will be recalled, arises in a context in which certain goals are widely shared by various classes in a democratic social structure, while it would have been less likely to occur where relevant goals *differed* by stratum or class. Less "democracy" would have generated less pain for a considerable part of the populace.[8]

The above perhaps already makes us receptive to the notion of strong affinity of structural-functional analysis with ironic perspective that Merton long ago suggested[9] and that Bruyn and Matza have rightly insisted upon in recent years. Bruyn writes that the effect of irony is "built into the theoretical pattern of functionalism" and draws particular attention to the matter of unintended consequences of social action; while Matza regards irony as "a central figure of functional analysis."[10] Matza reinforces his case by quoting Davis on prostitution, to the effect that "increased prostitution may reduce the sexual irregularities of respectable women. This, in fact, has been the ancient justification for tolerated prostitution—that it 'protected' the family and kept the wives and daughters of the respectable citizenry pure. . . . Such a view strikes us as paradoxical because in popular discourse an evil such as prostitution cannot cause a good such as feminine virtue, or vice versa.''[11]

But something on the order of structural-functional analysis with an accompanying focus on unintended or unanticipated consequences and the concomitant suggestion of an ironic perspective long antedates formal and self-conscious structural-functional analysis in sociology. Merton on social structure and anomie and Davis on prostitution particularly may serve to remind us of the striking anticipations of the ironies likely to arise in a functionalist kind of orientation that are to be found in the work of Bernard Mandeville (a true ''early sociologist,'' if ever there was one), as in his disquisitions on the social consequences of the ignorance of certain social classes, of prostitution (Mandeville's argument is ''the ancient justification'' that the unchastity of some women preserves the chastity of others—of course), and of dueling.[12]

Not only is it true that Mandeville adumbrates present-day functionalist ironies, but in so doing he is constantly likely to confront us with his very suggestive views about how vice, in one or another form, leads to virtue in one or another form. It is conventional, in this connection, to refer to Mandeville's ''paradoxes.'' But paradox here again has a general sense that at least brings it very close to irony. Economists have not forgotten Mandeville, and while sociologists do not remember him with quite the same sense for his relevance beyond his day, his mark within our discipline is nevertheless also traceable (even if not much attended to recently). The point here is to utilize Mandeville as a symbol for an ironic outlook that has even directly and with some frequency influenced sociologists.

Max Weber was well aware of Mandeville's ironic thought. He refers explicitly to *The Fable of the Bees,* cites the famous formula, ''private vice, public benefits,'' and also refers aptly to *''jene Kraft die stets das Böse will und stets das Gute schafft.''*[13] (In Priest's adroit English translation of Goethe, we get ''that power which would evil ever do and ever does the good.'') We return to Robert K. Merton, of whose knowledge of Mandeville's work there can be no doubt.[14] Merton turns the quotation regarding good and evil about, in a context of discussion of unlooked-for effects of the work of the Protestant reformers which damaged their original values. He refers to ''the essential paradox of social action—the 'realization' of values may lead to their renunciation''; and he writes of *''die Kraft die stets das Gute will und stets das Böse schafft.''*[15] The same Merton, many years later, reverted to the original form of Goethe's statement, observing that ''evil intent *can* generate benign consequences.''[16]

So vice can lead to virtue and virtue to vice. Evil can produce good and good, in turn, evil. Prostitution, it is argued, can sustain chastity. Ambition can help induce deviance. Religion can nourish science that ultimately devlops values and theses that challenge the religion that gave it strength. Such "paradoxes" may appear as part of the very ground on which functionalist ironies build, part of the foundation on which they are reared. To put it a bit differently, they need not be "additional" components in a functionalist and ironic position but rather an important portion thereof.

But it is hardly needful to confine one's self to structural-functional outlooks or adumbrations thereof in order to find significant ironic perspectives. Another position in sociology in which irony has played an important role is that of so-called labeling theory, which we turn to with a particular eye to its ironic component.[17]

Labeling Theory and Irony

Matza states what he calls "the neo-Chicagoan irony" succinctly as the irony that "systems of control and the agents that man them are implicated in the process by which others become deviant."[18] The general character of labeling theory[19] is thus represented aptly enough. Labeling theory does stress the role of labelers or definers of deviance who act— fatefully, one might say—upon a deviance already existent. But they do not act upon a deviance already existent.[20] Although there may be some confusion in the matter, there is certainly a saving awareness at least that not all deviant behavior is explicable as an outcome of labeling. Thus, Becker is careful to write that "it would be foolish to propose that stick-up men stick people up simply because someone has labeled them stick-up men or that everything a homosexual does results from someone having called him a homosexual."[21]

The notion of a deviance already existent on which more deviance is piled has been phrased in terms of a distinction between primary and secondary deviation. Lemert writes that "secondary deviation refers to a special class of socially defined responses which people make to problems created *by the societal reaction to their deviance.*"[22] The distinction is an important one, for it would seem to allow easier avoidance of such absurdities as the notion that all crime is caused by policemen—an absurdity to which few would subscribe formally, but one suggestive of excesses to which labeling theory is sometimes liable. It runs some danger, in its more careless representatives, of offering the vision of a radically mentalized universe in which phenomena like crime and mental illness have no reality *except* as they are superinduced by the very agents supposed to prevent or control or "cure" them or *except* as they are accorded a ghostly sort of existence because of the arbitrary labeling of persons who possess power,[23] with an element of the self-fulfilling prophecy suggested as some among the powerless tend to become that which the labelers say they are.[24]

This is said not because the writer fancies himself an expert on labeling theory (which he certainly is not) or feels called upon to pontificate about it. The point is, rather, precisely, that there are instructive ironies involved in the labeling outlook which could only be destroyed or lose all force in a mentalistic travesty of social realities. Again, it seems that the distinction of primary and secondary can be helpful. Even Szasz, whose work on madness in mental institutions has so marked a labeling flavor, argues that there is such a thing as "conceptual psychiatry," a psychiatry set in operation when persons who will often have had no deleterious influence exercised upon them by hospital personnel and who, therefore, in some sense have "emotional problems" antecedent to or independent of any institutionalization,[25] make private arrangements with psychiatrists for treatment.[26] The point, of course, is the implied concession of the existence of some kind of "primary" mental illness.

When a certain rationality and realism are preserved in these matters, there is clear value in the stress that some sociologists have afforded on, say, the role that it is possible for psychiatrists to play in shaping the perception and self-perception of mental patients, without benefit to the latter or to their positive harm (and, some will also stress, without attention to the initial self-perception of the latter). "Rewards" such as approval may be forthcoming to patients once they accept the quite arbitrary diagnoses that psychiatrists may impose, which again do patients no good whatever.[27] Szasz has persuasively sustained an older physician's view that "barbarous" and "unphilosophical" treatment of "mental indispositions" in asylums will have the effect of inflating even originally small aberrations "into the full and frightful monstrosity of madness."[28] There is a measure of real power and cogency in such views; they do not rest on a wholly arbitrary reading of pertinent evidence. The ironies within this sphere become tragic and savage. The tinge of comedy so persistent in irony now disappears and the wry smile of the "knowing" observer now readily becomes an outright grimace.[29]

The case of mental illness in particular has been taken up in this context because of the inevitable suggestion of the "medical" which has been conventionally associated with such illness. Insofar as the psychiatrist intensifies the illness that he is supposed to cure or alleviate, through his professional ministrations (regarded as medical), we are confronted with the phenomenon of iatrogenesis. The whole matter of the ironies on which labeling theory has touched[30] calls for some consideration of iatrogenesis. There is, indeed, so much continuity between central labeling-theory concerns and the sphere of iatrogenesis that it would be ill advised for sociologists *not* to ponder their connections. But it will be remembered that the range of phenomena labeling theory touched on extends well beyond mental illness, taking in such various things as crime, delinquency, prostitution, drug addiction, homosexuality, and stuttering.

Iatrogenesis

Iatrogenic diseases are now recognized as very important.[31] Within the area of iatrogenesis, medical interest has been heavily concentrated on drugs. The authors of a comprehensive recent monograph on iatrogenic diseases write, "In correlating the data for this book, it has been apparent that two factors are the major contribution to the manifestation of iatrogenic disease. These are the abnormal patient reaction to a drug, and the development of unexpected toxicity when the several drugs are given in combination."[32] This sounds almost like a loose equating of iatrogenesis with drug-induced maladies (the drugs being medically prescribed, always), but, however large may be the role within iatrogenesis of drugs,[33] it is certain that current medical usage extends the meaning of iatrogenesis well beyond anything having to do with the medical administration of drugs.

The phenomena suggested by the term as currently used are very old. Medical dictionaries today will often define the term as meaning medical generation of illness or physician-induced illness (when the physician is working as a physician). In this general sense, the famous case of Ignaz Phillip Semmelweis (1818-1865) and puerperal fever will clearly qualify as a case of iatrogenesis. It may be recalled that Semmelweis probed to the bottom of a Viennese hospital situation in which physicians, coming from the performance of autopsies to attend their patients in the last stages of pregnancy, would transmit lethal germs from the corpses to the living women.[34]

But if we include the transmission of disease as well as drug-induced illness under the rubric of iatrogenesis, we are still far from taking in the full reach of the term. Inspection of medical bibliographies indicates the publication, for example, of recent articles on "iatrogenic depression" and "iatrogenic anxiety" in journals such as the *Journal of the American Medical Association* and the *Psychiatric Quarterly*. "A Note on the Possible Iatrogenesis of Suicide" appeared in a recent issue of *Psychiatry*.[35] Wain's compilation on the origins of medical terms refers, under "iatrogenic," to "the production of a psychosomatic illness by overemphasis and exaggeration of the patient's true condition," aside from a standard mention of drugs.[36]

When the surgical blade slips and "the healing knife" destroys more tissue than it should, we also get cases plainly coming within the general meaning of iatrogenesis. The phenomena covered are various. There are evidently different types of iatrogenesis. The modes and mechanisms of iatrogenesis call for close inquiry, just as do modes and mechanisms of those secondary deviance-generating processes in which labeling theorists are interested. Yet the sheer scope or range of things fitting under the title of iatrogenesis suggests a certain comparability or parallelism with the scope of things that concern labeling theorists: on the one hand, a range of phenomena that includes crime, prostitution, mental illness, homosexuality, drug addiction, stuttering, among others: on the other, medical involvement and agency in disease transmission, generation of uncomfortable or parlous or suicidal mental strates, unintended and unwanted effects of drugs, slips of the surgical knife. (There are certainly some possibilities of medical and sociological overlap of interest, as in the case of mental illness, notably.)

There is further suggestiveness in the juxtaposition of iatrogenesis and labeling perspective in that in both medicine and sociology it is quickly apparent that something like a distinction between primary and secondary "difficulty" is indispensable. If a drug is medically administered and intensifies the illness it is designed to treat or has unwanted side effects, obviously it does not follow that the drug generated the initial disease it was prescribed for. One of the dictionaries of medicine or nursing that the writer inspected under "iatrogenic" explicitly takes the term to refer to "a secondary condition arising from a treatment of a primary condition."[37]

It was remarked parenthetically, just above, that there are possibilities of medical and sociological overlap of interest. There are cases of iatrogenesis that strongly feature social situations that could easily come within the purview of the sociologist and presumably be analyzed with a fair degree of accuracy of penetration just in terms of his discipline. A case in point would be the social interaction between doctor and patient in which the doctor's conveying to the patient of his discovery that the latter has a mild hypertension that has had no significant damaging effect and is readily controlled by standard medication leaves the patient in an unnecessary panic. This is clearly a matter of social relationships that simply happen to fall within a medical context. For certain sociological purposes, the particular medical context may not be important. There is hardly a question of medical "analogies" when both doctor and sociologist would be concerned with a problem in social intercourse.

(Henderson noted several decades ago that physician and patient make a "social system."[38]) There is no deviance here, and, accordingly, this sort of case has not interested labeling theorists. But this sort of case has entirely unmistakable continuity with the "social system" case presented by, say, interaction of psychiatrist and patient in a mental institution. Sociologists have not hesitated to discern a large "sociological" element here, and with evident justification, aside from the matter of special competences that psychiatrists may have.

Finally, the juxtaposition of labeling and iatrogenesis raises a point about the vulnerability of experts in general, within our society, which will be taken up in the next section. In the interim, given the dominant concern of this paper, it is appropriate to be insistent on the marked susceptibility of matters covered in both iatrogenesis and labeling theory to interpretation in ironic terms. Things are not as they are "supposed to be." They come out in ways unintended or unexpected, although there is also the suggestion that there are various audiences (often, indeed, more than just two) or observers privy to what is going on in varying degrees, some not "wise" at all. And ironies of interest for both labeling theory and iatrogenesis may well be intensified by the presence of flaws in those supposedly especially competent to "cure" or alleviate, while the flaws are both veiled by and involved in the qualities or features that are considered as the marks of competence itself.[39]

Iatrogenesis, Labeling, and the Ironic Vulnerability of Experts in General

What is "medical" and what is not? How seriously shall the idea of cure or of alleviation of illness be taken in certain contexts that are not indubitably "medical"? Should we decide in various cases that statements about "cure" are so barrenly rhetorical or so unequivocally intended for advertising uses that the statements simply cannot be taken seriously? Where if anywhere do medical "analogies" with situations encompassed in labeling theory warrant a more determined effort to establish continuities or strong affinities with the therapeutic and alleviative efforts of physicians? Where else may there be overlap, such as was suggested above, where there is no question of analogies at all and labeling theory and iatrogenesis converge on the same data?

Asking what is "medical" and what not, one is constained to extend further the scope of inquiry into irony-laden situations that bear evident resemblances to those mentioned thus far. As has been noted, there are various types of iatrogenesis, as there are various ways in which labeling may get its effects. But we have stayed within certain limits. Suppose, however, we should consider the case of a middle-class teacher who inadvertently discourages lower-class students by the very exercise of skills and approaches that help her effectiveness among children of her own class background. Perhaps she has expectations about dress and comportment that make middle-class children comfortable with her but puzzle and disconcert those of lower-class background and impair their learning.

There are familiar presumptions about the job a teacher is supposed to do, and ironies lurk in the situation just described. But is it really worthwhile to try to assimilate it to a medical category such as iatrogenesis? One might well hesitate to do so, while recognizing points of resemblance. Modern society has, of course, witnessed the rise of a great variety of specialties in which there are requirements for considerable training and in which there is constant contact with a public supposed to be benefited by the specialist's services. A vast field for ironies has been opened up here. That is evident enough, whatever one may decide on the applicability of medical categories. There is a *pervasive* irony centering on the inadvertent (and sometimes arrogant) incompetence of competence. "You hurt where you are supposed to help, and you show some aptitude for doing so via the instrumentalities and skills that are supposed to be helpful." Internists, psychiatrists, youth counselors, teachers, and numerous others—all might at times be so addressed.

In this connection, it is worth remembering that the unwanted side effects of medically prescribed drugs have been referred to as "diseases of medical progress," as a part of the price that has to be paid for the achievement of improved medication. "In each prize, some sad germ of evil lies."[40] The ironies or difficulties that arise in connection with the incompetence of competence in areas ordinarily viewed as well removed from the medical sphere may be regarded as a price we must pay for the modern growth of expertness.

In the end, one must ask not only what is medical and what not but even what is ironic and what not. The term "ironic" can be extended in ways that are quite useless and silly. Fowler's *Modern English Usage* (second edition), toward the end of its article on irony, has this: "For practical purposes a protest is needed against the application of 'the irony of Fate,' or of 'irony' for short, *to every trivial oddity*" (italics added). There are areas of "expertness" in some sense (as, say, in hairdressing) where "simulation" of irony would very often presumably not be worth consideration.[41]

Limitations on the Ironic Perspective

The point just stated suggests further cautions. Some dangers to which labeling theory is liable have already been noted. Those dangers, however, are not the only ones.

So-called common sense no doubt has its failings. And the sociologist always has an understandable desire to make a distinctive contribution to the analysis of social phenomena. He has an understandable desire to get away from the obvious, to penetrate deeper, to be analytically resourceful, to bring enlightenment. In his discussion of manifest and latent functions, Merton wrote: "There is some evidence that it is precisely at the point where the research attention of sociologists has shifted from the plane of manifest to the plane of latent functions that they have made their distinctive and major contributions."[42] Merton's own documentation of this assertion gives it good support and, in general, the present writer has no real disposition to quarrel with it. Yet one has to recognize that, precisely because of desire to attain a more penetrating view of things, common sense may be unduly slighted and sociologists may reach for strained interpretations.

Some of the materials with which labeling theorists present us are hard to judge. Problems of sheer evidence loom large here. The writer lacks the space to handle them in any significant way nor is he well qualified to do so. Let us put things naively: Is *everything* that occurs in mental hospitals destructive to the patient's emotional equilibrium? Put in this bald way, these questions can only evoke an offhand, "of course not" response, while they appear to leave labeling theory intact. But there is some force in what would appear the commonsense argument (bearing on the illustrative sphere of delinquency)—counter to the theme of secondary deviation—that "maintains that until the delinquent is caught, charged, and forced to face directly the fact of his delinquency, he will not be motivated to put an end to it."[43]

An important residue, a valuable contribution still remains in labeling theory. One merely seeks to preserve an essential sanity when one adds, simply, that there can be such a thing as irony-mongering or paradox-mongering, brought on by being excessively intrigued and finally bemused by the ironic perspective. With all the importance of iatrogenesis, doctors *do* cure people and alleviate their ailments. Teachers *do* teach numbers of children some things worth teaching. Policemen *do* do some of the work by way of public protection that TV has them doing practically exclusively. This may seem like undue agitation about the perfectly obvious. It does no harm, given certain unhappy potentials in the peculiar enthusiasm that sometimes arise in our field.

But the excesses suggested are not necessary. With appropriate restrains that disciplined sociologists should be able to exercise, ironic outlooks, we have argued and continue to argue, can be highly stimulating to sociological thought.

Irony and Humanistic and Scientific Values

In one of the most gracefully stated arguments that we have for a humanistic bias in the field of sociology, Robert Bierstedt proposed that the field (whatever its status as science might actually be or should be) "owns a rightful place in the domain of humane letters and belongs, with literature, history, and philosophy, among the arts that liberate the human mind."[44] Irony has long been a potent component in works of literature, history, and philosophy. Its humanistic associations are obvious. No serious preoccupation with it on the part of a sociologist could possibly keep it free of such associations; nor is there any compelling reason that anyone should try this impossible thing.

At the same time, it is clear that the careful pursuit of the nuances, the twists and turns of irony in social life could well encourage detailed inquiry that moves toward the scientific kind of enterprise. It is not that men of letters, say, or philosophers, must lack analytical rigor by comparison with sociologists. That is palpable nonsense. But the matter that has been gone over in the present paper may perhaps give a sufficient sense of the feasibility of undertakings of analysis—and of empirical investigation—that are in thorough harmony with the best the sociological tradition has to offer and that take advantage of and are stimulated by ironic outlooks. (Such undertakings have clearly already emerged, and one may hope that they will be carried further.) It may be suggested that the whole area of things here covered lends itself especially well to a blending of humanistic and scientific values in sociology.[45]

Notes

1.   As we turn to the meaning of irony, it must be said that there are some matters that it seems best to avoid on this occasion. There are, for instance, interesting problems having to do with irony as an outlook or stance on the part of an observer of things versus irony as somehow inherent in the nature of things observed, which will not be taken up. It would be too much of a distraction to try to alert the reader constantly to shifts from observer's perspective to quality of things observed. (The idea of a "double audience," referred to in note 3 below, it may be remarked, draws attention to irony as perspective or stance on the part of an observer.) It should also be understood that we shall not return faithfully and regularly to the

detail of the specification of irony to be offered. The specification presents a set of convenient reference points for the reader.

2. Severyn T. Bruyn, *The Human Perspective in Sociology* (Englewood Cliffs, N.J.: Prentice-Hall, 1966), p. 151.

3. This view of irony draws on a number of sources. It is influenced by Bruyn, *Human Perspective*, pp. 150-57, and by David Matza, *Becoming Deviant* (Englewood Cliffs, N.J.: Prentice-Hall, 1969), passim. It receives support from the idea of a "double audience" (one "in" on things, one not, while the former is also aware of the latter's incomprehension) as set out in Fowler's *Modern English Usage*, 2d ed. (New York: Oxford University Press, 1965), s.v. "irony." The exemplification of the powerful and weak draws from a statement by Reinhold Niebuhr, *The Irony of American History* (New York: Scribner's, 1952), p. 154, as quoted in Matza, *Deviant*, pp. 69-70. There is, of course, much discussion of irony and its literary congerers by literary critics: see, for example, Northrop Frye, *Anatomy of Criticism* (Princeton, N.J.: Princeton University Press, 1957), passim. It is evident that irony is both a rich and occasionally somewhat elusive term. A strong sense—even too strong a one—of this richness and elusiveness is expressed in the preface to A. E. Dyson, *The Crazy Fabric: Essays in Irony* (New York: St. Martin's Press, 1965).

4. The relations of irony to paradox, in particular, would be worth exploring. But the senses of the two terms do in fact often overlap, and for the purposes of this paper, the writer is inclined toward a casual association of them, although there is little incidental comment about the relations of the two in what follows.

5. Robert K. Merton, *Science, Technology, and Society in Seventeenth-Century England* (New York: Harper & Row, 1970), p. 58 n. 6. Max Weber as everyone knows, had stressed the same paradox in the field of religion-and-economy independent of religion-and-science—a most important precedence.

6. Matza, *Deviant*, p. 77.

7. Robert K. Merton, *Social Theory and Social Structure*, enl. ed. (New York: Free Press, 1968), ch. 6. (Hereafter referred to as *STSS*.) Cf. Matza, *Deviant*, p. 77.

8. To interpret this as "opposition to democracy" would patently be nonsense. It is well known that Merton's work on social structure and anomie has been subjected to much criticism in recent years. One can only suggest here that it retains at the very least a measure of historical validity that has to do with the central irony about democracy that it rests upon. Thomas and Znaniecki, it may be observed, anticipated Merton's pertinent views in a limited but interesting way. They pointed out that Polish peasant girls immigrating to the United States who became sexually deviant here would not have been so tempted to deviance in their old-world situation, where the near impossibility of attainment of the marvels of "high life"—a class-conditioned near impossibility—would have been less upsetting to their tendency to be "good girls." It should be noted that this argument in no way rests on hostility toward a lower class or anything analogous thereto. See William I. Thomas and Florian Znaniecki, *The Polish Peasant in Europe and America* (New York: Dover, 1958), 2:1820-21. (Thomas and Znaniecki's argument is a bit more complex

than this would suggest, but it clearly incorporates the contention indicated.)

9. Merton, *STSS*, p. 122, where Merton himself writes of "paradox." The affinity of functionalist outlook and irony, it should, however, be added, is decidedly more evident in that variant of the outlook that has interested Merton than it is in the variant that has been developed by Parsons.

10. Bruyn, *Human Perspective*, pp. 151-52; Matza, *Deviant*, p. 77.

11. Kingsley Davis, "Prostitution," in Robert K. Merton and Robert A. Nisbet, eds. *Contemporary Social Problems* (New York: Harcourt Brace Jovanovich, 1961), pp. 283-84, as quoted in Matza, *Deviant*, pp. 77-78. The "functions" of prostitution will shortly be alluded to again. It is worth noting that the supposed happy effects of prostitution in a larger social framework are apparently not altogether a matter of "latent functions." The reader may detect significant ironies in the circumstance that prostitutes themselves can verge on something like functionalist views of prostitution. Thus: "We girls see, like I guess you call them perverts of some sort, you know, little freaky people and if they don't have girls to come to like us that are able to handle them and make it a nice thing, there would be so many rapes . . ."; or: "I could say that a prostitute has held more marriages together as part of their profession than any divorce counselor." James H. Bryan, "Occupational Ideologies and Individual Attitudes of Call Girls," *Social Problems* 13 (Spring 1966):442, as cited by Edwin M. Schur, *Labeling Deviant Behavior* (New York: Harper & Row, 1971), p. 76.

12. See Bernard Mandeville's *The Fable of the Bees*, ed. F.B. Kaye (Oxford: Clarendon Press, 1924), 1:passim, for ignorance; 1:95-100, for prostitution; 1:219-22, 2:102, for dueling. On Mandeville's functionalist outlook generally, see Joseph Spengler, "Veblen and Mandeville Contrasted," *Weltwirtschaftliches Archiv* 82 (1959):35-65 [and ch. 1 of the present volume—Ed.]. Mandeville did incline to cynicism and it is worth repeating that irony is *not* to be identified with that.

13. Max Weber, *Gesammelte Aufsätze zur Wissenschaftslehre* (Tübingen: Mohr, 1951), p. 33.

14. See Merton, *STSS*, pp. 20-21, 475.

15. Merton, *Science, Technology*, p. 101 (italics added).

16. Robert K. Merton, *On the Shoulders of Giants* (New York: Free Press, 1965), p. 14. Edward Shils writes that "although anomic actions are often pernicious in themselves and in their consequences there are some which may be pernicious and immoral in themselves and most beneficial in their consequences." This is classic Mandevillean doctrine. Shils adds to this statement the following one, in parentheses: "This was the view of Mandeville and Adam Smith, but it has not entered very centrally into modern sociology and particularly into the ethical-political outlook of modern sociologists." Edward Shils, *Selected Essays* (Chicago: University of Chicago Department of Sociology, 1970), p. 61n. One cannot be sure how justified Shils is in the first part of this latter parenthetical statement, regarding centrality, although he seems to be on strong ground in the portion of the statement relating to the ethical-political outlook of sociologists.

17. Structural-functional analysis has its limitations. If the writer did not think it had a residual value that goes beyond these, he would certainly not con-

sider it worthwhile to trace the ironic strands in it. The same general statement holds for labeling theory.

18. Matza, *Deviant,* p. 80.
19. The phrase *labeling theory* is used despite some evident discomfort over the two gradiose suggestions of the word *theory* in it. See Howard Becker, *Outsiders* (New York: Free Press, 1973), p. 178. The following outline of labeling theory is designedly most economical and inevitably made in the light of present interests.
20. Here is one of the points on which this sketch is sketchy indeed. The question of what part norms play in labeling theory conceptions of deviance is not taken up. (We do not even consider the grounding of "primary" deviance.) The question is considered by Jack Gibbs, "Issues in Defining Deviant Behavior," in Robert E. Scott and Jack D. Douglas, eds., *Theoretical Perspectives on Deviance* (New York: Basic Books, 1972), ch. 2.
21. Becker, *Outsiders,* p. 179.
22. Edwin M. Lemert, *Human Deviance, Social Problems, and Social Control* (Englewood Cliffs, N.J.: Prentice-Hall, 1972), p. 63 (italics added).
23. Compare the aptly phrased strictures of Gerald D. Suttles, *The Social Construction of Communities* (Chicago: University of Chicago Press, 1972), p. 114.
24. There are also other reasons for reserve about labeling theory, as indicated below in the section "Limitations on the Ironic Perspective."
25. No special view of mental illness is here being intimated or tacitly or insidiously supported. There is not even any bias against the possibility that ultimately it may prove sensible and scientifically justifiable not to regard such "illness" as illness at all. What is argued is simply that, whatever mental illness is, it is not to be considered as unreservedly and totally the product of the work of psychiatrists.
26. See Thomas S. Szasz, *The Manufacture of Madness* (New York: Harper & Row, 1970), pp. 127-28.
27. See Thomas Scheff, *Being Mentally Ill* (Chicago: Aldine, 1966).
28. See Szasz, *Madness,* pp. 127-28.
29. It is of interest that just as prostitutes appear to show some awareness of "functions" of prostitution, so it may be intimated in relevant literature that mental patients can get some inkling that it is possible that psychiatric personnel will hurt them by their ministrations. Thus, Goffman comments that, in the patient's outlook, "psychiatric staff are sometimes seen not as discovering whether you are sick, but as making you sick; and 'Don't bug me man' can mean 'Don't push me to the point where I'll get upset.' " Erving Goffman, *Asylums* (Garden City, N.Y.: Doubleday, 1961), p. 154n.
30. Again, we have had to omit much. A fuller discussion of labeling would have taken into account the significant detail of stereotyping, retrospective interpretation, and negotiation (see, for example, Schur, *Deviant Behavior,* ch. 3), and utilized such detail for the further exhibition of ironies.
31. The writer has made no effort to find recent studies of the incidence of iatrogenic illness. Barber reported in 1966 "a recent study" of the medical service of a university hospital, in connection with which "the house staff found that 20 percent of all patients developed some iatrongenic trouble." See Bernard Barber, *Drugs and Society* (New York: Russell Sage, 1967), p.

182, n. 52, for the source of Barber's information.

32.   P. F. D'Arcy and J. P. Griffin, *Iatrogenic Diseases* (London: Oxford University Press, 1972), "Preface," p. 5.

33.   In the study Barber refers to (see note 31), more than half of the patients who were found to have iatrogenic troubles "sufferred from iatrogenic complications originating in drugs that had been administered routinely" (Barber, *Drugs,* p. 182). We should here at least mention explicitly the matter of inadvertently medically initiated drug addiction, following from legitimate medical use of drugs for analgesic or sedative purposes. There is evident reason for regarding this sort of thing as iatrogenic. But it is, to be sure, one of the iatrogenic phenomena of which there is thorough medical awareness.

34.   A convenient, brief account of Semmelweis and his work is in Henry Sigerist, *The Great Doctors* (New York: Dover, 1971), pp. 354-59. There is irony in the hostile response from physicians that Semmelweis's epoch-making study of childbed fever evoked.

35.   See "A Note on the Possible Iatrogenesis of Suicide," *Psychiatry* 36 (May 1973):213-18.

36.   Harry Wain, *The Story Behind the Word: Some Interesting Origins of Medical Terms* (Springfield, Ill.: Thomas, 1968).

37.   Helen A. Duncan, *Duncan's Dictionary for Nurses* (New York: Springer, 1971). The particular language of two other dictionaries is also of interest in this light. *Dorland's Illustrated Medical Dictionary* (Philadelphia: Saunders, 1957), under "iatrogenic," refers to the generation of "additional problems" that result from the activity of physicians; while the *Encyclopedia and Dictionary of Medicine and Nursing,* ed. Benjamin F. Miller and Claire B. Keene, (Philadelphia: Saunders, 1972), defines an iatrogenic disorder as one produced inadvertently in consequences of medical treatment "for some other disorder."

38.   See L.J. Henderson, "Physician and Patient as a Social System," in Henderson's *On the Social System* (Chicago: University of Chicago Press, 1970), pp. 202-13.

39.   At the end of this section on iatrogenesis, a word may be allowed on *serendipity* and *iatrogenesis.* The former term has been a favorite of Merton's as all acquainted with his work know, and it it utilized with some frequency in *Social Theory and Social Structure* and in *On the Shoulders of Giants.* It will be recalled that serendipity, in scientific usage, refers to discovery of an unexpected or unanticipated but actually helpful datum which works toward modifying or initiating theory. Outside scientific investigations, the term refers to a happy faculty of inadvertently stumbling on good things. In both serendipity and iatrogenesis there is the element of the unexpected or unanticipated, but if serendipity refers to a faculty of stumbling on good things, much iatrogenesis may be said to involve the fact of stumbling on bad ones. (Intention in both cases may be taken to be unexceptionable.) A seriously conceived ironic outlook must take seriously the job of constructing types and families of ironies and of discriminating variants and neighbors thereof and deceptive resemblances thereto. In such an outlook comparison of terms like serendipity and iatrogenesis may be considered to stimulate more than verbal play.

40.   See the quoted matter from an article on drug toxicity in G. Zblinden, in

the Preface to L. Meyler and A. H. Herkheimer, *Side Effects of Drugs: A Survey of Unwanted Effects of Drugs Reported in 1965-1967* (Baltimore: Williams & Wilkins, 1968), p. 5, and the poetic lines quoted in Fielding H. Garrison, *Contributions to the History of Medicine* (New York: Hafner, 1966), p. 546. I am indebted for the Meyler-Herkheimer reference to my friend Morton Ziskind, M.D., of the Tulane Medical School.

41. [Here Schneider appears to have overly compressed his thoughts. He is pointing to a solution to a problem that was of explicit concern to him—and continues to be of concern to students of the ironic focus— that is, the question of what distinguishes latent outcomes from specifically ironic ones. In this brief paragraph he suggests that it is a difference of degree (at least), analogous to the difference between the respective degrees of "expertness" of the physician and the hairdresser. This seems to us fairly unsatisfactory and, importantly, it misses a key connection between humanistic and scientific approaches to irony taken up in the concluding section of this chapter. In a related discussion ("Irony and Technology" in *Social Science Quarterly* 63 [June 1982]:293-311), we have explored this distinction in terms of the *dramatic* character of those special latent outcomes we term "ironic." Since concern with the dramatic may thus obviously be shared by the sociological ironist and his literary counterpart, the ironic focus could be counted as a key linking method between the sciences and the humanities. Ed.]

42. Merton, *STSS*, p. 120.

43. Stanton Wheeler, "Deviant Behavior," in Neil J. Smelser, ed., *Sociology: An Introduction*, 2d ed. (New York: Wiley, 1973), p. 681.

44. Robert Bierstedt, "Sociology and Humane Learning," *American Sociological Review* 25 (February 1960):4.

45. [Schneider's last sentence, deleted from the text for obvious reasons, reads: "Unless I am badly mistaken, the work of the man in whose honor the present volume has been put together moves strongly in the direction of such blending." Ed.]

Part III

RELIGION IN SOCIETY: SCOPE, FUNCTIONS, AND CONTRADICTIONS

Introduction

The final four chapters of this volume include some of Schneider's major writings on the sociology of religion. The main outlines of his approach are already fairly evident from the considerable use made in Parts 1 and 2 of illustrations from the religious sphere. But in this section we also get the opportunity to observe Schneider at work in "his area": the subdiscipline in which he did his most recognizably sociological empirical research and in which his texts *(Sociological Approach to Religion* and *Religion, Culture and Society)* were—and continue to be—widely adopted for use in university undergraduate and graduate sociology courses. We thus find, in addition to the expected references to Mandeville and the Scots (though there are only a few of these here), to Durkheim, Weber, Marx, and Sorokin and the characteristic attention to the ironic, the dialectical, and the unanticipated side of social relations, Schneider's most detailed analyses of conrete historical phenomena and his most explicit expressions of concern about contemporary social issues.

These essays share a common purpose that to a great extent informs all of Schneider's work on religion. It is to delimit the religious "element" or "factor" as a sociological phenomenon; to pose and seek answers to a series of questions that will give clues about such matters as: What is "authentic" religion and at what point does it become inauthentic? In what specific historical contexts—places and times—does religion wax or wane? What does religion "do" for individuals, groups, and societies (i.e., what are its functions)? And, how do these functions resemble and how do they differ from functions performed by other systems of belief and practice, such as magic, law, and psychiatry?

It is instructive, even to those whose interest in religion is at best remote, to see how a scholar of Schneider's calibre—one who is well grounded in the classics and who has developed therefrom a very strong sense of what sociology ought to be (interdisciplinary, "ambitious," etc.)—approaches a fairly conventional, well-worked sociological specialty. Indeed, Schneider is well aware that his suggestions may have a bearing on the research programs of other subdisciplines—though these chapters are consistently and explicitly addressed to students of religion —as when, for example, he underscores some important parallels between the sociologies of religion and crime (Chapter 13). In the course of his quest for the boundaries of "the religious," Schneider has much that is original and useful to say to all social scientists about this elusive and archetypically controversial social force.

Chapter 11 is an early review essay coauthored by Schneider and Sanford Dornbusch in which are discussed the methods and findings of their major study *Popular Religion*. The value of this ingenious, partly historical and partly content-analytical study clearly justifies inclusion of the article here, despite the fact that—more than in any other chapter of this volume—the story is in the footnotes, for the text is sparse and sketchy, little more than an outline. The subject of the study is the "inspirational" religious literature that has been popular, especially in the United States, for several generations. Authors of books of this genre include Ralph Waldo Trine, Henry C. Link, and—of very special interest— Norman Vincent Peale. We have already noted instances in Schneider's writings on the history of social theory and on dialectic and related themes in which he contrasts, on the one hand, insightful sociological perspective on motives and, on the other, Peale's "Power of Positive Thinking" approach. In the work with Dornbusch, Peale and his "philosophy" are dissected and debunked at length, including shots at Peale's literary ancestors and near-relatives. Because many of the ideas and slogans of America's popular religionists are blatantly simplistic and —from the standpoint of one immersed in Mandevillean thought— sociologically naive, the reporting of this research has a note of sarcastic whimsy to it.

This is not to say that Schneider and Dornbusch see nothing of value in Peale's exhortations "to accentuate the positive." In fact, as the title indicates, the point of the article is to show how this type of religion plays a large part in American life, that it has functions (and dysfunctions), latent and/or manifest, that may be very far-reaching. But there is another bit of background "noise" that caused Schneider (at least) to take Peale and his brand of theology seriously, despite their utter lack of regard for dialectical, ironic, Smithian, Mandevillean, or other properly sociological thought, that is, the fantastic numbers of copies of these books that are sold. Schneider was well aware of this "strain" in the publishing business, and this awareness is often expressed with fascination.

The main finding of this study is that popular religion is a "spiritual technology" that not only has a market but also gets certain "results"— it works, though through indirect means. As sociologists know, religions of the more conventional types perform certain integrative functions for individuals and primary groups, despite the fact that they may be oriented not to individuals and groups but to "larger" entities like congregations and, ultimately, God. Peale and the other popular religionists urge their audiences to pursue these functions directly: to seek happiness, to be popular or influential, to be a "success" in life, through prayer, devotion, belief in a "sacred" realm, and the other trappings of religion. As traditional religion is "for God," popular inspirational literature is intentionally "for man."

Here we have what appears to be a clear case of the latent in religion being made manifest. This discovery prompts what Schneider, here and elsewhere, identifies as a key empirical question in sociology: Can outcomes be expected to be the same when the latent becomes manifest? The suggestion in the case of popular religion is that "the drive to make religion useful is possibly self defeating" (from the abstract, published with the original article).

Clearly, there are presumptions here that might be questioned. There is even some self-contradiction because, in the same article, popular religion is identified as an *effective* lower-middle-class substitute for psychiatry; that is, the opposition between the "for God" and the "for man" orientation in religion may here be forced and artificial. It is substantially documented that all religions in all times have had a "mixed" technology, some specific techniques designed for remote and/or transcendent ends (though as Schneider points out in later chapters, some Buddhist sects deny anything like a "for God" orientation) *and* some techniques to bring immediate personal gain. In all of the religions of India, every day, gods are bribed for concrete "favors" *and moksha,* salvation, or some such "remote" end is sought.

Thus, the books by Peale and the others may not be the best place, after all, to begin to look for an outright "self-defeating" strain in religion. But such a study does at least allow us to expand our perspective, to see that religion exists—even thrives if sales records are any indication—outside "normal" religious organizations and doctrines.

Following a brief introductory statement on theory and method, Chapter 12 turns directly to religion outside normal organizations, to "the shift of attention of a number of students in the field to nonchurchly forms or manifestations of the religious." Among the nonchurchly forms subsequently discussed in the five numbered sections of this chapter are civil religion, including the celebration of America, Marxism, antinomianism, and secularized Protestantism. The chapter concludes with a plea, sounded earlier in relation to sociology generally and here the sociology of religion, for broad, interdisciplinary, encompassing approaches to phenomena of interest. This means that the sociologist of religion cannot avoid and should not attempt to avoid theological issues, poetic interpretations, etc.

Written some twelve years after the study of popular religion was completed, this exploration of "some areas of theoretical potential" is clearly the work of a seasoned professor. A great range of material is drawn together in an effort to direct researchers to areas likely to bear fruit in reconciling "big ideas"—which Schneider believes to be virtually absent in work on religion done after Parsons's *The Social System* (1937)—with rigorous methods, which he believes to be the virtually exclusive and essentially meaningless preoccupation of some practitioners of the sociology of religion. The tone of the chapter is, thus, forthrightly prescriptive, notwithstanding some highly original thoughts on substantive features of religion (and a note on the possibility that the prescriptive task is best approached indirectly).

Structural-functional perspectives figure significantly in this chapter, beyond the mention of Parsons as a possible author of some "big ideas." In fact, the five areas of potential share the premise that *religion is as religion functions.* In considering the work on civil religion of Robert Bellah, W. Lloyd Warner, and Harvey Cox, Schneider suggests that "pulling together elements of 'religion' that may be found at various loci" may "provide a chance for functionalist thought to give evidence of further vitality." From these comments, specifically, and from Schneider's work on religion as a whole, it is hardly remarkable to conclude, as most of his colleagues and students (critics among them) have, that he is, basically, "a functionalist." But, as is clear in the treatment of Marxism and antinomianism that follows these remarks, to so label him is to miss the very special relationship that he sees—and puts into practice—between functionalism, dialectical approaches, and the like. Moreover, as observed in earlier chapters, he has some strong objections to the types of vulgarization to which functionalism is apparently prone. Thus, it seems fair to think of Schneider's approach to religion as functionalist only if it is also remembered that he was very much a "plain" functionalist, who might equally be termed a dialectician or, even, an ironist.

"Antinomianism" in its etymological roots describes the "creed" and practice of the religious outlaw. It is the belief that some states of religious "excellence" can be achieved—and here the shades of meaning of the term become evident—either despite or in the extreme because practitioners break the rules *(nomos)* by which people are ordinarily expected to abide. The term makes a brief appearance in Chapter 12, specifically in connection with Anne Hutchinson's movement in the

United States, in order to illustrate a kind of ultimate perversion of religion that, nevertheless, continues to *function* as religion. In Chapter 14, antinomianism is featured as an instructive subject for the application of dialectical approaches, and we shall have more to say about it presently.

In a carefully qualified exploration of the commonly voiced claim (or "charge") that Marxism is a religion, Schneider continues the project undertaken in Part 2 of separating the useful from the spurious in Marxist sociology. Here, as in Chapter 9, his patience appears to be strained by "Marxist pieties," "mythology," "hypostatizing," "stultification." There is an indication here (which is fully explicated in Chapter 13) that Marxism suffers from idolatry, or that there is at least an "idolatrous tendency" in the worship of the working class and the "history loading" practiced by many Marxists. But also, as in earlier chapters and here with strong emphasis, Schneider wishes to preserve the "genuine scientific contribution[s] of Marxism," especially the concept of the fetishism of commodities.

This discussion leads to consideration of the problem of "meaning" — religious meaning in nonreligious contexts and nonreligious meaning in religious ones. The problem was identified in Chapter 6, among other places, where Schneider suggests that Sorokin may have made too much of mere surface differences between forms of speech and other cultural items, treating them, incorrectly, as indicators of major differences in world views, values, etc.; that, in brief, two differently stated propositions from two apparently different cultures can still have the same "meaning." In attempting to clarify how Marxism—and antinomianism, civil religion, etc.—can have religious "meaning," Schneider is once again impressed by the fact that there are several (three are listed) ways in which two distinct belief systems—say, Marxism and "normal" Judaeo-Christian religion—might have the *same* meaning. It is of some interest that Ludwig Wittgenstein, in a different but not wholly unrelated set of *Philosophical Investigations*, also came to this sort of conclusion.

The "meaning" problem arose in another quarter of Schneider's research, that on the dissident priests of San Antonio (see Chapter 12, note 9 for detailed reference). In that study, intensive interviews were employed, historical background was gathered, and Manfred Kuhn's Twenty Sentence Test (complete the sentence "I am . . ." in twenty separate statements) was administered. Data from all of these sources pointed fairly conclusively to a religious or "priestly" definition of the situation (especially the events surrounding their demand for the resignation of the archbishop) that, nevertheless, had the "same meaning" as the manifestly nonreligious definitions of situations of other counter-cultural dissidents of the late 1960s and early 1970s. Thus, the "meaning" problem arises both in Schneider's most general cultural, philosophical interests and his most "hard-nosed" empirical research (complete with malfunctioning tape recorders and equally balky interviewees). This problem also relates to Schneider's general concern with "bounding" religion: What does religion "mean" to individuals, to society?

A belief system (e.g., Marxism) can have religious "meaning" in the sense of "manifestation," and/or "reduction," and/or *"plus ça change . . .,"* and in other ways. There is ample cause for tension, opposition, and contradiction among such levels of meaning. These are features of religion—in relation to society—upon which a dialectical approach can shed much light. Here some familiar examples are used to illustrate the workings of contradiction, self-defeat, and other dialectical principles in the religious sphere: Weber's analysis of the Protestant ethic, antinomianism, the general advantages of indirection in planned social change, and, what was known to Schneider's students as a classroom favorite, "the monk's success story." This story, in essence the "Saint Paul effect" mentioned by both Schneider and Sorokin in their exchange, highlights the manner in which ascetics, in mastering their other-wordly disciplines and thereby achieving the "success" of religious excellence, subsequently come to attract followers. But the followers tend to partake in various this-worldly practices in connection with their religious worship. Organizations are established, resources are marshaled and closely budgeted, a bazaar grows up near the place where the ascetics gather, and, in a neat dialectical sequence, the spirit becomes flesh.

As noted, the chapter concludes with the general injunction to the sociologist of religion to avoid a narrow, disciplinary focus. In assessing the theological potential of dialectical approaches and the other areas, it is evident that the study of religion in society is sufficiently complex to demand, in addition to the ordinary sociological tools and frameworks, a good background in history, anthropology, poetry, and theology. In an adumbration of this injunction on the first page of the chapter, Schneider shows that he is sensitive to the magnitude of the task thus assigned to the individual sociologist of religion; that perhaps the subdiscipline (like other subdisciplines) is best approached "in the way of teamwork for men of different talents." But however put into practice, it should never be far from the researcher's consciousness that a strictly sociological account of the functions and "meaning" of religion is necessarily a woefully partial one.

Chapter 13 continues and refines the exploration of religions outside the church, again with the overt purpose of providing "theoretical nourishment" to the field of sociology of religion, including through "repeated contact with theological issues." Three areas are selected here for special consideration: private religion, idolatry, and magic and the occult. Like Peter Berger, whose work is cited at several points in this last section, Schneider discerns "A Rumor of Angels" in these and other quarters of modern society commonly held to be secular.

The subject of prayer arises in connection with the first of these, private religion—of the type dispensed, for example, in the books of Norman Vincent Peale. Prayer is in some respects essential to "normal" religion: it is a form of communication between the individual and something larger than, and outside, himself. It affirms the existence of God or a sacred force insofar as it posits a receiver, a "divine listener"; and it has ethical consequences in that it forces the faithful to review—and, under some circumstances, to atone for—their moral conduct. In these ways it is one of the principal mechanisms whereby religion performs its widely recognized integrative functions. But then, one might ask, can prayer even exist, does it have "religious meaning" without a church and creed to support and channel it? Schneider's answer is simply, yes— prayer and the pursuit of private religion itself are, in principle, authentic. In coming to this answer, he provides a convincing and widely applicable anecdote about a certain man of "irascible temper" who storms out of the house in the morning in righteous indignation but who, during the course of the day, comes to regret his acts, promises himself to repent for them, and, by the evening, has resolved to change his ways: he is "a new man." For Schneider's purposes, despite the absence of God, church, and scripture, this may still qualify as a religious experience, that is, the experience called prayer. As he observes for the sake of his philosophically oriented readers, what is being sought here is a "real"—not a nominal—definition of prayer (and of religious elements generally). The question of the scope of the religious factor is precisely a sociological one in this sense; empirical, operational procedures are required to establish presence, absence, intensity, and its other features, that is, *prayer* is as *prayer* functions.

This functionalist thrust is present also in Schneider's interesting little byplay on faith in psychiatry—and in his informative section on Sutherland's concept of white-collar crime. Since, Schneider reasons, the concept has been so fruitful—sadly so, he notes, in the Watergate days during which this chapter was written—because it draws attention to crime committed outside normal "criminal circles," it is likely that much is to be gained with a parallel concept of nonchurchly religion, that is religious acts "committed" outside normal religious mileux. As

Schneider indicates, this analogy has some obvious limitations, [1] but at a minimum, its mention and related notions in psychiatry, civil religion, etc. help us to keep in view how *function* (functional equivalence, etc.) influences the scope of the religious factor.

In some further remarks on civil religion, Schneider encounters the phenomenon of idolatry.[2] The connection between civil religion and idolatry is nicely brought out in an exchange that occurred in the early 1960s between Edward Shils and Norman Birnbaum, in which Shils is—at least indirectly—accused of using an alleged analysis of the religious functions of the monarchy in England as a mask for a highly conservative, biased account. Without entering into the exchange, Schneider gleans from it a possibility, i.e., that civil religion in England, the United States, and possibly everywhere, *may* under some circumstances become a politically conservative ideology, in which case it is also tantamount to idolatry. Though not identified as such, there is an obvious distinction drawn here between "healthy" civil religion (e.g., in which the nation is subjected to moral scrutiny on the basis of higher values) and pathological, "idolatrous" civil religion (e.g., in which the nation is worshipped above any transcendent principles). In any case, Schneider does suggest that idolatry may be the "seamy side" of civil religion.

Indeed, other entities than the state may be the object of misplaced religious worship, for—as suggested in Chapter 12—there is a pronounced tendency in Marxism toward *class* idolatry. Humanity itself, as in the case of Comte's doctrine, may become the repository for religious sentiment. By giving to idolatry such a broad domain—even to taking seriously such things as the worship of sex or some other "impulses"—Schneider believes we can understand idolatry as a *perversion* of the religious factor.

Because there is also much that is valuable in Marxist views of the working class, and, when read with sympathy, in Comte's religion of humanity as well, it is important to distinguish between what is scientific and what is tainted by "idolatrous leanings" in such doctrines. And all of this indicates a useful role for a sociology of idolatry, a curiously unexploited field.

The chapter concludes with some comments on magic and the occult, including the very popular—and diffuse—current literature (and movement) that deals with ESP, communicating with the dead, and contact with extraterrestial beings. These and all manifestations of magic—ancient and recent—share a strong accent on the power that comes with control of supernatural forces. Yet significantly, they also invariably exist against a background of "high" religion. This suggests that magic may well be the obverse and complement of such high religion: The former emphasizes the "for man" and latter the "for God" phases of what is, after all, a unitary religious impulse. (Here Schneider has begun to qualify his views on the opposition between these two phases noted in Chapter 12.)

As Firey observed in his memorial to Schneider, he was "at the peak of his career" when he died. Chapter 14, the last of his works that he saw in print, is perfect proof of this. As the title suggests, the chapter explicitly connects Schneider's work on dialectical (and related) themes with his research on the sociology of religion; as should be evident by now, this also means that the views of Mandeville and the Scots are likely to be brought to bear, at least implicitly (and, in fact, Mandeville is cited). In this way, "Dialectical Orientation and the Sociology of Religion" summarizes and epitomizes this collection and, indeed, Schneider's work as a whole—as much as any one article can. Here Schneider also reveals in the strongest possible terms his interest in antinomianism and like phenomena. Though this topic is taken up at various points in earlier chapters, the discussion here is singular for the intensity of Schneider's fascination, for the dramatic character of the examples and "cases" he chooses to analyze, and, not least, for the vast amount and range of material that is drawn upon in support of his points.

To put it (perhaps too) briefly, in this paper, Schneider has "discovered" the tantric or kabbalistic dimension of religion. Perhaps it is a wholly predictable "discovery"—knowing his general interests in the boundaries of the religious factor—but at the same time, it is obviously a beginning of a new, higher intellectual stage in Schneider's life that he had no time to develop. (It might also be observed that, though we find Schneider's characteristic profuse citation of related works in at least a dozen fields, here the story *is* in the text; there are *no* footnotes in the original version of this chapter.)

The chapter begins with the distinction, first introduced in Chapter 9, among three related things to which the term "dialectic" (and its inflected forms) can refer: (1) the action of elements within a system, (2) the action of elements without special reference to a system, and (3) a language or grammar of social life. These three "meaning clusters" are then directly brought to bear on issues in the sociology of religion.

In each sense of dialectic, attention is focused on pairs of elements so related that "excessive movement" toward one member of a pair brings about movement toward the other; and within religion one can discern striking shifts between extremes that fit this pattern. In a broad sense religion consists of what have been called "gnostic" and "bhaktic"—rationalist and nonrationalist—strains. In some readings of the history of religion, these strains appear to alternate in a dialectical rhythm over the years and over the centuries. In other respects, from a more *social-*

historical perspective, these two tendencies appear always to be co-present: The same religion that man uses to denounce the world he also uses to seek God's help to change the world (for his benefit). Tibetan Buddhism, the Parsi religion of Zoroastrianism, and perhaps a few other creeds are, in fact, very explicit about God's *dual* character.

With this formulation Schneider eliminates most traces of artificiality in his treatment of the "for God"/"for man" opposition that arose in his earlier views on popular religion. Following an informative comparison of the views on religion of Durkheim and William James—who, with important qualifications, could be counted as an intellectual "forefather" of Norman Vincent Peale—Schneider acknowledges that problems can arise in identifying instances of "true" opposition, that the dialectic, for all its value, has at least this limitation.

In working through these problems at some length, it is once again observed that "dialectic," "latent function," and "indirection" are closely related terms in the sociologist (of religion)'s vocabulary. One evident cause of the difficulties that arise in attempting to sort out the true "opposites" in religion—subject/object, God/man, spiritual/material, etc.—is that such pairs of elements actually coalesce: they suggest what in linguistics is known as "oxymoron," the close juxtaposition of antonyms for dramatic effect (e.g., "deliberate speed," "foolishly wise"). And here we reach the core of this discussion and, thus, of this stage of Schneider's intellectual development. As he puts it here, "Virtually the whole of this present chapter may be allowed to suggest the salience of oxymoron in phenomena of interest to the sociology of religion."

In a similar vein, antinomianism, the quest for religious goals through disregard or outright violation of "law," is identified as a natural interest of "anyone with a dialectical orientation toward religion." Indeed, in something of a continuation of the remarks in the preceding chapter on the affinities between the sociologies of religion and crime, antinomianism is here proposed as an instance of "religious deviance" par excellence. In a wide variety of reports about and documents from antinomian creeds—such as the *Consolamentum,* or last rites, of the Catharists—there is a prevalent notion that through faith and activity one can be freed from obligation to religious and moral law. What is actually considered impure action or unconventional comportment is, for antinomians, justifiable or even excellent because of their "dialectic of purity."

For Schneider, contemplation of antinomianism is a veritable wellspring of sociological insight into deviant behavior, the religious sphere, and the workings of the dialectic. The mere listing of selected historical instances of antinomianism suggests much about the scope of the religious factor, etc.: the Catharists, the Ranters, the Great Awakening (in New England), the (Adventist) Millerites, Hasan's (Muslim) Millenium, certain Sufi tendencies in Islam, Hindu and Buddhist Tantrism, and the Sabbatai Zevi Coming in Judaism. These, indisputably marginal yet also so universal, tendencies within religion reveal things great and petty about human relationships: How people can be profoundly inspired by the celebration of the end of law, but also how the experience of antinomian purity is often translated into righteous hatred of the impure.

There is a little bit of antinomian in all of us,[3] just as there is a little bit of criminal. For this reason the analysis of this "marginal" phenomenon is bound to be of interest to any social scientist. In fact, in a later reference to meaning (3) of "dialectic," Schneider refers to it as a means of understanding "the distinctive language which social phenomena speak."

This chapter also contains a long section on Tantrism, a group of cult-beliefs in India and neighboring countries with decided antinomian tendencies. The oxymoronic quality of the Tantric creeds is described in the Sanskrit word *nirdharma* (lawlessness). Basing his view largely on the findings of religious historians (B. Walter, Ken Ch'en, and Edward Conze), Schneider sees some revealing, common themes among the "left-handed" Tantric cults, such as the Hindu Saklas, Nathas, and Kaylas, and the Buddhist Vajrayawas, and Kaichakrayanas. Of special note is an apparent mixture of awe and guilt among practitioners, that is, it appears that one must be conscious of doing "wrong" in order to attain Tantric spiritual rewards, which in turn suggests the oxymoron "holy sinner."

This seeming paradox also figures significantly in the movement associated with the "Coming" of the apostate messiah Sabbatai Zevi. Sabbatai Zevi (1626-1676) gathered a following as the annointed one in the Mideast and Eastern Europe, before his conversion to Islam—i.e., an ultimate breach of Jewish law. This cult continued after his apostasy until his death, and has reappeared in Jewish and Muslim communities from time to time to this day. In his fantastic story "The Destruction of Kreshev," Isaac Bashevis Singer tells of a young man, a native of the seventeenth-century *Shtetel* of Kreshev, who reveals—in a synagogue—how:

> he had joined the ranks of the Cult of Sabbatai Zevi while still a boy, how he had studied with his fellow disciples, how he had been taught that an excess of degradation meant greater sanctity and that the more heinous the wickedness the closer the day of redemption.[4]

As Singer, Gresham Scholem, and other students of diaspora Judaism have noted, the doctrine of Sabbatai Zevi, though certainly an aberrant offshoot of the messianic tradition, also has traceable roots in kabbalism (both the Orthodox and the "Luranic" strains), and thus in the Talmud and Torah itself. For this reason, such apostasy in Judaism and, by extension, antinomianism in any religious culture, remains an authentic—if, in principle, illegitimate—part of that culture and of the religious sphere as a whole. It is this part/whole relationship that, Schneider feels, is of very special interest to the sociologist—of religion and in general. Somewhere in the background (or underground) of the major world faiths—Judaism, Christianity, Islam, Buddhism, and Hinduism—there always lurks the "hypothesis" that although good and evil are opposites there is also a very special connection, an affinity, between them.

As indicated, this chapter and this volume conclude with Schneider's expressed hope that he has advanced the development of a sociological *perspective,* identified in Chapter 10 as the ironic focus and here as the dialectical approach: a "grammar" of social relations in which figures of speech such as irony, oxymoron, and synechdoche can be viewed as forms of action. Thus, with due and characteristic qualifications concerning these limits—especially as so far developed—Schneider closes with the hope that he has "at least hint[ed] at the profundity such a grammar might have. . . ."

Notes

1. But, as we note, the analogy was revised effectively by the time Chapter 14 was written.
2. One might raise objections to the term *idolatry,* which Schneider appears to share. That is, it tends to belittle, to class as inauthentic, religions—like Hinduism—in which idols are "worshipped." The point is that one may, it appears, include idols in religious ceremonies without the "misplaced concreteness" or—and perhaps this is the better covering term after all—fetishism associated with "idolatry." Anyway, my dictionary distinguishes between meanings "(1) worship of idols" and "(2) excessive devotion to or reverence for some person or thing," whereas in the text Schneider uses the term exclusively in the second sense—with, as noted, due recognition of the problem.
3. Within certain kabbalistic interpretations the search for the end of law begins at the moment of The Fall, as reported in Genesis. To this extent, every messianic movement arising in the Judeo-Christian tradition is thus (directly or indirectly) antinomian; at least indirectly, every Jew and Christian is seeking restoration of Eden—i.e., the state of man before tasting the fruit of the tree of knowledge of good and evil—and is thus also antinomian.
4. "The Destruction of Kreshev," reprinted in *The Spinoza of Market Street* (New York: Penguin Books, 1981), p. 180.

11
Inspirational Religious Literature:
From Latent to Manifest
Functions of Religion
(1957)

The inspirational religious literature is known to be enormously popular. The books of Norman Vincent Peale today, of Bruce Barton a generation ago, and of numerous of their close intellectual relatives and imitators have achieved staggering sales.[1] Sociologists have left comment on it to journalists or theologians or gifted outsiders.[2] But it is of significance for the analysis of "cultural drift," with broad general implications. In this article, a brief survey of the inspirational religious literature and a summary of its dominant trends and themes, attention is given to a special phase that is of considerable sociological import.[3]

Description of the Literature

The literature is by no means unitary, but strains or trends in it exhibit prominent elements of unity.[4] Ralph Waldo Trine's *In Tune with the Infinite,* Bruce Barton's *The Man Nobody Knows,* Henry C. Link's *The Return to Religion,* and Peale's *A Guide to Confident Living* and *The Power of Positive Thinking* suggest for purposes of definition four criteria to which the items of literature should conform: (1) They assume the general validity of the Judeo-Christian religious tradition; (2) they aim to inspire with the hope of salvation here or in an afterlife; (3) they recommend use of techniques to achieve salvation, in whatever sense salvation might be understood; and (4) they address themselves to the "everyday problems" of "everyday people." The books vary in the balance among the four points.

The general validity of the Judeo-Christian tradition is assumed among these works with significant vagueness. Specific theological doc-

---

Coauthored with Sanford M. Dornbusch

trines, such as of Christ's soteriological mission, or specific theological discussions, as of Christ's status as a member of the Trinity, are hard to find. More likely, there will be found discussion of a transcendent "something" about which a professed theologian could say practically nothing. Daniel Poling confesses, "I began saying in the morning two words, 'I believe'—those two words with nothing added."[5]

The literature also holds forth the hope of some kind of salvation. In the seventy-five years covered in the survey eschatological interest has declined. But, while concern with the next world fades increasingly, salvation comes quite conclusively to mean salvation in this world: release from poverty or handicapping inhibition in personal relations or from ill health or emotional disequilibrium. But salvation in this secular sense is held forth as a definite hope and even a promise.[6]

The inspirational literature bristles with techniques to attain peace and power which range from putting one's self "in tune with the infinite" by some intuitive twist of the psyche to sensing a deity in the chair by one's bed at night; from reconstructing failure as trifles or even as successes to whispering to one's self a promise of good things to come. These practices, finally, are represented as helpful to ordinary men and women in solving their everyday problems, but this point needs no elaboration here.

Elements of this kind may be found in a variety of places, for example, in Augustine's *Confessions* or Thomas à Kempis's *Imitation of Christ*. But these documents differ in affirming faith unequivocally. Moreover, the salvation they envisage is not of this world. The ends they set out lack the concrete, tangible quality of such goals as business success or emotional "adjustment," and, consequently, they hardly bristle with the techniques with which the modern literature is filled. True, in a certain sense, there is some overlap, as, for instance, in the case of prayer, which is often recommended; but there are obvious differences between devotional prayer and prayer that, not very subtly, is instrumental.[7] On the other hand, the literature, not only on its own recognizance, is in some sense "religious." Advertisements that promise to add six inches to the chests of scrawny men are "inspirational" in tone, but they make no pretensions to being religious and cannot qualify as inspirational religious literature.

A dominant trend in the literature through the decades is secularization; for instance, suffering has lost its "meaningfulness" and more and more is described as senseless misery, best gotten rid of. No longer divinely or transcendentally significant, suffering figures as a pathological experience calling for a psychiatrist or a minister trained in counseling. Again, the deity as represented in the literature is in process of transformation: his existence in some objective sense is no longer insisted upon, and he often approximates a consciously useful fiction. The "hero" appears more and more as the "well-adjusted" man, who does not question existing social institutions and who, ideally successful both in a business or in a professional sense,[8] feels no emotional pain. Finally, there is a strong bias against the "unscientific" and for equating religion and "science."[9]

In American thought William James,[10] in effect, substituted, "I believe because it is useful" for "I believe because it is so"—or even, with Tertullian, "because it is impossible"—an idea that abounds in the inspirational religious literature. Or the best is made of both worlds in a combination such as "I feel it is absurd; but, since it is useful, I shall insist that it is true." Thus, Henry Link avers, "I believe in God because I have found that without the belief in someone more important than themselves, people fail to achieve their own potential importance." And he adds later, "Agnosticism is an intellectual disease, and faith in fallacies is better than no faith at all."[11] Writers like Harry Emerson Fosdick will go on a certain distance in this direction. Fosdick asserts:

> The explanation of the rise of cults like Christian Science and New Thought is obvious. While the old-line churches were largely concerning themselves with dogma, ritual, and organization, multitudes of folk were starving for available spiritual power with which to live. These cults arose to meet this need, and with all their mistaken attitudes . . . they have genuinely served millions of people by *translating religion into terms of power available for daily use.*[12]

But if Fosdick is willing to go only this far, others are willing to go beyond him. The literature consistently emphasizes "God-power" as divine flow into men, sustaining and aiding him in some materially useful sense to the point where the deity often becomes simply a psychological device. The strain toward instrumentalization is so strong in Peale, for example, that one must by inference from his work assign to God as a primary function the dispensing of divine vitamins to men eager for health and wealth.

A kind of spiritual technology has also been developed, inseparable, of course, from the instrumental element. Standard religious procedures like prayer are constantly recommended, although often with a characteristic twist, as in Peale when he urges, "Learn to pray correctly, scientifically. Employ tested and proven methods. Avoid slipshod praying."[13] Self-exhortation, another frequently suggested procedure, undoubtedly has affinities with more "classical" religious procedures, for example: "I believe," "Christ is with me," "In everything I do God helps," "I cannot lose." Again, stress is placed on special psychic states, perhaps with physical props simultaneously suggested—for example, a state of receptivity to "God-power." A notable set of recommendations depends upon converting spiritual principles into magic. Thus, as in some of the work by Lloyd Douglas, which is frequently only a fictional transcript of inspirational religious literature, he who gives without letting anyone know it is repaid a thousandfold, both magically and materially; he becomes a great success. An outcome not only of impossible physics but—in the light of the principle "cast your bread upon the waters" and cognate exhortations—of a dubious spirituality, this can be described as spiritual technology.

Other trends include, as the quotation above from Fosdick illustrates, a definitely antiritualistic,[14] antidogmatic, anti-institutional (antiorganizational) strain. The stress is most emphatically on religious "experience" as might be expected.

Manifest and Latent Functions of Inspirational Religion

In marking the transition from latent to manifest functions of religion, one must distinguish between a *primary* and a *secondary* religious sequence. A good enough text for the primary sequence is afforded by the biblical prescription and promise, "Seek ye first the Kingdom of God, and all these things shall be added unto you." "Faith" is thus urged, but it is urged as primary; its possible "fruits" are only hinted at. The notion that Job might have been seeking to be "well adjusted" simply on the basis of the *Book of Job* is incongruous. The primary religious sequence may be roughly rendered, then, as follows: Faith⟶ Action⟶ "Results" (for example, emotional equanimity).[15]

But the modern inspirational literature more or less deliberately reverses the sequence. It starts from the observation (here assumed to be correct) that what is loosely called "faith" *can* bring about "peace of mind" and cognate desired ends. It does not, so to say, start with "the Kingdom of God," that is, with what might be called "classical" religious belief, because the belief is thought to be *true*. (Of course, it may incidentally hold out for the truth of such doctrine as it happens to retain.) It relies on a secondary sequence that begins with a projection or presentation of the desirability of all manner of "good things," mainly wealth and emotional of physical health. This secondary sequence becomes, then, "Results" (in prospect) ⟶ Action⟶ Faith (or, possibly, also "Results"⟶ Faith⟶ Action), "action" being largely on the lines of spiritual technology. The modern spiritual technology may in a number of ways be a substitute for older religious ritual. If it is acknowledged that at times, when men have believed sincerely and devotedly, serenity or calm has come to them, it has clearly often come as a *by-product.* Serenity, calm, and the like have been latent functions of religious faith and devotion. It is not necessary to claim that they have been *unqualifiedly* latent; differences of degree may well be crucial. But the inspirational religious literature makes these latent functions of religion manifest and pursues them as aims.

The shift from latent to manifest raises the question: Can the same "results" be obtained? A task facing sociological theory is the classification and explanation of cases in which the transition has different kinds of results. If, say, factory workers can be inspired by a demonstration of the full nature and final uses of the product to which their seemingly disjointed individual efforts have led, it does not follow that an analogous service will always be performed by a demonstration to the religious that their efforts to "find God" afford them "peace of mind." Nor is there any reason to think that faith will be enhanced if it is also shown, directly or by implication, that gaining peace of mind is the point of religious practice in the first place. Here, too, differences of degrees are important. That the inspirational religious literature does not always make an outright and unqualified shift from latent to manifest but often stops short of an uninhibited assertion that the *object* of faith is to attain power or peace of mind is of sociological interest.

But the sheer fact that there has been a shift on the lines indicated is easily documented and, for that matter, not only in the inspirational religious literature. Thus, Marshall Sklare notes a similar development in Conservative Judaism:

> According to tradition, the Jew should observe the Sabbath because it is God's will that he do so. In appealing for a reinvigoration of the holiday, Conservatism, however speaks in terms of *social utility*—in this case the potential contribution of observance to better mental health. Only secondarily is it suggested that the Sabbath may have something more than therapeutic significance, and, furthermore, no Divine sanctions are inferred. The performance of a religious obligation becomes a technique for achieving personal adjustment.[16]

Thus, curiously, the religious begin to look on their own activity in the manner of functionally oriented sociologists and psychologists. The question is whether, in doing so, they do not endanger the religious function; or perhaps these are all signs that faith has already lapsed, the efforts to exhibit its virtues being proof. In this connection it is pertinent to look back to a recent paper by William Kolb, who poses a "moral dilemma" for sociologists of religion who affirm the "integrating" function and necessity of belief in ultimates while themselves holding that belief to be illusory:

> To spread the idea that a belief in ultimate validity of values is necessary but illusory would be to destroy society through destroying or confusing this belief. Yet to urge people to accept the idea that there is an ontic realm of values while believing oneself that such an idea is false is deliberately to deprive people of the knowledge necessary for their freedom and dignity.[17]

Many of the purveyors of inspirational religion may represent a kind of halfway house. At one extreme we would find followers of the "old-time religion," unreserved believers that their creed has objective validity, who, at times, incidentally reap material benefits from it. At another extreme are "positivistic" functional sociologists, quite prepared to find religion increasing the solidarity of the group, drawing the deviant individual back to it, and so on, while unconvinced themselves. Inspirational religion is somewhere between these extremes, somewhat fluctuating and unsure, yet with a powerful instrumental bent. Faith, again, is "the answer"—enjoined in the first instance not because the religious content that it affirms is above all "true," but just because it is "the answer." The concentration on "the answer," the results, already half-suggests an "illusion." The presumed primary "truth," put into the background from the very absence of attention to it, becomes the more dubious the less stress it receives and the vaguer it gets. The impulse to make religion "useful" is understandable, but the deliberate effort to do so may be self-defeating.

Notes

Grateful acknowledgement is made to the Center for Advanced Study in the Behavioral Sciences, Inc., and to the Laboratory of Social Relations of Harvard University for their support of the project which this paper reports in part. We are also grateful to Miriam Gallaher, Margaret Swenson, David Feldman, and Bruce Finney.

1. A two-page advertisement in the *New York Times Book Review* (April 8, 1956) announces that Peale's *The Power of Positive Thinking*, "the best-loved inspirational book of our times, reaches its 2,000,000 copy anniversary." A generation ago it could be remarked that "few realize that the field of religious books often furnishes the most spectacular and continuing records in book sales. While novelists may vie with each other for records of a hundred thousand, there are continually springing up in the field of religious books titles that go far beyond that, and even into the million" *(Publisher's Weekly,* February 19, 1921, p. 513).

2. See, however, Everett C. Parker, David W. Barry, and Dallas W. Smythe, *The Television-Radio Audience and Religion* (New York: Harper, 1955), for a sociological analysis of the output of inspirational religion on televi-

sion and radio in New Haven. Other discussions are: William Lee Miller, "A Passionate Faith in the Great Whatever" (review of Edward R. Murrow's *This I Believe), Reporter* 10 (April 1954):46-48, and "Some Negative Thinking about Norman Vincent Peale," ibid. 12 (January 1955):19-24; and Gustave Weigel, "Protestantism as a Catholic Concern," *Theological Studies* 16 (June 1955): 214-32.

3.   It reports part of a study of a sample of over thirty best-sellers published since about 1880.

4.   Individual writers differ, e.g., there are marked differences between Peale and Harry Emerson Fosdick and between them and Bruce Barton or between all three and British writers who have found a sizable American public, like Harold Begbie, who in *Twice-born Men* (Boston: Revell, 1909) praised the "inspiration" afforded the poor of the London slums by the Salvation Army more than a generation earlier, or like Daphne du Maurier, who ranges herself, in *Come Wind, Come Weather* (New York: Doubleday, Doran, 1940), with the followers of Frank Buchman. Catholic writers, like Bishop Fulton Sheen, are in quite a different universe, to which the characterization below will not apply well. This should not, however, suggest that there are no important resemblances between Catholic and other writers; many, for example, share the view that "social salvation" or social reform is to be achieved more or less exclusively through the reform of the individual and increased numbers of reformed individuals. Thus, Bishop Sheen, who avers that "world wars are *nothing but* macrocosmic signs of the psychic wars waging inside microcosmic muddled souls" *(Peace of Soul* [New York: Permabooks, 1954], p. 8; italics added), allies himself on this point with Daphne du Maurier and Henry C. Link.

5.   Quoted from *Parade: The Sunday Picture Magazine,* September 19, 1954, by Will Herberg, *Protestant-Catholic-Jew* (New York: Doubleday, 1956), p. 282.

6.   So Emmet Fox, "If only you will find out the thing God intends you to do, and will do it, you will find that all doors will open to you; all obstacles in your path will melt away; you will be acclaimed a brilliant success; you will be most liberally rewarded from the monetary point of view; and you will be gloriously happy" (*Power Through Constructive Thinking* [New York: Harper, 1932], p. 23).

7.   A qualification rather unusual in the literature is: "Too often the whole value of a prayer is judged by emotional awareness of change in one's inner states, and if one does not feel differently after having prayed, he begins to wonder if there is anything to it." The writer adds, in even more unusual vein, that, "to make such a test is to forget that prayer is directed toward God, not toward ourselves" (Georgia Harkness, *Prayer and the Common Life* [Nashville: Abingdon-Cokesbury Press, 1948], p. 66).

8.   Bruce Barton in one strategic sentence sets off two dominant strains in the literature in speaking of the life of Christ: "Stripped of all dogma, this is the grandest achievement story of all" (*The Man Nobody Knows* [Indianapolis: Bobbs-Merrill, 1925], p. 9). Surprisingly little attention has been given by sociologists to the success theme and the support for it in American religion, especially in view of the leads given by Weber and Tawney. The Reverend Russell H. Conwell's "Acres of Diamonds" speech contains the forthright assertion that "the foundation principles

of business success and the foundation principles of Christianity, itself, are both the same" (*Acres of Diamonds* [New York: Modern Eloquence, 1901], pp. 138-68). On page 148 is a pertinent and well-known
item, but Weber would also have been interested in numerous similiar
items, such as the contention of Mrs. Stetson, the Christian Scientist, that
poverty is a form of evil and error, while prosperity is both symbol and
consequence of spirituality (see E. S. Bates and J. V. Dittemore, *Mary
Baker Eddy: The Truth and the Tradition* [New York: Knopf, 1932], p.
381).

9. Perhaps simply an exaggeration of an already fundamental strain in Protestant philosophy of religion and theology (Cf. George F. Thomas, *Protestant Thought in the Twentieth Century,* ed. Arnold St. Nash [New York:
Macmillan, 1951], pp. 99-100).

10. Cf. his *Varieties of Religious Experience* (New York: Longmans, Green,
1902) and *Essays on Faith and Morals* (New York: Longmans, Green,
1949). From James comes, apparently, much of whatever intellectual stock
in trade the inspirational literature manifests. "Believe," he says at one
point, "that life *is* worth living, and your belief will help create the fact"
(Essays, p. 31). However, the literature, taking the stance that "faith is the
answer," hardly bothers with instances in which the most devoted faith has
not brought emotional calm or brought it only after long struggle, such as
are often found in James.

11. *The Return to Religion* (New York: Macmillan, 1936), pp. 34, 63. This may
also be simply an exaggeration of trends found throughout American Protestantism (cf. Willard L. Sperry, *Religion in America* [New York: Macmillan, 1947], pp. 153-54).

12. *As I See Religion* (New York: Harper, 1932), pp. 17-18; italics added.

13. *A Guide to Confident Living* (Englewood Cliffs, N.J.: Prentice-Hall,
1948), p. 114.

14. Cf., e.g., E. Stanley Jones: "Nothing is essential but God, and no rite or
ceremony is essential in finding him" (*The Christ of Every Road* [Nash-
ville: Abingdon Press, 1930], p. 150).

15. An anthropologically or psychologically simplistic view is not being suggested. If "faith" can lead to "action," under "action" including ritual or
ceremonial behavior, there is no implication that this is a *necessary* sequence. It is quite possible for "action" to reinforce "faith" or for each to
reinforce the other. Moreover, it is not suggested that a *necessary* outcome
of "faith" is "peace of mind"; merely that this is sometimes the outcome.

16. *Conservative Judaism* (Glencoe, Ill.: Free Press, 1955), pp. 121-22. Sklare
also quotes from a wall poster that avers that Sabbath has afforded the Jew
"a blessed opportunity for personality adjustment" and the opportunity,
furthermore "to preserve our psychological, physical, and spiritual
equilibrium" amid the tensions of daily stress (ibid., p. 122).

17. W. L. Kolb, "Values, Positivism, and the Functional Theory of Religion:
The Growth of a Moral Dilemma," *Social Forces* 31 (May 1953):309.

12
The Sociology of Religion: Some Areas
of Theoretical Potential
(1970)

The sociology of religion, whatever else it may be, is sociology. Being sociology, it can be held to a notably difficult ideal for the analysis of social data generally, namely, the ideal of marrying "big," important ideas with rigorous methods. Because of the difficulty of the ideal and of the high demands of a training that shall embody it there is a certain danger of fragmentation. Some sociologists will be tempted to go off into special speculation, philosophy, or history. Others will be tempted to develop fine measurement instruments, redoubling their strictly technical efforts when they have lost hold of any larger nontechnical aims. There is now considerable and acute awareness of, and sophistication about, these things. There are many sociologists not particularly liable to the temptations noted. There are possibilities in the way of teamwork for men of different talents. But sociology does not thereby at once become an easy endeavor, with promise of great success soon to be attained.

It is not that there is warrant to sag hopelessly before the challenge that sociology presents. However, it is not surprising if its practitioners are often concerned about its progress or failure to progress, and this holds in the sociology of religion as elsewhere in the general field. The sociology of religion has suffered much from lack of data on matters of essential interest. On the whole it has thus far made use of rather rudimentary methods in a technical sense, although this may not have been altogether disadvantageous, given its general condition of underdevelopment. Yet despite this underdevelopment, the field has had the benefit of a number of reasonably "big" ideas.

"Big" ideas have indeed been a rather conspicuous feature of the sociology of religion. Everyone knows that two of the authentic giants of modern sociology—Durkheim and Weber—made important contributions in the field. In the historical background there loom figures like Marx and Freud, shining lights in their time (with all their perversities, I, for one, would add), who did relevant and provocative work. If anthropologists like Malinowski and Radcliffe-Brown lack the stature of these four men, they are still far from dwarfish in their own right. The considerable intellectual tradition this suggests has been continued (although with small debt to Marx) by that very capable "idea" man, Talcott Parsons. But the big ideas have not been replenished or greatly developed for some time. With all due respect to Parsons and with full regard to the significance of his work for the sociology of religion, it can be plausibly argued that he never went much beyond a synthesis of Durkheim, Weber, and perhaps one may say Freud, as far as basic insights are concerned.

A good deal, of course, depends on what one means by basic insights. The concern here is particularly with the major functionalist tradition, a tradition heavily dependent in its background on Durkheim and the anthropologists mentioned. One of the great achievements of functionalism was the demonstration of the importance of the nonrational in human social life, of certain elements in the orientation of the actor (for the matter can be put in this way) different from scientific elements, not cognate with the latter and not in any sense "inferior" to them. Parsons may be said to have consolidated this victory on the basis of the work of Durkheim, with help from Pareto, in *The Structure of Social Action* in 1937.[1] It would not be unreasonable to regard this as the last main instance of theoretical development in, or pertinent to, the sociology of religion in the functionalist line. Or one might take statements in *The Social System*[2] relating to religion and *Ausgleich* ("the ultimate balancing of the motivational moral economy"), or religion and tension management, and regard these as such a final main instance of development. This would perhaps be generous, but the point could be argued. One is certainly not free to overlook the relevance to analysis of religion of Parsons's ideas of structure, of his applications of cybernetic notions, of his development of concepts like that of "fundamentalism." It would not be difficult to defend the view that there is much interesting and even brilliant work here. And others besides Parsons have contributed to the sociology of religion in the functionalist line. It is hardly necessary to contend that there has been hopeless stagnation. In fact, there has been a good deal of capable reinforcement and refinement, and a measure of advance, but these things are not the same as major steps forward.

With this absence of really large advance in a crucial line of theory, we inevitably ask how we can move ahead. The ultimate ideal for the field remains, and must remain, an effective consolidation of significant idea and acute method. It would be an achievement to dredge up from the sociology of religion as it has developed up to now the materials for a spectacular consolidation. But it is an unlikely achievement, given what the field up to now can offer. Perhaps one could effect some really strategic combination of functionalism, and, say, phenomenology, to help toward the ultimate ideal. But functional theory alone stands in need of further development on its own terms, to say no more. Or one might bring into the field from outside some quite new, smashing theoretical outlook that would reorder and systematize it to its lasting scientific benefit. We could not withhold admiration from anyone capable of doing such a thing, but it cannot be brought appreciably nearer by being wished for. One might at least hope for a stylish new notational scheme that would present old insights in a fresh, economical way and thereby create the prospect of catching significant things previously uncaught. Even this is not offered here.

It is of course not difficult to be critical of the sociology of religion. But it is not always easy to be "constructive." I do not pretend to do more in the following five notes than to point to a few areas of theoretical potential for the field. They rest largely on the simple conviction that the field is likely to gain from broadening its outlook and, indeed, the last of the notes directly advocates a deliberate effort to broaden outlook and is somewhat different from the foregoing four, which address themselves to more particular matters from whose consideration a broadened outlook might emerge. The ultimate ideal of consolidation of significant idea and effective method is not forgotten, but the main design of the subsequent remarks is to offer a limited set of suggestions that may conceivably be helpful on the "idea" side. However conscious sociologists may be at various times of falling short of their ultimate ideal, that ideal still cannot be forced, and it is not necessarily always best advanced by endeavor strictly undertaken in the light of it alone. The ways of indirection can be profitable in a discipline aspiring to scientific status also. In correspondence with the relatively "relaxed" spirit in which the following is set out, it is assumed that it is sometimes profitable even today to look back to older or pioneering work even while one appreciates the point that the past may become oppressive and constrictive.

1. A first matter has again to do with functional theory. One of the most conspicuous developments in the sociology of religion in the last few years has been the shift of attention of a number of students in the field to nonchurchly forms of manifestations of the religious. A bare review of this development is quickly given. Bellah noted in his familiar article on religious evolution that it is misleading to concentrate on the church "in a discussion of the modern religious situation," for "it is precisely the characteristic of the new situation that the great problem of religion . . . is no longer the monopoly of any groups explicitly labeled

religious."[3] And in another familiar article the same writer outlined the elements of a civil religion in America, in its way drawing on but certainly not identical with the heritages of Christianity and Judaism.[4] Lloyd Warner, of whom Bellah was naturally aware, was clear on the point that he used the word "sacred" not only with reference to the specifically, conventionally religious sphere of the Christian faith but used it also to apply "to objects and phases of life to which the special reverence arising from religion in general has been extended."[5] Peter Berger's *A Rumor of Angels*[6] turns away from what its author sees as a conventional churchly supernaturalism in decline and toward examination of a number of possibly constant sources of religious impulse—one might say intimations of the divine—that could give nourishment to religion in all sorts of nonchurchly loci. Luckmann[7] is another of the sociologists disposed to look for manifestations of religion outside specialized religious forms or institutions. This extrachurchly orientation is hardly confined to sociologists. Thus, Harvey Cox, the theologian, cites Bellah, Berger, and Luckmann with evident approval and writes: "Just as education is not by any means confined to schools, so religion cannot be equated with what goes on in churches. Any theologian must today be something of a theologian of culture."[8]

This statement by Cox actually touches on something most significant for theoretical development in the sociology of religion. If the concern with the nonchurchly forms of the religious or sacred has any merit at all, then the functionalist theory, in particular, would appear to face a considerable task of "aggregating" the religious, marking out its components in a variety of places and "packaging" them properly for analytical purposes. Just as the "political" has to be aggregated and packaged or put together, since it is not confined to "state" or "government," so a similar problem arises for the religious. This is the more important since Parsonian theory, in particular, has in recent years given so much stress to interchanges (as between culture and personality systems within the large "action" context). It is hard to see how any very full or impressive theory of interchange could be built without pulling together the elements of "religion" that may be found at various loci.[9] Even if we are not concerned with interchange in particular, the entire preoccupation with the nonchurchly religious still awaits a full, distinctive functionalist development. It seems fair to say that there is a large challenge here and possibly a chance for functionalist thought to give evidence of further vitality.

2.   But the wanderings of the religious or sacred are hardly done with yet. It has become virtually banal to suggest that movements like Marxism need serious consideration in the light of the question whether they

are religious or contain religious components.[10] No more than beginnings
are made with the question when, on the one hand, one notes within
Marxism such things as the presumption of a loaded historical process
that in the end makes for an inevitable triumph of good over evil or notes
the presence within Marx himself of a passion for social justice of quite
possibly religious origin breaking through an ostensibly scientific socialism; or, on the other hand, such things as Berger suggests when he
observes that "the wisdom of Marxism is unlikely to afford much comfort to an individual facing a cancer operation."[11] No one would want
confusion introduced into a field that is in any case difficult enough.
Why go chasing after "religious elements" in a phenomenon like Marxism when there are at least surface indications that in some respects it can
well be argued *not* to be religious and there is sufficient work to do elsewhere? But the matter is not so easily disposed of and it would hardly do
to shirk a necessary task. Birnbaum reminds us that Friedrich Engels
observed that, in a religious epoch, "even revolutionary ideas have to be
expressed in a religious rhetoric."[12] Then perhaps in a political epoch (if
that is what ours is) even religious ideas have to be expressed in a political
rhetoric. If we're not going to be fooled by forms or appearances, let's
not be fooled by them.

Whatever conclusions we may ultimately reach in regard to the
religious character of Marxism, the entire notion of the diffusion of the
religious is suggestive in other ways. It may serve to remind us of the
need for doing things that we have tended to put aside. In the present
context of reference to Marxism, it is worth recalling that Marxism *does*
have a scientific side. Marx was one of the significant modern contribu-
tors to the idea of religion or myth (not necessarily "religious") as arising out of social circumstance. When he discussed the fetishism of commodities, as is well known,[13] he afforded a powerful delineation
(however obsolete the relevant framework of economic analysis has
become) of how the results of men's actions in economic context confronted them as phenomena which they could no longer trace to their
authentic human sources. He wrote of the producers in the capitalist
economy that "to them their own social action takes the form of the action of objects which rule the producers instead of being ruled by
them."[14] The elements of a sociology of knowledge and of economic and
political myth are certainly present in his work. Economic and political
mythology has hardly ceased to be important. Myths about races and
ethnic groups, too, are notoriously widespread in the modern world.
Processes of hypostatizing, personifying, and demonizing are constantly
at work in a kind of "natural" mythological development, a kind of bad

poetry—bad because it rests on false or inaccurate perceptions and on a literal understanding of its own metaphors.[15] An economic depression can still seem to be something like a hostile visitation from another world —an arbitrary, self-willed, autonomous thing—although no doubt this perception differs by societies and other groups. Witches, devils, and angels in human form are always with us.

The idea that the realm of politics, for example, is a realm of myth is not a novel one by any means.[16] Nationalism has often been scrutinized for its possible religious content. But there is a potential here to which the sociology of religion has hardly been sufficiently alert. The possibilities of close affiliation with the sociology of religion of studies of race prejudice and its ideologies, of the psychodynamics of politically significant personality types have not begun to be properly explored. Political mythology should be of prime interest to sociologists of religion. Perhaps the rather impoverished state of economic sociology explains something of the reluctance of sociologists of religion to look for legitimate objects of concern in the economic realm. Students of Marxism have long been aware of the possibility of turning its own weapons of sociological analysis against it and exploring the character and foundations of its own mythical components.

Three points are worth stressing at the price of some repetition. First, it is not being unequivocally, flatly contended that "Marxism" (a complex, various thing) is a "religion." Rather, that proposition needs (and will undoubtedly get) further serious analysis. Second, it is certainly not contended that the area of political, ethnic, economic mythology, with the above referred-to processes of hypostatizing, personifying, and demonizing it presents, necessarily must be a "religious" area. The religious or sacred in some fairly strict sense may be more to the fore in some of the things to be studied in this area and much less to the fore in others. But the whole idea of the diffusion of the religious, of its extension to nonchurchly spheres, may be utilized to motivate us to be more alert than ever to common mythic elements shared by things religious and certain things nonreligious. Third, it is recognized that words like *religious* and *sacred,* even if many of us still regard them as indispensable, give us a lot of trouble already. There is no desire to allow them unwarranted further extension. It is merely one of the circumstances attesting the underdevelopment of the sociology of religion that its vocabulary is not up to the clear statement of its problems.

3.   Cox has been quoted as saying: "Any theologian today must be something of a theologian of culture." It would seem desirable for the sociologist of religion to be more than a little of a student of culture in general. It is important for him to be this in following the movement of

religion, in itself and in relation to other things. Broadly speaking, we have thus far exploited some possibilities of considering the religious or sacred to be more diffused or pervasive than it has been considered to be up until recently, at least in a good deal of Western thought, and even the previous note, with its suggested reservation that much in the realm of political and economic mythologies is not religious (even if it is mythical), was to some extent motivated by the same notion of diffusion of the religious. But is is also true that much that "looks" religious is, or has been cogently argued to be, only superficially so. In facing up to such contentions, we would be greatly aided by a really penetrating theory of culture.

To indicate what is intended here, it is well to note that there are at least three meanings that may attach to the assertion that certain things are only superficially religious—meanings that may be here designated as reduction-meanings, manifestation-meanings, and *plus ça change plus c'est la même chose* meanings.

Charles Francis Adams, in his study of the so-called antinomian controversy of 1636-1638 in Massachusetts, the controversy centrally involving Anne Hutchinson, remarks that that controversy was "in reality not a religious dispute, which was but the form it took." Adams thought that the controversy was properly seen as "the first of many New England quickenings in the direction of social, intellectual and political development—New England's earliest protest against formulas."[17] Quite independently of Adams, Belfort Bax, in his often cited study of the Anabaptists published soon after the turn of the century, writes of "the religious garb" of movements of the Anabaptist type and time—a garb which "allows us plainly to see through to the deeper-lying social discontent which constituted [their] real substance."[18] Bax tends to be defensive of the Anabaptists, more particularly with regard to their conduct in Münster, and sees men like Münzer, Jan of Leyden, and Jan Matthys, "with all their shortcomings" as in a sense "forerunners of Modern Socialism."[19] But what is of interest here once more is the tendency to think that the "real signfiicance" of certain ostensibly "religious" phenomena is not "religious."

Adams and Bax have been drawn upon rather than other men who might do equally well because of certain interests I have at the present time.[20] But others could certainly have been drawn upon. Neither Adams nor Bax makes his meaning very clear in statements crucial for present purposes. Each man might conceivably be interpreted as talking about a manifestation, within the religious sphere, of things also to be perceived elsewhere, outside the religious sphere. Thus, Adams might be construed to be saying that there was a general, widespread movement, at the time he writes of, against rigid modes of thought and behavior that showed itself *in* religion as elsewhere. This suggests a kind of simultaneous, more or less "equal" operation of generic forces in different specific areas. Bax might be interpreted in much the same way. The "deeper-lying social discontent" of which he writes might then, once more, be manifesting itself *in* religion as elsewhere. In this interpretation, one might well wonder about the "religious" character of what one sees in the religious sphere. What one sees in that sphere might merely be a specifically religiously colored form of a more general reality. Dissident Catholic priests today complain about hierarchy, authority, structure, and hardened institutions, but they share precisely these complaints with alienated college students in large public universities. The priests' perceptions and ideology could very plausibly be interpreted as manifestations *in* the religious sphere (and perhaps given a somewhat peculiar coloring in that sphere) of more general phenomena "equally" appearing in other spheres.[21]

Adams and Bax might be differently interpreted. Their meaning might be, not a manifestation-meaning, but a reduction-meaning. This is perhaps particularly the case for Bax. In a reduction-meaning, one could hold a bias to the effect that a kind of false consciousness, a kind of illusion appeared in the case of, say, the Anabaptists at Münster. Their fantasies would need translation into another language. We would be in the presence of false renderings or derivations of the realities of class conflict and the like. Whatever portion of truth this may contain and however subtly that might have to be worked out, it is of interest that a shrewd present-day Marxist (Gerhard Brendler) takes Karl Kautsky to task on the subject of Anabaptism and writes of "religious motives not reducible without remainder to economic reasons for action"; while just prior to this he remarks of Kautsky's work (in language mercilessly orthodox but intelligently cautious): "His economic reductions of ideological realities eliminate the ruling dialectical reciprocal action between economy and ideology and negate the relative independence of ideological phenomena."[22] But a reduction-meaning still must involve at least a *component* of reduction, as in the sense above suggested. The religious appearance is in some measure deceptive in that it is, precisely, an appearance that cannot be taken simply at face value.

In a third possible interpretation, Adams and Bax (or others who write in rather similar terms) might be conceived to be saying that we can see the significance of the New England antinomianism of 1636-1638 and of Anabaptism and its travail at Münster some hundred years earlier if we recognize that they were only *religious expressions* of transhistorical or transcultural impulses which might at other times and in other places take a nonreligious form. We would accordingly be fooled by them if we took their "religious" character too seriously. Adams remarked provocatively that to call a man an antinomian in Anne Hutchinson's time and place was "merely another way of calling him a lawless libertine or a ferocious revolutionist."[23] There is reason to think that there is much similarity between statements such as "She is a witch" and "She is neurotic" when these statements are transhistorical or transcultural.[24] This is emphatically not to deny that the verbalization "She is a witch" may be accompanied by very different consequences from those that accompany "She is neurotic." And those different consequences are obviously important. But there can still be a powerful strain toward cross-cultural similarity in that the statements or verbalizations address themselves to the same or quite similar phenomena. *Plus ça change plus c'est la même chose.* It is not merely that when a shift does in fact occur from "witch" to "neurotic"[25] something like "secularization" may be at work. That need not be denied. It is that a different language and a different interpretive frame translate much the same experience.

There are striking cases where relevant shifts are hard to misinterpret. I have suggested elsewhere, after F. J. E. Woodbridge, that a pious man of an earlier day might have called sweetheart or wife "a handmaiden of the Lord." But the woman would in time become "a very fine girl"; and, in further time, "quite a kid." The language involved in "handmaiden of the Lord" could have rather little religious significance and might be hardly more than an archaic way of saying "a very fine girl." The religious quality of the early language could be but a thin veil cast over a sentiment substantially the same over several centuries.[26] Granted, not all our cases are in principle so simple.[27] Granted, too, that the threefold distinction developed above could stand a good deal more explanation than it has received here. It has received enough, it may be allowed, to suggest the gains that might come to the sociologist of religion from a developed theory of culture. The "character" of different cultural spheres, the relative autonomy of those spheres, their tendency to change at the same or different times and the measurement of the time differentials, the rationale for regarding various phenomena as transhistorically or transculturally "equivalent"—these are all relevant things. Religion cannot be adequately studied in isolation from its cultural neighbors. The threefold distinction introduced points to jobs that could yield considerable theoretical gains. They are jobs that will have to be done (with whatever help can be gotten from other disciplines) if a successful historical and comparative sociology of religion is ever going to emerge.

4.   The sociologist of religion cannot afford to forget the simple, very general point that certain things that occur in the religious sphere also oc-

cur elsewhere. Religion is a sphere rife with paradoxes, dilemmas, "contradictions," oppositions. In this broad sense, it is eminently dialectical.[28] One may study religious statements alone for evidence of stress on counterbalancing themes of entities and forces, and one can also study religion in a more comprehensive sense—religion in action—for evidence of similar things. Consider a forest hermitage in Ceylon referred to by Obeyesekere.[29] Monks had come to live in caves at the hermitage. But they could not remain isolated in meditation and free of the world. Their fame brought the world (involving laymen and alms) to them. The state of holiness of the monks could greatly benefit laymen, but the very availability to laymen that would accord the benefit would at the same time reduce the monks' holiness. Paradox, dilemma, "contradiction," opposition are thus readily suggested. Consideration of these can cast considerable light on religion and on the connections and affinities of religious with nonreligious phenomena.

The entire subject of dialectic in religion is an immense one. But let us just stress opposition or oppositeness in two roughly discriminated contexts. One is a "logical" context, which may be illustrated by antinomianism, although it is not necessary to refer again to the weak form of it that appeared in New England in 1636-1638. Antinomianism crops up in religion with some frequency. It is certainly not confined to Christianity. But it is often described in terms that suggest a peculiar religious tension and opposition. Thus, Bax includes among phenomena that "alike found their place in the ranks of the Anabaptists and of the later sects of the sixteenth and seventeenth centuries" *both* "the mortification of the flesh of the anchorite" *and* "the unbridled lasciviousness of the libertine." (He remarks that "religious asceticism in sexual matters has invariably throughout history carried its own reaction with it. It has always tended to pass over into its opposite.")[30] Opposition is further suggested by the common theme that to the pure all things are pure, for it implies that the pure can harmlessly, without peril to their spiritual welfare, give themselves over to all kinds of impurity.[31] Dollinger, in his vivid account of the medieval Gnostic-Manichean sects, points out how, via the institution of the Consolamentum among the Catharists, with which a "good end" indispensable to salvation was made, antinomianism was encouraged, for one who was certain of salvation at the end of life *could* afford to be unrestrainedly licentious until the end (although by no means all were).[32] It is significant that the Catharists generally rejected marriage and contended that a married man, too, looked upon his wife with lust and was accordingly sinful.

A more recent student of Catharist morality, in touching upon the dualistically grounded notion of liberation from this evil world, notes that one could scorn the flesh in libertinism or punish and repress it in asceticism.[33] That the soul is untouched by what the body does is a common antinomian idea. Koch observes: "The origins as well as the goals of libertinism were the same as those of asceticism. The two orientations were but two poles of a fundamental disposition, which proposed disdain for matter."[34] In politics, the fundamental rejection of the notion that a social order is susceptible of any considerable reform may unite extremists of the right and left.

In a second context in which opposition or oppositeness may be stressed, we become especially alert to various processes and mechanisms. This "processual" context may be conceived to overlap with the "logical." Cohn, writing on the persecution of the Anabaptists, observes: "This persecution in the end created the very danger it was intended to forestall."[35] This is a quite commonplace example of suggestion of mechanisms whereby the opposite of something intended is brought about. The religious sphere constantly exhibits this kind of thing. So do other sociocultural spheres. Certain paradoxes in the sphere of religion suggest that processes of indirection often will in fact "work" better than direct efforts to attain various goals or results. Thus Battis voices the at least plausible suspicion that "the most substantial strides toward religious freedom have generally been made, not by the dedicated and articulate proponents of that end, but rather by the strenuous endeavors of innumerable sectarians . . . to gain religious freedom for themselves." He adds: "In the long run religious heterogeneity and the force of numbers were more powerful persuaders than rational arguments in producing this great social change."[36] Heimert's work on American religion features a thesis to the effect that it was precisely orthodox or conservative ("evangelical") religion that carried strong democratic seeds within itself and afforded impulse or energy to popular activity—not "liberal" religion.[37] (Generally relevant in the present discussion is the circumstance that Max Weber's work in the sociology of religion was imbued with a deep sense of how men constantly brought about results that they had never contemplated and that could even—à la the notion of "the tragedy of the idea"—*contravene* their intentions.)

Paradox, dilemma, contradiction, opposition, or oppositeness are indeed broad notions. It may seem almost as if the above is designed to suggest that sociologists of religion should work in the field of the sociology of religion. But a fuller statement than has been possible here would make it quite plain that a major result to be hoped for from dialectical sensitivity is the discrimination and precise description of particular patterns of "logic" in religion that are also important elsewhere (as in the case of the "logic" of libertinism-asceticism); and of processes and mechanisms that are only dimly grasped or quite unknown now. All this could conceivably make a large contribution to what Merton calls "theories of the middle range," in the particular case of the sociology of religion—regardless of whether or not one is inclined to think present-day sociology should especially concentrate on attaining theories of the middle range.

5.   In a somewhat different vein, finally, it may not be amiss to stress that it is profitable in the sociology of religion to pay close attention to more or less comprehensive views of religion for their sociological suggestiveness. In this connection, it is worth recalling, for example, that there have been various statements of what it is well to label a "poetic" view of religion. Some important tendencies in this are suggested by the work of the early Santayana, who set out the notion that "religion and poetry are identical in essence and differ merely in the way in which they are attached to practical affairs," poetry being called religion "when it intervenes in life," while religion, "when it merely supervenes upon life, is seen to be nothing but poetry."[38] On the basis of this outlook, Santayana thought it well for religion not to claim to deal analytically with the "empirical" world, since it had "ideal" functions different from, and in principle not in conflict with, those of science. It was accordingly possible for him to say that "science should be mathematical and religion anthropomorphic";[39] the former rigorously precise in its language, the latter utilizing poetic symbols.

Santayana offers us an instance of a transparent bit of "poetry" or myth: "Punishment, limping on one leg, patiently follows every criminal."[40] The personifications here cannot be missed. This is a way of saying that there is a rough or lagging tendency for criminals to be caught up with. As Santayana puts the matter, in stating the myth he has "expressed a truth of experience and pointed vaguely to the course which events may be expected to take under given circumstances."[41] The poetic view of religion takes much religious language as metaphorical statement of a variety of truths. It is clear that the poetic view in one form or another has had considerable influence in theological work and in work on mythology and literature. Max Muller's old theory that religion was in a way due to a corruption of language has plain affinities with the poetic view.[42] The poetic view has an evident pertinence to demythologization. To say that there is a lagging tendency for criminals to get caught up with is indeed to demythologize Santayana's little myth. The poetic view is likely to be accompanied by a certain friendliness toward religion and a disposition to notice its functional—i.e., eufunctional—aspects (as well as by a certain discomfort about or antagonism toward such conventional supernatural features as it may have). A philosopher like Santayana, something of an authentic poet himself, is likely to be inimical to what he takes to be poetry in action. It is in line with the entire tendency of Santayana's outlook on religion that he should treat prayer, for example, in a functionalist manner. He insists first that "no chapter in theology is more unhappy than that in which a material efficacy is assigned to prayer." It is simply not the case that "the most orthodox and hard-praying army wins the most battles." But prayer has its "true uses," for "it clarifies the ideal"; "it reconciles to the inevitable"; and "it fosters spiritual life by conceiving it in its perfection." Prayer will not bring rain, "but until rain comes it may cultivate hope and resignation and may prepare the heart for any issue."[43]

The larger philosophical context, of Santayana's thought in particular, within which this so briefly stated view comes, the precise relation of Santayana's poetic view to that of other and more recent thinkers, the matter of just how "transcendence" may be accommodated in a poetic view of religion, the question that James B. Pratt so keenly presented of how one might get "benefits" from prayer without belief in premises upon which the act of prayer is grounded—these and other interesting things have to be left aside. I do not pretend to evaluate Santayana's views here. I am for now more concerned with their suggestiveness. The need to study aesthetic objects in relation to religion is clearly suggested. It is small wonder, in the poetic view of religion, that men of letters, for instance, should often be greatly interested in religion for their part. And the sociologist can ill afford to reject possible help in comprehending religion *qua* cultural form. Something is perhaps suggested also by the poetic view with regard to the attitudes of "the common man." The views of philosophers are often entertained in less articulate, less systematic form by more ordinary persons. It is at any rate possible that a certain amount of "poetic" sympathy with religion is concealed under ostensible rejection of it and that a certain religious potential is accordingly underestimated in a population that is asked questions that are too simple. The need for study of hypostatization or reification of the poetic is reinforced. Archaic language (or archaism generally) is suggested as a field of study in the sociology and psychology of religion, and the ancient question of whether new wine can be poured into old bottles is posed in a new richness, when religion is perceived as "poetic."

There could clearly be dangers in taking a poetic view of religion, including the danger of forgetting that religion in action can be devastatingly "unpoetic," as when it is exploitative or submissive to the powers that be. Adherents of a poetic view can learn something from those more determined to show "unfriendliness" toward religion. The poetic view points us to things that are of sociological interest, true, but it might be said that we could come upon them by other ways and that they are in any case not startlingly novel, even if a certain novelty may be present here and there. Moreover, sociologists of religion are already well aware of the need to "broaden" themselves, in such fields as theology, for instance (and a number of them are theologically more than passably informed). All this may be acknowledged. But it does no harm whatever in an area like the sociology of religion to stress again and again the utility of broad outlooks. The sources of such outlooks, and their richness, may differ. If we could and should ever develop a sociology of religion without appreciable affinities with history, culture theory, theology, perhaps even philosophy and literature, it would hardly be worth having.[44] This is *not* to forget the indispensable need for the sociology of religion (as for sociology in general), in the end, to combine vision with sound method. It is only to remember that sociology (and the sociology of religion more so than most other subfields thereof) is a difficult discipline.

The above notes have drawn on a number of analytical traditions. This I believe to be unavoidable in a richly problematic area like that of the sociology of religion. The notes may seem remote from "empirical" concerns. The obvious suggestion can be made that they will seem less remote if "empirical" is not defined with arbitrary narrowness. Why turn back to past thought so much? Is not the object to move ahead? No antiquarianism has been intended here. If one does go back, it is precisely in the hope of finding a better way ahead.

Notes

1. Talcott Parsons, *The Structure of Social Action* (New York: McGraw-Hill, 1937).
2. Talcott Parsons, *The Social System* (Glencoe, Ill.: Free Press, 1951), p. 164.
3. Robert N. Bellah, "Religious Evolution," *American Sociological Review* 29 (June 1964):372.
4. Robert N. Bellah, "Civil Religion in America," *Daedalus* 96 (Winter 1967):1-21.
5. W. Lloyd Warner, *The Living and the Dead* (New Haven: Yale University Press, 1959), p. 5.
6. Peter Berger, A Rumor of Angels (New York: Doubleday, 1969).
7. Thomas Luckmann, *The Invisible Religion* (New York: Macmillan, 1967).
8. Harvey Cox, *The Feast of Fools* (Boston: Harvard University Press, 1969), p. 173. It is of interest in connection with the concern of nonsociologists for certain extrachurchly religious phenomena that Marty suggests that Bellah tended to "slight the historians' [pertinent] contributions in dealing with the past" when he discussed civil religion and that Williams writes that Bellah is "unaware . . . of the extensive historical literature on this subject

and even of a quite articulate contemporary exposition: Duncan Howlett, *The Fourth American Faith* (Donald Cutler, ed., *The Religious Situation: 1969* [Boston: Beacon Press, 1969], pp. 31-493). The present interest in this of course has to do with the nonchurchly religious or sacred beyond the circle of sociologists. Theologians are obviously also similarly concerned. The philosophical Huston Smith looks penetratingly for shifts in the locus of the sacred on the contemporary scene (Donald Cutler, ed., *The Religious Situation: 1968* [Boston: Beacon Press, 1968], ch. 16). Writers such as Joseph Campbell, who functions in a college department of literature, and Frederick Elder, a minister by profession, do work that is most suggestive with regard to the extension of the religious beyond conventional frameworks and categories (Cutler, *Religious Situations 1968,* ch. 17; *1969,* chs. 18, 2). Marty notes popular-periodical indications of new religious (and magical) concern. The most recent indication of such concern in a popular periodical to come to the writer's attention is "The Search for Faith," in *Life* for January 9, 1970. The larger backgrounds of this whole development are beyond the scope of this article.

9.   Parsons has been receptive to the idea of the diffusion of the sacred insofar, at least, as he has taken up Bellah's notion of civil religion, which he does with some enthusiasm in his "Religion in a Modern Pluralistic Society," *Review of Religious Research* 7 (1966):125-46. His expectable affirmative stance toward Bellah's paper on evolution (which contains the statement we have quoted on religion as no longer monopolized by "groups explicitly labeled religious") is indicated in Cutler, *Religious Situation 1968*, p. 688.

10. Some pertinent matters are covered by Mary-Barbara Zeldin, "The Religious Nature of Russian Marxism," *Journal for the Scientific Study of Religion* 8 (1969):100-111.

11. Berger, *Angels,* p. 32.

12. Cutler, *Religious Situation, 1968*, p. 917. [Schneider does not bring up Sorel and the Franco-Italian line; but they do illustrate the point that Marxists have been interested in Marxism as a religion—and, as noted in Chapter 5, they developed Marxism's psychological dimension in other ways. Ed.]

13. Karl Marx, *Capital* (New York: Modern Library, 1936), 1:81-96; *Capital* (Chicago: Kerr, 1909), 3:962-68.

14. Marx, *Capital* (1936), p. 86.

15. This is not to deny that there can be spontaneous social production of "good" poetry. Any effort to interpret, say, touchy race relations exclusively in terms of poetry, without reference to the terrible social and personal consequences or concomitants of "bad" poetry, would obviously be disastrously wrong, if it is really necessary to say this.

16. Note Claude Lévi-Strauss's interesting reference to "myth and what appears largely to have replaced it in modern societies, namely, politics." (See Lévi-Strauss in William E. Lessa and Evon Z. Vogt, eds., *A Reader in Comparative Religion* [New York: Harper & Row, 1968], p. 563).

17. Charles F. Adams, *Three Episodes of Massachusetts History* (New York: Houghton Mifflin, 1892), 1:367. Contemporary treatments of the controversy are to be found in Emery Battis (*Saints and Sinners* [Chapel Hill: University of North Carolina Press, 1962]) and in Kai T. Erikson (*Wayward Puritans* [New York: Wiley, 1966]). It may be noted in passing

that however disturbing Anne Hutchinson's religious enthusiasm may have been among her contemporaries, she was not much of an antinomian. As Battis (*Saints,* p. 287) remarks, "Certainly with Mrs. Hutchinson and her colleagues the deeply implanted inhibitions of Puritan morality precluded the grosser behavioral possibilities of the Antinomian position." Erikson *(Puritans,* p. 85) remarks, "Anne Hutchinson may not have been an Antinomian in the purest sense. . . ."

18. Belfort Bax, *The Rise and Fall of the Anabaptists* (London: Swan Sonnenschein, 1903), pp. 133-34. See also Adams *(Massachusetts,* pp. 166-67), where the phrase "religious or theological garb" is again used in the same sense. This inevitably reminds us of Engels's observation that in a religious epoch even revolutionary ideas have to be expressed in a religious rhetoric.

19. Bax, *Anabaptists,* p. 391. Bax, incidentally, has some interesting comments on antinomianism. The Anabaptist movement has had particular attention paid to it in recent years by Marxists, and the impulse for this evidently goes back to Engels's view of the Reformation disturbances in Germany as heralds of the bourgeois revolution. See Otthein Rammstedt's sociological analysis of Münster (*Sekte und Soziale Bewegung* [Cologne: Westdeutscher Verlag, 1966], p. 118) and the Marxist dissertation by Gerhard Brendler *(Das Täuferreich zu Münster: 1534-1535* [Berlin: VEB Deutscher Verlag der Wissenschaften, 1966]).

20. [Most fully discussed in Chapter 14. Ed.]

21. These observations have their grounding in interviewing of a group of dissident priests done by the writer in 1968-1969.

22. Brendler, *Täuferreich,* p. 49.

23. Adams, *Massachusetts,* p. 432.

24. Thomas F. O'Dea, *The Sociology of Religion* (Englewood Cliffs, N.J.: Prentice-Hall, 1966), p. 112.

25. I recognize that there may be a good deal of simplifying in this quick formulation.

26. Cf. Louis Schneider in George K. Zollschan and Walter Hirsch, eds., *Explorations in Social Change,* 1st ed. (New York: Houghton Mifflin, 1964), pp. 371-400. I am convinced that Sorokin's *Social and Cultural Dynamics* is now underrated in American sociology, but it was one of the limitations of Sorokin's work that he often took at face value ostensibly considerable cultural "differences" that analysis could show to be rather superficial.

27. The whole point involved here should not be labored, but it may be reinforced by reference to folk sayings, where equivalences are often, admittedly, ridiculously easy to see. One group says, "The grass is always greener in the other fellow's field"; another "Other men's women are always the prettiest ones." We might want to make the obvious reservation that one group has had agricultural experiences in its eye and the other, shall we say, amatory experiences, but we cannot doubt that the statements are merely different forms of rendering the same sentiment—or perhaps one can say, without cynicism, the same perception. And when we find that still another group says, "There it is good where we are not," we can only applaud this gifted generalization of the *same* sentiment or perception. The different expressions of the same thing do not deceive.

28. Edmund R. Leach, ed., *Dialectic in Practical Religion* (Cambridge: University Press, 1968).

29. Ibid., p. 37.
30. Bax, *Anabaptists,* pp. 14, 204.
31. Norman Cohn, *The Pursuit of the Millennium* (New York: Harper, 1961), Appendix.
32. Ibid., pp. 211-12, 216-17.
33. Gottfried Koch, *Frauenfrage und Ketzertum im Mittelalter* (Berlin: Akademie Verlag, 1962), p. 107. This is formally a Marxist work, but its scholarship and its analysis are not stultified by Marxist pieties.
34. Ibid., p. 116.
35. Cohn, *Millennium,* p. 275.
36. Battis, *Saints,* p. vii.
37. Alan Heimert, *Religion and the American Mind* (Cambridge: Harvard University Press, 1966).
38. George Santayana, *Interpretations of Poetry and Religion* (New York: Harper, 1957), p. v.
39. George Santayana, *Reason in Society* (New York: Scribner's, 1936), p. 204.
40. George Santayana, *Reason in Science* (New York: Scribner's, 1936), p. 12.
41. Ibid., p. 12.
42. See the analysis in Emile Durkheim, *The Elementary Forms of the Religious Life* (London: Allen & Unwin, 1926), pp. 71-86.
43. Santayana, *Interpretations,* pp. 41-47.
44. One need not overlook the point that a science may sometimes move ahead and develop a powerful paradigm, a theoretical model commanding great consensus within a field, in Kuhn's sense, while it narrows its range. See Thomas S. Kuhn, *The Structure of Scientific Revolutions* (Chicago: University of Chicago Press, 1962). But the narrowing is not necessarily permanent. We go on the presumption that a sociology of religion that shall in some sense be scientifically adequate sooner or later will have to deal with problems that in a present view involve appreciable affinities with the areas mentioned.

13

The Scope of "The Religious Factor" in the Sociology of Religion: Notes on Definition, Idolatry, and Magic

(1974)

The question of the scope of "the religious factor"[1] has concerned sociologists of religion, as indeed it has concerned a large variety of other students of religion. There has long been present in thought about religion, generally, some propensity to extend the meaning of that term beyond what are conventionally, and virtually without dispute, regarded as "properly" religious phenomena. That sociologists have appreciably shared this tendency is something quite plain and not at all difficult to document. A single instance of the tendency may suffice for the moment. Shils points to human need for contact with the sacred or charismatic in politics, law, education—"as well as in the churches"—and urges that the ways in which this need is manifested are more "elusive" and yet more "fundamental" for a sociological theory of religion than conventional phenomena of church attendance and the like. Shils adds that both Durkheim and Weber had a "wonderful sense" for the extraconventional sacred or charismatic.[2]

The propensity among sociologists preoccupied with religion to widen the scope of the religious factor beyond the conventional churchly constitutes, then, the backdrop of this paper. To the fore is the circumstance that the present-day sociology of religion stands in need of theoretical nourishment.[3] The observations or notes that follow are designed to clarify—at least to a modest extent—what we do when we make various extensions of the religious factor and to suggest that there is theoretical point in constantly keeping before us questions as to its sheer scope.

I say "designed to clarify," but at once add "at least to a modest extent." It is simply honest to make this addition. Failure to assert or at any rate suggest it should at once be suspect in the present state of our knowledge of a number of the matters here taken up. In a recent essay on religion as a cultural system, Geertz urges in effect that "we abandon that sweet sense of accomplishment which comes from parading habitual skills and address ourselves to problems sufficiently unclarified to make discovery possible." Geertz then refers to significant contributions to his subject by Durkheim, Weber, Freud, and Malinowski; but he would wish to move beyond the starting points afforded by these men. Yet he is aware of the dangers involved—"arbitrary eclecticism, superficial theory mongering, and sheer intellectual confusion."[4] It may well be that such dangers will be sensed in the course of the following comments.

Another preliminary word may not be amiss. Robertson, who has afforded a pertinent and stimulating discussion of "basic problems of definition" in the sphere of sociology of religion, observes that a definition of religion that is restrictive or exclusive and is resistant to the notion of the wide scope of the religious factor has been attractive to some sociologists "because they find that the claim that certain phenomena are religious is a special case of pleading for religiosity, a manifestation of an anxiety about an areligious world."[5] This is shrewdly put and may well have some foundation. But it obviously raises a question of motivation and does not settle substantive issues raised by suggestion of the wide scope of the religious factor. Nor does it hint that there may be a quite different kind of "anxiety" lest embarrassing words like "religious" get extended to areas where they "don't belong." In any case, it need not inhibit the present concern with some issues of definition (but also transcending definition) that appear in connection with what for lack of a better term I may call private religion; with the matter of "idolatry" as that has been particularly alluded to by current discussions of civil religion; with the matter of magic, which is again forcibly obtruded on our attention by occultism.

In the Realm of Definition—and Beyond

The willingness, in principle, to allow wide scope to the religious factor—to allow at least the possibility of broad, nonexclusivist definitions of religion—evidently may present a chance to achieve a deepened understanding of "religious" attitudes.

One cannot help noting the diffuse character of a variety of activities that deal in culture. It is absurd to think that education is confined to schools.[6] It is equally absurd to think that, say, art is confined to such things as formal or peculiarly self-conscious performances by "painters" or "writers" or "actors." Authentic artistic endeavor goes into a performance by a college student who tries to write an eloquent term paper or presents a well-stated apologia for not having written one. What amounts to one of the more impressive recent efforts by a sociologist to exploit for the case of religion this rudimentary insight into the diffuse character of a variety of cultural activities is found in Peter Berger's well-known essay, *A Rumor of Angels*.[7]

In expounding his view of "signals of transcendence" Berger states that he means by such signals "phenomena that are to be found within the domain of our 'natural' reality." In developing his "argument from ordering," Berger calls attention to "the most routine experiences of life," which do not "depend upon any religious preconceptions." Or again, when he considers what he takes to be the special significance of play for his concerns he asserts that "the experience of joyful play is not something that must be sought on some mystical margin of existence."[8]

I would reinforce Berger's strong sense of the presence of religious attitudes in the very midst of daily life. In discussing prayer in his *Reason in Religion*, Santayana suggested that prayer "clarifies the ideal," "reconciles to the inevitable," and "fosters spiritual life by conceiving it in its perfection."[9] A man quarrels at the beginning of a day with wife or son or daughter. The quarrel leaves him with a disturbed, anxious feeling. He thinks it over on his way to work, feels deeply about it during his lunch break, and has achieved some clarity on it by the time he is on his way home. He should have been more just, more charitable. He conceives a better relation to wife or son or daughter and imagines the warming love he might give and receive in such a relation. The conception and the concomitant feelings are profoundly serious. He realizes, too, that he can gain only a certain measure of control over his rather irascible temper and that it is vain to expect his children to be precise moral replicas of himself.

If one insists on explicit supernaturalist or "superempirical" assumptions in prayer or will not allow the broad interpretation of "spiritual" I have obviously slipped into the above, then this sort of thing is not prayer. Otherwise, on Santayana's terms, it seems very close. One might also contend that there are hidden premises about, here, that amount to something like supernaturalist assumptions. My claims as a theologian must be even more subdued than the already subdued ones Berger makes and I shall not try to probe on theological lines. (I do not, however, see how the sociology of religion can avoid repeated contact with theological issues.) It is enough, even if the thing itself is fairly evident, to have suggested the sheer proximity of what I have described to what we think of as prayer. If anyone should now add, "But in this sense everybody prays," it is not necessary to shrink from this conclusion merely because it might alleviate the stress of those eager to feel that religion will never be entirely "lost" or might offend the sensibilities of those inclined to recoil at mere use of such a word as religion. But even if one should not resist the notion that "everybody prays," one may still feel constrained to reflect that some pray more than others and that modes or styles in prayer may well be different.

There is of course a verbal or nominal element in all this when we raise the question of definition. Is the private, nonchurchly activity described "prayerful" and "religious"? One might resolve that it is or that it is not. But there are clearly other than verbal issues also. There is an invitation here to engage in close, deep scrutiny and comparison of Prayer 1 (conventionally regarded as prayer) and Prayer 2 (not so regarded). Precisely what is prayer, in any case, or a prayerful attitude? The question is of course intended to point to empirical realities, not to mere verbal resolutions; toward a "real" instead of a merely "nominal" definition.

The same kind of question arises with respect to, say, the larger matter of faith. In this connection, it is in point to add a little to Berger's particular "argument from ordering." Berger writes of a child's awaking frightened in the night and being comforted by a mother who assures him that all is well, all is in order, "everything is all right." The experience again is ordinary, everyday. In the sense of effective removal from conventional religious frameworks, so is ordinary psychoanalytic or cognate psychiatric treatment. A young man has been brought up by a mother or father who filled him with quasi-paranoid suspicions of other people. There is a current of psychiatric theorizing that holds roughly that after sufficient contact with a qualified psychiatrist in a kind of resocialization process the suspicious attitudes of such a young man should be mitigated. The psychiatrist "proves" he can be trusted. He is so consistently trustworthy in situations that effectively test trustworthiness that this finally "gets through" to the patient, who then becomes a different man, decidedly less suspicious of his fellows—all to the accompaniment of much emotion.

Let us assume that this actually happens, that it is more than an engaging psychiatric fable. Its foundation in "faith" must be obvious. Did the patient take a sample of people generally to test their trustworthiness? Is he entitled on empirical grounds to the view that his splendid psychiatrist is a typical or modal kind of person? His "conversion" is not statistically based. There is no guarantee that he will not emerge from the psychiatrist's office after a long course and then encounter any number of betrayers in succession. The psychiatrist might be quite atypical. Of course, in making his initial, early-career "decisions" about people, the young man did not take a sample either, but came to "believe" as he did on the evidence he got from a parent who was a distorted human being. (In deliberately using the word "distorted," without quotation marks, one suggests for one's self something of the faith that the patient comes to have in virtue of his cure.) But in the old, bad days, all was not well, not in order, not right. Now it is. The world of people, at least, is ultimately as it should be. It is not hard to imagine that in a case of this sort our young man would feel strongly the wrongness of his previous quasi-paranoid attitudes and have a powerful commitment to the rightness of his new ones, the rightness of his new "ultimate" stance toward others.

Again we appear to be dealing with a phenomenon sufficiently close to orientations no one would hesitate to call religious to raise the question whether the kind of "faith" discussed is religious or not. No doubt, that is again partly a verbal question. No doubt, different consequences follow on different answers to the question. No doubt, those consequences would call for careful consideration. No doubt, one may employ terms like "secular faith" or "surrogate faith." There is still the fairly obvious but quite important matter of possible gain from close scrutiny and comparison of different "kinds" of faith if one will have it that they are indeed different.

I would of course like to make some contributions on the line of deepening understanding of prayer and faith and cognate things by the comparisons suggested, if I could. But this suggests large tasks from which I draw back in these notes, just as I draw back from any theological issues that my cases above may imply. But I may still indulge a speculative sociological turn that is suggested by the cases and by the whole tendency to widen the scope of the religious factor.

It has apparently not occurred to anyone working in the sociology of religion that something as seemingly far removed from consideration of the scope of the religious factor as Edwin H. Sutherland's classic work on white-collar crime may actually have some pertinence to it. It will be recalled that Sutherland greatly broadened the scope of "the criminal" by including, under crime, violations of the criminal law committed by business and professional people in connection with their businesses and professions and also by recognizing a dimension of white-collar criminality in politics. Is white-collar crime "really" crime? Sutherland faced the question directly.[10] In order to answer it affirmatively, as he did, he had to supplement the conventional criterion of criminality—conviction in a criminal court—in several respects.[11]

Is the sort of thing Berger talks about in *A Rumor of Angels* or that we talk about in reference to prayer and psychiatric experience "really" religious? Is civil religion "really" religious? Sutherland was persuasive to many criminologists and others in sociology because of the compelling character of his proposed supplementation to the criterion of conviction in a criminal court. More than nominal issues in definition were involved in his work. One could nominally resolve to use the term *crime* exclusively for what Sutherland called lower-class criminality or action involving conviction in a criminal court. But Sutherland's expansion of the scope of the criminal meant real gain in analysis and perspective and his wider view of crime has been highly adopted.

More than definitional issues in any narrow sense are again suggested. The notion of white-collar crime, just at present, when we witness the spectacles of Watergate and military malfeasance, must strike us with renewed impact. Sutherland already made the quite fundamental point that white-collar crime is especially disorganizing because it violates trust and is engaged in by community leaders who are ordinarily looked up to as upholders of strategic values and norms. White-collar crime looms as in many ways more important than what Sutherland called lower-class criminality. How about nonchurchly, nonconventional religious phenomena in relation to conventional ones? The category of "nonconventional" religious phenomena is of course very large and might take in much whose religious character would be more readily conceded than that of the private religion we have so far discussed, but certainly the question we ask may be conceived to cover private religion if the reality thereof is allowed. Is there, let us say, anything in such religion, if that is what it is, that is more "important" than conventional or churchly or institutionalized religion?

It is possible that at this juncture the sociology of religion could use the special talents of a Sutherland. At the conclusion of his seminal paper of 1940 on white-collar crime[12] Sutherland stated five propositions that summed up his argument. The first four of these propositions suggest analogous matters in the sociology of religion in the problem area on which these notes bear.

Sutherland's proposition 1: "White-collar criminality is real criminality, being in all cases in violation of the criminal law." *Query:* Are various forms of activity (including what we have referred to as private religion) up to now excluded from, or only precariously allowed inclusion under, the rubric of religion, religion or not, and by what criteria?

Sutherland's proposition 2: "White-collar criminality differs from lower-class criminality principally in an implementation of the criminal law which segregates white-collar criminals administratively from other criminals." *Query:* Precisely how do various forms of religion that may qualify as religious, although they are not conventionally taken as such, differ from each other and from the conventional form?

Sutherland's proposition 3: "The theories of the criminologists that crime is due to poverty or to psychopathic and sociopathic conditions associated with poverty are invalid because first, they are derived from samples . . . grossly biased with respect to socioeconomic status . . . second, they do not apply to the white-collar criminals . . . third, they do not even explain the criminality of the lower class since [they do not point to] a general process characteristic of all criminality." *Query:* What might be discerned as the serious limitations of theories of the foundation of conventional religion in the light of hypotheses that allow very broad scope to the religious factor?[13]

Sutherland's proposition 4: "A theory of criminal behavior which will explain both white-collar criminality and lower-class criminality is needed." *Query:* Can we formulate a theory of religion that will explain or clarify both conventional and nonconventional forms, assuming the reality of the latter?[14]

One additional comment may be made. For those sociologists who may be uncomfortable with the notion that the sociology of religion constantly and inevitably touches on theological issues, it may be well to observe that serious pursuit of criminology sooner or later involves one in consideration of criminal law.

Idolatry: Civil Religion—and Beyond

The matter of civil religion has occasioned some of the most salient efforts to extend the scope of the religious factor among sociologists. We have noted a pertinent statement by Shils. It is over half a century since Durkheim intimated that there is "no essential difference" between an assembly of Christians celebrating dates in Christ's life or Jews recalling the Exodus or the Decalogue, on the one hand, and "a reunion of citizens commemorating the promulgation of a new moral or legal system or some great event in the national life," on the other hand.[15] After Durkheim, Warner applied the word "sacred" not only to Divine Being "and the central experience and sacraments of Christian faith, but to objects and phases of life to which the special reverence arising from religions in general has been extended."[16] Bellah's familiar essay on civil religion plainly calls for mention here.[17] Shils's paper with Young on the coronation of Queen Elizabeth in 1952 purports to discern in the coronation a component of communion with the sacred that occurred as national value commitments were reaffirmed and fortified.[18] Verba notes that a large proportion of the American population reacted to the assassination of President Kennedy with prayer or church attendance, while "religious ceremony and imagery abounded in the events of the weekend." A religious dimension for state activities is thus intimated, and Verba sees religion and politics as closely related in the United

States, averring that "many of the functions that religion and religious symbolism perform elsewhere in holding society together are performed in the United States by central political symbols."[19]

These are only some of the writings bearing on the notion of civil religion, which will unquestionably get further attention from sociologists and others.[20] There have been various misgivings about the notion. There are those who are disturbed by what they sense as a possible threat to formal separation of church and state when talk about civil religion occurs. There is sensitivity on the point that scholars writing about how a nation is drawn together in solidarity by a coronation ceremony or, say, by public prayer for guidance in public policy may become overenthusiastic and endorse morally questionable goals or procedures. Rightly or wrongly, Birnbaum responded to the Shils-Young piece on the coronation with an item of his own which ended on the note that "it is a considerable disservice to sociology to present our discipline as a useful handmaiden of the current effort to make a conservative ideology once more orthodox and unquestioned."[21] It is certainly a legitimate question —and often an extremely difficult one to answer—how much national consensus, say, lies behind civil religion or how much consensus that religion creates. And an ear for sheer rhetoric is not a useless possession in these premises. Some indeterminate amount of various expressions in civil-religion context may well have little more than rhetorical significance.

The more talented writers on civil religion have been well aware of these things. I go here on the broad notion that "civil religion," as in the United States, has some real substance that survives various qualifications that need to be made about it. But I wish above all to make the hardly recondite suggestion that the idea of civil religion presents fine motivation for sociologists to think through, and get some theoretical profit from the entire conception of idolatry.

The conception of idolatry is of theological and philosophical provenance.[22] It evidently implies a certain—shall we say critical—stance toward lower "deities" (or nondivine deities) or their worship or, in a more generalized sense, refers to adherence to what are only relative rather than absolute or final goods. In the more generalized sense, idolatry may be concisely described as the worship of the actual rather than the ideal. Bellah indicates his awareness that civil religion in America always has a potential of turning to worship of what "the American way" actually is. He had latterly again been concerned to stress that he conceives "the central tradition of the American civil religion" not as "a form of national self-worship" (which would unequivocally be idolatrous) but rather as "the subordination of the nation to ethical principles that transcend it and in terms of which it should be judged."[23] The sheer effort to make sacred what is actually done by America as a nation would be thoroughly repugnant to many, precisely as a sort of shameless idolatry. (And such feeling might be particularly acute at the present time [1974].) Whatever the "central tradition" Bellah refers to actually has been, the meaning of idolatry in this context seems fairly clear.

But the notion of idolatry also clearly ramifies beyond this context. We began with civil *religion*. The notion of civil religion extends the scope of the religious factor. But consideration of civil religion quickly suggests idolatry, forms of what one might call "the perversion of the sacred." If the religious factor or the sacred is "perverted," it is still the religious factor or the sacred that is perverted. The type of perversion here labeled idolatry may be conceived to include the sort of worship of narrow nationalistic goals that constitute the seamy side of civil religion. It may also be conceived to include worship of a particular class, worship of humanity, on certain terms, worship of a variety of human impulses.

In connection with worship of a class I mean to suggest particularly the metaphysic of history—toward which there has been a plain tendency in Marxism—whereby the historicoeconomic cosmos is due to sweat out certain results in society whether man wants them or not, results on the line of ensuring the victory of a proletariat that becomes the bearer of all excellence, all worthwhile values. (I reserve a further brief word about this for later.)

In connection with worship of humanity I mean particularly to suggest constructions of the type of Comte's religion of humanity.[24] It has been, I would argue, a mistake on the part of sociologists that they have so readily dismissed this religion of Comte's as matter for ridicule.[25] Comte's detailed development of his religion in the fourth volume of his *Positive Polity* expresses a great deal that is of intrinsic interest for the sociology of religion. The bias toward using religion as an instrument of social control and particularly to enhance "altruism"; the obvious borrowings from Catholicism based on a much shrewder understanding of its "functions" than superficial students of Comte are likely to realize; the powerful sense of the importance of tradition and "the dead" in human social life—these and other features of Comte's construction are still of importance as casting light on the character of religion in the broadest sense (aside from matters of intellectual history or questions about Comte's views as peculiar to Comte). But it is the feature of idolatry in Comte's construction, taken as an example of tendencies in "social religions," that is of prime significance here. In precisely what sense is idolatry involved? Of course it is idolatrous to worship humanity or a Great Being from some orthodox religious point of view, such as that of Catholicism. But that is hardly the end of the matter. We recall that the humanity or Great Being to be worshipped was, after all, in Comte's conception a cleansed and purified humanity or Great Being, its constituent human units being persons, as Comte phrased it, "purified by death." The Great Being is clearly supposed to be a spiritually ideal being. But all this raises the most significant problems still with respect to the sacralizing and rigidifying of particular forms of society or social organization.

In connection with worship of a variety of human impulses, I mean to suggest something far removed from the "civil" in any sense—remote from nation worship or class worship or humanity worship. I have in view here simply the sort of thing one intends when one speaks of "worship of sex" or the like.

The idolatries referred to all extend the religious factor or the scope of the sacred—precisely in the form of "perversions" of the sacred. I suggest that it may be theoretically useful for sociologists to concern themselves quite deliberately with a whole category of idolatries and types thereof. What causes the peculiar sort of shifts that we encounter in the idolatries, when indeed it is clear that there are shifts from the nonidolatrous to the idolatrous? What unites the various idolatries? Salomon argued a generation ago that the sociology of religion "can and does relate the drama of the defeat of the religious intention."[26] He had in view the involvement of religion in "the world," the subordination of creeds to the uses of class conflict, and the like. O'Dea's much cited paper on dilemmas in the institutionalization of religion[27] deals penetratingly with certain aspects of "the defeat of the religious intention." In this general context, a sociology of idolatry might well take a very important place. The sense of my title for this chapter broadens and "the scope of the religious factor" takes in also the scope of "perversions" of the religious factor (in the sense of the sacred).

Two further comments on idolatry need to be made. One is that the term *idolatry* itself is most compelling and even obvious, when we are close to some context where there is a kind of primordial contrast between "false gods," which of course are "idols," and "true gods." In the case of the American civil religion as discussed by Bellah, for example, a Jewish-Christian set of references to the divine is still close at hand, granting that the civil religion is neither Judaism nor Christianity. There is still ready reference to "this nation under God." The civil religion is supposed to have to do with a national obligation to carry out God's will on earth. God's elevated moral and spiritual requirements hover in the immediate background to afford a ground of judgment for merely relative goods or morally dubious nationalistic enterprises.

There are, to be sure, other contextual circumstances where primordial religious references are less evident and where accordingly the term *idolatry* moves toward its philosophical rather than toward its pristine theological or religious side. Philosophically, one might regard the tendency to idolize a proletariat as idolatrous but the sense would not be on the line of absolutizing a relative good, without a Judeo-Christian God or a like presence in the background. From this point of view the history-loading, working-class-idolatrous component in Marxism might be taken as a sort of "secular" idolatry, if one wishes to use such language. On the other hand, it does not seem entirely foolish to recall, as commentators on Marx repeatedly do, the religious background of his own family. His measurelessly bitter expostulation, "Accumulate! accumulate! That is Moses and the prophets!"[28] creates its own distinctive impression. In the case of Comte the Catholic background simply cannot be overlooked. Comte's own preoccupation with Catholicism and the profound influence the repudiated religion exercised upon him are not to be mistaken.

A second comment has to do particularly with the plausibility of extension of the notion of idolatry to a variety of things. Here I want only to note that the sheer persuasiveness of a term like *idolatry*, the initial sense of its fitness or lack thereof, is dependent on how "seriously" any possible rivalry between a nonidol and an idol is taken. No doubt there are those who would contend that gluttony is spiritually dangerous. A fat parishioner in a "religious" novel popular several decades ago is adjured by her Catholic pastor to eat less because the gates of heaven are narrow. And there is a certain currency of phrases like "making a god of one's stomach." But perhaps it is not too far off the mark to say that in the modern West at any rate, looked at in a religious context, gluttony tends to be taken not very seriously. Sexuality appears to be a more serious business, more enticing, much more repressed, more liable to "demonic" temptation. "Mammon" presumably is not to be reduced to a status like that of mere gluttony, in this context. Nation, class, and humanity all evoke a certain real seriousness. What it is that men treat idolatrously has more than theological interest and it is hardly extreme to take it as a matter important for the sociology of religion.[29]

Magic and Religion

The scope of the religious factor is easily conceived to take in much of what goes by the name of the occult. Insofar as the occult involves the supernatural or superempirical one would expect little quarrel about the matter. Whatever particular theological judgments on occult manifestations might then be, those manifestations would be within the "religious" realm. In a publication like the popular magazine *Fate,* which is heavily devoted to the occult, one will find stories or other items that deal with haunted houses, with witches, with banshees wailing to announce forthcoming deaths, with ghostly apparitions at the beds of the dying. That range of the "occult" that covers phenomena like flying saucers, dowsing, and vexed questions in the area of ESP and that is also of interest to *Fate,* on the other hand, does not necessarily come within "religious" definitions. If someone should want to call the supernatural-occult "antireligious," that is hardly of importance; for our present purposes it would still be within the "religious" realm.

There is a certain preoccupation with the occult today. At the least one can stay it is appreciably popular. The popularity in the United States of Blatty's recent novel *The Exorcist* is well known, and items like *Rosemary's Baby* have had their considerable success. Too much of the information we have regarding the occult today and actual devotion thereto and practice therein is sporadic and anecdotal. Some of the best work in the entire area of the occult has been done by historians and by anthropologists working with primitive materials. But the area has rather obvious intrinsic sociological interest and is bound to evoke more sociological talent than has yet been devoted to it. I want to emphasize in connection with it the whole broad range of activities and fantasies to which we apply the label "magical" and to recall the accent on power, control, manipulation that is so evident in much magical activity. I should then add that when I refer now to magic I do not refer to phenomena of the type of sleight of hand or of the type of an "empirically" based palmistry, without supernatural or superempirical elements. I mean to refer to magic that is supernaturally based or tinged. (Here a certain "exclusiveness" seems necessary.)

The accent on power referred to is at once evident from relevant literature on religion and magic and witchcraft.[30] The literature reveals this striving for power, for control, for manipulation in a large variety of enterprises. The striving will compass magical-supernatural devices to make a maiden restless in her sleep "until she be eased of her maidenhead" and operations to transfer destructive effects from mere effigies to the persons whom they represent.

It is helpful to make a distinction between a "for God" and a "for man" orientation within what I may call a total religiomagical complex.[31] There is on the one hand a drive "toward complete and total extinction of all self-interest," a kind of "extreme spiritual teaching," and on the other hand a stress on "the tangible and visible advantages which [may come] in this very life here and now."[32] Conze makes this contrast with reference to particular Buddhist documents, but it is a far more general one within religion in the broadest sense. Men undoubtedly "want" things from their religions—health, wealth, peace of mind, among others. Their strivings in religious context can also be eminently "spiritual" and self-abnegating. The "for God" principle, by contrast with the "for man" principle, is taken to great lengths in a case referred to by Knox, who writes of "a young priest who asked God in set terms to send him to hell, so that the Divine justice and the Divine glory might be more fully manifested."[33] The "for man" principle is illustrated well enough in efforts to "utilize" religion for practical advantage and daily-life purposes ranging from the still "spiritually" resonating instrumentalism of a William James to the cruder instrumentalism of those who have purveyed religion to help achieve business success and the like.

"Religion" generally is saturated with both "for God" and "for man" principles or orientations or components. Empirical, actual religion *is* simultaneously religious and magical. The blending of the two principles seems to be unstable.

> When the "for God" element in religion recedes into the background and men's own needs are clamorously to the fore and when various manipulative techniques come into play (such as using the name of a spiritually exalted figure to obtain power over that figure for one's own practical purposes), we shall . . . say that we have to do with magic. . . . When the emphasis within the [religiomagical] complex moves toward the "for God," non-technique and nonmanipulative side, there is movement toward "religion" rather than toward "magic."[34]

In setting out this view of religion or magic, which can here be indicated only very sketchily, I further noted in the same passage I have just drawn on that "magic as here understood . . . arises in a cultural situation where there is at least some 'high-level' comprehension of what a 'for God' orientation means." Accordingly, not all kinds of magic are covered by the view I set out. It does not cover "primitive" magic or any cases where the cultural background of a "high religion" is absent.

But I would urge that the kind of magic that I do point to is particularly relevant in the sphere of the occult today, as within the United States. The scope of the religious factor, again, is inevitably enlarged. Given the tendency to pervasion of religion generally with magic and some tendency for magic to be pervaded by religion, it becomes entirely indispensable to extend the religious factor to include magic—entirely indispensable and, I believe, theoretically fruitful. But there are several matters in this whole connection that are worth further comment, however brief it must be.

In his large-scale study of religion and the decline of magic, Thomas points out that while popular magic in England in earlier centuries performed certain limited functions, "it never offered a comprehensive view of the world, an explanation of human existence. . . . It was a collection of miscellaneous recipes, not a comprehensive body of doctrine."[35] Even granting this, within modern Western societies magic still has the potential capacity of drawing on Jewish-Christian theological notions, including notions about the devil, and orienting itself to them, just as in Islamic societies there has been the option of "understanding" pre-Islamic supernatural forms against the background of the exalted figure of Allah and his prophet. The view of magic I have suggested states, as has been indicated, that magic exists against a background of at least some comprehension of "high level" religion. To precisely what extent and in precisely what way the intellectual options thus offered would affect magic in any sense is an empirical question I do not pretend even to try to answer broadly in this place.

"Religion" and "magic" in the sense in which they have been discriminated just here are of course abstract types. It cannot be too strongly stressed—it is indeed part of my thesis—that empirically they will tend to overlap. Again to refer to Thomas, he writes: "But even in the years after the Reformation it would be wrong to regard magic and religion as two opposed and incompatible systems of belief. There were magical elements surviving in religion, and there were religious facets to the practice of magic." This is precisely to the point. When Thomas goes on to make such important observations as the one that "for the magicians themselves the summoning of celestial beings was a religious rite, in which prayer played an essential part, and where piety and purity of life were deemed essential,"[36] his statement is entirely in line with the view of religion and magic that I have set out. Once more: "Religion" is full of "magical" components and "magic" may well have considerable "religious" components. If there is nothing startling about this view, I can hope that I have brought it out more sharply than is usually done.

Finally, the brevity of the present statement must leave a sense of certain ambiguities. I am aware that terms like *instrumentalism* and *instrumentalization* need clarification.[37] There may be "uses" of religion, of "God" that are magical and manipulative only in the most dubious sense. And I do not mean to suggest a rigorist, purist view of religion. One would not have to contend unreservedly, for example, that for religion to be authentically "religion" it must never be of "help" to men or never be more or less deliberately drawn upon by them as resource in need. But even my awareness of certain ambiguities that derive at least partly from overbrevity must be briefly stated.

There is a great deal that a paper on the scope of the religious factor might cover that I have not even mentioned in these observations. But if I expanded this statement to include considerably more illustrative matter, I would still incline to much the same conclusion about the character of religion. The scope of the religious factor can be argued to be very wide indeed as soon as one sees religion as involving a certain orientation or set of attitudes. That orientation, it is here suggested, is very diffuse and accordingly may be found in a large number of "places." Institutionalization in ecclesiastical forms is then only an incident in the flow, or the wanderings, of the religious factor.

The specific concern in the above has been to stress the flow or "scope." But I take it that a good deal needs yet to be learned about the religious orientation. And better knowledge of it should help us to penetrate its more specious manifestations, or to state, when it is appropriate to do so, that it does *not* exist although by conventional labeling it seems to. I take it, too, that "perversions" of the religious orientation are always likely to have a special interest for the sociologist, among others.

Notes

1. I realize only too well that this is a loose phrase and I do not intend to make simplistic equations of "the religious factor" and "the sacred" or engage in similar simplisms. I believe that taking single phrases within their larger contexts, in these notes, will make my meaning plain enough.
2. Edward Shils, "The Calling of Sociology," in Talcott Parsons et al., ed., *Theories of Society* (New York: Free Press, 1961), 2:1445.
3. [See Chapter 12 of this volume. Ed.]
4. Clifford Geertz, "Religion as a Cultural System," in Donald R. Cutler, ed., *The Religious Situation: 1968* (Boston: Beacon Press, 1968), p. 640.
5. Roland Robertson, *The Sociological Interpretation of Religion* (New York: Schocken Books, 1970), p. 37.
6. See Harvey Cox, *The Feast of Fools* (Cambridge: Harvard University Press, 1969), p. 173.
7. Peter L. Berger, *A Rumor of Angels* (Garden City, N.Y.: Doubleday, 1969).
8. Ibid., pp. 53, 55, 60.
9. George Santayana, *The Life of Reason* (New York: Scribner's, 1905), vol. 3, *Reason in Religion,* pp. 43-45. In Chapter 12 I made a somewhat different use of Santayana's view of prayer from that made here.
10. Note the title of one of his seminal papers: "Is 'White-Collar Crime' Crime?" *American Sociological Review* 10 (February 1945):142-49. This title is also given to chapter 3 of Sutherland's book *White Collar Crime* (New York: Dryden Press, 1949).

11. See his "White-Collar Criminality," *American Sociological Review* 5 (1940):5-7.
12. Ibid., pp. 11-12.
13. Sutherland's threefold proposition 3 suggests more than the query I append to it, but my limited query must suffice for the present.
14. Sutherland's proposition 5 reads: "An hypothesis of this nature is suggested in terms of differential association and social disorganization." I do not try to suggest a corresponding query here.
15. Emile Durkheim, *The Elementary Forms of the Religious Life* (New York: Macmillan, 1926), p. 427.
16. W. Lloyd Warner, *The Living and the Dead* (New Haven: Yale University Press, 1949), p. 5. This appears to assume a certain "origin" for the sacred which itself could easily be made problematic.
17. Robert N. Bellah, *Beyond Belief* (New York: Harper & Row, 1970), ch. 9.
18. Edward Shils and Michael Young, "The Meaning of the Coronation," *Sociological Review* 1 (December 1953):63-81.
19. Sidney Verba, "The Kennedy Assassination and the Nature of Political Commitment," in Bradley S. Greenberg and Edwin B. Parker, eds., *The Kennedy Assassination and the American Public* (Stanford: Stanford University Press, 1965), pp. 348-60, at pp. 352, 353. Note also in the same volume pp. 161-63, 180, 190.
20. An interesting recent study utilizing historical material and employing content analysis of relevant documents is Keith M. Wulff's unpublished master's thesis, "The Civil Religion of Texas," University of Texas at Austin, December 1972.
21. Norman Birnbaum, "Monarchs and Sociologists: A Reply to Professor Shils and Mr. Young," *Sociological Review* 3 (July 1955):5-23, at p. 23.
22. The reader will rightly suspect by now that this occasions no great disturbance on my part.   .
23. Bellah, *Belief,* p. 168n.
24. See particularly Donald G. Charlton, *Secular Religions in France, 1815-1870* (London: Oxford University Press, 1963). As bearing on the question previously suggested in these observations whether we can properly speak of the religious where the supernatural or superempirical is not specifically involved, it may be noted that Anatole France has a comment pertinent to the religion of humanity that is worth remembering: "Le positivisme est un catholicisme sans dieu, et, *dans toute religion, c'est toujours le dieu qui importe le moins"* (quoted by Richard L. Hawkins, *Positivism in the United States* [Cambridge: Harvard University Press, 1938] p. 40, n. 3; italics added).
25. See the comments by Roland Robertson in T. J. Nossiter et al., eds., *Imagination and Precision in the Social Sciences* (London: Faber & Faber, 1972), pp. 62-63.
26. Albert Salomon, *In Praise of Enlightenment* (Cleveland: World, 1962), p. 389; italics in the original.
27. Thomas F. O'Dea, "Five Dilemmas in the Institutionalization of Religion," *Journal for the Scientific Study of Religion* 1 (October 1961):30-39.
28. Karl Marx, *Capital* (New York: Modern Library, 1936), 1:652.

29. My colleague, Joe R. Feagin, makes some shrewd observations about prophecy as opposite of idolatry, but I am not prepared at this writing to do them justice within my framework.

30. Among relevant newer books, see Keith Thomas, *Religion and the Decline of Magic* (New York: Scribner's, 1971); among somewhat older ones, see George Lyman Kittredge, *Witchcraft in Old and New England* (Cambridge: Harvard University Press, 1929). These are but two items of a very large literature.

31. The distinction is elaborated in Louis Schneider, *Sociological Approach to Religion* (New York: Wiley, 1970), ch. 7.

32. Edward Conze, *Buddhism* (New York: Harper, 1959), pp. 84-85.

33. Ronald Knox, *Enthusiasm* (New York: Oxford University Press, 1961), pp. 272, 273. Cf. Schneider, *Sociological Approach,* p. 142.

34. Schneider, *Sociological Approach,* p. 152.

35. Thomas, *Religion and Magic,* p. 636.

36. Ibid., pp. 267, 268.

37. See Schneider, *Sociological Approach,* pp. 152-53.

14
Dialectical Orientation and the Sociology of Religion
(1979)

The thesis of this chapter is that a dialectical orientation will guide us to important areas of religion that we might otherwise bypass too easily and will afford us a notion of how such areas may be usefully approached or studied. The term *dialectic*, itself, has been the object of much dispute and disagreement. This chapter sets out for brief exploration three meanings that the term has certainly had. In one sense, *dialectic* refers to study of the action of elements within a system, with an accent on *system* (although it may be useful to refer to such action itself). In a second sense, the term refers to analysis of the play of "opposites." In a third sense, dialectic is to be understood as a kind of "language" or "grammar," which here has special application to social life. These several senses of the term are not to be taken as suggesting hard, inviolable distinctions. Rather, they suggest aspects of dialectic that one may wish to stress at one time or another. The first and second senses are very intimately connected, as will soon be evident, and the third may be constantly in the near background or on the verge of articulation when the first and second are being explored. The reality of overlap will be clearer from our account. The second sense will be explored in close association with the concept of antinomianism.

In the first sense, then, dialectic involves the idea of a system or totality in which elements—say, A and B—that demand some kind of "satisfaction" are in tension and in which "excessive" movement toward either—toward A or toward B—will tend to generate movement toward the other. Thus, Diesing writes on a certain one-sidedness in the methodology of science that is illustrated by a definition of science exclusively in terms of rigor and precision. Diesing argues that science needs a certain amount of "vagueness" and "suggestiveness" as well as rigor and precision. He finds that actual scientific traditions show a balance of precision and vagueness but that different traditions apportion the two in different ways. "The various kinds of balance serve the conflicting scientific needs of creativity and control: Vagueness and suggestiveness facilitate creativity, and precision and rigor are means of control, either empirical or logical."[1] The outcome of an exaggerated stress on rigor and precision is likely to be "theoretical stagnation and empirical preoccupation with detail," while an excess of vagueness leads to "diffuse and uncontrolled speculation." In a broad sense, then, science as a totality or system unites the "opposites" of rigor or precision *and* vagueness or suggestiveness. These opposites are never "perfectly" balanced but are in a tense interrelationship, and, as balance shifts, either may crowd out the other, to the detriment of the whole scientific enterprise. The interrelationship may also be called *dialectical.* (The reference to "opposites" already indicates the close affinity between our first and our second meanings of *dialectic.)*

The general pattern of thought—the orientation, if one will—thus suggested with regard to science is easily extended beyond science to include phenomena that are of interest in the sociology of religion. Religion can also be profitably regarded as a realm of elements in tension that are constantly productive of conflict (although also showing movement toward accommodation). But at this point we must not lose sight of system, totality, or larger context, although it is often hard to define this context with any precision in relation to religion.

Within the religious realm, we frequently discern striking swings from one "extreme" to another. Sheldon Shapiro, in an interesting article on religious reformations, develops a contrast between "gnostic" and "bhaktic" strains toward salvation by faith[2] or by what Glasenapp calls "believing surrender to God."[3] But Shapiro sees more than the two strains. He also discerns a rhythm or alternation. The reaction to stress on salvation by knowledge or wisdom (or on that alone) may be noted in the popular Mahayana Buddhism, which opened a path of salvation by faith to great multitudes—or indeed, in Methodism, with its reaction in favor of religious feeling against a "rationalistic," "formalistic," and "dry" religion.

We simplify Shapiro's account in the interest of presenting a sharp contrast, which, we believe with him, is basically defensible. Gnostic or cognitive has vied with bhaktic or devotional repeatedly and in religions remote from one another in space and time. But our interest in the contrast is now also connected with the notion of a religious system or totality. The swing between bhaktic and gnostic may occur over centuries. What is the time span to be allowed for a single system that can be handled in analytically useful terms by sociologists or other? And how delicately can we discriminate "elements" in which we are interested? Will a really subtle analysis show that, while the notion of alternation or rhythm has some point, it is also true that the elements or extremes between which there is movement are always still substantially *co*-present? It is certainly a plausible notion, at any rate, that gnostic and bhaktic represent quite fundamental human religious orientations that are *constantly* at work within numerous totalities that may be fairly accurately delimited.

We are thus motivated to look for the simultaneous presence of "conflicting" or "opposite" religious impulses, not merely for alternations or rhythms (granted that we may theoretically bring even the notion of centuries-long swings within the compass of the general idea of system). This all ties in with questions about just who the adherents of a religion are, what their class affiliation is, and to whom the proselytizing endeavors of a religion, if such there are, are addressed. Particular strata may accept religious activity and thought that will not appeal to others. But religions that take in large and socially varied portions of humanity clearly appear to have a certain likelihood of catering to a variety of religious strains or impulses and of sustaining the tension of struggle among them. Conze, a close student of Buddhism, writes, perhaps somewhat testily, that "of course, if one makes up one's mind that 'original' Buddhism was a perfectly rational religion, after the heart of the 'ethical society,' without any touch of the supernatural or mysterious," then certain developments within it (say, on the lines of magic, for instance; Conze himself here refers to the Tantra, of which we shall say something later) "will become an incomprehensible 'degeneration' of that presumed original Buddhism. In actual fact, Buddhism has always been closely associated with what to rationalists would appear as superstitutions."[4]

Conze forthrightly criticizes a contempt for magic that may be harbored by educated people as "a serious obstacle to our historical understanding of the past." He continues, in context still of discussion of Buddhism, "In order to live, in order to keep its feet on the earth, a religion must to some extent serve the material occupations of the average man. It must be able to insert iself into the rhythm of communal life which in the past was everywhere permeated and dominated by magic. Then, as now, the average man was deeply absorbed in the problems of everyday life. . . . He expected *that same religion which was based on the reunciation of all things of the world,* to provide him with that control over the unseen magical forces all around him, which would guarantee or at least assist the secure possession of the things of the world."[5]

Indeed, Conze is willing to generalize his pertinent observations and contend that "no known religion has become mature without embracing both the spiritual and the magical. . . . If . . . religion rejects the magical side of life, it cuts itself off from the living forces of the world to such an extent that it cannot even bring the spiritual side of man to maturity."[6] And, referring once more to Buddhism itself, the same writer observes that "among all the paradoxes with which the history of Buddhism presents us, this combination of spiritual negation of self-interest with magical subservience to self-interest is perhaps one of the most striking. Illogical though it may seem, a great deal of the actual life of the Buddhist religion has been due to it."[7] Tambiah's study of Buddhism in a Thai village, which develops such "dualities" or "paradoxes" (the language is that of author of the study referred to) as the one in which a community of Buddhist monks renounces the world and life, while *at the same time* the monks tap powers adaptable to the life needs of laymen, constitutes in its way a brilliant confirmation of Conze's thesis.[8]

That thesis might conceivably be more precisely stated, but there is substantial historical and comparative support for the view that religions will often at once feature "splendid heights" and accommodation even to the "grossest" inclinations. Appropriate scholarly statements may be found elsewhere than in the work of Conze. But it is an irresistible temptation to quote a pertinent statement on Tibetan Buddhist temples made by Maraini in a popular, although still substantial, work: "In a Tibetan Buddhist temple, there is darkness, mystery, magnificence, and filth; the stink of yak butter; a love of death and horror; a strange, twisted mentality, sex mingled with mystical exaltation; barbarous couplings combined with extreme asceticism; magic and gnosticism; a multiplication of arms, heads, and symbols; unbridled audacity and imagination; a continuous metaphysical shudder."[9]

Neither yak butter nor other things Maraini mentions are present everywhere. But "magnificence and filth," "sex mingled with mystical exaltation" (even Western religious history suggests a certain affinity of these "opposites"—if that is what they are—for one another), and "barbarous couplings combined with extreme asceticism"—these must in themselves strike us strongly. A dialectical orientation in the analysis of religion will enhance our sensitivity to the tendency of religion to do some sort of "justice," to render some sort of "satisfaction," to a variety of different or conflicting or "opposite" needs, impulses, and strains. If there is no overt sign of "sex," it is what one might call a bit of dialectical sagacity, not cynicism, to obey the behest *"Cherchez la femme,"* at least until it seems quite certain that it is profitless to do so. If God is represented as an oblong blur or the essence of all essences, it is sagacious to look for indications somewhere that he is also regarded as a supplier of bread and meat.[10] Again, it will be wise to be alert to the possibility of tensions, conflicts, alternations, and rhythms as the deity is passionately represented as of one nature or another, simultaneously and over stretches of time.

But we wish to revert once more to the notion of system. It is noteworthy that, in some of the central theoretical work that students of religion and society have at their disposal, the significance of that notion is suggested. We have here in view, particularly, two studies that have been very influential in the sociology of religion; namely, James's *Varieties of Religious Experience*[11] and Durkheim's *Elementary Forms of the Religious Life*.[12] It is well to recall each of these scholars' very mode of apprehending religion. Religion, writes James, shall mean for him and his audience "the feeling, acts, and experiences of individual men in their solitude, so far as they apprehend themselves to stand in relation to whatever they may consider the divine."[13] For Durkheim, on the other hand, "a religion is a unified system of beliefs and practices relative to sacred things; that is to say, things set apart and forbidden—beliefs and practices which untie into one single moral community called a church all those who adhere to them."[14]

James is interested above all in a God who is on the firing line of human experience, as it were, a God who is approached via firsthand experience in a terribly compelling desire for his help. James's book may be said to resound with the cries of sinners and saints and mystics seeking their own distinctive encounters with a divine existence that they must contact merely in order to live. It is not hard to get from James the impression that "church" was for him a rather negative symbol, connected with "ecclesiastical institutions with corporate ambitions of their own" and "the spirit of politics and the lust of dogmatic rule."[15] Durkheim had different purposes from those of James. Each man had considerable sensitivity to much of the range of religious phenomena, but there is certainly a bias toward a different sort of appreciation of religion in the two. Where James might well see barren dogmatism and uncongenially fixed religious practices or structures, Durkheim saw powerful forces indispensably strengthening group solidarities, ensuring group morale, and the like. These were things from which James might consider the spirit had departed, leaving only institutional lumber.

Febrile, vibrating personal experience, we might say, is thus contrasted with the experience of social sustainment in reliable ritual and ceremony. Thus stated, the contrast is rather too simple, if only because in Durkheim's depiction of primitive Australian religion, in his *Elementary Forms,* religious ceremonies reaffirming group strength and bolstering morale could also be very quickening, "exciting" performances. But we would venture the suggestion that both "religion as living personal experience" and "religion as ritual or ceremony" are likely to be "needed" in a religious system or totality.

We may, however, catch a strong warning in these premises that we must not be satisfied too easily that we know precisely what the "opposites" within a religious system are. A dialectical orientation will be useless if it betrays us into glibness and superficiality about ostensible opposites. James is immensely interested in mind cure, in the psychotherapeutic effects of religion. He is very much concerned with persons who have "gone to pieces" emotionally and who reach out to something transcendent that they can, as it were, get on board of, transcedent yet in active contact with some portion of themselves. We might then think, on the one hand, of pressing individual needs where, for example, any considerable psychotherapeutic help, if available at all, *might* be available, let us say, only from religion, and, on the other hand, of a religion so fixed in its ritual-social orientation, so uncompromisingly churchly or ecclesiastical, that it will not be inclined to seek to provide therapeutic resources for individuals. Or, again, we might think of a contrast between the latter sort of ritual-social orientation and impulses to individual religious experience having to do not so much with psychotherapy as with cultivating novel and titillating religious adventures or "kicks," in turn connected with certain kinds of social protest or rebellion not congruous with conventional churchliness. The differences here are obvious enough, but they might hide under the common cover of what might well become *too* loose a contrast of rigid social forms and "living individual experience."

But a dialectical orientation need not betray us into foolishness or neglect of pertinent empirical realities. Its stress on system is a heuristically useful one, and when it comes to concentrate on the subtle relations of "elements in opposition" *without* particular reference to system (thereby featuring the second sense in which we deal with dialectic) it can also be most stimulating, as we shall seek to show. James Bissett Pratt makes a distinction that at once points back to our own concern with dialectic in the second sense.

In a series of able books, Pratt worked out very shrewdly the contrast between "objective" and "subjective" worship.[16] The contrast is rich with implications but it may be concisely described as one between (1) a religious attitude concerned with the divine or sacred or transcendent or the like, in itself or for itself, such as one may note in ceremonies whose object is to "gratify the gods," and (2) a religious attitude concerned with the effects of religion on the self or the members of the social group. In subjective worship, one seeks psychological benefit for oneself or benefit to the emotions of the members of the group. Pratt, another keen student of Buddhism, found cases, particularly in Buddhism and Jainism, where the subjective stress was very strong and where religious activity was maintained explicitly because it was psychologically beneficial. Pratt regards traditional Catholicism to be relatively more oriented toward objective worship than Protestantism.

But, thus far, we might say that Pratt is pointing to certain realities that are not at all difficult to think of in system terms. Within many religious systems or totalities, there will be tension between "worship of God for himself" (God being an appropriate symbol here that will serve also for cases where "a god" is not involved) and worship of God so that one may gain psychic benefit. (One may wonder how much Pratt's thought was affected by William James.) One might expect the usual tensions, strains toward extremes, returns to "equilibrium," and so on, but the subjective and the objective would presumably both be needed components within system or totality. However, Pratt's analysis probes the relation of subjective and objective more carefully. Another sense or aspect of dialectic is now intimated, not at all incompatible with the first but making salient the connections of the "elements in opposition." Pratt notes that where one wants and is exclusively concerned with (beneficial) subjective effects there is danger of getting no effect at all. To pray for something for one's own benefit can become exceedingly difficult when "that to which" one is somehow supposed to pray is actually believed not to exist. Pratt, as earlier stated, found a strong strain of objectivity in Catholicism but suggested that the subjective effect of Catholic religious activity was considerable *because* it was not directly aimed at. (Paradoxically, one might get more "peace of mind" by religious ventures not addressed to getting it than by ventures squarely aiming at it.) By this analysis, objectively oriented religious exercise addressed to and concerned with the divine, the sacred, the transcendent, or something cognate at least has some fair chance of bringing subjective "benefit." Subjective "benefit" has little chance of being obtained without some modicum of faith that there is "something" that is "really there," objectively existent as divine or sacred or transcendent. At the same time, one could ask how perduring any objective worship would be if it brought no subjective results. There are thus powerful connections of objective and subjective. Each depends on the other, and, because they tend markedly to come together, they may in a sense even be said to "coalesce" and exist in unity.

The coalescence or sheer closeness of opposites (or seeming opposites) is important and will engage us shortly. But we will proceed more effectively with it, and the effort to exhibit the heuristic value of dialectic will be facilitated, if we now examine the specific phenomenon of antinomianism in relative detail. (The very choice of antinomianism as a matter to attend to here is, we believe, a choice that might well be expected in anyone with a dialectical orientation toward religion.) We define antinomianism generally as either the doctrine that faith frees one from obligation to the religious or moral law or as activity that is significantly determined by such doctrine.

Adherents to antinomian views have, inevitably and repeatedly, shown "deviant" behavior, behavior that violates a variety of commonly held norms. It is a matter for astonishment that a field with so ostensibly great an interest in "deviance" as sociology has so largely neglected antinomianism, which has been intimately bound up with the emergence of sects and the occurrence of schisms. Perhaps the neglect of it is partly explained by a continuing reluctance on the part of numerous sociologists to engage seriously in historical and comparative study. In any case, antinomianism is a very salient "nay-saying" phenomenon in the framework of religion. It is by its very character oppositional, and it would be matter for surprise if some consideration of it did not allow us to develop somewhat further the sense of a dialectical orientation in the sociology of religion.

The incidence of antinomianism is so considerable that it is impossible in a short chapter to do more than refer to a relatively small number of cases of it, necessarily omitting some very important ones. But we may at least illustrate its scope. The history of medieval sects within "Christianity" is most instructive in regard to antinomianism. With foundations in Gnostic and Manichean teachings, these sects presented numerous doctrines most radically uncongenial to Roman Catholicism. There was Catharist teaching that "worldly authority and administration of justice are not admissible among true believers and constitute an alien invention not deriving from the good God and that accordingly members of the true church are under no obligation of obedience to worldly princes and judges." Knowing this much, we are not altogether unprepared to learn that the institution of the *Consolamentum* among the Catharists, whereby one made a "good end" sufficient for salvation, encouraged antinomianism: One who was assured that he would receive the Consolamentum on his deathbed could, before he got there, engage in unrestrained behavior and gratify all lusts—although, certainly, not all persons did so.[17]

Barbour, in his treatment of the early Quakers, writing of the seventeenth-century Ranters, with whom the Quakers were often confused, notes that the Ranters "claimed that, since they were led by the spirit, they could do no wrong and so followed impulses into all kinds of immorality and anarchy. Some went further, saying that no man could be freed from a sin until he had committed that sin as if it were not a sin.''[18] Cohn has presented documents that back the view of the Ranters thus suggested. Strong among them was the doctrine that to the pure all things were pure. (So, presumably, was that very likely concomitant of the sense of being pure: aggressive and contemptuous feeling toward the ordinary "impure.") Adultery and fornication could not defile them, nor, apparently, could incest or murder. Cohn regards it as beyond doubt that some Ranters genuinely taught total amoralism. There was some patent Ranter bias toward regarding the most "deviant" acts as identical with the act of prayer itself.[19]

Let us fill out the picture for English speakers a little. Gaustad, writing on the Great Awakening in New England, warns us of "the ambiguity of a word like *antinomianism*" yet does not hesitate to suggest a sufficiently clear general sense for the same word when he avers, "The antinomian could be sure that *faith without the law* was enough to save him.''[20] And about the existence of such people as "antinomians" in this sense in mid-eighteenth-century New England there is no question. Wilbur Cross, in his study of enthusiastic religion in Western New York in the first half of the nineteenth century, pays attention to the (Adventist) Millerites, among other groups, and notes that "many of the most zealously sincere" in their ranks were led into "remarkable extravagances." There appears once more a notable and frequent tendency for those who regard themselves as especially sanctified to believe or aver that what is usually considered impure action or unconventional comportment is justifiable or even excellent for *them* because of *their* distinctive purity.[21]

We move very briefly to the Muslim world. Hasan II, lord of Alamut near the Caspian Sea, in the twelfth century proclaimed the millennium, announcing a message of liberation from the bonds of holy law. The word was received in Syria, and there too the faithful celebrated the law's end. Lewis writes of "the solemn and ritual violation of the law" as a (millenarian and) antinomian tendency "which is recurrent in Islam and has obvious parallels in Christendom."[22] And Grunebaum observes that Islam, too, had "had to counteract those antinomian tendencies which everywhere and at all times accompany the process of interiorization of the religious experience." It is also of interest that Grunebaum notes something of a Sufi tendency to claim or presume freedom not only from ritual but also from moral precepts.[23]

There is admitted danger in thus ranging over the world while relying on a simple rubric such as antinomianism as we have thus far described it. Moreover, we intend even to increase the danger by reference also to the extremely interesting cases of Tantrism and the antinomian activity of the seventeenth-century mystical Jewish "messiah," Sabbatai Sevi. We have noted Gaustad's saying that antinomianism is an ambiguous word, although he can also give it a rather unambiguous definition. There are differences among antinomianisms. But at least some of these various movements appear to have much in common. Let us venture some remarks bearing on common features, in the sense of dialectical orientation, before describing additional cases.

The coalescence or closeness of opposites now virtually obtrudes itself on us. The cases we have thus far reviewed suggest a remarkable coincidence of opposites: a remarkable tendency for those who strive for special, really extraordinary holiness *and* those who are by all usual standards wicked people who engage in heinous behavior, people in any case "abandoned of the Lord," to act in the same way, a way thoroughly reprehensible in the ordinary view. Thus, the religiously zealous or pious and the hopelessly abandoned come together. If anything, the religiously very zealous perhaps can exceed the wicked in the awfulness, the reprehensibility of their performances. Opposites, or ostensible opposites, meet or coalesce.[24]

Of course, in some few cases, it may be possible to explain such coalescence on the ground that the exceptionally zealous were fakes or hypocrites all along. In his learned treatise on the Tantric tradition, Bharati notes that Hindu and Buddhist critics of Tantric teaching and conduct "have constantly suggested that the Tantric uses religion as a mantle for sexual desire and debauchery"; but he also records the rather convincing answer of the Tantrics that the complex, elaborate, and very difficult procedures they follow "would not at all be necessary to gratify sexual desire, whose objects are much easier to obtain without any logic trappings."[25] It is always possible that there are some few attracted to "wild" doctrines and practices for the sheer joy of the wildness, but there is far too much to suggest intense zeal and profound commitment to make plausible the notion that "wild" religious impulses are in any general way covers for mere desires to engage in crime, indulge in drink, and commit fornication, adultery, and incest. The affinities between uncommon religiousness—supererogatory religiousness, one might say—and the ways of the unqualifiedly ungodly must be sought at deeper levels.

What, then, brings together—makes "coalesce"—great holiness and flagrant wickedness? It is noteworthy that *within* sectarian contexts themselves both holiness and wickedness may make their appearance. Koch, a much more recent student of Catharism than von Döllinger, notes that by antinomian standards with a certain philosophical base one could be either ascetic or libertine on the ground that matter is utterly worthless and spirit possesses all merit. Then one could express one's contempt for the urges of the flesh (a part of matter) by refusing, ascetically, to gratify all desire; but if one indulged the flesh one was merely giving way to something entirely contemptible and one's soul would be untainted by the actions of the body.[26] The doctrine of the so-called dualistic Cathari, then, disdaining matter and exalting spirit, might go some way toward explaining both holiness and wickedness. (Yet it should be said that statements made about the Cathari in this chapter are not beyond controversy. Not all present-day scholars would be easy with the notion that the Cathari came to libertine conclusions from their depreciative view of the flesh.) I remarked earlier that Grunebaum noted some Sufi antinomian tendencies. He connects this with belief: "The unreality of this world entails the nothingness of all its attributes. What, then, could the statutes and demands of society, what the tenets of this or that specific truth, mean to him who had seen through the meaningless mirage?"[27] The "statutes and demands of society"—these, too, are unreal, and violation of them accordingly would mean nothing.

It is not claimed that this solves all problems that may arise in this context. It does, of course, suggest that it might be profitable for sociologists of religion to entertain the notion of particularly close affinities between ascetic and orgiastic sects. And numerous other factors may throw light on the affinity we have noted, including psychological factors such as reaction formation. A bit of wit from Bernard Mandeville, although it is perhaps rather nasty, may have its point. Mandeville writes that to conquer his sexual desire (his "domestic enemy") St. Francis was capable of throwing himself into an ice-filled ditch or a heap of snow (or of scourging himself). Mandeville comments that "the fever of lust must be very high where such violent coolers are required."[28] Again lust and asceticism are connected. But sociologists studying such phenomena, like historians, would be alert to the possible relevance in these matters of a variety of social circumstances, including class origins, the status of women, and the character of their opportunities in a particular social order, and level of education.

From the cases of Catharism and Sufism, we see that religions may contain components that unite "opposites" and in this sense exhibit a dialectical bias or structure. The foundations for a "unity of opposites" were apparently also present among the Ranters, by Barbour's account. The Ranters were redeemed and led by the spirit and could do no wrong; hence, anything "wrong" that they did was not really such, and "right" and "wrong" were thereby at one. (It is a particular sort of "unity" that the Ranters insisted on. We do not claim that everything that might come in some sense under the rubric of "unity of opposites" would necessarily result in a sheer obliteration of distinctions.) This is actually a very common antinomian tendency, also manifested by the Millerites, for example, as we noted earlier: What the sanctified do is by the same token sanctified. For another American example, Anne Hutchinson, the seventeenth-century New England religious leader, would have found it difficult, according to Battis, "to abandon her conviction that once God's children have been sealed in His love, the seal could not be removed," which suggests that, once God's love has been sealed, if the seal cannot be removed then no matter what his children may do, they will retain their sanctity.[29] Outside America, Knox notes that it would appear that at least some of the medieval Beghards were antinomians, "extending the principle of perfectionism so as to hold that actions normally regarded as sinful were not sinful in the perfect."[30]

Despite differences among antinomianisms, the literature does encourage one to think that it is worth trying out hypotheses about shared features. And a dialectical orientation may make us fruitfully curious. By now, we may be prepared to look with renewed curiosity at something that was quoted earlier from Barbour, who noted the view of some Ranters that no man could be free of a sin until he had committed it as if it were not a sin.[31] Perhaps the relations of "opposites" are more subtle than we have thus far suspected. Antinomianism might reveal not only their tendency to "come together," to "coalesce," but also other intimate relationships between them. Thus, not only may antinomian doctrine refuse to see any differences between what is called good and evil but it also might conceivably premise some sort of special connection between them.

We turn to some aspects of antinomianism in India, seeking to expand our bare survey of the phenomenon while we do not forget our suspicions about special connection just intimated. "The idea that a man is not necessarily bound by the moral law, and can reach a state that takes him beyond its precepts, is prominent in the Indian religions, particularly in the left-hand Tantric cults like those of the Saktas, Nathas, Kaulas, and Kapalikas among the Hindus, and the Vajrayanas and Kalachakrayanas among the Buddhists. The Sanskrit equivalent for the term *antinomianism* is *nirdharma*, 'unrighteousness,' which implies a lack of regard for the norms of religion and conventions of society. Tantriks believe that the goddess Sakti is gratified in all forms of antinomian activity."[32] Kenneth Ch'en writes of a Tantric Buddhist text whence it appears that a bodhisattva, dedicated as he is to the serving of all sentient beings, would find it his duty, to a woman who had fallen in love with him and was about to sacrifice her life for him, to "save her life by satisfying all her desires." The bodhisattva does not ever sin. "For this reason, it is repeatedly stated in the texts that there is nothing that the bodhisattva should not do for the salvation of others. Since the intentions and motives of the bodhisattva are noble and virtuous, whatever deeds he performs are also virtuous."[33] This certainly has a familiar sound in the mansions of antinomianism.

Walker notes a widely prevalent antinomianism in Hindu sex mysticism ("unequivocally condemned by Hindus of advanced thought"), refers to "the worship of the linga of Siva and the yoni of the Mother Goddess," and writes also that "tantrism affirms that spiritual union with god can best be attained *through sexual union* in the flesh" (emphasis added). Here we already have a significant intimation about "special connection." The "high" can be reached best *through* the "low." Further, again within the Tantric context, the ideal union is "the unconventional and perilous intimacy of a man with a woman with whom he can never unite; an antinomian adventure in defiance of the laws of society. . . . Such unions bring into play that element of awe and guilt accompanied by heightened tensions so necessary to satisfying Sakti." Union with low-caste women, dancing girls, and prostitutes is yet more to be commended for its breaking of the bonds of caste; and "if this type of intercourse is accompanied by *feelings* of revulsion, all the greater is its spiritual merit" (emphasis added). Awe—and guilt: one must clearly be conscious of doing wrong, and yet this is clearly also associated with getting close to the divine or transcendent or the like. The greater the revulsion (revulsion being grounded in the consciousness of "wrongdoing," of violating powerful norms), the greater the spiritual merit. Religious excellence, apparently, can be attained precisely through the "vilest" sort of behavior. (Note that "the feelings of revulsion" or the guilt alluded to are *not* simply imputed by Western scholars or observers on the basis of their own values.)[34]

Tantrism can be rather spectacularly antinomian. There are in it elements of support for incest, best of all with one's mother. It has, further, associations with diabolism and black magic and "preoccupation with ordure and other scatological substances, with cadavers, graveyards, and cremation grounds."[35] Since this may indeed seem extreme, it is perhaps well to add that students of Tantrism have protested that antagonistic attitudes toward it have inhibited careful examination of it. It is interesting in this connection that Walker, for all his vivid description of the "left-hand" religious activities he describes, can also say that "Tantrism contains the loftiest philosophical speculation side by side with the greatest obscenities; the more rarified metaphysics with the wildest superstition."[36] This is undoubtedly promoted in part by the desire to be fair, but it is also a correct statement in itself. By this juncture, we might in fact be saying, "Of course! What else would one expect? In religion, it's virtually a dialectical 'law' that opposites should beget one another."

We do not pretend to give a rounded representation of Tantric religion. We do, of course, wish to stress antinomianism and the bias toward attaining "good" via "evil." The well-informed Conze, who is not in principle unfriendly to "deviant" religious forms, has made observations much like some of those made by Walker. Conze notes that the scriptures of the left-handed Tantra appear to push in the very opposite direction to that taken by Buddhist asceticism. "Just the most immoral, the most tabooed actions, seem to have a particular fascination for the followers of this doctrine. . . . One must feed on the flesh of elephants, horses, and dogs, and all food and drink should be mixed with ordure, urine, or meat."[37] But Conze finds all this essentially quite understandable. He calls attention to the purpose of bringing the senses into contact with stimulating objects. We may come fully to realize the "vanity and relativity" of the sensual pleasures by full exposure to them. (We may add that on the same principle an extreme involvement with the world, getting one's fill of it and more, may be just the thing needed to turn from it, in the end, with utter aversion.) Overlooking nuances important in themselves but not especially to the point here, Bharati, too, appealing to the aim of "freedom from the misery of attachment," suggests that in their radical way, Tantrics move toward that aim.[38]

The Tantric way still is "radical" and the sort of "justification" given by Conze, say, may still strike us as far from explaining the full character of Tantrism, but it does make in some degree understandable the Tantric juxtaposition of "good" and "evil" and what would seem to be a certain disposition to reach good *through* evil. And our understanding is also aided when Blofeld writes of responding to the promptings of desire "in order to profit from the subsequent disillusion and gradually lay desire to rest."[39] In the context of discussing Tantrism, sexual activity or the emotion and bliss that accompany it should, Blofled writes, be "made to contribute to [one's] realization of not being an individual cut off by his envelope of skin from the rest of phenomena. During enjoyment, he must visualize his desire as a companion to voidness-bliss; that is to say, as an integral part of the universal play of void functioning through him but not belonging to him."[40] It may not be reading too much into this—or too much of a simplification—to suggest that, at least where the sexual activity Blofeld thus refers to is of a highly "deviant" sort, a metaphysical or religious excellence is represented as reachable (or even best reachable) through "vileness." This hardly means that in tension between the high metaphysical or religious impulse informing antinomian activity, on the one hand, and the temptation to indulge in that activity for its own sake, on the other, the "elevated" impulse will always win out. That would be quite implausible.

One more relevant account will bring to a close our conspectus of antinomianism and allow us again a glance at how good is presumed to be advanced through evil. We draw on Gershom Scholem's monumental study of Sabbatai Sevi (1626-1676), the mystical Jewish messiah. Sabbatai was a complex character who, Scholem was quite certain, suffered from manic-depressive psychosis. But Sabbatai's doctrines and behavior require more explanation than this, and Scholem provides us with relevant theological background, particularly in kabbalism (in which Isaac Luria Ashkenazi, 1534-1572, played an important part; Scholem employs the term "Lurianic kabbalism"). Orthodox kabbalism had some notion that a messiah had in himself "something of the 'evil side.' " This became very important in Sabbatai's case. Sabbatai, the great hope and light of very many Jews in the seventeenth-century world of the Near East and Europe, became an apostate under pressure, converting to Islam. He "bought his life at the price of apostasy."[41]

This was unavoidably terribly shocking to multitudes of Jews. What worse, what more profoundly wrong, than apostasy? Faith in Sabbatai would then be (and was) taken by numbers of previous adherents as a sad illusion. One *could*, however, seek to believe in an apostate messiah, as some did. But so to believe would be "to build one's faith on foundations of paradox and absurdity, which could only lead to more paradoxes . . . . The Sabbataian paradox . . . was not that of a saint who suffers and whose suffering is a mystery hidden with God, but of a saint who sins. Its dialectical premise of necessity begets conclusions that are equally marked by the dialectics of paradox."[42]

Even before his apostasy, Sabbatai had engaged in various "strange," antinomian actions. But the apostasy was something that required quite special justification, and it had to be justified in terms based on traditional Judaism, even though, inevitably, the new justifying doctrine was heretical by those very terms. The complexities of kabbalism get involved here. Scholem expounds background-relevant Lurianic kabbalism, which had taught a mode of spearating "holy sparks" from "the clutches of evil in which they were held." If these sparks were released and "raised," evil, by itself without power (which it obtained only from good), would simply be wiped out. And just at this point Sabbataian doctrine introduced a dialectical turn into "the Lurianic idea." Scholem notes that it was no longer enough, in the new Sabbataian version of things, to extract the sparks of holiness from the realm of impurity. The power of holiness—as embodied in the messiah—had to go down into impurity, and good had to assume the form of evil, that holiness might carry out its mission. Sabbatai had to become a Muslim in order to fulfill his very messianic task and do ultimate, final good. He was truly a "holy sinner."[43]

In time, it even came to be contended by Sabbataian radicals that "only the complete transformation of good into evil would exhaust the full potential of the latter and thereby explode it, as it were, from within. This dialectical liquidation of evil requires not only the disguise of good in the form of evil but total identification with it."[44] Nathan of Gaza, Sabbatai's "prophet," put major emphasis on the theme of the descent of the righteous one into the realm of evil, the realm of "the other side." We find in Sabbatai the paradox of "the messiah who saves the world by himself transgressing the law."[45] Antinomianism has nourished such development elsewhere, also. But what we would again especially emphasize is that aspect of Sabbataian doctrine whereby evil becomes the instrumentality of good. Despite all differences, the similarities with tendencies we have already noted in Tantrism is striking.

We must always expect a certain skill in argument on the part of significant antinomian figures. Medieval antinomians in Europe, often drawing on Gnostic or Manichean ideas, could present imaginative mythological and theological justifications for their beliefs. Nathan of Gaza, with a mind nourished on kabbalistic writings, was clearly a man of some ability in handling the theological subtleties pertinent to the vindication of Sabbatai. Even antinomians with what would appear to be relatively modest talents can present, if they do not originate, such distinctions as that between "carnal" union and "spiritual" union, the former being bad even in marriage, while the latter would be good even outside of marraige. Cross reports that one Lucina Umphreville took up this distinction in 1835 while at about the same time one Maria Brown "decided to demonstrate that her piety could overcome lowly desires by proving that she could sleep chastely with her minister."[46] But again and again the "dialectic" of the antinomians themselves will strike us as replete with paradox, ambiguity, and play with contradictions. This brings us to the last sense in which we wish to discuss dialectic.

Paradox, ambiguity, contradictions—up to this point, we have been concerned with the opposition of elements within a system, giving emphasis to the idea of system, precisely, and we have allowed the notion of opposition to lead us into a discussion of antinomianism, this time not stressing the idea of system but letting that fade into the background while allowing ourselves to be guided to a number of significant questions and "interesting phenomena" suggested by "opposition" itself. But it has surely been evident throughout that a dialectical orientation is markedly an orientation to the paradoxical, the ambiguous, the contradictory, the dilemmatic. There is a meaning of dialectic that now may emerge more distinctly.

Social phenomena, including phenomena of central interest in the sociology of religion, speak to us in a distinctive "language," it may be proposed—a language we are as yet far from understanding thoroughly. Dialectic can then be conceived as a striving to understand just that language—or as an effort to set out a "grammar" of that language, a conspectus of the fundamental rules by which it works or by which its expressions are controlled.

In the study of literary productions, as we know, there has long been developing a specialized and sophisticated set of terms for the description and understanding of what students encounter. This set of terms and the manner in which they are used can be very suggestive to the analyst of religion. One of the best-known terms here referred to is *synecdoche*. Kenneth Burke characterizes it as "the figure of speech wherein the part is used for the whole, the whole for the part, the container for the thing contained, the cause for the effect, the effect for the cause, etc. Simplest example: 'twenty noses' for 'twenty men.' " To this, Burke then adds these interesting words: "The more I examine both the structure of poetry *and the structure of human relations outside of poetry,* the more I am convinced that this is the basic figure of speech and that it occurs in many modes besides that of the formal trope" (emphasis added).[47]

Given a dialectical orientation, the literary term *oxymoron* must impress us as very significant. One might almost be tempted to risk a statement just like Burke's, substituting *oxymoron* for *synecdoche* as "the basic figure of speech." Indeed, even Burke himself might sympathize with this. The view that the oxymoron is "the basic figure of speech" does not really seem very alien to him (despite what he has said about synecdoche) when we consider the interest he has had in "perspective by incongruity," an idea that strongly suggests oxymoron.[48]

It is well to remind ourselves that, as for example Webster's *Unabridged Dictionary* (second edition) indicates, an oxymoron is, etymologically, a "sharp-foolish" or, in more colloquial language, a "smart-dumb." Webster's gives the instances of "cruel kindness" and "laborious idleness." We have quoted Cross on the subject of one Maria Brown, a woman who would prove she could "sleep chastely with her minister." The moral and lexical context in terms of which we would understand such phrasing would readily suggest oxymoron. A woman does not sleep "chastely" with a minister (of all people!) who is not her husband. Sabbatai's status as a "holy sinner" will be recalled.

Dictionaries of literary terms define the oxymoron as a figure of speech—for instance, as "a figure of speech consisting generally of two apparently contradictory terms which express a startling paradox"[49] or as "a figure of speech which combines incongruous and apparently contradictory words and meanings for special effect."[50] But, to be sure, as regards our interest here much more than a figure of speech is involved. Human action in the religious sphere often takes on a kind of oxymoronic form. One "sleeps chastely" with one's minister, and the phrasing points beyond its own character as phrasing. We have a *situation* in which a woman so represents matters to herself, in virtue of some peculiar or distinctive religious construction, that to her a conventionally "unchaste" act ostensibly becomes quite pure. The Tantric adept does something abhorrently "bad" by conventional standards in the light of something, or to achieve something, that is in no way reprehensible but rather superlatively good. (Clearly, oxymoron, like synecdoche, occurs "in many modes besides that of the formal trope.") And the sociological significance of his oxymoronic comportment will presumably be more readily or immediately seen in interactions with partners where these occur, as in the case of sexual partners. Virtually the whole of the present chapter may be allowed to suggest the salience of oxymoron in phenomena of interest to the sociology of religion.

The term *dialectic* has often been associated with the idea of irony, which is, of course, a standard item in a lexicon of literary terms and even likely to be treated at some length in such a lexicon. Irony is not all of a piece, but we refer here particularly to what is often called *dramatic irony,* which features outcomes of action incongruous with the expectations of actors involved and perceived as incongruous either by spectators of action or by actors themselves. A classic instance is afforded by Weber on the relation between certain premises of Calvinist theology and methodical this-worldly activity. Phenomena of this ironic *type* are frequently recurrent in the sphere of religion. Heimert seeks to show how, on the American religious scene, it was *orthodox* or conservative ("evangelical") religion that harbored democratic seeds and gave strength to popular activities—*not* the "liberal" religion that might, more congruously, have been expected to do so.[51] Here, too, there may well be material for the elaboration of a dialectical grammar in the meaning of a special sort of "grammar" of human relationships (with special reference to the sphere of religion).

The resources of literary terms and conceptions alone, for the development of such a grammar, may still not have been sufficiently tapped, despite brilliant suggestions by writers such as Burke. It would be pleasing and no doubt rewarding to set out the fundamentals of a grammar such as is proposed, in clear and very precise terms. There are severe limitations on what can be done on such lines. If human social and cultural life "speaks" to us, in the sphere of religion as in others, a dialectical *orientation,* solely, is not enough to enable us shrewdly to compass all the speech or language thus poured out and derive a systematic grammar for it. But we abide with the heuristic value of a dialectical orientation. It can sharpen our awareness of the sheer possibility of such a grammar. It can grope for "paradigms" and illustrative matter that may be useful for the development of such a grammar. It can at least hint at the profundity such a grammar might have and constitute a provocative substitute for it until such time as we may possibly attain to a better approximation to "the real thing." We also cherish the hope that the heuristic value of a dialectical orientation has been yet more widely suggested in the earlier portions of this chapter.

Notes

1. Paul Diesing, *Patterns of Discovery in the Social Sciences* (Chicago: Aldine, 1971), p. 221.
2. Sheldon Shapiro, "Patterns of Religious Reformations," *Comparative Studies in Society and History* 15 (1973):143-57.
3. Helmuth von Glasenapp, *Von Buddha zu Gandhi* (Wiesbaden: Harrassowitz, 1962), p. 24.
4. Edward Conze, *Buddhism: Its Essence and Development* (New York: Harper & Row, 1959), p. 175.
5. Ibid., p. 82 (italics added).
6. Ibid., p. 84
7. Ibid., p. 85.
8. S. J. Tambiah, "The Ideology of Merit and the Social Correlates of Buddhism in a Thai Village," in E. R. Leach, ed., *Dialectic in Practical Religion* (Cambridge: Cambridge University Press, 1968).
9. Fosco Maraini, *Meeting with Japan* (New York: Viking, 1960), p. 162.
10. See James Bissett Pratt, *The Religious Consciousness* (New York: Macmillan, 1920), pp. 200, 207.
11. William James, *The Varieties of Religious Experience* (New York: Collier, [1902] 1961).
12. Emile Durkheim, *The Elementary Forms of the Religious Life* (London: Allen & Unwin, [1912] 1926).
13. James, *Varieties,* p. 42.
14. Durkheim, *Elementary Forms,* p. 47.
15. James, *Varieties,* p. 267.

16. James Bissett Pratt, *India and Its Faiths* (Boston: Houghton Mifflin, 1915); *Religious Consequences* (New York: Macmillan, 1920); *The Pilgrimage of Buddhism* (New York: Macmillan, 1928); and *Eternal Values in Religion* (New York: Macmillan, 1950).

17. J.J.I. von Döllinger, *Beiträge zur Sektengeschichte des Mittelalters,* 1st part (New York: Franklin, 1971), pp. 183, 211-12, 216-17.

18. Hugh Barbour, *The Quakers in Puritan England* (New Haven: Yale University Press, 1964), p. 119.

19. Norman Cohn, *The Pursuit of the Millennium* (New York: Oxford University Press, 1970), Appendix.

20. Edwin S. Gaustad, *The Great Awakening in New England* (New York: Harper & Row, 1957), pp. 95, 95 (emphasis added).

21. W. R. Cross, *The Burned-Over District* (Ithaca, N. Y.: Cornell University Press, 1950), pp. 314-15.

22. Bernard Lewis, *The Assassins: A Radical Sect in Islam* (London: Weidenfeld & Nicolson, 1967), p. 73.

23. Gustave von Grunebaum, *Medieval Islam* (Chicago: University of Chicago Press, 1953), pp. 136-37.

24. Ronald Knox, whose book *Enthusiasm* contains much that bears on our theme here, provocatively quotes Bishop Bossuet's shrewd exhortation never to believe good of those who outdo virtue itself. *Enthusiasm* (New York, Oxford University Press, 1961), p. 104.

25. Agehananda Bharati, *The Tantric Tradition* (London: Rider, 1965), p. 292; see also p. 284, where Bharati observes that "no one has to undergo the excessive hardships, the degree of control, the tedium of initiation, of ritualistic perfection, and of minute detail [involved in Tantrism] in order to have fun, even in Puritan India."

26. Gottfried Koch, *Frauenfrage und Ketzertum im Mittelalter* (Berlin: Akademie Verlag, 1962), p. 107.

27. Grunebaum, *Islam,* p. 137.

28. Bernard Mandeville, *Free Thoughts on Religion, the Church, and National Happiness,* 2d ed. (London: Brotherton, 1729), pp. 216-17.

29. Emery J. Battis, *Saints and Sinners: Anne Hutchinson and the Antinomian Controversy in the Massachusetts Bay Colony* (Chapel Hill: University of North Carolina Press, 1962), p. 16; it is of interest, however, to note Battis's opinion that, with Mrs. Hutchinson and her colleagues, "the deeply implanted inhibitions of Puritan morality precluded the grosser behavioral possibilities of the antinomian position" (p. 287).

30. Knox, *Enthusiasm,* p. 125.

31. Barbour, *Quakers.*

32. G. Benjamin Walker, *The Hindu World: An Encyclopedic Survey of Hinduism,* 2 vols. (New York: Praeger, 1968), 1:51.

33. Kenneth Ch'en, *Buddhism in China* (Princeton, N.J.: Princeton University Press, 1964), p. 332.

34. Walker, *Hindu World,* 1:52-53.

35. Ibid, 2:484.

36. Ibid.

37. Conze, *Buddhism,* p. 195.

38. Bharati, *Tantric Tradition,* p. 285.

39. John E. C. Blofeld, *The Tantric Mysticism of Tibet* (New York: Dutton, 1970), p. 93.
40. Ibid., p. 227.
41. Gershom Scholem, *Sabbatai Sevi: The Mystical Messiah* (Princeton, N.J.: Princeton University Press, 1973), p. 678.
42. Ibid., pp. 690-91.
43. Ibid., p. 706.
44. Ibid., p. 801.
45. Ibid., p. 808.
46. Cross, *Burned-Over District,* p. 243.
47. Kenneth Burke, *The Philosophy of Literary Form* (New York: Vintage, 1957), pp. 22-23.
48. See Kenneth Burke, *Permanence and Change* (Indianapolis: Bobbs-Merrill, 1975), chs. 3, 4.
49. Karl Beckson and Arthur Ganz, *A Reader's Guide to Literary Terms* (New York: Noonday Press, 1960), p. 144.
50. John A. Cuddon, *A Dictionary of Literary Terms* (New York: Doubleday, 1977), p. 462.
51. Alan E. Heimert, *Religion and the American Mind* (Cambridge: Havard University Press, 1966).

Bibliography:
Published Writings of Louis Schneider

Books Authored or Coauthored by Schneider

1948.   *The Freudian Psychology and Veblen's Social Theory.* New York: King's Crown Press.

1954.   *Power, Order, and the Economy.* New York: Harper (with M. B. Ogle and J. W. Wiley).

1958.   *Popular Religion: Inspirational Books in America.* Chicago: University of Chicago Press (with Sanford M. Dornbusch).

1970.   *Sociological Approach to Religion.* New York: Wiley.

1973.   *Popular Religion: Inspirational Books in America.* 1958. Reprint. Chicago: University of Chicago Press, Midway Reprints.

1974.   *The Freudian Psychology and Veblen's Social Theory.* 1948. Reprint. Westport, Conn.: Greenwood.

1975.   *The Sociological Way of Looking at the World.* New York: McGraw Hill.

1976.   *Classical Theories of Social Change.* Morristown, N.J.: General Learning Press.

1979.   *Como la sociología va el mundo* (Spanish translation of *The Sociological Way of Looking at the World*). Buenos Aires: Editorial Paidós.

1981.   *Human Responses to Social Problems.* Homewood, Ill.: Dorsey Press (with Cookie Stephan, Louis Zurcher, Jr., and Sheldon Ekland-Olson).

Books Edited or Coedited by Schneider

1963.   *Problems of Economics and Sociology: Essays by Carl Menger.* Urbana: University of Illinois Press.

1964.   *Religion, Culture, and Society: A Reader in the Sociology of Religion.* New York: Wiley.

1967.   *The Scottish Moralists on Human Nature and Society.* Chicago: University of Chicago Press.

1973.   *The Idea of Culture in the Social Sciences.* Cambridge and New York: Cambridge University Press (with Charles M. Bonjean). This volume is based on the September 1972 issue of *Social Science Quarterly,* of which Schneider was coeditor.

1976.   *Social Science in America.* Austin and London: University of Texas Press (with Charles M. Bonjean and Robert M. Lineberry).

Articles and Chapters Authored or Coauthored by Schneider
(Date in italics indicates that the paper is included in this volume.)

1942.   "Toward an Institutional Psychology." *Journal of Social Philosophy and Jurisprudence* 4:344-57.

1949.   "Some Psychiatric Views on 'Freedom' and the Theory of Social Systems." *Psychiatry* 12:251-64.

1950.   "An Industrial Sociology—For What Ends?" *Antioch Review* 10:407-17.

1951.   "The Contribution of Cultural Anthropology to Problems of Guidance." *Purdue University Studies in Higher Education,* no. 76, pp. 1-10.

1952.   " 'Deficiency' and 'Conflict' in Industrial Sociology." *American Journal of Economics and Sociology* 12:49-61 (with Sverre Lysgaard).

1953.   "The Deferred Gratification Pattern." *American Sociological Review* 18 (April):142-59 (with Sverre Lysgaard). (Reprinted as No. 250 in the Bobbs-Merrill Reprint Series in the Social Sciences, and elsewhere.)

1954a.   "A Sociological Perspective on Education." In *Introduction to Educational Psychology,* edited by H. H. Remmers et al., pp. 187-222. New York: Harper.

1954b.   "Additional Discussion" of paper by Ralph Linton. In *Aspects of Culture and Personality,* edited by Francis L. K. Hsu, pp. 215-28. New York: Abelard-Schuman.

1954c.   "Three Views of Religion." *Harvest,* Hillel Foundation, Purdue University (Spring), pp. 2-4.

1955.   "Some Notes on Moral Paradoxes in Race Relations." *Phylon* (2nd Quarter):149-58 (with A. J. Brodbeck).

1957.   "Inspirational Religious Literature: From Latent to Manifest Functions." *American Journal of Sociology* 62:476-81. (Reprinted as No. 249 in the Bobbs-Merrill Reprint Series in the Social Sciences, and elsewhere.)

1962a.   "The Role of the Category of Ignorance in Sociological Theory." *American Sociological Review* 25 (August):492-508.

1962b.   "Race, Reason and Rubbish Again." *Phylon* (2nd Quarter):149-55.

1964a.   "Toward Assessment of Sorokin's Views of Change." In *Explorations in Social Change,* edited by George K. Zollschan and Walter Hirsch, pp. 371-400. New York: Houghton Mifflin.

1964b.   "Problems in the Sociology of Religion." In *Handbook of Modern Sociology,* edited by Robert E. L. Faris, pp. 770-807. Chicago: Rand McNally.

1968.   "Pitirim A. Sorokin: Social Science in the 'Grand Manner.' " *Social Science Quarterly* (June):142-51.

1969a.   "Ideological Conflict between Clergy and Laity: Another Interpretation." *Social Science Quarterly* (March): 925-27.

1969b   "On Frontiers of Sociology and History." *Social Science Quarterly* (June):6-24.

1969c.   "The Scottish Moralists Reconsidered: Rejoinder to a Review." *Studies in Burke and His Time* (Fall):1373-78.

1970a.   "Mandeville as Forerunner of Modern Sociology." *Journal of the History of the Behavioral Sciences* 6 (July):219-30.

1970b.   "The Sociology of Religion: Some Areas of Theoretical Potential." *Sociological Analysis* 31 (Fall):131-44.

1970c.   "Toward Understanding the Catholic Crisis: Observations on Dissident Priests in Texas." *Journal of the Scientific Study of Religion* 9 (Fall):197-207 (with Louis Zurcher, Jr.).

1970d.   "Max Weber: Saggezza e Scienza in Sociologia." *Rassegna Italiana di Sociologia* (October - December):527-43.

1971a.   "Dialectic in Sociology." *American Sociological Review* 36 (August):667-78.

1971b.　　"Max Weber: Wisdom and Science in Sociology." *Sociological Quarterly* 12 (Autumn):462-72 (revised translation of 1970d).

1971-72.　　"Tension in the Thought of John Millar." *Studies in Burke and His Time* 13 (Winter):2083-98.

1972a.　　"On Eighteenth-Century Scottish Sociology." *Contemporary Sociology* (September):410-13. (Review essay.)

1972b–73　　"Controversial Comments on the Idea of Culture." *Social Science Quarterly* (September):337-52, and in *The Idea of Culture in the Social Sciences,* edited by Charles M. Bonjean and Louis Schneider, pp. 118-43. Cambridge and New York: Cambridge University Press.

1974.　　"The Scope of the 'Religious Factor' and the Sociology of Religion." *Social Research* 41 (Summer):340-61.

1975a.　　"Ironic Perspective and Sociological Thought." In *The Idea of Social Structure: Papers in Honor of Robert K. Merton,* edited by Lewis A. Coser, pp. 323-37. New York: Harcourt Brace Jovanovich.

1975b.　　Introduction to and translation of a paper by Max Weber, "Die Grenznutzlehre und das 'Psychophysische Grundgesetz,' " tr. as "Marginal Utility Theory and 'The Fundamental Law of Psychophysics.' " *Social Science Quarterly* 56 (June):21-36.

1976a.　　"Toward Assessment of Sorokin's View of Change." In *Social Change: Explorations, Diagnoses, and Conjectures,* edited by George K. Zollschan and Walter Hirsch, pp. 552-82. New York: Wiley (revised version of 1964a).

1976b.　　"The Social Sciences in America: Some Comments on Past, Present, and Future." In *Social Science in America,* edited by Charles M. Bonjean, Louis Schneider, and Robert M. Lineberry, pp. 208-21. Austin & London: University of Texas Press.

1979a.　　"Adam Smith on Human Nature and Social Circumstance." In *Adam Smith and Modern Political Economy: Bicentennial Essays* on The Wealth of Nations, edited by Gerald P. O'Driscoll, Jr., pp. 44-67. Ames: Iowa State University Press. (Revised version of Harry Girvetz Memorial Lecture on Adam Smith, University of California at Santa Barbara, February 12, 1976.)

1979b.　　"Introduction" to *An Essay on the History of Civil Society* by Adam Ferguson. Transaction Reprints of Social Science Classics, pp. x-xxviii. New Brunswick, N.J.: Transaction Books.

1979c.　　"Dialectical Orientation and the Sociology of Religion." *Sociological Inquiry* 49:49-73. (Reprinted in *Religious Change and*

Continuity, edited by Harry M. Johnson. San Francisco: Jossey Bass.)

Book Reviews Written by Schneider

1954.   Sartre, Jean-Paul. *Existential Psychoanalysis.* Translated and with an introduction by Hazel E. Barnes. New York: Philosophical Library, 1953. *Phylon* 15 (1st Quarter):109.

1956.   Fromm, Erich. *The Sane Society.* New York: Rinehart, 1955. *Social Problems* 4 (October):181-82.

1958a.   Harris, Dale B., ed. *The Concept of Development.* Minneapolis: University of Minnesota Press, 1957. *Marriage and Family Living* 20 (February):97-98.

1958b.   Dobriansky, Lev E. *Veblenism: A New Critique.* Washington, D.C.: Public Affairs Press, 1957. *American Sociological Review* 23 (June):345.

1959.   Miller, Daniel R., and Guy E. Swanson. *The Changing American Parent: A Study in the Detroit Area.* New York: John Wiley and Sons, 1958. *Marriage and Family Living* 21 (August):303-5.

1960.   Dowd, Douglas F., ed. *Thorstein Veblen: A Critical Reappraisal.* Lectures and Essays Commemorating the Hundredth Anniversary of Veblen's Birth. Ithaca: Cornell University Press, 1958. *American Sociological Review* 25 (Frebruary):119-20.

1962.   Lenski, Gerhard. *The Religious Factor: A Sociological Study of Religion's Impact on Politics, Economics, and Family Life.* Garden City, N.Y.: Doubleday, 1961. *Sociological Quarterly* 3 (January):73-75.

1964a.   Kateb, George. *Utopia and Its Enemies.* New York: Free Press of Glencoe, 1963. *American Sociological Review* 29 (June):427-28.

1964b.   Goffman, Erving. *Behavior in Public Places: Notes on the Social Organization of Gatherings.* New York: Free Press of Glencoe; and London: Collier-Macmillan, 1963. *American Sociological Review* 29 (June):427-28.

1965.   Miyakawa, T. Scott. *Protestants and Pioneers: Individualism and Conformity on the American Frontier.* Chicago: University of Chicago Press, 1964. *Social Forces* 44 (December):283.

1966.   Whitley, Oliver R. *Religious Behavior: Where Sociology and Religion Meet.* Englewood Cliffs, N.J.: Prentice-Hall, 1964. \merican *Journal of Sociology* 71 (January):442.

1968a.   Stark, Werner. *The Sociology of Religion: A Study of Christendom.* Vol. 1: *Established Religion.* New York: Fordham University Press, 1966. *American Sociological Review* 33 (April):305-6.

1968b.   Leach, E. R., ed. *Dialectic in Practical Religion.* Cambridge Papers in Social Anthropology. Vol. 5. Cambridge: Cambridge University Press, 1968. *Sociological Analysis* 29 (Summer):106-8.

1970.   Streissler, Erich, ed. *Roads to Freedom: Essays in Honour of Friedrich A. von Hayek.* New York: Augustus M. Kelley, 1969. *Social Science Quarterly* 51 (December):783.

1971a.   Nisbet, Robert A. *Social Change and History.* New York: Oxford University Press, 1969. *Journal of the History of the Behavioral Sciences* 7.

1971b.   Schwartz, Gary. *Sect Ideologies and Social Status.* Chicago: University of Chicago Press, 1970. *Annals of the American Academy of Political and Social Science* 395 (May):258-59.

1973.   Woods, Frances Jerome. *Marginality and Identity: A Colored Creole Family Through Ten Generations.* Baton Rouge: Louisiana State University Press, 1972. *Journal of Southern History* 29 (August):470-71.

1974a.   Goode, William J. *Explorations in Social Theory.* New York: Oxford University Press, 1973. *Contemporary Sociology* 3 (March):114-16.

1974b.   Horowitz, Irving Louis. *Foundations of Political Sociology.* New York: Harper & Row, 1972. *Social Forces* 52 (March):416-17.

1974c.   Couch, William T. *The Human Potential: An Essay on Its Cultivation.* Durham: Duke University Press, 1974. *Annals of the American Academy of Political and Social Science* 415 (September):272-73.

1975a.   Hill, Michael. *The Religious Order: A Study of Virtuoso Religion and Its Legitimation in the Nineteenth-Century Church of England.* New York: Crane, Russak, 1973. *Journal for the Scientific Study of Religion* 14 (June):210-11.

1975b.   Turner, Bryan S. *Weber and Islam: A Critical Study.* London: Routledge and Kegan Paul, 1974. *Social Science Quarterly* 56 (June):151-52.

1975c.   Bierstedt, Robert. *Power and Progress: Essays on Sociological Theory.* New York: McGraw-Hill, 1974. *Contemporary Sociology* 4 (July):436-37.

1975d.   Laslett, John H. M., and Seymour Martin Lipset, eds. *Failure of a Dream?: Essays in the History of American Socialism.* Garden City, N.Y.: Anchor Press/Doubleday, 1974. *Journal of Political and Military Sociology* 3 (Fall):248-50.

1975e.   Shils, Edward. *Center and Periphery: Essays in Macrosociology.* Chicago: University of Chicago Press, 1975. *Journal for the Scientific Study of Religion* 14 (December):417-20.

1976.   Veblen, Thorstein. *The Theory of the Leisure Class: An Economic Study of Institutions.* New York: Modern Library, 1934. *Social Science Quarterly* 57 (June):218-21. (Review essay.)

1977a.   Bryant, Christopher G. *Sociology in Action: A Critique of Selected Conceptions of the Role of the Sociologist.* New York: John Wiley, Halsted Press, 1976. *Social Forces* 55 (March):817-18.

1977b.   Burger, Thomas. *Max Weber's Theory of Concept Formation: History, Laws, and Ideal Types.* Durham: Duke University Press, 1976. *Social Science Quarterly* 58 (June):172-73.

1977c.   Reisman, David A. *Adam Smith's Sociological Economics.* New York: Barnes and Noble, 1976. *Contemporary Sociology* 6 (July):497-99.

1978a.   Ben-David, Joseph, and Terry Nichols Clark, eds. *Culture and Its Creators: Essays in Honor of Edward Shils.* Chicago: University of Chicago Press, 1977. *Social Forces* 56 (June):1254-55.

1978b.   Smith, Adam. *The Theory of Moral Sentiments.* Indianapolis: Liberty Classics, 1976. *Journal for the Scientific Study of Religion* 17 (June):189-90.

1978c.   Hirschman, Albert O. *The Passions and the Interests: Political Arguments for Capitalism Before Its Triumph.* Princeton: Princeton University Press, 1977. Symposium review with Lewis A. Coser ("A Superb Contribution to the History of Ideas") and Gianfranco Poggi ("Economy and Polity: A Chastened Reflection of Past Hopes"). Louis Schneider review titled "On Human Nature, Economy and Society." *Contemporary Sociology* 7 (July):400-402.

1978d.   Lehmann, William C. *Scottish and Scotch-Irish Contributions to Early American Life and Culture.* Port Washington, N.Y.: Kennikat Press, 1978. *Contemporary Sociology* 7 (September):645-46.

1978e.   Smith, Anthony. *Social Change: Social Theory and Historical Processes.* London and New York: Longman, 1977. *American Journal of Sociology* 84 (November):774-76.

Other Publications

1964.   "Church," "Institution," and "Sociology of Religion." In *A Dictionary of the Social Sciences,* edited by Julius Gould and William L. Kolb, pp. 86-87, 338-39, and 683. New York: Free Press.

1966.   Report on "The Interdepartmental Program in Religious Studies at the University of Illinois." In *Newsletter of the Society for the Scientific Study of Religion* (June):1, 4 (with C. E. Dawn).

Completed but Not Published

a.   "Paradox and Society: The Work of Bernard Mandeville (book manuscript)

b.   "The Heritage of Sociology" (book manuscript)

c.   "Religion, Culture, and Society" (new edition)

d.   "Religion as Culture" (a chapter for a projected volume on culture)

Index

Gain through indirection, 205n23
Gallaher, Miriam, 268n
Galpin, Charles J., 158n7
Ganz, Arthur, *A Reader's Guide to Literary Terms* (with Karl Beckson), 327n49
Game theory, 203n3
Garfield, Eugene, xiii-xivn6; *Citation Indexing: Its Theory and Application in Science, Technology, and the Humanities,* xiiin6
Garrison, Fielding H., *Contributions to the History of Medicine,* 247n40
Gaustad, Edwin S., 315, 316; *The Great Awakening in New England,* 326n20
Gay, Peter, *The Enlightenment,* 95n18
Geertz, Clifford, 303n4; quoted on religion as cultural system, 289-90
Geller, Nancy L., xivn6
Ganeral systems theory and research, xxvi
Gerard, Ralph, xxvi
Germany: idealism, 210; industrializing, 217; philosophy, 213; pre-Nazi, 173; its *Wirtschaftswunder,* 169, 217
Gesammelte Aufsatze zur Wissenschaftslehre (Max Weber), 181n28, 226n10, 244n13
Geschichte der Neueren Historiographie (Edouard Feuter), 227n28
Gibbon, Edward, 79, 86; *The Decline and Fall of the Roman Empire,* 87
Gibbs, Jack, 245
Giddens, Anthony, 74-75n31
Gillin, John P., xxvi
Gini, Corrado, xliii, 171
Girvitz Memorial Lecture on Adam Smith (1976), xxxi, xlii, xliii, 10
Glasgow Lectures (Adam Smith), 72n1
Glasgow University, 91
Glasenapp, Helmuth von, 308, 325n3
Glenn, Norval D., 5, 7
Gnostic: the bhaktic strains in religion, 259, 308; and Manichean ideas, 322; Manichean sects, 280, 314
"God power," 256-66
Goethe, Johann Wolfgang von, 72n9, 234
Goffman, Erving, 224; *Asylums,* 245n29
Goldsmith, M.M., "Mandeville" in

International Encyclopedia of the Social Sciences, 43n1
Gouldner, Alvin, 5, 195, 206n28
Grammar, dialectic as, 323, 325; of human relationships, 324-25; of social life, 226, 259, 307; of social relations, 262
Grampp, William, 72n6
Grand theory, 157
Great Awakening, 261, 315
(The) Great Awakening in New England (Edwin S. Gaustad), 326n20
Great Being, 298
(The) Great Doctors (Henry Sigerist), 246n34
Greece, as a "seed-bed" society, 167
Green, A. W., 145n20,n24, 145-46n25
Greenberg, Bradley S., *The Kennedy Assassination and the American Public* (with Edwin B. Parker), 304n19
Gregg, D., 146n29
Gregoire, F., 42n1; *Bernard de Mandeville et la "Fable des Abeilles,"* 43n1
Griffin, J.P., *Iatrogenic Diseases* (with P.F. D'Arcy), 246n32
Grote, George, 213
Group solidarity, 187
Grunebaum, Gustave von, 315, 317; *Medieval Islam,* 326n23,n27
(A) Guide to Confident Living (Norman Vincent Peale), 263, 269n13
Gumplowicz, Ludwig, 20, 89; *Die Soziologische Strattzidee,* 95n13
Gurvitch, George, 122, 209; *Twentieth Century Sociology* (with W. E. Moore), 146n26; *Dialectique et Sociologie,* 226n1,n5,n8
Gusfield, Joseph, 5

Hall, Roland, 209, 226n4
Halley, Edmund, xxxix
Harkness, Georgia, *Power and the Common Life,* 269n7
Harmony, in Smith's work, 63-68
Harvard University, xvi, xxxvi, 80, 149; Laboratory of Social Relations, 268n; Research Center in Creative Altruism, 149

DATE DUE